JAPAN'S COLD WAR

JAPAN'S COLD WAR

Media, Literature, and the Law

Ann Sherif

Columbia University Press   New York

Columbia University Press
Publishers Since 1893
New York   Chichester, West Sussex

Library of Congress Cataloging-in-Publication Data
Sherif, Ann.
    Japan's Cold War : media, literature, and the law / Ann Sherif.
        p.   cm.
    Includes bibliographical references and index.
    ISBN 978-0-231-14662-3 (cloth : alk. paper)
    ISBN 978-0-231-51834-5 (e-book)
    I. Japan—Intellectual life—1945–   2. Cold War—Social aspects—Japan.   I Title.

DS822.5.S426 2009
952.04—dc22

                                                              2008034133

Columbia University Press books are printed on
permanent and durable acid-free paper.
Printed in the United States of America
c 10 9 8 7 6 5 4 3 2 1

References to Internet Web sites (URLs) were accurate at the time of writing. Neither the author nor Columbia University Press is responsible for URLs that may have expired or changed since the manuscript was prepared.

Contents

Acknowledgments

The long history of this book started with a conversation with Wendy Kozol at the World War II Memorial at Oberlin College. I am grateful for her friendship and intellectual companionship over the years.

I dedicate this book to Leonard Smith and Ian Wilson. Thank you for your love, support, and patience.

I am indebted to many others as well: Davinder Bhowmik, Michael Bourdagh, Rebecca Copeland, Henry David, Norma Field, Aaron Gerow and Ono Seiko, Will Hammel, Ken Ito, Abé Mark Nornes, Leslie Pincus, Atsuko Ueda, Stephen Filler, Ted Fowler, Jim Fujii, Laura Hein, Heather Hogan, Yoshikuni Igarashi, Kozawa Setsuko, Helen Liggett, Ted Mack, Marukawa Tetsushi, Richard Minear, Sharalyn Orbaugh, Michael Raine, Jay Rubin, Jordan Sand, and Sone Hiroyoshi. I am grateful to Kamei Hideo for his guidance and to Ito Rei, who generously shared his memories of his father and his own erudition. I was inspired by Kozawa Setsuko's impressive work on the Marukis and appreciate her advice and time. Julie Davis, always a kind friend, gave me an opportunity to present my research, as did Mark Williams, Rachel Hutchinson, and Tomi Suzuki.

I had the opportunity to meet many people in Japan who supported and informed my research: Yasuda Kazuya and the volunteers at the

Daigo Fukuryūmaru Foundation; Suzuki Yoko and Okamura Yukinori of the Maruki Gallery for the Hiroshima panels; the staff of the Otaru bungakukan; Hayashi Atsuko of Chugoku shinbunsha; Narusawa Katsushi and Hirota Ikuma of the Kobe City Koiso Memorial Museum; Ishii Kazue of Shinchosha; Yokoe Fuminori of the Museum of Contemporary Art in Tokyo; Abe Yutaka, Yano Kazuyuki, and Asakawa Shiho of the Yamagata International Documentary Film Festival; and Tochigi Akira of the National Film Center. From teaching "Living with the Bomb" at Oberlin, I learned a great deal from Wendy Kozol and the students in our classes, and I benefited from conversations with the Kohno seminar students at Nihon University. Many thanks to Pam Snyder at Oberlin.

My colleagues and students—especially Suzanne Gay, Amy Redden, Ikuko Kurasawa, and Sheila Jager—in the East Asian Studies Program at Oberlin College have provided a wonderfully supportive environment. I thank my family for their encouragement and support, particularly Sue Sherif, Joan Sherif, Tulin and the Aydins, the Uzawas, and the Wilsons.

I am most grateful to the two reviewers of the manuscript for their extremely helpful suggestions and to Jennifer Crewe, Margaret B. Yamashita, and the staff of Columbia University Press.

I thank the staffs of many libraries and archives: Mudd Library, Oberlin College; Waseda Main Library and International Center Library; Nihon University Library; Doshisha University Library; Kawasaki Shimin Museum; Hiroshima Peace Museum; Nagasaki Peace Museum; National Diet Library; Daigo Fukuryūmaru shiryō sentaa; and Tōkyō sensai shiryōkan.

I was fortunate to receive generous funding from the Japan Foundation, the Northeast Asia Council of the Association for Asian Studies, and Oberlin College. I am deeply indebted to Kohno Kensuke of Nihon University and Kanai Keiko of Waseda University for their support, friendship, and hospitality.

A version of chapter 2 appeared in *Japan Forum*, and parts of chapter 5 were included in *Representing the Other in Modern Japanese Literature: A Critical Approach*, edited by Rachael Hutchinson and Mark Williams (New York: Routledge, 2007). The other chapters appear here for the first time.

In loving memory of Uzawa Toshiko and Hiroshi Miyaji.

Chronology of the Early Cold War

This following chronology covers the period explored in this book, although scholars offer divergent opinions on the start date of the Cold War, ranging from 1917 (the Russian Revolution) to 1949. This book uses 1945 as the beginning of the Cold War, and the years covered in this chronology correspond to Shōwa 20 to Shōwa 38. The cultural events that I discuss here are noted in boldface.

1945	War ends in Europe; at Yalta, the Soviets agree to enter the war three months after Germans surrender; fire-bombing of Tokyo and dozens of other cities.
June	Battle of Okinawa.
July 16	Trinity test, the Manhattan Project's first test of a nuclear device at Alamogordo, New Mexico; at Potsdam, USSR occupies Poland.
August 6 and 9	Atomic bombings of Hiroshima and Nagasaki.
September 15	Instruments of surrender signed aboard the USS *Missouri*.
	Occupation forces arrive in Japan; Japanese Empire is dissolved; colonies are liberated; military is demobilized.

1946   Occupation authorities' purge of politicians. U.S. begins formulating policy of containment of USSR; tension between U.S. and USSR intensifies; Winston Churchill delivers "Iron Curtain" speech.

Kamei Fumio's documentary *A Japanese Tragedy*.

John Hersey's *Hiroshima;* Japanese documentary film *The Effects of the Atomic Bomb on Hiroshima and Nagasaki*.

1947   Postwar Japanese constitution is promulgated; Truman Doctrine expressing U.S. defense of "free peoples" around the world, U.S. Marshall Plan to revive European economy, liberal Occupation reforms, and Truman's loyalty program to keep Communists out of U.S. government all established.

Maruki Toshi and Maruki Iri's A-bomb panels; Hara Tamiki's "Summer Flowers"; World Convention for Peace in Paris.

Kurihara Sadako's poems.

1948   Reserve Course commences; U.S. defies Soviet blockade of Berlin.

Politicians purged and military officers accused at the Tokyo trials.

Matsukawa's trial; Hara Tamiki's "Feet of Fire."

1949   NATO (first U.S. military alliance in peacetime) formed; Soviets' possession and test of nuclear device disclosed; People's Republic of China founded.

Partisans of Peace World Conference held in Paris; Hiroshima designated "City of Peace." Funds allocated for Hiroshima museum.

Japanese translation of Hersey's *Hiroshima*.

1950   U.S. Senator Joseph McCarthy becomes prominent in "Red scare"; Korean War begins; Truman orders increases in development of thermonuclear weapons; National Security Council Paper no. 68 (NSC68) predicts "an indefinite period of tension and danger"; Stockholm appeal.

Itō Sei's translation of *Lady Chatterley's Lover;* Tokyo police seize copies of Japanese translation of *Lady Chatterley's Lover* from bookstores; Hara Tamiki's "On the Shore of a Beautiful Death."

1951	Peace treaty and United States–Japan Security Treaty signed; Truman announces possible use of nuclear weapons on Korean Peninsula.
	Lady Chatterley trial at Tokyo Municipal Court; Hara Tamiki's "Land of My Heart's Desire"; Hara Tamiki commits suicide.
1952	First U.S. thermonuclear test at Eniwetok, South Pacific; official end of Occupation.
	Lady Chatterley trial's first-round verdict and appeal; Shindo Kaneto's film Children of Hiroshima; Dr. Kusano Nobuo's "The Corpses Resist."
1953	Stalin dies; Dwight Eisenhower becomes U.S. president; Korean War armistice signed, dividing north and south, which officially remain at war; USSR tests its first thermonuclear device.
	Marukis' A-bomb panels begin international tour (to 1964); Kamei Fumio's feature film, A Woman Walking Alone on the Earth.
1954	Japanese Self-Defense Forces established.
	Test Bravo in Marshall Islands, South Pacific.
	Vietminh defeat French at Dien Bien Phu; Geneva Accords signed; Vietnam partitioned at seventeenth parallel.
	U.S. Senator Joseph McCarthy censured by Senate; hysteria over Communists recedes.
March	Tuna on Lucky Dragon no. 5 contaminated with radioactive fallout from A-bomb test; mass protests and petition drive against nuclear testing.
September	Lucky Dragon crew member Kuboyama Ai dies.
	Shunkotsumaru surveys radiation concentrations in South Pacific.
	Honda Ishiro's Godzilla; Odagari Hideo's and Abe Tomoji's The Atomic Problem and Literature.
1955	Japan's Liberal Democratic Party founded; Nikita Khrushchev becomes head of the Soviet government, which is de-Stalinized; twenty-nine African and Asian countries meet regarding nonalignment; Khrushchev rejects inevitability of war with capitalist world; Warsaw Pact established.

First International Conference against A-bombs and H-bombs held in Hiroshima; Kurosawa Akira's movie *Record of a Living Being* released; Ishihara Shintarō's *Season of the Sun* wins Bungakukai literary prize; book version of *Season of the Sun* published; movie version of *Season of the Sun* released; Kamei Fumio Sunagawa's documentaries *The People of Sunagawa* and *Wheat Will Never Fall* and Nicholas Ray's movie *Rebel Without a Cause* released.

1956   Egypt's Gamal Abdel Nasser seizes Suez Canal from the British; Khrushchev delivers de-Stalinization speech; USSR crushes Hungarian revolution; Suez Crisis marks decline of Great Powers.

Kamei Fumio's atomic documentary *Still It's Good to Live;* Sunagawa documentary *Record of Blood: Sunagawa* and Nakahira Ko's *Crazed Fruit* released; *Season of the Sun* wins Akutagawa literary prize.

1957   Kishi Nobusuke becomes prime minister with conservative agenda.

Sputnik launched; space race begins.

Kamei Fumio's atomic documentary *The World Is Terrified* released.

1958   Citizen protest against revisions of police protection law.

Wakai Nihon no kai formed.

1959   Demonstrations against United States–Japan Security Treaty; Ho Chi Minh leads struggle to take over South Vietnam.

Kamei Fumio's *Voice of Hiroshima;* Alain Resnais's *Hiroshima Mon Amour.*

1960   Mass demonstrations against United States–Japan Security Treaty continue, but treaty ratified; Kishi cabinet dissolved; Prime Minister Ikeda Hayato's income doubling and economic development plans.

1961   USSR builds Berlin Wall; Bay of Pigs fiasco in Cuba.

Kamei Fumio's *Toward a World Without Arms* released.

1962   Cuban missile crisis.

1963   Limited test ban treaty ratified.
              Ōe Kenzaburō's *Hiroshima Notes* **published.**

The dissolution of the Soviet Union between 1989 and 1991 is widely considered the end of the Cold War, although some historians believe it ended earlier in some countries.

JAPAN'S COLD WAR

But aren't we all afraid of H-bombs ourselves? But we're just not as afraid as
that man.   —Kurosawa Akira, *Record of a Living Being*

Introduction *The Strange Tension of the Cold War*

This book explores the interaction between postwar Japanese
culture and the global geopolitical and ideological conflict known as the
Cold War. At the height of the Cold War in the late 1940s and 1950s,
Japan found itself at the same time scarred by war and made new by
the Allied Occupation. In reframing its identity, the nation seemed to
embrace a splendid pacifist isolation in response to the bombings of Hiroshima and Nagasaki. Even the cultural imagination appeared to com-
ply with a vision of Japan as a safe haven in a precarious world, as in
the movie *Godzilla* (*Gojira*, 1954), which showed a Japan whose scientific
ingenuity, art, and self-sacrifice enabled it to overpower a monster awak-
ened by H-bomb testing.[1]

The Cold War has been an important point of reference in cultural histories of Japan's Asian neighbors—Korea, China, and Taiwan—as well as
those of its geographically more distant but diplomatically closer allies in
Europe and the United States.[2] Far less frequently, however, have Japan's
literature, film, and art been tied to the Cold War. Instead, critics and cultural historians most often have posited Japanese cultural production as
taking place in an insular peacetime Japan while emphasizing a cultural
identity that can never escape the memory of the traumatic Asian and
world wars of the 1930s and 1940s.

The superpowers' violent proxy war during the 1950s was fought not in Japan but on the Korean Peninsula. Unlike countries in Europe, Japan shared no land borders with potential communist foes.[3] But even though Japan was not situated in a geographical hot spot, we should not assume that Japanese culture was insulated from the Cold War. In analytical terms, the framework of the Cold War offers a productive alternative to the retrospective, morally laden discourse centering on the past war and empire, as well as to the perspective of privatized domesticity dominant in much of post-1945 criticism and art.[4]

My book positions Japanese culture in the context of the Cold War in order to better understand that era's social, cultural, and ideological changes and creativity. Accordingly, cultural events, iconic figures, and texts that may appear anomalous or subversive in standard postwar cultural histories make much more sense when viewed through the lens of the Cold War. Moreover, seeing Japan as part of the global battle allows us to understand its culture in relation to *contemporary* domestic and foreign social and cultural change, in other words, in relation to the current events following World War II.

Long Hot Summer: Artists in Mid-1950s Tokyo

Most summers in Tokyo are hot and humid, but the summer of 1955 was exceptionally brutal. The renowned film director Kurosawa Akira did not allow the heat to dampen his creative spirit that summer. Instead, he decided to feature the high temperatures in his current project. In *Record of a Living Being (Ikimono no kiroku,* 1955), a film about a man taken to court by his own family because of his obsession with the threat of nuclear weapons, Kurosawa uses heat to great effect by showing us the judge and the Nakajima family constantly fanning themselves and wiping their brows.[5] Along with the close camera framing, this suggestion of extreme heat adds to the oppressive atmosphere of both the courthouse and Japan under the cloud of thermonuclear tests in the South Pacific. At the end of the film, the now deranged Nakajima stares out the window at the setting sun and exclaims, "Oh, my god. It is burning; the earth is burning." Echoing his late collaborator, the composer Hayasaka Fumio, Kurosawa commented that the film's lack of a clear message about the proper response to the nuclear arms race reflected the times: "The world has come to such a state that we don't really know what is in store for us tomorrow. I wouldn't even know how to go on living—I'm that uncertain. Uncertainties, nothing but uncertainties."[6] During the 1950s, these uncertainties arose from the superpowers' contest to accumulate the most powerful arsenal of weapons of mass destruction as well as from the awareness of larger global dynamics called the Cold War.

During that hot summer, many other artists shared Kurosawa's and Hayasaka's feelings of uncertainty. The waves of heat confirmed the conviction of writer Abe Tomoji (1903–1973) that he must speak up against nuclear arms. Yet he also was aware that the Cold War complicated both his activism and his cultural work.[7] Before the war, Abe chose to study English and established himself as a novelist, literary critic, and prolific translator of H. G. Wells, Emily Brontë, and Sir Arthur Conan Doyle's Sherlock Holmes series and as a scholar of British literature and modernism more generally.[8] But then, during World War II, English became the enemy language. Even after the war, Abe's political views did not accord with those of Japan's English-speaking occupiers, as he had long been interested in Marxism and progressive thought.[9]

Abe's journey to the site of the first atomic bombing became fraught with political significance. In April 1950, Abe traveled to Hiroshima with eighteen other writers (including Kawabata Yasunari) for a special meeting of the Japan PEN Club, at which he delivered a lecture entitled "War and Peace." If in retrospect Abe's topic seems innocuous, recall that in 1950 both the use of the term "peace" and the visit itself were highly political and ambiguous in Japan, and speaking out against nuclear weapons and testing was by no means a politically uncontroversial matter. Along with many other artists, Abe had to moderate his critiques of the U.S. ally or praise of the Soviet foe during the Cold War's most tense and volatile years.

In 1949, the year of the revelation of Soviet possession and testing of the atomic bomb and of the founding of the People's Republic of China, the Allied Occupation began purging socialists and communists from Japan's schools and civil service jobs as part of its strategy of shielding Japan from communism. Significantly, leftists and labor unionists figured prominently in the early peace gatherings in Hiroshima, but at that time, many on the Left extolled the Soviet Union as the protector of peace and the United States as the warmonger. Others condemned the possession of nuclear weapons by any nation. In this polarized atmosphere, Abe and others—as citizens of the currently occupied but soon to be sovereign Japan and as citizens of the world—worked to construct new modes of activism, art, and identities.

Even after the Occupation drew to a close, Abe Tomoji and his fellow writers continued to be cautious about their activism and their creative activities. In his preface to *Atomic Power and Literature,* Abe wrote that Japanese writers and artists were working under an extraordinarily "strange tension," which he linked specifically with the Cold War.[10]

The very title of this anthology of essays, *Atomic Power and Literature,* suggests the strangeness of the age. The mainstream publisher Kodansha released the volume in 1955, at the height of the thermonuclear arms race between the United States and the Soviet Union. The dangers of radioactive fallout from recent superpower nuclear tests dominated the headlines that year, as did the unending threat of extreme and apocalyptic violence from hydrogen bombs. Why, then, does the title contain the mild phrase "atomic power" rather than the alarming "atomic bomb"?

The Occupation had ended, but the Japanese state's alliance with the United States blossomed in the 1950s, culminating in the highly controversial ratification of the United States–Japan Security Treaty in 1960. As I will discuss later, the consolidation of conservative forces domestically, along with the evolving needs of the United States and major shifts in the Eastern bloc and international communism, affected cultural production in significant ways. The editors of *Atomic Power and Literature* thus knew that even with the rise of a mainstream antinuclear movement in the aftermath of the highly publicized incidents of radioactive pollution, they had to be cautious about expressing antinuclear opinions or risk being branded as "Red." By the same token, a dedicated Communist Party member who criticized Soviet testing might incur the wrath of the party hard-liners at a time when the Left was increasingly splintered.

In tandem with the frightening arms race, the promise of productive uses of atomic power and even an atomic utopia emerged. Even if one abhorred the hydrogen bomb, the allure of a limitless power source that could light up cities and cure diseases was hard to resist. In his preface to *Atomic Power and Literature,* Abe Tomoji alludes to these conflicting discourses and clashing political rivalries rather indirectly, under the rubric of the Cold War. By attaching to the book the optimistic phrase "atomic power" rather than "bomb," the editors aspired to a neutrality that was, in fact, unattainable in the ideologically volatile 1950s.

Abe's concern with the "strange tension" created by the Cold War (and not just by the arms race) reminds us that the "war of nerves" had a variety of manifestations: some bloody confrontations but more often battles fought through words and images and aimed at expanding the superpowers' respective realms of ideological and cultural influence. In those days, many major forces of social change stemmed directly from global Cold War dynamics, including the course of the Allied Occupation of Japan, the Korean War, the testing and stockpiling of hydrogen bombs, and the United States–Japan Security Treaty of 1960.[11] Similarly, many political processes arose from the Cold War: anti-Stalinism, anticommunism, anti-Americanism, containment, and decolonization.

Abe's concern with a pervasive, complex conflict of ideology and culture encourages us to view in a new light the subsequent dominant national allegory of Japan as an observer of, rather than a dynamic participant in, the Cold War.[12] This allegory arose partly from the widespread public and state affirmation of the values set forth in Japan's postwar "peace" constitution and, in later decades, its vigorous rejection of the nuclear arms race.[13] At the height of the Cold War, however, many Japanese engaged in ideological and cultural struggles directly linked to a broader range of Cold War dynamics, which, in turn, contributed to the formation of their cultural identity during this period.

In Japan's culture, confrontations tempered by the Cold War's unsettled global order and its bipolar worldview sometimes appeared in public arenas of political activism or courts of law, such as when citizens grappled with attempts, by either foreign or domestic authorities, to narrow or expand the scope of protest, dissent, or freedom of speech. Such public processes contributed to the country's newly democratic ideological and cultural foundations. The primacy of free-world values led to a fascination with the various cultural values and identities advocated in the Western bloc, such as rebellious youth, domesticity, conformity, and masculinity as articulated in both mass and elite cultures. As an alternative (or sometimes as a complement) to a Marxist–Leninist worldview, American social sciences emerged as a potent tool in public debates about values and culture. At the same time, many artists—along with scientists, journalists, and ordinary citizens—responded to the Cold War in their own work. Some became embroiled in controversies over ideological allegiances to international communism or to the postwar Western allies. Others contributed to the construction of new types of knowledge about novel nuclear technologies, science, and radiation, as well as the human and environmental costs of the nuclear regime. Writers, artists, and critics in Japan saw themselves as deeply involved in the discourses of the Cold War. Abe Tomoji's activities thus exemplify the ways that many writers and artists revealed their awareness of the Cold War, which, in turn, influenced their creative and intellectual lives.

In 1949, partly in an effort to bolster its own moral standing and to redefine peace on its own terms, the United States encouraged the designation of Hiroshima as a "city of peace." Abe knew about the antinuclear demonstrations in Hiroshima and the opposing ideologies of the West and the East that clashed in the bombed city. In an effort to curb domestic political debate and dissent, the Occupation authorities banned the peace ceremony held annually in Hiroshima on August 6, the anniversary of the bombing.

If progressive individuals keenly felt the influence of the Cold War in both their work and their lived experience, so did artists and intellectuals of other persuasions. When Ishihara Shintarō debuted as a novelist in the mid-1950s, his fiction, films, and public persona spotlighted the social phenomenon of rebellious youth and new cultural values, such as the valorization of adolescence, privatization, and depoliticization.[14] Around the same time, James Dean, the iconic figure of the young rebel, appeared in many countries of the Western bloc, becoming a symbol of the emancipatory promise of free-world liberal democracy and capitalism and of resistance to the demands of conformity, and, by extension, totalitarianism.[15] Living in Japan during this phase of the Cold War, furthermore, meant witnessing "the consolidation of a massive . . . urban middle class in the 1950s and 1960s under the auspices of capitalist modernization," which Kristen Ross has described as also occurring in contemporary France.[16] Ishihara's meteoric rise as the bad boy of 1950s film, literature, and the new medium of television was closely linked to the promise of a middle-class life and the free-world values of family, gender, and mass culture.

The Cold War was, among other things, an ideological clash between liberal capitalism and state socialism, manifested as a battle of propaganda in which the superpowers vied to expand their spheres of influence. Images and words became the primary weapons. During the late 1940s and 1950s, waves of fear, conflicting ideological messages, demonstrations of changing technologies, and new cultural and social orders spread over the globe and even through Japan. In addition, the rapid decolonization of much of the world's population gave rise to a Third World that was a key player in what is usually regarded as a bipolar struggle.[17]

In partnership with Japan's establishment, America strove to contain communism and to fashion Japan as a model free-world ally during the Allied Occupation (1945–1952). Japan's importance to the United States derived not only from its status as conquered enemy but also from the key part it could play in America's Cold War vision of the global order, which depended on the strategy of containment. Even after the Allied Occupation came to an end in 1952, the Japanese state fell in step, culturally as well as militarily, with many of the conditions set by the alliance with America. It is easy to forget the then-powerful allure of the Soviet utopian vision and Marxist–Leninist thought during the 1940s and 1950s. Whether Marxists or progressives, many citizens resisted the conservative state's drive to align with capitalist America. As we shall see, however, artists and writers in Japan did not blindly conform to Western- or Eastern-bloc values, politics, and aesthetics during the peak of the Cold War. Instead, many of them fought to negotiate a third way.

During the decades after World War II, the war, its dramatic end, and its unexpected aftermath continued to occupy a prominent place in public and personal memory. Yet the past war was far from the sole preoccupation of individuals and the public as a whole. Abe Tomoji and his readers also lived with the tension arising from a terrifying yet curiously invisible Cold War. Although Abe continued to work for change and to resist the totalizing narrative of deterrence and superpower, he acknowledged a widely shared anxiety when he wrote that "what follows this age of fear [may] be the suicide of all of humankind."[18]

Cold War Politics

From the early stages of high economic growth in the 1950s, the aura of Hiroshima and Nagasaki as centers of peace and that of Article 9 of Japan's postwar "peace constitution" contributed to the seeming disappearance of the Cold War from culture. Not until a half century later, after the end of the Cold War, Marukawa Tetsushi in his book *Cold War Culture* (2005) revealed the continuing dominance of the discourse defining Japanese culture as an oasis away from the Cold War. But even as Marukawa examined "Cold War culture" (*reisen bunka*), he admitted that pairing the phrase "Cold War" with Japanese culture seemed jarring. Scholars and the media more conventionally use the Cold War as a framework for interpreting Japan's politics and diplomatic relations after 1945, but seldom in relation to culture.

Marukawa's discomfort about pairing the Cold War and culture raises a question: If the Cold War influences on Japanese politics, economy, and military were undeniable, how could Japanese culture be shielded from those same sociocultural processes? Put another way, why were Cold War discourses reinterpreted in the cultural realm chiefly in terms of the postwar? The postwar periodization had the effect of obscuring the struggles and debates—the cultural change and work—that transpired on the way to arriving at what later would be understood as consensus. This consensus appears in various forms: as the postwar literary canon, what constituted art, what was obscene, modes of expressing knowledge and values, and the role of the artist in shaping society.

Marukawa Tetsushi first recognized the amnesia regarding the impact of the Cold War on Japan's culture when he was studying the literature of Taiwan and Korea during the 1990s. If scholars defined Taiwanese and Korean literature and art after 1945 in terms of liberation (from Japanese colonialism), they also frequently invoked the influence of the Cold War on cultural production. Because the Cold War had been important to Korean and Taiwan, its end resulted in shifts in culture as well. Yet in neighboring Japan, mention of the Cold War in its culture was strangely absent.

My book reconsiders this erasure of the Cold War. In what ways was the Cold War part of Japan's social imaginary? What did the Cold War mean in the lived experience of people in Japan? How can we understand the significance of the end of the Cold War in Japan or elsewhere if we do not explore the cultural meanings of the conflict?[19]

The Cold War and Popular Culture

In simple terms, the Cold War was a geopolitical and cultural conflict that dominated the post–World War II world, driven by powerful narratives of good and evil that predicted an apocalyptic disaster between two titans and their satellites. Even though opinions diverge about when the Cold War started, I consider 1945 and, in particular, the American deployment of nuclear weapons as the beginning of the Cold War.[20] Its end coincides with the dissolution of the Soviet Union and the fall of the Berlin Wall, from 1989 to 1991.

This book focuses on Japan's culture during the high Cold War, which here refers to the period from the end of World War II to the early 1960s. No other years of the postwar era were as unstable. It was during these years that many qualities, subsequently understood as natural aspects of the Cold War, emerged in sometimes thrilling but more often in grotesque and disturbing ways.

Historian James Hershberg describes the first phase of the Cold War, between the late 1940s and 1963, as a time when "the tensions that had been accumulating since the end of World War II sharpened and intensified through a series of crises that repeatedly appeared to bring the globe to the precipice of nuclear war."[21] Not only was the U.S.–Soviet rivalry fierce, but the early postwar "anarchic international system conjured up unprecedented threats and opportunities for leaders in many nations."[22] The Berlin blockade of 1948/1949 and the U.S.–Soviet sparring over Europe's fate provided a dramatic demonstration of the animosity between the two superpowers, as well as the uncertainty of the future for the potential allies and satellites of each. In contrast, the hot war in Korea was far more violent, messy, and lacking in symbols of American triumphalism. Although it was fought with conventional weapons, the Korean conflict also was haunted by threats of atomic bombs. In those days, no one yet knew what fierce loyalty the philosophy of deterrence would earn from all the players in the conflict.

Distinct from battles defined by tanks and bullets, the seemingly endless Cold War was fought with the goal of winning "hearts and minds," that is, of convincing people of the superiority of one system and ideology over another. President Dwight D. Eisenhower announced in 1954 that "the world, once divided by oceans and mountain ranges, is now split by hostile concepts of man's character and nature." Eisenhower, himself a five-star general, defined the Cold War as "a war for the minds of men."[23] Distinct from World War II, the Cold War featured astounding new weapons and communications technologies, as well as relatively limited, geographically contained battles such as the proxy wars in Korea, Vietnam, and Afghanistan. From the American and the Soviet perspectives, however, as Ellen Herman notes, the Cold War "was, above all, a psychological phenomenon, just as total war [in World War II] had been."[24]

The ideological components of the conflict appeared in a long, drawn-out propaganda war, in which both superpowers claimed the ability to deliver peace to a war-weary and fearful world. In this setting, peace took on a perverse meaning because the champions of peace were enthralled with the project of fetishizing and normalizing thermonuclear weapons.[25] Under the nuclear regime, fear intermingled with the thrill of the nuclear sublime.

During the high Cold War, popular culture offered a means of pro-
cessing and exploring these anxieties and fears. Some of the films and
literature fell in step with state propaganda efforts, while other works offered parodies of Cold War dilemmas or action-packed, radioactive duels.
In the American and Western European cultural imaginations, the Cold
War conjured up images of menacing communist infiltrators, duck-and-
cover propaganda films, and campy monster movies. In Britain, by then
in possession of its own bomb, the Cold War provided excellent material
for action-packed entertainment. During the 1950s, British novelist Ian
Fleming wrote the series of adventure thrillers featuring the virile secret
agent James Bond.

In contrast, the single most famous product of Japan's Cold War culture is the movie monster Godzilla or perhaps the film *Hiroshima Mon
Amour* (1959), a French romance about the scars of World War II Europe,
with a setting offering just the right touch of the nuclear sublime. Cultural production emanating from the high Cold War did not stop at big
movie studios. As we shall see, in its various manifestations, the Cold
War also compelled artists, writers, and filmmakers to take action.

The year 1955, when Abe Tomoji offered his description of the strange
political and cultural Cold War climate, marked the tenth anniversary of
the end of World War II. What was happening in Japan and in the world
that explains Abe's perception of his age? A consideration of social change
during this time will help us answer that question. Historians identify the
mid-1950s as a major turning point in Japanese domestic politics and in
the recovery of the nation's economy after the war. Specifically, even after
the 1951 San Francisco peace treaty, which restored Japan's sovereignty
and placed the country under the U.S. security umbrella, the amalgama-
tion of conservative political forces in 1955 further strengthened the nation's bonds to the Western bloc. Economic and physical recovery, along
with the progress toward economic growth that started in earnest during
the Korean War (1950–1953), were inextricably linked to American Cold
War security goals of containing the threat of Soviet and Chinese communism by fashioning Japan as an essential part of the "great crescent"
stretching from Northeast Asia to the Middle East.[26] Starting with Prime
Minister Yoshida Shigeru in 1946, successive administrations articulated
goals in line with advanced capitalism, including economic growth and
the doubling of the GDP and personal income.[27]

This book discusses a few of the well-known artists and events connected with the Cold War. Although I chose to focus on the nuclear age

and the influence of Anglo-American culture in Japan, I am not attempting to force Japan into the United States's Cold War cultural mold. Rather, because I regard Japan as part of the Cold War's global nexus, my study centers on some of the intersections between Japan and one other part of the world. I look at local cultural responses to and articulations of the uncertain, often frightening, and sometimes exciting international Cold War. This thrilling phase of the Cold War was full of possibilities and therefore was culturally productive.

Chapter 1 looks in greater depth at the historical dimensions of the high Cold War and considers some of the cultural manifestations of Cold War tensions in Japan. In particular, I discuss the Occupation and post-Occupation evolution of the concept of peace, the ethical dimensions of nuclear exceptionalism, and the geopolitical, military, and cultural manifestations of containment. Other significant Cold War themes are domesticity, constructions of masculinity and the private realm, and the evolving discourses of liberal democracy in courts of law and the media.

Each of the next four chapters examines either an individual artist or a cultural event both sustained and transformed by the ideological and material dimensions of the Cold War. These include an avant-garde poet whose identity became entangled with his survival of the Hiroshima bombing and then the anxiety of the Cold War, and an activist filmmaker who created new types of knowledge about science, radiation, and hydrogen bomb testing. Similarly, two widely publicized public events that involved artists, the media, and the state in struggles over cultural discourses and politics highlight the dynamics of a public sphere buffeted by the Cold War. One of these, an obscenity trial, tells us much about the conflict and negotiation that followed in the effort to determine the parameters of art and free speech in a society that had pledged to join the ranks of Western-bloc liberal democracies. The second spectacle was a media controversy over the quintessential Cold War figure of rebel youth, a debate in the media that reveals the reasons why this icon fulfilled a variety of cultural needs.

Chapters 2 through 5 proceed in a roughly chronological order, beginning with the *Lady Chatterley's Lover* trials (1950–1959), the famous legal case about obscenity that also became a showcase for debating the merits of liberal democracy and social science. In chapter 3, I consider Hara Tamiki, one of the best-known *hibakusha* (atomic bomb survivor) writers, and how his canonization as the "first victim of the atomic age" and his avant-gardism contributed to the myth of nuclear exceptionalism. Chapter 4 concerns the production and reception of a group of atomic films by the renowned filmmaker Kamei Fumio. Kamei's mid- and late-1950s documentaries gave rise to new views of radiation and the nuclear regime at a time when states were trying to suppress such knowledge. Finally, chapter 5 delves into the controversial mid-1950s debut of one of Japan's best-known writer-politicians, Ishihara Shintarō, who launched his public career as a novelist, filmmaker, and bad-boy darling of the media. I use methods from cultural and literary studies to situate all these cultural events in the Cold War cultural field of post-1945 Japan.

The apotheosis of simulation: the nuclear. However, the balance of terror is never anything but the spectacular slope of a system of deterrence that has insinuated itself from *the inside* into all the cracks of daily life. . . . It is not the direct threat of atomic destruction that paralyzes our lives, it is deterrence that gives them leukemia. And this deterrence comes from the fact that *even the real atomic clash is precluded*—precluded like the eventuality of the real in a system of signs. . . .

The risk of nuclear annihilation only serves as a pretext, through the sophistication of weapons . . . for installing a universal security system, a universal lockup and control system whose deterrent effect is not at all aimed at an atomic clash (which was never in question, except without a doubt in the very initial stages of the cold war, when one still confused the nuclear apparatus with conventional war). (italics in original)

—Jean Baudrillard, *Simulacra and Simulation*

1   The Meanings of War and Peace After 1945

Since the early 1990s, the post–Cold War world has witnessed the dismantling of some Cold War foundational narratives and the reconsideration or erasure of others. Major shifts in the global hierarchy of power resulting from the end of the Cold War and newly available resources in the form of declassified documents and archives have combined to stimulate a great deal of scholarly and popular interest in the Cold War as history. While diplomatic history and international relations theory have long dominated the research on this phase of the twentieth century, intellectual approaches diversified in the post–Cold War era. For example, Rana Mitter, Patrick Major, and Kenneth Osgood have promoted the project of studying "the socio-cultural aspects of that era systematically and paradigmatically, rather than as an afterthought to the analysis of high politics." Such an approach would necessarily include "the propaganda, psychological, cultural, and ideological dimensions of the Cold War."[1]

The Cold War was a battle to win "hearts and minds." For both the superpowers, the psychological and discursive battle had several goals: the prevention of domestic "subversion," the allegiance of peoples in satellite countries, and the conversion of those captive to the opposing ideological and political system. During the 1950s, it became clear that the stockpiling of nuclear weapons functioned partly to bolster the primary goal of ideological allegiance. Conventional weapons, after all, had proved inadequate to capture either land or people's minds, as the war in Korea (and later in the Vietnam War and in more recent wars) amply demonstrated. Seen in this way, culture during the Cold War reveals itself as the primary front, or battlefield, the desired site of transformation and conviction. High politics, while more dramatic and thrilling, must therefore be understood as a means to an end. For this reason, this study examines a variety of artistic media and cultural discourses.[2]

The specific level of participation of the press and popular culture varied greatly because the media in the Western bloc had relatively more autonomy than those in the Soviet bloc, where governments commonly exercised much greater control over cultural apparatuses. In the case of Japan, the United States fashioned the country, through its postwar constitution, as a laboratory of democracy, with a free press and guaranteed free speech. Whether or not citizens and the media in fact fully enjoyed these rights, the image of a free press was promoted as a cornerstone of the free world.

Both cultural production and lived experience during the Cold War differed greatly in the Eastern and Western blocs, from country to country, and even within a single nation. Arguably, the most thoroughly studied national variant of Cold War culture to date is that of the United States, with its well-documented and often entertaining civil defense projects (duck-and-cover drills), the commercialization and commodification of symbols of the atomic era, and McCarthyism.[3] In every country, however, the media and artists had a major role in cultural mobilization—that is, in rallying citizens to the cause and maintaining their loyalty. Moreover, because the Cold War was an invisible war or "armed truce," the media and artists who sided with the government's agendas also had the task of convincing the public that there was a war was going on in the first place.[4] At the same time, oppositional voices—not all of which were progressive—emerged to critique the dominant Cold War discourses.

Because both the United States and the Soviet Union tended to regard Europe as the focus of the Cold War battle to win hearts and minds, many scholars have concentrated on its manifestations in both Eastern and Western Europe.[5] Since the dissolution of the Soviet Union, considerable scholarly energy has been devoted to learning about the Russian experience of the Cold War, at both the diplomatic and the cultural level, from newly declassified documents.[6] Until recently, however, scholars have paid far less attention to the cultural Cold War in East Asia. As Charles

Armstrong maintains, the Cold War "was 'hotter' [in East Asia] than any other place on the planet from the late 1940s to the mid-1970s." Despite the persistence of "vestiges of the Cold War" found on the Korean Peninsula, for example, East Asia "has been almost entirely neglected in the emerging literature on the cultural Cold War, with a few exceptions." Armstrong acknowledges that the "importation of the nuclear theme into Japanese popular culture . . . [has] already received critical attention."[7] Certainly this is true of the excellent work of John Dower, Lisa Yoneyama, Norma Field, Abé Mark Nornes, and Yoshikuni Igarashi, among others. The identification of Japan as significant mainly in its role as a nuclear authority, however, is more a lingering symptom of the Cold War than an illumination of a broader picture of it. Indeed, the majority of scholars have approached even the bomb in Japan from the perspective of a nationally specific *postwar* history rather than Cold War history.[8]

In the United States, where the cultural imaginary of the 1950s is dominated by images of middle-class conformity, repression, and rabid anticommunism, the notion of the 1950s as a time of domestic and international "ideological conflict" and "political, social, and economic change" may seem to be an anachronism. Nonetheless, many social and cultural trends that we now take for granted started to take root in the 1950s, including urbanization, growth of an urban middle class, economic recovery, and certain inflections and emphases of popular culture.[9]

In this book, I do not dwell on the politics and culture of the Allied Occupation (1945–1952), since there already are many excellent historical and cultural studies of that era.[10] But owing to the considerable overlap and continuity from the Occupation to independence, I do consider some events in the late Occupation. Despite the so-called Bloody May Day demonstrations of 1952, when activists and unionists marched in the streets and clashed with police, no abrupt break or radical change marked the year ending the Occupation and beginning Japan's sovereignty. My main concern is what the high Cold War, the early and most intense phase, meant for art, literature, film, and culture in Japan.

The 1960s, 1970s, and 1980s have received more scholarly attention because they were the decades of intense high-speed growth, capped by the achievement of global superpower status and a concomitant nationalistic pride (exemplified by Ishihara Shintarō's *Japan That Can Say "No"*). During the so-called economic miracle era, a "revived capitalist workshop" Japan came to maturity as a producer of material goods as well as cultural artifacts for both domestic and foreign consumption.[11] In contrast, the post-Occupation 1950s seem to many observers as a bland transitional phase leading up to the more ebullient and significant 1960s.

The Beginning of Peace?

In 1949, the Soviets' possession of nuclear weapons marked the start of the arms race and altered the nature of U.S.–Soviet relations and, indeed, the global power structure. In that year, the founding of the People's Republic of China (PRC) presented a formidable and seemingly united international communist bloc, whereas previously the Soviet Union had towered as the single worthy communist opponent to the United States. The PRC also altered the face of East Asia. For Japan, this new political arrangement had long-range implications, as the Korean War and the United States's strategy of containment demonstrated. Culturally, many progressive artists and intellectuals regarded the Soviet Union and the newly founded PRC as promising alternatives to American might.

In Japanese movie theaters during the late 1940s and 1950s, newsreels showed the initially inevitable and subsequently controversial U.S. military bases, as well as scenes of the U.S. and Japanese authorities firing communists from their jobs as teachers and civil servants. It is important to remember that the battle between communism and capitalism dramatized in both U.S. and Soviet propaganda did not result in writers and artists, along with other citizens, lining up blindly on one side or the other of the imagined boundary between good and evil. On the contrary, at the height of the Cold War, many activist artists and writers reexamined their political affiliations and values, a task complicated by vestiges of discourses of imperial Japan.[12]

It is easy to forget that many activist literary writers, critics, and film-makers who were confronted with choosing among different ideological visions ("free" versus "Red") considered themselves independent Marxists, progressives, or conservatives who did not adhere strictly to any party line. The late 1940s and 1950s were early stages in what must be thought of as a long process by which eventually the "massive polarization staged by the contest between the so-called free world and the totalitarian dictatorships—between democracy and Marxist–Leninist communism—narrowed the compass of competing alternatives, forcing them out of the field of contention or encouraging their assimilation into one pole or the other."[13] In other words, differentiating the superpowers in black and white terms of good and evil, characteristic of the "evil empire" rhetoric of President Ronald Reagan in the 1980s, was not necessarily part of early Cold War discourse. In the words of one historian, "To frame international politics in the initial post-war years as a struggle between Soviet tyranny and American freedom is to simplify reality and distort the way most peoples around the world understood events."[14]

The career of the well-known writer and conservative politician Ishihara Shintarō shows the influence of the many significant shifts marking these years. In political terms, 1955 marked the rise to power of Japan's Liberal Democratic Party and thus the establishment of "a domestic political structure characterized by an internally competitive but nonetheless hegemonic conservative establishment and a marginalized but sometimes influential liberal and Marxist opposition."[15] During his earliest years of involvement with politics, Ishihara aligned himself with the newly formed party as it pursued an agenda of maintaining the reactionary "Reverse Course" of the Occupation period.[16] It was during the 1950s when the Liberal Democratic Party, headed by Kishi Nobusuke, "clearly aimed at rescinding the postwar reforms and strengthening the power of the state over citizens."[17] The party also advanced the Cold War agenda of the United States by identifying itself "first, and above all else, as anticommunist."[18]

Even more relevant to the consideration of literature and art in the 1950s is the view of 1955 as a milestone in the evolution of mass culture. By mass culture, I mean the "administered, commodified culture pretargeted and produced for large numbers of consumers."[19] Although the interwar era also witnessed the rise of mass culture, the scale and pace of postwar mass culture vastly exceeded earlier manifestations.[20] Marilyn Ivy describes 1955 as a year that "marks the true advent of 'mass culture' as a particular historical formation associated with advanced industrial societies. . . . The cultivation of high-level consumer desires via innovations in production and marketing went forward on the basis of a newly acceptable 'privatism,' 'productionism,' and 'modernism,' values fully entrenched by the more affluent late 1960s and 1970s." This rise of a new type of mass culture also signals a "great inversion of the entire prewar social formation."[21] The novelty of postwar mass culture can be found, too, in the newly defined relationship between state and citizen in an emerging democratic, capitalist nation-state, in contrast to the authoritarian imperial state's extensive limitation of the rights of subjects. Postwar mass culture furthermore found its basis in the building of an unprecedentedly large middle class whose members would participate in the democratic process and be active consumers.[22]

Some important mechanisms of this postwar mass culture are the incredible popularity of weekly magazines or tabloids (*shūkanshi*) with huge circulations, publishers' increased interest in attracting mass audiences with inexpensive paperback novels, the continued prosperity of the film industry, and the rapid spread of the relatively new medium of television. In particular, the proliferation of *shūkanshi* contributed to the emergence of a "new middlebrow culture" (*chūkan bunka*), which Katō Hidetoshi (among others) views as eventually absorbing elite and "lowbrow" culture. During the 1940s and especially the 1950s, such patterns of development were associated primarily with the "free world." The 1959 Soviet–U.S. "Kitchen Debate" exemplified the centrality of consumer goods in the conception of Western freedom when Vice President Richard Nixon proudly pointed out to Premier Nikita Khrushchev, "There are some instances where you may be ahead of us, for example in the development of the thrust of your rockets for the investigation of outer space; there may be some instances in which we are ahead of you—in color television, for instance."[23] The Soviet bloc concentrated on the development of heavy industries rather than on consumerism and a large middle class. In Japan, middle-class values included new concepts of the family, identity, and gender.

My main concern in this book is how the high Cold War, its early and most intense phase, affected cultural production in Japan, particularly film, art, and literature. I will start with Kurosawa Akira's film *Record of a Living Being* (*Ikimono no kiroku*, 1955).

Kurosawa Akira's View of the Cold War

Often described as an antinuclear film, *Record of a Living Being* evokes the paralysis created by faith in the "direct threat of atomic destruction," as well as by the malaise or nihilism arising from belief in the balance of terror and other Cold War currents pervasive in everyday life. Kurosawa's film depicts Nakajima, a wealthy industrialist obsessed with his plan of escaping the dangers of H-bomb testing and radioactive fallout by moving his entire extended family—wife, children, mistresses, and illegitimate children—to Brazil.[24] His family, content with their increasingly middle-class lifestyle, not only refuses to leave Japan but resorts to having the

patriarch declared incompetent in a court of law. The themes of conformist domesticity, threatened masculinity, political apathy, nuclear nihilism,
insanity, and fear of apocalypse all are directly linked to Cold War values.
Both Kurosawa and his critics found the film problematic, not only for
formal reasons, but also precisely for this revelation of the disconcerting
concerns of the early Cold War.

Unlike his family, Nakajima feels as certain about the "direct threat
of atomic destruction" as he does about his own power to resist a force
greater than any one person. Initially, his resistance takes the form of outrage. He sits with his back to the camera, shoulders firm, and declares
resolutely to the judge, "I don't feel fear [fuan]. I refuse to be killed by
them [anna mono ni korosarete tamaru mon ka]. Cowards just tremble and
close their eyes—like my children."[25] His anachronistic masculine identity as patriarch, as his family's protector and provider, contribute to his
sense of hubris and control. Once stripped of the means by which to steer
his own destiny, however, Nakajima descends into insanity. Still sincerely
believing in the bomb as apocalyptic, he is transformed into a trembling
creature, stooped, timid, and obsessed.

In keeping with the notion of the 1950s as an "age of fear," Kurosawa
represents the problem of nuclear weapons in psychological rather than
ideological or political terms. Despite the mass grassroots antinuclear
movement in Japan in the mid-1950s, the director dramatizes the extreme
reactions to the arms race—either obsessive fear or total apathy—but excludes political and moral views of the bomb in order to avoid having to
choose sides in the ongoing debates over nuclear weapons.

At the same time, Kurosawa uses the Nakajima family as a means of
exploring a broad range of contemporary social concerns, many of which
were linked specifically to the Cold War. Set during a period of accelerated
economic recovery in the aftermath of the Korean War, the film highlights
a range of discourses central to Western liberal democracy, including the
use of courts of law to assert the rights of women and the family (against
the patriarch) and the growing attachment to domesticity and the middle-
class family. Both the courtroom and the Nakajima home evoke the promise of youth and the rejection of the older generation. In the courtroom,
furthermore, the language of social science, specifically of psychology,
is employed as a means of challenging a regressive notion of patriarchy.
Kurosawa includes hints of the role of the mass media in creating knowledge about the new atomic age. Echoing the polarized political climate of

the age, the director hesitates to show more than a fleeting sympathy for the plight of the workers who are deprived of their livelihood after Nakajima burns down the factory.

Likewise, Kurosawa engages in what might be called self-censorship. In a film so focused on the nuclear arms race, there is not a single mention of the rivals in that competition: the United States and the Soviet Union. The sense of confusion that *Record of a Living Being* conveys derives partly from the aged Nakajima's fear of A-bombs and H-bombs, evoked brilliantly in the performance of the young and usually daring Mifune Toshiro, and partly from the dissonance between Nakajima's family's complacency and his extreme (yet logical) perspective. The audience also feels uneasy because of the unsettled notion of family and masculinity evoked in the film.

As Donald Richie notes, Nakajima is "an old-fashioned, rigid, paternal, traditional Japanese father."[26] He fancies himself the head of a family that is an inviolable unit, as in the pre-1945 concept of *ie* (family). Only with the advent of the postwar constitution and legal system did the individual come to the forefront. Under the new rules of postwar society, the father is no longer able to impose his will on the family as a whole. Accordingly, Nakajima's family rejects his plan to emigrate to Brazil, not only because it does not fit with their own, but also because they are able to challenge him under the new legal system. In the family court, Nakajima angrily berates the judge and mediators: "I don't understand why you must butt into a family affair [*Nande oyako no mondai ni tanin no anata gata wa kuchi o dasu no ka*]." Even though the patriarch's acute anxiety about the bomb is completely in tune with the times, his concept of masculinity and fatherhood is rooted in pre-1945, predemocratic Japan. The film exhibits the novelty of family members taking legal action against one another.

The language of the family court (*katei saibansho*) and the discourses of psychology and the social sciences also show the new liberal democratic values of the Western bloc. The Nakajima family, now individuals in an open society, seeks a psychological classification of "quasi incompetence" (*junkinchisan*) for Nakajima. But Harada, one of the court mediators (played by the great actor Shimura Takashi), questions the court's decision to grant the family the classification because, he believes, Nakajima's fear is shared by all: "But aren't we all afraid of H-bombs ourselves? But we're just not as afraid as that man. So we don't build underground shelters. Nor do we plan to go to Brazil. But we can understand how he feels, can't we? It's a feeling shared by all of us Japanese to some degree. We can't punish him simply because he's overly concerned." Another mediator, however, affirms the court's decision on the basis of new democratic values: "We can't make [the family] go. It's against human rights [*jinken mondai da*]."

Nakajima's family is ungainly and confusing because it contains elements of the prewar family (the authority of the patriarch, his mistresses, and their children). Nakajima has demonstrated his virility time and again with his own wife and with his three mistresses, the youngest of whom is around the same age as his teenage daughter.

Nakajima's eventual descent into insanity is caused partly by his extreme fear of the bomb and partly by his stubborn conviction that he, as patriarch, can maintain control of his family and of the world. While both his family and viewers have difficulty empathizing with this obstinate, authoritarian, and obsessive man, Kurosawa also shows us his caring side. The camera catches Nakajima trembling and crouched over his infant son (by his mistress), attempting to shelter him from a bright burst of lightning that he has mistaken for the *pika* flash of the atomic bomb. On a scorchingly hot day when the family is waiting in the courthouse to meet with the judge, Nakajima disappears, only to bring back soft drinks to the very same relatives who are attempting to remove his financial power and authority. "I'll take care of everybody," he declares later to his family and even to his workers. The deranged Nakajima prostrates himself before his large family and begs them to allow him to take them to Brazil. Such humility on the part of the patriarch is, in Richie's words, "unheard of" in an extended Japanese family with a powerful father like the one portrayed in the film.[27]

Nakajima's wife is his partner in sustaining the fiction of his absolute patriarchal authority and paternalism. Even though she reluctantly participates in her children's plan to gain legal control over Nakajima and his fortune by allowing her name to be used as the chief plaintiff in the case against her husband, she also occasionally reverts to the role of stoic wife.

The renowned actress Miyoshi Eiko convincingly conveys the streak of subservience by maintaining a stooped posture and walking with a shuffle, her face sour from years of self-sacrifice. The still camera shows Nakajima in the foreground as he pleads with his large family for the final time.[28] As Nakajima's speech falters—when none of his family responds to his urgency—his wife chimes in: "I'll beg you [to go to Brazil] too," she cries out. "Please, let's go with him. You know Father has never been wrong. He's always planned our future." She, however, is almost entirely obscured from the camera by Nakajima's body, so that when she does speak, it appears that her voice is coming from his body, like a ventriloquist. At the very moment in *Record of a Living Being* when the wife seems to speak with conviction—even if it is only to urge her family to acquiesce to Nakajima's plan of emigration to Brazil—Nakajima loses his own voice and collapses, never to return to normalcy.

The film offers a source of resistance to patriarchal authority: outspoken and rebellious youth. Nakajima's illegitimate teenage child, the son of his dead mistress, would be recognizable to contemporary audiences as a member of the defiant Sun Tribe (Taiyōzoku), with his fashionable haircut and shorts in a flashy, Hawaiian print.[29] When Nakajima barges in on him and demands to see his savings account passbook, the adolescent turns his back on him. Pointedly ignoring his father, the teenager puts a popular tune on the record player and turns up the volume. Nakajima's youngest daughter, Sue, also behaves saucily. She talks back to her brothers and declares loudly in the presence of her aged mother and her father's young mistress that no one is bothered by the presence of the mistress or her son.

Kurosawa's film also evokes the political climate of the age, though mostly by omission. Even though Nakajima's iron foundry is one of the main settings in the film, the representation of the workers there is understated, to say the least. In the mid-1950s, the rabid anticommunism of Japan's American ally and its own conservative forces led to a stigmatizing of overly sympathetic portraits of laborers and the labor movement, as was typical in socialist realism. In *Record of a Living Being,* the workers have few lines and appear mostly in the background. Only briefly does the film make the viewer feel empathy for the laborers, when they arrive at work only to find that their boss has burned down the factory.[30] Horrified, an elderly worker challenges him, "Master, are you saying that you don't care what happens to us? You don't care if we starve?" These words force Nakajima to the ground, where he grovels in a muddy puddle left by the fire trucks and pounds his own head with his fists. As he did before his family, Nakajima humbles himself before his employees: "I was wrong. Forgive me. I'll find a way to take you all."[31] While Kurosawa made what can only be called progressive films in the immediate postwar years (such as *No Regrets for Our Youth*), he no longer worked in a time sympathetic to such messages. In addition, he omitted any mention of the role of the United States and the Soviet Union in the nuclear arms race, which was at its peak in the 1950s.

The Western bloc's values figure in the resistance by Nakajima's families (legitimate and not) to his plans. In a brilliant sequence, the blissfully inebriated father of his youngest mistress advises Nakajima to "make peace with your family and get as much [money] as you can." And Nakajima's children express satisfaction with middle-class life and their new conception of family. Jiro, one of the sons who wishes to preserve his comfortable family life in Tokyo, tells the court, "I feel that he has no regard for our present lives. Think about how we feel. We're actually quite satisfied here. Why must we go?" When exposed in public, many of the children frown on the father's many lovers and their children.

In *Record of a Living Being*, then, the director uses the Nakajima family as a means of exploring a broad range of contemporary social concerns, many of which were linked specifically to the Cold War. Japan's involvement with the nuclear arms race was not the only intersection with the changing world. Although Kurosawa never refers directly to the superpowers' rivalry, he describes throughout the film the concerns and tensions related to the global dynamic, including the spread of discourses of Western liberal democracy, such as the use of courts of law to assert the rights of the individual and the growing influence of the social sciences. Resonating with free-world ideals and the notion of containment, the family asserts its growing attachment to domesticity and the middle-class family. We also detect hints of a new, privileged, youth culture and the evolving mass culture and media. Kurosawa's detachment of both nuclear weapons and the working class from politics is another sign of the cautious self-censorship demanded in this polarized environment.

Japan as a Front: Military Bases and Cities of Peace

In a famous scene from *Record of a Living Being*, Nakajima follows with his eyes the sound of airplanes as they streak overhead. His young mistress, though, seems oblivious to the roar of their engines as they cut low over the house. To audiences used to thinking of the film as an atomic film, the planes may suggest the bomb. But these planes have nothing to do with the bomb; they are not B-29s like the *Enola Gay* or *Bock's Car* from 1945. Instead, they are fighter planes from one of the hundreds of U.S. military bases in Japan in the 1950s. No contemporary audience member would have to be reminded of the growing controversy over the stationing of U.S. military facilities in Japan during the Occupation, then the Korean War, and then in the post-Occupation era, or of the security treaties that allowed the U.S. presence. Only four years after this film, Tokyo witnessed the rise of massive anti–security treaty protests in anticipation of its renewal in 1960. Even as Nakajima slipped away from sanity, he knew that these were not high-altitude bombers of the type that would drop a hydrogen bomb.[32]

The controversy over the U.S. military bases is often forgotten or dismissed as a local affair. But along with the symbolic authority of Article 9 of the postwar constitution and the mainstreaming of peace education, the early postwar transformation of Hiroshima and Nagasaki into cities of peace contributed heavily to the understanding of Japan as a cultural oasis independent of Cold War tensions.[33] Popular imagination fashioned Hiroshima and Nagasaki into sacred spaces buffered from external rancor, reinforcing the idea of Japan's insulation. Indeed, so powerful are these long-standing images of the cities as symbolic centers from which a pacifist Japan has risen that they overshadow the presence of the numerous U.S. military facilities on Japanese soil, some close to the cities of peace.[34] Nonetheless, these military bases were essential to America's global strategy of containment during the Cold War.

In short, both Japan and the United States conceived of Hiroshima and Nagasaki as having universal meanings. In contrast, the cultural and political implications of American military bases in Japan were downplayed as merely local in nature, despite (or perhaps because of) Japanese anti-base activism.[35] Yet those very bases had a central function in American Cold War foreign policy. The imbalance in the cultural significance of the pacifist and martial spaces in Japan does not, however, appear so contradictory if we think of Hiroshima and Nagasaki spatially and symbolically as battlefronts in the Cold War. Even the advocacy of peace had specific political, partisan meanings early in the Cold War.

I regard Hiroshima and Nagasaki as Cold War centers because they are central to Japanese culture as both sites of memory and barometers of change in the arms race, the antinuclear movement, and cultural production related to nuclear technology. Lisa Yoneyama links Hiroshima's postwar status with deterrence, asserting that in the eyes of the U.S. military occupiers, the

> commemorative city of Hiroshima was . . . designed specifically to demonstrate the interchangeability of "the atomic bomb" and "peace." Remembering a link between the bomb and peace fostered

the conviction that without use of the atomic weapon, peace in the Pacific could not have been achieved in a timely manner. . . . The textual production of Hiroshima as the A-bombed city that revived as a mecca of world peace thus helped disseminate the view that the world's peaceful order was attained and will be maintained not by diplomatic efforts or negotiations, but by sustaining a menacing military force and technological supremacy.[36]

In 1949, numerous cultural and military events revealed the extent to which the project of rebuilding Hiroshima as a city of peace conformed to America's aims of shifting its international image from the first user of atomic weapons to a supporter of peace. From early 1949, indications of the Soviets' development of nuclear arms spelled an end to the U.S. monopoly. The Soviets' possession of nuclear weapons may have reduced the absolute power of the United States as the sole possessor, but it also had the effect of spreading the moral burden for dubious uses of a powerful technology for military purposes. At the 1947 Communist International, the Soviet Union had declared itself a "bearer of peace" (*heiwa no ninaite*) and further stated that it reflected "in its policies the hopes of all progressive people in the world who do not wish to take part in the new wars that are the purview of capitalism."[37] Beginning in 1949, however, the arms race between the United States and the Soviet Union exposed the lie behind the promise that either system was capable of creating a world ruled not by violence but by justice. For its part, the United States strove to improve its moral standing in the international community by propagating the image of Japan as a peace-loving ally.[38]

The cultural Cold War was fought in Hiroshima and Nagasaki by means of a wide variety cultural practices, including commemorative acts, political protest, art exhibitions, and the repetition of visiting, returning to, and seeing these cities. Many antinuclear groups, individuals, and the cities rightly saw their own activism as resistance. For many leftists, the Marxism of the Soviet Union and the newly created People's Republic of China offered credible strategies for ending war and forming a peaceful socialist society. One strain of the antinuclear movement, however, created an image of itself as nonaligned, independent, antimilitarist, and prodemocratic rather than as complicit with the U.S.–Japanese security alliance.[39] Under the overarching goal of "peace," people from a broad range of political backgrounds joined together to celebrate Hiroshima. In affirmation of the peace constitution, Hiroshima's mayor, Hamai Shinzō, declared August 6 as a "Day of Peace in 1949." Would the Cold War structure tolerate such a nonaligned political force? If anything, the fate of the peace movement in Hiroshima and Nagasaki points to the difficulties of achieving neutrality and working as an effective political force during the Cold War. As Rana Mittner points out, "Intellectual dissidents . . . conscious of the irony of national security states invoking discourses of freedom while applying ever greater controls, sought to avoid polarization and steer a middle course: the so-called 'third way.' This was always a precarious position given the fatal either/or logic of the Cold War."[40] Although along with and through their satellite states, the United States and the Soviet Union waged an aggressive war of propaganda, no government dictated Cold War discourse, which also emanated from cultural production by artists and critics and as part of a broad conversation that took place across national borders.

Although antinuclearism became a truly nationwide movement from around the time of the Bikini incident in the mid-1950s (a U.S. H-bomb test that resulted in extensive civilian exposure to excessive radiation, also known as the *Lucky Dragon* incident), it is important to keep in mind that this popular wave of protest stemmed from the mostly the leftist-led activism of the late 1940s. The movement never spoke with a single ideological voice and not only took the form of protest and marching in the streets, but also depended in critical ways on the activism of artists, writers, and critics, as well as links between these cultural figures and political organizations, especially the communists and socialists.

In the English-language literature, the Occupation and moderate activists have been regarded as the main molders of the notion of an apolitical, universal peace. In fact, many leading Japanese artists, intellectuals, and citizens in the movement were inspired by socialist ideals. Many of the individuals whom I consider in these chapters—the painters Maruki Iri and Maruki Toshi, the critics who supported writer Hara Tamiki, and the filmmaker Kamei Fumio—were strongly influenced by Marxist thought and had ties to the Communist Party. During the early postwar era, a leftist ideology surfaced, partly as remnants of the idealistic progressive thought and activism that had been brutally repressed and eventually silenced by the imperial government and thought police, and partly under the influence of international communism. Soviet rhetoric supplied progressive critics with an alternative vision of peace based on a socialist historical model. Japanese activists also had links with European antinuclear movements, which were heavily influenced by Marxist thought and communists.

Koiso Ryōhei, poster for foreign audiences promoting the image of Hiroshima as the city of peace. (Courtesy of Kobe City Koiso Memorial Museum)

Citizens sign antinuclear petitions, Tokyo, May 1955. (From Daigo Fukuryūmaru Foundation, ed., *Compiled Materials on the Bikini H-Bomb Incident* [Tokyo, 2004]. Courtesy of Daigo Fukuryūmaru Foundation)

It is hardly coincidence that the planning for Hiroshima as a city of peace coincided with the push for the remilitarization of Japan under the security arrangements with the United States. A crucial component of Japan's remilitarization was the guarantee of an extensive network of U.S. military bases. As part of its policy of containment of the Soviet Union, the United States regarded air bases close to the Asian continent as a high priority, especially before the introduction of the B-52 Stratofortress in the mid-1950s, the first long-range, intercontinental bomber. If Japan could house bombers loaded with nuclear weapons, then it could also espouse the peace that the United States was trying to preserve with those bombs. Two factors—Article 9 of the Japanese constitution, which was the legal barrier to the country's full remilitarization, and the ethical realization of the bomb's significance—made the creation of a city of peace in a Cold War ally of the United States both desirable and useful.[41]

Thus the international city of peace initially seems to espouse a nonideological notion of universal peace, but the planning itself took place under the watchful eye of the Allied Occupation. Sanctioned cultural products and practices tended to emphasize liberal democratic and capitalist ideals, not communist and socialist notions of peace. During the decade after the war, the list of famous visitors to Hiroshima was dominated by well-known Americans such as Eleanor Roosevelt, Norman Cousins, and Helen Keller. With Allied Occupation censorship easing up in the late 1940s, Japanese people had greater leeway to express their views concerning nuclear weapons and politics. Yet this seemingly liberal stance may have had benefits for the United States as well, as the promotion of a positive image.

During 1949, the American and Japanese authorities' collaboration in taking advantage of the seemingly nonaligned message of peace is especially evident. Not only would the remaking of Hiroshima help change the image of the United States from atomic warrior to protector of peace, it would also help the future sovereign Japan overcome its past militarist expansionist image. Accordingly, in early April 1949 the Japanese crown prince paid a visit to Hiroshima. Then on May 2, 1949, in still-occupied Japan, the Japanese Ministry of Construction allocated ¥2 billion for the Hiroshima Peace Museum. In Japan, the notable nuclear-related events that month (the start of the fiscal year) included the publication of the Japanese translation of John Hersey's *Hiroshima* (Hōsei University Press) and an exhibition of the Hiroshima Peace Bell (sponsored by Hiroshima Prefecture) and photographs of Hiroshima from *Life* magazine (in the Mitsukoshi Department Store in Tokyo's Nihonbashi district). The Tokyo exhibition was aimed at promoting tourism to Hiroshima. In addition, the Japanese Diet passed a bill in May 1949 that designated Hiroshima and Nagasaki as international cities of peace and of culture, respectively. Locally, 65 percent of Hiroshima residents voted in favor of this designation and urban plan. Then on August 6, 1949, an exhibition of atom bomb photographs opened at the Chūgoku Shinbun Hall in Hiroshima. Also in 1949, Tange Kenzo's design for the peace museum was chosen.[42]

The timing of the founding of Hiroshima as a city of peace seems all the more extraordinary when one considers the escalating arms race and bellicose posture of the United States and the Soviet Union at that time. On April 6, 1949, President Harry Truman told the press that he might order the use of atomic bombs if that were necessary to protect democracy. Despite his reservations about atomic weapons, Truman publicly refused to rule out their use. Indeed, in Europe, Truman's comment, along with the possibility of a Soviet bomb, led to the Partisans of Peace World Conference held on April 20. Neither an antinuclear petition presented to President Truman by the city of Hiroshima on June 5 nor the slogan "No More Hiroshimas," which was coined by an American, was banned by the Occupation, nor did they have a significant effect on the all-out arms race that was about to commence. In late September 1949, President Truman announced to the world the news of the Soviet Union's first nuclear tests earlier that year.

Every year since the bombing in 1945, a memorial ceremony has taken place on August 6 in Hiroshima. The second anniversary was broadcast on NHK radio in Japan, and on CBS in the United States. In 1948, the anniversary of the bombing changed from a local observance to a larger-scale ceremony, with delegates from abroad and even a message from the Supreme Allied Commander, General Douglas MacArthur. In 1949, as if in anticipation of the end of the Allied Occupation, Prime Minister Yoshida Shigeru was the leader offering the message.

If the cultural meanings of nuclear weapons and the discourse of the Cold War began to be presented in 1949 in complex and contradictory ways in international diplomacy and national politics, what transpired at the local cultural level? Many made the journey to Hiroshima for rituals of remembrance and mourning as well for political protest against the escalating arms race. A number of critics and artists also left Hiroshima, the Cold War front, with the aim of disseminating knowledge and creating a broader discourse about nuclear weapons and the Cold War, a dialogue "separate from the official statist narratives."[43]

Confusing Nuclear Weapons

As a category of periodization, the notion of an atomic age flows from technological concepts of time and a belief in linear scientific progress, divorced from moral and political categories. In contrast, the framework of the Cold War forces us to look at sociocultural and political complexities that evolved over the second half of the twentieth century. Even after the end of the Cold War, the "system of deterrence" has so "insinuated itself from *the inside* into all the cracks of daily life" that we can barely imagine a time when the apparent threat of nuclear apocalypse was not a part of our daily life. We cannot conceive that anyone could have "confused" nuclear weapons with conventional weapons. In the early stages of the Cold War, however, that was precisely what happened. During the crucial years between Hiroshima/Nagasaki and the Cuban missile crisis, deterrence had not yet become an imperative, and the Cold War was starting to become apparent in "all the cracks of daily life."

Outside Hiroshima and Nagasaki, how did Japanese audiences perceive the atomic present? For Walter Benjamin, in the modern age "each new means of destruction . . . also required a greater level of social anesthesia to normalize its impact on everyday life."[44] The first time that a newsreel of a hydrogen bomb test was shown in an American movie theater, on April 1, 1952, it "followed its terrifying ten-minute report on the H-bomb with an upbeat 'Hollywood Fashion Holiday,'" in which starlets modeled swimsuits and leisure wear.[45]

Even with the strong U.S.–Japanese alliance after the Occupation, the U.S. government no longer strictly controlled the narrative concerning the bomb. Nor was there immediate consensus in Japan on the moral and practical meanings of nuclear weapons. Instead, the complex nature of nuclear weapons meant that cultural production was one of the prime conduits for learning about and understanding the bomb. Given the Occupation's censorship of atomic materials and the lack of a comprehensive civil defense campaign in Japan, what did people know about the bomb?[46] How did artists and critics deal with the nuclear issue in their work during this unstable period in the Cold War?

In 1952, not long after the Occupation's ban on A-bomb topics officially ended, the Japanese public had the opportunity to see images of the testing of nuclear weapons that dwarfed those used in 1945. Professor Watanabe Kazuo of Tokyo University watched the United States's first test of a hydrogen bomb, on the screen of a movie theater:

> The other day, I saw a newsreel of the first hydrogen bomb test [conducted on November 1, 1952, in the Marshall Islands]. As we watched the atomic cloud billow high in the sky, the friend who was with me commented, "It's a stanza from an epic poem." In my eyes, though, the test seemed nothing like an epic poem. It felt like something truly horrible, something hideous, something frightful that greatly complicates our responsibility as human beings. It literally made me shudder with fear. Please keep in mind that my friend is not a man who idealizes war. He loves peace and possesses much clearer opinions about the current push to remilitarize Japan than do I. In respect to nuclear weapons, he of course regards them as inevitably leading mankind to great misfortune. I can only guess that his spontaneous description of the film as "a stanza from an epic poem" came from his perception of some kind of beauty there. Or perhaps he felt fear, and chose to express his fear with a literary, aesthetic (!?) turn of phrase.[47]

As Watanabe suggests, even sensitive people were confused about the proper reaction to the H-bomb and its display. The Marshall Islands test was separate from warfare and was presented as a spectacle. What were the broader contexts of this representation and viewing of a powerful weapon? Before discussing the specific dynamics of 1950s culture in Japan, we will look at the broader—indeed, global—discursive field of atomic culture.

Nuclear discourse was made possible by new technology as well as by the elaboration of a preexisting discourse of progress, the broadly held notion that harnessing the energy of the atom would contribute to the advancement of science and, in turn, would benefit humanity. The fact that military applications—specifically the 1945 atomic bombs—preceded peaceful uses of nuclear technology does not contradict this claim. Indeed, stories of the coming atomic utopia, replete with amazing cures for disease and nuclear-powered cars, began appearing in both the Japanese and the American press very soon after the Hiroshima and Nagasaki bombings.[48] Of course, this was partly a tactic meant to divert attention from the difficult issues surrounding the weapons. Yet the notion of positive uses for nuclear technology was by no means a novel fantasy but instead a logical extension of the idea of progress.

The concept of an "atomic age" thus contained both the ominous threat of nuclear annihilation and the exhilarating prospect of a bright future brought about by technology. The creation of an atomic utopia with limitless energy, however, depended on the idea that people could remain in control of the technology as well as the by-products of its use. In addition, the ideology of progress suggested that this innovative technology would radically transform the nature of war and, in turn, give rise to new articulations of culture. In specific historical terms, the social meanings of atomic weapons were inextricably linked with the Allies' victory over fascism and the defeat of imperial Japan. For this reason, many people in both the former Allied countries and colonized Asia regarded the A-bomb in a positive light, practically and morally. If we remember the high Cold War as the "age of fear," we should not forget that it was also the age of the triumph of science.

In the 1940s and 1950s, although the imagination of a positive nuclear culture existed in tandem with memory of Fat Man and Little Boy, the names of the bombs dropped on Hiroshima and Nagasaki, neither governments nor citizens knew much about nuclear technology, constructive or destructive. As a U.S. military spokesman pointed out at the first postwar atomic bomb test, on July 1, 1946, "We expect to learn facts of great value. As a final word, I hope that the public will adopt the same attitude as we do in Joint Task Force One. . . . There is much more to learn."[49] Given this paucity of information, how could the bomb and the atomic age be understood? Diverse types of knowledge about the bomb ranged from emotional, visual, and moral knowledge based on firsthand or mediated experience to empirical knowledge stemming from scientific or medical research. In addition, socially committed artists and critics played a central role in promoting various understandings of the technology, science, morality, and experience of nuclear weapons.

The New Age, Witnesses, and Secrecy

From the start of the Cold War, it was customary to describe the atomic bomb as possessing a destructive power far beyond that of conventional weapons and also as ushering in a new age in human history. Accounts by people who had direct experiences of the Hiroshima and Nagasaki bombings conveyed authority partly because they belonged to this new world order, one dominated by miraculous nuclear weaponry rather than crude conventional armaments. One result of the evolving discourse that emphasized the narration of A-bomb experiences as exceptional was the severing of the A-bomb from the twentieth-century international culture of extreme violence based on aerial warfare, the very culture that had given rise to the invention of nuclear weapons in the first place.[50] The fierce determination of, first, the United States and, later, the Soviet Union to develop weapons more destructive than the atomic bombs contributed to the public imagination of violence and apocalypse as inevitable.

This myth of atomic uniqueness arose from a modernist discourse of progress, an understanding of the A-bomb as the triumph of man and science and furthermore as a sign of human proximity to the sacred. Positive regard for nuclear technology was not associated exclusively with conservatism or with a single ideology. In 1954, the progressive intellectual Watanabe Kazuo, while horrified about the continued testing of H-bombs, declared without irony that "harnessing atomic power is a triumph for mankind. Humans have become a successful Prometheus."[51]

The literature and the visual record of the August 1945 atomic bombings were extensive, and the project of creating and sharing knowledge about the bomb was remarkably broad based—indeed, global in scale. We know far less, however, about the Cold War discourse in Japan surrounding new thermonuclear weapons technologies and the dissemination of knowledge about the weapons.

In contrast to previous military technologies, the atomic and hydrogen bombs were studied broadly by civilians. For example, many Japanese physicians and scientists undertook projects designed to ascertain the levels of fallout in the atmosphere, rain, water, and food supply resulting from atomic testing. In the late 1950s, university students served as the crew of the *Shunkotsumaru,* a ship that surveyed levels of radiation in the South Pacific.[52] While some studying the bomb were motivated by their opposition to nuclear weapons, the presence of civilians and military personnel as witnesses to nuclear testing became central to the propaganda value of the tests.[53] In other words, the unusual Cold War practice of inviting observers to tests of nuclear devices meant that civilians and ordinary soldiers played an important role in the development of the weapons and in the discourse of deterrence. In this way, many sectors of society—from civilian physicians to novelists, from the military to university researchers, from activists to *hibakusha*—participated in generating knowledge about the weapons. The relatively open exchange concerning nuclear weapons contrasts greatly with the arcane language and realist worldview that subsequently defined weapons research and strategy. Nuclear possessor nations soon recognized that control over nuclear-related information was the key to dominance in the Cold War.

Much attention has been paid to the Allied Occupation's censorship of A-bomb–related texts in Japan and to the Atomic Bomb Casualty Commission's (ABCC) refusal to provide medical treatment for the *hibakusha* who were its research subjects. While the ABCC's posture is difficult to defend in moral terms, it serves as a reminder that at the time, the U.S. government itself was in the process of acquiring basic knowledge about nuclear technologies and especially about the effects of radiation. Owing to the invisibility and unfamiliarity of radiation, the government was able to play down the dangers, and for the same reason, scientists and citizens were hard-pressed to convince people about the unique threats posed by massive doses of radiation. Part of the *hibakusha*'s most valued experiential knowledge was their intimate understanding of the harmful, often lethal, effects of radiation. It is in this respect that their stories differ most from those of the survivors of conventional urban warfare.

The tardiness in the government's acknowledgment of the deleterious affects of massive doses of radiation on the human body was compounded by a general lack of awareness of the dangers of environmental pollution. From the late 1940s through the early 1960s, both the United States and the Soviet Union almost exclusively tested nuclear bombs aboveground, despite the huge release of radioactive fallout into the atmosphere. The high doses of radiation resulting from this type of test traveled through the atmosphere to populated areas, causing injury and death. In addition, in many parts of the world, the fallout contaminated rain and water and entered the food chain. Eventually, awareness of airborne radioactive particles as pollution contributed to the rise of the environmental movement.[54] The careless and reckless handling of radioactive materials also resulted in fatal accidents and high levels of radioactivity around nuclear weapon production and storage facilities in both the United States and the Soviet Union. The continued failure to maintain safety in nuclear power plants furthermore demonstrates the ignorance of the dangers of excessive radiation. Thus the hubris that encouraged the United States and other countries to design and test larger and larger lethal weapons like the hydrogen bomb was combined with their vision of human mastery of nature that prevailed before the rise of the environmental movement.

Part of the knowledge related to the Hiroshima and Nagasaki bombings was the accounts of those who had lived through the bombings. These nonmilitary accounts of air war emerged at the very end of the war and at the start of the uneasy peace that came to be called the Cold War. Among all the stories of war, the testimonies and narratives concerning Hiroshima and Nagasaki attained a special status. How did this exceptionalist discourse develop?

In contrast to the testimonials of soldiers about the hell of the battlefield and trenches, accounts by nonmilitary personnel who survived war from the air dominated the post-1945 narratives about the horrors of the war. If anything was new about the world war in the 1930s and 1940s, it was the extent to which aerial bombing made battlefields of cities and towns of all sizes and exposed civilians to the violence of war in their own homes and neighborhoods. In an age of total war, governments enlisted all citizens and all spaces for the national military effort, and consequently no person was a civilian. Rather, citizens were either combatants or noncombatants mobilized in the service of the state. In the rhetoric of total war, a city was no longer considered a city. Immediately after the atomic bomb was dropped on Hiroshima, when President Truman described the city as an important Japanese military base, he did so not out of ignorance or as a means of averting guilt for what the United States had just done. Rather, his description was fully consistent with the discourse of total war that gripped the world.

With the cessation of hostilities and the cultural demobilization of the apparatuses of total war, the narratives of the long militarized period included tales of both the great land and naval battles and the air war in the cities. During the 1940s and 1950s, at the height of the Cold War, the most prominent and widely circulated accounts of experiences of air war focused on Hiroshima and Nagasaki. Although the conventional air attacks caused far more destruction of property and fatalities in Chinese cities such as Nanjing and Shanghai; European cities such as London, Hamburg, and Dresden; and dozens of Japanese cities, including Tokyo, Osaka, and Yokohama, we find many fewer accounts about them. How can we explain this?

Both President Truman and the Japanese emperor labeled the atomic bomb a "new" weapon, one possessing such awesome power that it seemed to have the capacity to bring a world war to an end and even to change the nature of war.[55] Indeed, the Allies had accomplished their mission with a single plane and a single warhead, rather than with hundreds of planes and thousands of canisters filled with napalm. The unstudied and thus surprising effects of radiation led to countless deaths and much suffering that continued for days, months, and years after the bombing. But as Michael Sherry observed, "Declarations of the past's irrelevance masked the persistence of old habits."[56] The August 1945 bombings were far from innovative in one important sense, as they were the logical consequences of the culture of violence of total war and of the repeated use of strategic bombing by most parties involved in the world war. The path to atomic weapons was not entirely separate from that of conventional bombs. As David Painter comments, "Changes in the technology of war reinforced shifts in the global balance of power. Conventional weapons had reached new heights of destructiveness during World War II. . . . The atomic bomb was especially frightening because it magnified the destructive force of warfare to a previously unimagined scale and concentrated that destruction in time." This concentration was not unique to weapons, however. Marshall McLuhan pointed out that "it is this trend toward more and more power with less and less hardware that is characteristic of the electric age of information."[57]

In 1945, the media similarly described the A-bombs as "new," even though since the early twentieth century, much had appeared in print

Mukai Junkichi, *Shadow (in the Suzhou Sky)*, oil on panel (1938). (Courtesy of Fukutomi Tarō Collection)

about radioactivity and the potential for the development of both nuclear power and nuclear weapons. In literature, H. G. Wells's novel *The World Set Free* (1914) predicted a world dominated by "atomic bombs," and beginning in the 1920s, the Japanese press featured scientists who had done research on physics and radioactivity, such as Albert Einstein and the Curies.[58] In fact, as if affirming the promise of the atomic age, a film from Hollywood about Marie Curie's life became a hit in Tokyo theaters in the early years of the Occupation.[59]

Whether or not one acknowledged the lingering suffering of radiation sickness, most people knew that the atomic bombs had caused grotesque and horrible varieties of instant injury and death, as well as the threat of apocalypse. From the start of the Cold War in 1945, however, the bomb also had positive attributes. Even though no good could come of other types of weapons of mass destruction, such as chemical and biological weapons, nuclear technology was understood as possessing a redemptive potential in material terms, as a means of generating power and as a tool with medical and engineering applications.

Literary critical habits also promoted nuclear exceptionalism. One of the most famous novellas about the bombing of Hiroshima and its aftermath, Hara Tamiki's *Summer Flowers* (*Natsu no hana*, 1947) has often been read as a literary expression of a man's realization of the new age and the horror of the new weapons. The narrator of *Summer Flowers* has never been to the battlefront, but he has some secondhand knowledge about air raids. After he realizes the bombing "that was bound to come to Hiroshima" has begun at last, he first believes that only his house has been hit. But when he comes out of his house, he realizes that the whole city had been leveled. Even though the descriptions of death from radiation sickness are horrifying reminders of the threat presented by nuclear weapons, much of the ruins and many of the injured people and corpses bear striking similarities to the destruction caused by conventional weapons like those that rained down on cities in strategic bombing raids. Far less frequently do we find descriptions of conventional bombing raids, making it easier to forget the many ways in which a conventional air war resembles an atomic attack.[60]

Sun and Speed: Cold War Youth

Although A-bomb art and activism in Japan have earned much attention as aspects of Cold War culture, the Cold War influenced cultural production in other ways as well. In Kurosawa's *Record of a Living Being*, both the rebellious illegitimate teenage son in his aloha shirt and Nakajima's saucy teenage daughter suggest the emergence of youth culture in society and the media. Several cultural events and personalities of the 1950s, such as the Sun Tribe (Taiyōzoku) cult of youth, illustrate the variety of ways that Western-bloc Cold War dynamics swayed mass culture, resulting in a new variety of middlebrow cultural values, aesthetics, and institutions. These changes came about partly because of the expansion and elaboration of mass culture, the booming consumerism, the changes in ideas about adolescence, and the demographic shifts contributing to an unprecedented expansion of the urban middle class.

Given the tremendous growth of mass culture after the war, it is not surprising that the Cold War battle of words and images found expression in the media and arts and letters. The valorization of consumerism, the flood of advertising, and the affirmation of middle-class values in the movies, on television, and in the press are indicators that Japan was firmly on the road to an economy of capitalist abundance after decades of the scarcity and sacrifice demanded by war and empire building. One sign of Japan's adherence to the Western bloc's Cold War values appears in the mass phenomenon of the adulation of youth culture.

Popular Japanese magazines from mid-1950s contain numerous photos of adolescents having fun on their motorboats, driving big fast cars, and holding each other tight, clad only in fashionable swimwear. In the pictures, the so-called Sun Tribe boys look bored, and they make a point of rebelling against their elders. The Sun Tribe shared many traits with James Dean and the rebellious youth seen in the American and Western European media of the same era. Novelist Ishihara Shintarō, the prototypical Sun Tribe youth, wrote books (such as the novel *Season of the Sun* [*Taiyō no kisetsu*, 1955]) and movies that made these teenagers seem appealing and stylish and not immoral. He and his production team referred to them as "Sun Tribe" rather than juvenile delinquents because it sounded sexier and promised to promote sales of his books and movies.[61] They also sensed the appeal of these nonconformist young people to a broad audience. Why would the Sun Tribe appeal to Japanese audiences of the day?

Doubtless, audiences in Japan loved (or were repulsed by) the wild aloha shirts, the hairstyles, and the surface. Below the surface, though, the lure of depoliticized rebellion, carefree and robust youth resonated with the rapidly changing culture. The political disengagement of the Sun Tribe fit well into a capitalist society on the brink of enormous growth, a society that did not encourage its young people to concern themselves with class struggle or socialist notions of peace. Ishihara's imagination of youth also struck a cord with audiences as a fantasy of adolescents who were thoroughly accustomed to abundance instead of the hunger and scarcity that still plagued Japan even years after the war. These were teenagers, who, if they chose to, could instantly gratify their lusts and desires with boats and cars and sex.

Even if slightly immoral, then, the possibility of material abundance and a carefree attitude made the Sun Tribe compelling. Ishihara's bright splash onto the 1950s cultural scene affirmed that sovereign Japan's postwar recovery would conform to Occupation goals of fashioning Japan as East Asia's capitalist workshop. In addition, this workshop was more than just an industrial powerhouse, as the cultural and social goals of its citizens started to match those of the discourse emphasizing individualism, consumerism, and private property. The Sun Tribe also expressed a movement toward what has been called "privatization," which Kristin Ross describes as the "movement inward . . . a movement echoed on the level of everyday life by the withdrawal of the new middle classes to their newly comfortable domestic interiors . . . to the enclosure of private automobiles." Such privatization found its basis in "an ideology of happiness built around the new unit of middle-class consumption, the couple," as well as in "depoliticization."[62]

Although we can easily identify prewar Japanese manifestations of these socioeconomic and cultural phenomena, the postwar versions took place on a far greater scale and differed qualitatively as well. During the 1950s, the young generation started to appear as both the primary subject of and the audience for the *après-guerre* mass culture. Its audiences were fascinated by the aesthetics and values of the rebellious youth. But older writers and critics still enamored of imperial-era configurations of the literary world expressed alarm at the media's role in popularizing the cult of youth, as did intellectuals who had been wary of the prewar fascist manipulation of mass culture. On an institutional level, Ishihara's mid-1950s fame forged a new interaction between the mass culture media of film and new journalistic formats such as, on the one hand, the weekly magazines and television and, on the other, the values and social practices of the elite cultural literary establishment, which were now understood to be linked to the social sciences and psychology. The rebellious Ishihara and his crew, however, offered few innovative models of gender roles and identity. Instead, they drew on the premilitarist fascination with speed as a cultural mode, a preoccupation with the glorious speed of trains and energy of machines, which had been championed early in the twentieth century by Italian futurists such as Filippo Marinetti and then in the liberal atmosphere of urban interwar Japan. The strongly gendered component of this cultural value also affirms virility and strength and advocates the destruction of elite cultural institutions.[63]

Discourses of Western Liberal Democracy

Kristin Ross proposes that "a convincing case" can be made that during the 1950s, "the foremost American export . . . was not Coca-Cola or movies but the supremacy of the social sciences."[64] The U.S. government's enormous financial and organizational support for the dissemination of social science methods and values abroad confirms that this country was actively promoting the spread of American-style sociology, psychology, and other disciplines during these early postwar decades. The motives for the U.S. strategy of containing Soviet communism translated not only into bombers or nuclear warheads pointed toward Soviet territory but also into the intellectual and "psychological containment of the progress of Marxism in the world."[65] The weapon of social science operated on several levels: in academia, in broad social concepts of authority and of youth, and in the most basic assumptions about the nature of the Cold War as a war.

On one level, the U.S. strategy of containment targeted intellectuals on the assumption that their conversion to American social science method and concepts might ensure greater allegiance to the free world. The social sciences, with their promise of scientific method and objectivity in the study of human society and behavior, might serve as a counterbalance to the systematic approach of Marxism. Abundant government funding helped elevate the status of sociology, psychology, and other related disciplines.[66] Although I will not examine the interaction among the social sciences in Japan here, I should point out that in Japan after 1945, American social science entered academia just as many other Americanizing influences—from material cultural to politics to popular culture—flooded into Occupied Japan. The Empire of Japan had incorporated the tools and discourses of social sciences, and so, as Andrew Barshay notes, the social sciences manifested as "technical expertise and planning as a form of engaged social science" were "already well established," even in early postwar Japan.[67] Yet the social sciences that dominate today in Japan are very much a postwar manifestation and must be understood in relation to the increasing dominance of American articulations of the social sciences and modernization theory that were introduced as part of the United States's Cold War agenda. Notably, Marxism long remained influential in much of Japanese scholarship and the universities even as its influence began to wane in other areas of society.

An Ominous Psychological War

Let us go back to Abe Tomoji's striking perception of the eerie tension that pervaded society at the height of the Cold War. The obsessive certainty that a catastrophic world war loomed in the near future, a battle that would annihilate all life on earth, certainly contributed to people's feeling that they were living in an age of fear. Remember, though, that Abe did not describe a straightforward emotion of pure terror but instead a more complex atmosphere and mind-set. *Bukimi,* the adjective that he used to evoke the mood of the day, implies something weird, ominous, strange. Similarly, in Kurosawa's *Record of a Living Being,* Nakajima speaks of his own reactions to the nuclear threat as *fuan,* a term that can mean "fear" but also "anxiety" and "uneasiness." We can better understand what gave rise to this complex tension once we realize that the terror of nuclear weapons was only part of what Abe found unsettling. The terror of the bomb existed in a discourse designed to instill a mind-set of constant vigilance in the face of awesome weapons and also a dark enemy threatening to contaminate one's very mind and soul. Compounded with the near chaos of the international scene, the prospect of an endless war of nerves (in French, *guerre de nerfs*) and the discourse of fear that inscribed it on every mind produced a disquieting peace.

The eerie tension also stemmed from the disturbing legacy of modern total war. Although World War II and the Cold War were fought by radically different means, the two conflicts had in common the belief that war was fundamentally psychological in nature. Owing to the invocation of total war by all the major players and the increasing dominance of air war, World War II came to be characterized by a blurring of "boundaries between military and civilian targets, between wartime and peacetime conflicts."[68] Both human identity and space were subject to this blurring. In total war, the fate of the civilian's body and social role started to merge with that of the soldier (as suggested by the close terms "combatant" and "noncombatant"). The increasing lack of differentiation between battlefields and the towns and neighborhoods where people lived and worked led to a breakdown of boundaries in spatial terms and ultimately in a psychological sense as well. As part of a world war that would eventually end, the unnerving mind-set (no place, no person, was safe) might have seemed temporary. In contrast, during the Cold War, these uncertain, shifting boundaries and the maintenance of the psychological assumptions of total war "took on an eerie permanence."[69]

In the U.S. military, "psychological operations experts were only stating what many Americans already felt when they pointed out that peace had lost much of its previous association with security: peace was 'simply a period of less violent war in which nonmilitary means are predominantly used to achieve certain political objectives.'"[70] Although Japan did not, of course, operate under precisely the same social and psychological assumptions as the United States did, the alliance between the two nations, as well as Japan's innumerable contributions to U.S. Cold War military strategy, meant that this psychological approach was not completely alien. Even pacifist Japan was deeply implicated in the battle of nerves. As I suggested earlier, the bombed, pacifist Japan served as a showcase for hope after nuclear war even as it tried to lead the world in the effort to ban the bomb.

Cold War combatants must employ psychological weapons, tools that experts in the fields of psychology and communication studies (among others) could provide. This strategy was not based on new Cold War assumptions about the nature of war for the U.S. military and its allies. Rather, the military was simply carrying on "the fundamental lesson learned during World War II: war should be treated as a psychological struggle and laboratory."[71] On the crudest level, this practice was demonstrated by the CIA's extensive use of psychological techniques of interrogation and treatment of "brainwashed" subjects (during covert operations in Korea, for example). Historians of social science like Ellen Herman remind us that this emphasis on psychology is based on the particular sociohistorical developments of the twentieth-century United States and should not be considered universal. Herman points out that "psychology's face is so familiar that it is tempting, but wrong, to consider it an ahistorical fact of life or an entity so amorphous and all-pervasive that it eludes definition altogether."[72]

For the occupation of Japan and the diplomatic relations that followed, the Western bloc's goal was not merely demilitarization and democratization aimed at eliminating the structures of a fascist, militarist society but also ideological and cultural "reorientation."[73] Throughout the Cold War, both the United States and the Soviet Union made extensive use of propaganda, and both sides also employed more subtle means of persuasion. For the United States, this included cultural exchanges and the activities of the Rockefeller Foundation or government agencies (the CIA, for example). Indeed, as early as 1947, if not earlier, both the United States and the Soviet Union instituted means of generating and disseminating propaganda and engaging in psychological warfare.[74]

Scholars have extensively studied the governmental and quasi-governmental projects of the United States and, to a lesser extent, those of the Soviet Union. For example, Frances Saunders, Joel Kotek, and others have investigated the influence of the Congress for Cultural Freedom in

Europe, a covert, CIA-funded organization whose purpose was to "inoculate the world against the contagion of Communism." Headed by a CIA agent, the congress operated more than thirty offices around the world from 1950 to 1967. [75] In Asia as well, the Asia Foundation, which funded and sponsored cultural activities, also had CIA connections.[76] As David Painter points out, "U.S. security policies were designed not only to protect the physical security of the United States and its allies but to preserve a broadly defined 'American way of life' by constructing an international order that would be open to and compatible with U.S. interests and ideals."[77] Even Japanese artists and critics who worked at a distance from the overt mechanisms of Cold War policy could not escape the broader social and ideological dynamics.

The Authority of Science in the Courts and Media

The emphasis on social science concepts applied to the most overt battles of the Cold War as well as to more subtle everyday processes in the new democratic Japan. Part of the Occupation's reforms had been the purging of militaristic and fascist elements of society and culture. Disciplines such as sociology, psychology, and communication studies played an important role in this, as they offered alternative models for enforcing liberal humanist values like individualism and for discouraging blind conformity. Soon after the war, Japanese intellectuals actively engaged with the social sciences, as demonstrated by the founding in 1946 of the influential Tokyo Institute for the Science of Thought (Shiso no kagaku kenkyūkai) by the leftist Tsurumi Shunsuke. In addition to disseminating recent findings and trends in European and American social sciences in the journal *Science of Thought* (*Shisō no kagaku*), Tsurumi and his colleagues also advocated "value-free" social sciences. In the new postwar legal system, the social science method and emphasis on objectivity also became valuable tools, and Kurosawa's film *Record of a Living Being* illustrates the use of courts of law as public spaces where individualism and human rights could be asserted openly.

In prewar practice, legal cases had often been dominated by the judge's own subjective opinions and by his assumed adherence to the empire's values and political goals. In contrast, the defense in the famous postwar obscenity trial of the Japanese translation of D. H. Lawrence's *Lady Chatterley's Lover* used social scientific surveys of attitudes and quantitative method as evidence. The accused—the publisher and translator of Lawrence's novel—were able to provide the basic data for the defense because they themselves had participated in a study carried out by social psychologists. The defense used the social psychologists' conclusions about sexual attitudes in order to fight what they viewed as the court's feudal, fascistic, and subjective attitudes, which, they deemed, were still stuck in the imperial mentality.

In a less obvious way, the views of American psychologists and sociologists found indirect expression in the popular culture of the Cold War. For example, the Sun Tribe boom in film and literature glorified youth, especially rebellious and troubled young people. Given Japan's earlier attitudes toward adolescence as a stage of life and conformity, it is remarkable that Ishihara Shintarō, his publishers and filmmakers, television, and even the literary establishment should collaborate—intentionally or not—in portraying these young people as attractive, even as role models.[78] Doubtless, the popular culture's expressions of wild young people were informed by (or perhaps informed) fundamental changes in the social scientists' understanding of adolescence. American attitudes toward teenagers underwent a striking change during the first two decades after the war. In the age of James Dean, influential psychologists such as Erik Erikson, whose works were known in Japan, contributed to a new interpretation of youthful rebellion. Rather than regarding nonconformity and extreme individualism as pathological, as they had been, Erikson and many of his peers began to view these traits as healthy signs of what they deemed a stage of necessary experimentation and independence on the road to adulthood. It is possible that social change in the aftermath of war and new popular cultural evocations gave rise to new interpretations. It is equally conceivable that the sanction of social science encouraged popular culture and young people to embrace the images of rebellious style. In any case, this interaction of media, culture, and social science had a tremendous impact in Japan and established the young rebel that Ishihara popularized (and later rejected) as an icon in Japan's Cold War culture.

The Spectrum of Cold War Culture in Japan

The cultural spectrum of the Cold War may easily be seen in the contrasting approaches of several important cultural figures: the progressive painters Maruki Toshi and Maruki Iri, the conservative critic Etō Jun, and the activist critic Odagiri Hideo. As Charles Armstrong wrote, "The cultural arena broadly conceived—from the realm of arts and letters to that of mass media and popular education—was the site of an intense political struggle in East Asia."[79]

At one extreme were Maruki Toshi (1912–2000) and Maruki Iri (1901–1995), painters devoted to leftist politics and art activism who toured the Soviet bloc. At the other end of the spectrum was the literary critic Etō Jun (1932–1999), who flirted with Marxism but then followed a path of affirming and even defining Japanese conservatism and nationalism. He also had close ties with the United States. This was a time when artists and writers felt compelled to anticipate an international audience, especially on certain topics like nuclear weapons. For example, the activities of critic Odagiri Hideo (1916–2000) illustrate the modification of both text and politics in response to potential audiences in a superpower bloc.

Maruki Toshi and Maruki Iri

As the Allied Occupation after Japan's defeat in the war drew to a close, artists Maruki Toshi and Maruki Iri traveled to nearly 150 cities and towns across the country in order to show their paintings of the atomic bombing of Hiroshima. In 1950, four years before the release of the popular movie Godzilla (Gojira, 1954), which became the best-known popular culture evocation of Japan's nuclear fear, the Marukis' A-bomb panels offered many in the Japanese public a first visual impression of the human cost of a nuclear attack.[80]

The Marukis' three monochromatic paintings—Ghosts, Fire, and Water—displayed during their first tour in 1950/1951 were provocative, to say the least. These large murals show large, nearly life-size nude figures with their scorched flesh, peeling skin, and frazzled hair, and a pile of burned corpses. During the 1950s, nearly a million people in Japan visited the A-bomb panels exhibitions, where they could look at the panels and listen to Maruki Toshi or university student volunteers talk about the Hiroshima and Nagasaki bombings of August 1945.[81] When the Japanese police and the Occupation forces came to tear down the posters and arrest the sponsors of the show, the Marukis and their assistants would roll up the scrolls, stow them in their rucksacks, and move on to the next venue. The authorities interfered with the A-bomb exhibition not only because they introduced the public to images that SCAP (Supreme Commander of the Allied Powers) classified as forbidden (that is, the damage caused by the American weapons) but also because the Marukis had joined the Japan Communist Party shortly after the war's end (as had many other artists and intellectuals). Like *Godzilla,* the couple's A-bomb paintings quickly gained international fame as part of the new Cold War nuclear culture. While *Godzilla*'s fantasy of human control of nuclear weapons appealed broadly to American audiences, the Marukis' paintings enjoyed a different foreign venue: Europe, the Soviet Union, and the still-young People's Republic of China. From 1953 to 1964, the A-bomb panels toured the Eastern bloc from Beijing to Moscow and were widely exhibited in London, Copenhagen, and other cities in NATO allies of the United States. As the world tour of the Marukis' paintings reveals, writers and filmmakers in Japan were well aware of the moral cachet that they derived from their status as witnesses, whether or not they were among the bombed.[82]

Etō Jun

In this period of international political flux and polarization, leftist artists and writers were not the only people in Japan who believed in the social role of art and literature. Later in his life, Etō Jun became one of Japan's preeminent literary critics and a prominent neoconservative political commentator. In the early postwar period, however, he, from a prominent military family, formed a Marxist reading group. When he was only sixteen, Etō and his peers experimented with Marxist theory as an analytical framework for literature: "We had heated debates about the great novelists— Akutagawa Ryūnosuke, Dazai Osamu. With our formalist Marxist method, we posited parallels between the causes of Dazai's recent suicide and Akutagawa's death [in 1927]. Both deaths, we felt quite certain, represented the tragicomedies of men who had suffered defeat to a new age." Etō's idiosyncratic nationalism and conservatism begin to manifest itself even at a young age. As a means of rejecting Marxism, he invoked the seemingly universal category of history, by which he meant Japan's cultural and intellectual history and his own desire to define those histories: "By then, however, I had come to the realization that my existence was part of history and knew that I had to resist anything that might separate me from history. I lost patience with our study group. What we need now, I thought to myself, is an activist movement [*jissen undō*]."[83]

Unlike that of the Marukis, Etō's concept of activism did not include touring the country and talking with the people about art and politics. In-

stead, his idea of a movement was grounded in the notion of writer as public intellectual whose deep understanding of the past would teach readers
pride in Japan's culture and modernity. During the first decade after the
war, therefore, Etō rejected the Left and the Eastern bloc, and in the 1950s
and 1960s, the conservative political climate welcomed this high-profile,
outspoken intellectual, cosmopolitan yet fiercely nationalistic. Etō was, in
a sense, the model free-world intellectual, who skillfully used the mass
media and persistently advanced his own political platform. He found inspiration in the convictions of Natsume Sōseki (1867–1916), the premier
novelist and intellectual whom Etō spent much of his career championing.

Although vastly different in their moral and political convictions, the
Marukis and Etō fiercely defended the optimistic notion that art and literature made essential contributions to society. Because they perceived literature and art as central to the intellectual and political life, they believed
that their work and beliefs would mold and benefit society as a whole. In
the context of the Cold War, both the Marukis and Etō took full advantage of the social potential of artistic and literary production in a liberal
democratic, capitalist society, engaging skillfully with the mass media.
They traversed the boundaries of mass and elite culture, categories transformed radically over the course of the 1950s by the huge growth of an
urban middle class, a new educational system, new forms of media, and
changes in the publishing industry.

In terms of political affiliation, however, they could not be more different. The Marukis had long ties with the Japan Communist Party, whereas
Etō found allies in the long-lived hegemonic conservative Liberal Democratic Party. Etō did research and taught at elite American universities
like Princeton, whereas the Marukis toured North Korea, China, and the
Soviet Union, where they exhibited their art to high acclaim. In contrast
to the Marukis' increasingly blunt critique of Japanese imperialism and
discourse of victimhood, Etō promoted a Japan that would find its own
voice and own story. Both the Marukis and Etō continued to be recognized by the public as important cultural and political figures throughout
their careers, which lasted well into the 1990s.

Odagiri Hideo

The dynamics of Cold War culture are evident as well in the many approaches of Japanese writers and artists to their international audiences.
Both the Marukis' painterly approach and their progressive political lean-

ings coincided with those of their Eastern-bloc hosts. Even though he was critical of the United States, Etō visited the United States many times and formed deep relationships with American scholars. For other writers and artists, however, contact with non-Japanese audiences required that they modify their work in response to rapidly changing Cold War politics. The well-known literary critic Odagiri Hideo, for example, displayed his consciousness of the anticommunist sentiment of the Western bloc in the carefully edited English translations of his potentially controversial writings on atomic power and literature, which appeared in the same volume in which Abe Tomoji's essay appeared.

The activism of critics like Odagiri reveals the variety of ways in which people became fighters in the "battle for hearts and minds," sometimes in strict conformity with Eastern- or Western-bloc agendas but more often as independent-minded thinkers. I think it fair to say that Odagiri was an independent progressive and Marxist because of the nuanced and independent thinking evident in his critical writings. Soon after Japan's defeat, he refused to accept that all Japanese people should repent for the war together, as Prime Minister Higashikuni Naruhiko had advocated. To Odagiri, group repentance would serve only to obscure "the fact that some of us bear a greater, more direct responsibility."[84] Although he is famous for his outspoken role in the war responsibility (*sensō sekinin*) debate, he also participated actively in Marxist circles and antinuclear groups. By the standards of American Cold War thinking, Odagiri would likely be branded a subversive, a fellow traveler obedient to Cominform. The fact that many intellectuals, writers, filmmakers, and artists joined the Japan Communist Party or embraced Marxist–Leninism after 1945, however, should not lead us to the automatic conclusion that they all were doctrinaire or conformist. It also is instructive to recall that in the early postwar era, there was widespread skepticism about capitalism owing to its prewar associations with fascism and the trauma of the Great Depression.[85]

We can find further evidence that Odagiri, although caught up in the political struggles of the Cold War, did not strictly toe the party line in his willingness to address diverse audiences on their own terms. Rather, with his goal of persuading readers of different political persuasions and nationalities, he modified his message considerably. In the 1950s when Odagiri was writing about controversial nuclear issues, he took into consideration at least three constituencies. First, his primary audience may have been other progressives, Marxists, and Communist Party members in Japan whom he knew would be receptive to his attack on the "atomic imperialism" of the United States, as well as his sympathy for what he and many at the time understood as the Soviets' goal of using nuclear energy primarily for constructive purposes.⁸⁶ But Odagiri also was clearly aware that certain contents and approaches would earn him the label "Red" in Japan's domestic political discourse, which was becoming increasingly anticommunist. Finally, Odagiri wished his strong antinuclear message to reach audiences outside Japan. Although he was not a survivor of the Hiroshima or Nagasaki bombing, he was fully aware that the mere fact that he lived in Japan, the bombed nation, would lend authority to his writings in the eyes of non-Japanese.

Odagiri's nuanced strategy for winning hearts and minds is evident in the two strikingly different versions of his renowned essay "The Atomic Problem and Japanese Literature" (Genshiryoku mondai to bungaku, 1954).⁸⁷ The original Japanese version appeared in 1954 in the mainstream progressive journal *Kaizō*, and the Japanese text and an English translation were included in a monograph the following year. In both versions, Odagiri condemns the current practice of testing nuclear weapons and warns against the dangers of radioactive fallout caused by the tests. He mourns the victims of the 1945 A-bombs, as well as those people living in the South Pacific who were suffering from radiation disease. In an essay about literature and the bomb, it is not at all surprising that Odagiri also highlights the testimonials of survivors of Hiroshima and Nagasaki. He believed that these texts and films about the bombings' aftermath could teach people about the horrors of nuclear weapons.

Readers of the English translation of Odagiri's essay would come away with this straightforward, seemingly apolitical message. The original Japanese essay, however, makes perfectly clear who is responsible for the "ashes of death" (radioactive fallout) that plague peoples in the South Pacific, and it furthermore is highly critical of the current American nuclear policy.⁸⁸ Odagiri offers a scathing critique of what he calls America's nuclear imperialism and praises what he understands as Soviet efforts to use nuclear technology in constructive ways.⁸⁹ The critic does not hesitate to lambaste President Truman's dangerous flirtation with nuclear weapons during the Korean War. In the following passages from Odagiri's essay, the sentences in roman are from the English translation, and those in italics are my translations of sections in Odagiri's original essay that were omitted from the translation:

On the other hand, in the South Pacific islands many natives are reportedly dying of an "ill-defined" disease, praying to God and taking it for an act of God. [*In other parts of the world*], *when the United States faced danger in the Korean War in December 1950, the American president acknowledged the possibility that the United States might use nuclear weapons if forced to. As a result, the British prime minister had to fly to Washington in order to prevent their use. During the fighting in Indochina as well, the U.S. military hinted that it was considering using nuclear weapons. The Soviets, furthermore, have begun using nuclear power generators and have started employing atomic power for massive earth-moving projects of unsettled areas.*[90]

This essay places emphasizes the pivotal role of the Japanese people in the global nuclear debate. In the English version, Odagiri singles out the testimonials of Hiroshima and Nagasaki *hibakusha* and the film *Children of Hiroshima* (*Genbaku no ko*, 1952). The Japanese text, however, offers many more examples of Japanese activism, describing at length the contributions of Japanese scientists, physicians, students, and ordinary citizens to research on the harmful effects of radiation and nuclear weapons:

The importance of the atomic energy problem has come to be realized by all the peoples of the world. Particularly, the Japanese people are most aware of the grim realities of the atomic age, as they were once treated as human guinea pigs at Hiroshima and Nagasaki for the first time in history, and recently the crew of the *Lucky 5 Dragon* became the first victims of the "death ash." *The horrific reality [of the bombings], previously covered up by the Occupation authorities, has now been brought out into the open, and Japanese people have pleaded for an end to war and demanded peace. At this crucial juncture, Japanese people have contributed to the investigation of the nuclear problem in a number of ways. First, respected Japanese physicists have participated in high-caliber scientific investigations. Ordinary Japanese citizens, furthermore, have shared their stories of actual nuclear attack as a way of demonstrating the tremendously destructive nature of these weapons for all of humankind. In the area of radiation sickness, the expertise and dedication of the Japanese medical profession and of individual physicians, stemming from their work since Hiroshima, have been amply revealed in the aftermath of the Bikini tests. . . . Professionals from many*

fields—eteorologists, radiological biophysicists, agronomists, marine sci-
entists, economists, political scientists, diplomatic historians, legal schol-
ars, and others—all have recognized the stark realities of the hydrogen
bomb and radiation. The efforts of these professionals have helped clarify
the enormous dilemma that we face because of the hydrogen bomb and
nuclear power.[91]

In contrast to the English version, which leaves the impression that
the Japanese and South Pacific peoples are helpless victims, the Japanese
version emphasizes the active participation and contributions of people
from all walks of life in Japan in a movement aimed at generating knowledge and fostering awareness of the dangers of nuclear weapons. As I
will show, this project was one that governments, activist groups, and ordinary citizens from around the world became involved in because of the
demands of the Cold War.

As a cultural critic, Odagiri did not forget to mention the crucial activities of artists and filmmakers, singling out the painters Maruki Toshi and
Maruki Iri. He also makes no bones about the links between the *Children*
of Hiroshima and the Japan Teachers' Union (JTU; Nikkyōsō):

> *The Japan Teachers Union and progressive filmmakers made* Children
> of Hiroshima *into a film. Akamatsu Toshiko and her husband painted*
> *the A-bomb panels (Genbaku no zu) and toured around the country*
> *with the paintings. . . . All these efforts have been made possible by the*
> *growing demands, whether direct or indirect, and support of the Japanese*
> *people in their quest for peace. None of this would have possible without*
> *the support of the people.*[92]

Most Japanese readers would have recognized Akamatsu Toshiko as
the maiden name of Maruki Toshi, whose A-bomb panels had already
started touring Eastern-bloc countries by this time. The panels had also
been shown in Western-bloc England, where Marxist critic John Berger
was an organizer of the London exhibition. Odagiri also draws attention to
the film *Children of Hiroshima*, directed by leftist director Shindō Kaneto
(b. 1912), whose sponsor, the JTU, was a leftist labor union.[93]

Finally, Odagiri highlights the dominant psychological modes in
the nuclear age: anxiety and terror. He contrasts the "nuclear nihilism"
caused by fear and feelings of powerlessness with the political resistance
of those who oppose "nuclear imperialism":

Children may have forgotten how they felt around the time of the Bikini test in March, *but the primal fear still remains deep in their unconscious and will never go away. The children's fear, in fact, is a reflection of the adults' fear. While resistance to nuclear imperialism grows among the younger generations, what might be called nuclear nihilism, however subtle, has also started to develop.*[94]

What do these alterations mean for Odagiri's Cold War political allegiances and ethics? His willingness to compromise in order to reach a broad audience shows a certain degree of independence. However we may judge Odagiri and his publisher for concealing their leftist politics in the translated work, we should keep in mind that the paranoia over communism in the Western bloc was at its peak when they were working. Odagiri and others who were concerned with the "atomic problem" knew well that this was not a local or an abstract concern but an issue that arose from the Cold War dynamics in which they lived and worked. What appears in the English translation as an early manifestation of the discourse of Japanese victimization turns out to be critical of American nuclear domination and laudatory of progressive activism in the original text.

As a result of its strong alliances with the Western bloc, Japan was absorbed into a new network of global culture and economy. Central to political, historical, and ideological change and stasis are cultural production and works of art, literature, and film. Any study of works of art must also take into account aesthetic response and formal aspects, yet that alone is not enough to help us understand why art matters in society.[95]

And in spite of antagonism, I put forth this novel as an honest, healthy book, necessary for us today.
—D. H. Lawrence, "A Propos of *Lady Chatterley's Lover*"

2 Sex and Democracy Lady Chatterley's Lover *in Cold War Japan*

On January 18, 1952, writer Itō Sei and publisher Oyama Hisa-jirō stood before the bench of a Tokyo courtroom awaiting the judge's de-cision. Both the defendants' formal clothing (a double-breasted suit and a tuxedo) and the huge crowd of journalists and spectators suggested the momentousness of the trial. The Allied Occupation was still in force in Japan, but two men were not being tried by the Occupation authorities. Instead, their countrymen were sitting in judgment. Itō and Oyama were accused of violating Japanese obscenity law by publishing a Japanese translation of British writer D. H. Lawrence's novel *Lady Chatterley's Lover.*

In Tokyo that day, many people were struggling to find their next meal, much less decent housing, and the ruins of firebombed buildings still were part of the cityscape. Reports of the Occupation's Red purge filled the newspapers. As an exasperated witness in the *Chatterley* case burst out early in the trial proceedings, "Doesn't the government have more important things to do than talk about whether a single foreign book is pornographic or not?" Why, so soon after Japan's defeat in a traumatic and tremendously disruptive world war, did the courts have time to fuss about something as seemingly trivial as "the private morality of the middle-classes"? In retrospect, the *Lady Chatterley* trial was far from frivo-lous, unfolding as a significant public debate over Japan's sexual, literary,

Itō Sei (*left*) and Oyama Hisajirō at the Tokyo Municipal Court, January 18, 1952. (Courtesy of Itō Rei)

and political identity in the most tumultuous years of the Cold War. Both the trial and the media's coverage contributed to the cultural production essential to constructing a sense of "private morality" befitting an unprecedented mass middle class. That huge urban middle class began to take shape in the early 1950s as citizens reaped the benefits of the Korean War's boost to Japan's industrial and economic recovery.

Although the trial concerned literature, many external social concerns and pressures also figured in determining what book would come to trial, the arguments in the court, and even the people present in the courtroom. The Occupation authorities initially promoted the ideals of an open, tolerant society, many of which were detailed in the new postwar constitution.[1] These progressive attitudes encouraged the *Lady Chatterley* defense team and many of the spectators to conceive of the trial as a novel type of public sphere in which the people could explore the new values of postwar democracy. At this juncture between occupied and independent Japan, the defense team insisted that as readers and writers, the people properly had a role in defining the concepts of art and obscenity, the public and the private, and the rights and responsibilities of citizens and the state.

At the same time, the United States had recently announced that as part of its strategy of containment (during and after the Occupation), it would mobilize Japan as a strong anticommunist presence in East Asia, a policy that resonated throughout the country. The contrast between the *Chatterley* trial of 1952, a "culture trial" *(bunka saiban)* highlighting such cultural figures as Itō Sei (1905–1969), and the overtly political Matsukawa trial *(Matsukawa saiban)* of 1949, another showcase trial of the Occupation period, illuminates the shift in political climate.[2] The earlier Matsukawa prosecution sought to demonize labor unions, which at that time were closely linked with leftism and communism. By the time of the *Chatterley* trial late in the Occupation, however, the authorities did not consider such public airing of volatile political issues to be prudent. Thus we encounter the seemingly apolitical, seemingly trivial, prosecution of Itō and his publisher.

In such a tense political atmosphere, the siege mentality among the artists and intellectuals who attended the *Lady Chatterley's Lover* trial was evident in the presence in the courtroom of both progressives, like Odagiri Hideo, and writers who had complied with the imperial state's wartime agenda, like Itō. Those assembled had much more on their mind than literary criticism or trifling bourgeois values. Pushing beyond literary discourses, the defense invoked the discourse and objectivity of the social sciences and contrasted them with the regressive subjectivity of the judges, thereby challenging the existing morality, not only about sex, but also about the viability of democracy in Japan.

The *Chatterley* trial also clearly demonstrates the ways in which the Japanese writing and publishing communities were being drawn closely into the Western bloc's network of print culture. Writers like Itō were able to reclaim publicly their connections with British literature after the long hiatus of the war, during which English was the enemy language. Yet even the significance of that connection was not self-evident, since English culture was not a static entity. What is more, the novel that Itō had translated was aesthetically and politically controversial, and its place in the canon was far from settled. In this way, the Japanese literary community entered into dialogue with its counterparts in the English-speaking world, which also coincided with Japan's Cold War allies.

Lady Chatterley's Lover had gained an aura unusual even among maverick modernist texts. One aspect of its controversial identity was its status as a contested book for more than twenty years in some part of the world while other comparably explicit texts had gained legal sanction and were freely distributed in the marketplace. In Europe and the United States, *Ulysses* and other works that had initially shocked audiences and critics had earned what amounted to canonical status in the 1930s, when the Great Depression encouraged writers to seek the patronage of universities. In legal terms as well, the courts in the early 1930s recognized James Joyce's *Ulysses* as art and denied that it was "dirt for dirt's sake." In Japan, in contrast, the canonization of Lawrence and other modernist writers (and all English-language writers!) had been deferred by the war.

Cultural expansiveness characterizes much of Japan's modern period, as evidenced by the huge influx of foreign art and literature through the media, exhibitions, and translations.[3] In the early postwar years, French literature and philosophy, especially the writings of Jean-Paul Sartre and Albert Camus, were extremely popular in Japan.[4] Similarly, many students of Russian, British, Chinese, and American culture had the opportunity to reassert their passions after the war's end. Of the many controversial novels that entered Japan during this period, *Lady Chatterley* became the focus of the most famous media trial. In the "Red scare" atmosphere of the Occupation, exposing Sartre or Camus to such public scrutiny would only have given publicity to their leftist thinking. Moreover, after the recent Chinese revolution and years of war with China, the conservative Japanese authorities did not want a spectacle concerning anything Chinese. The British may have spoken English, but they were not the dominant occupier of Japan. Besides, Lawrence's novel originally became controversial because British publishers and legal system would not publish it. British readers had to get it from French and Italian publishers. Thus it was the prudish public discourse in England that provided an excellent opportunity to challenge prevailing—or obsolete—moral scruples and laws.

The purpose of this chapter is not a rereading of *Lady Chatterley* as a text. Instead, I am interested in the ways that "a text becomes subject to the various, unstable forces that shape the public sphere" and the "competing interests" that arise as part of that sphere.[5] These trials offer us a rare, detailed view of the ways in which a varied group of readers interpreted *Lady Chatterley's Lover* and the formation of meaning around this text in post-Occupation Japan. Accordingly, following Roger Chartier and Peter McDonald, I treat the novel here as a "mediated material artifact" and not just as an "abstract linguistic form."[6]

The stern judge of the first round of the trial delivered the following verdict to Itō and Oyama: Itō, as only the translator, was innocent of obscenity charges, but Oyama was found guilty for publishing with salacious intent. Oyama decided to appeal, and so the trial continued into the post-Occupation period. Many of the issues that arose in the first round persisted as the case was tried in higher courts, all the way to Japan's highest court.

The Tokyo Case in Brief

Novelist and critic Itō Sei first prepared a Japanese translation of D. H. Lawrence's *Lady Chatterley's Lover* in 1935, about seven years after the novel first appeared in Europe.[7] Considering the extent of government censorship in 1930s Japan, it is not surprising that Itō published only an expurgated translation of the novel then. Not until 1949, four years after Japan's defeat in the world war, did Itō entertain the request of publisher Oyama shoten to produce an unexpurgated translation as the first volume in a collection of Lawrence's best-known novels.[8] During the Allied Occupation, publishers could not easily anticipate the police's reaction to new publications.

The initial release of the two-volume Japanese translation of *Lady Chatterley's Lover* in 1950 resulted in impressive sales figures: volume 1 sold 80,029 copies, and volume 2, slightly fewer, 69,545 copies. Itō's translation enjoyed these tremendous sales in just two months, from mid-April through late June 1950.[9] During the Occupation, texts concerning political thought, activism, A-bombs, fraternization of GIs and Japanese, and the image of the United States and the Occupation all had been strictly censored by the Occupation's Civil Censorship Detachment (CCD). The CCD, however, made public its official policy that "it had no concern with material obscene or pornographic, providing that material was not detrimental to Occupation objectives."[10] The fact of the Allied victory and the Cold War agenda of the United States and its allies had a profound effect on political and artistic discourse (the "Reverse-Course" crackdown on leftist writings comes to mind).[11] Nonetheless, in contrast to imperial practice, when "total state control of the arts was formed on a legal and organization-institutional basis," the Occupation-era censorship left some areas of cultural production relatively untouched.[12] Thus, while the *Lady Chatterley* obscenity case took place during the Occupation, it was in fact a Japanese legal case and not under SCAP's jurisdiction.

The Tokyo police invoked Article 175 of the "still-operative Meiji criminal code, which threatened purveyors of obscenity" with a fine and, in accordance with a postwar revision, a possible prison sentence.[13] On June 26, 1950, the Tokyo police made its first move on what promised to be a highly publicized prosecution, confiscating the few copies of Itō's translation still in circulation. The police then charged both translator Itō and publisher Oyama Hisajirō (b. 1905) with violating Article 175. On May 8, 1951, the court of the first instance convened in Tokyo Municipal Court, with the trial not ending until January 18, 1952, just as the Occupation was drawing to a close.

Cold and Hot Wars, Sex, and the Novel

It is not coincidental that this crucial court case, on the eve of Japan's independence in the Cold War world, pertained to D. H. Lawrence's ideas about sex and representation. During his lifetime, Lawrence (1885–1930) relentlessly voiced his opinions about morality, politics, modernity, and art, in both his literary works and his criticism. He was aggressive, even abrasive, in anticipating his opposition, which, broadly defined, was contemporary British society, and he regarded the censors as an especially obnoxious symptom of the nation's diseased state. By the 1920s, therefore, publishers had already pegged Lawrence as dangerous because of his early obscenity conviction for *The Rainbow* (1915).[14]

Many generations of critics have analyzed Lawrence's complex and often contradictory thinking about sexuality, Christianity, empire, and gender, and I will not review that here.[15] But several aspects of Lawrence's thought and career are relevant to understanding the nature of the novelist's appeal to Japanese audiences soon after World War II. Lawrence was particularly outspoken about his views on the connection of national identity, morality, and sexuality. In his essay "A Propos of *Lady Chatterley's Lover*" (1929), Lawrence analyzed the nature of that link:

I cannot see any hope of regeneration for a sexless England. An England that has lost its sex seems to me nothing to feel very hopeful about. . . . [T]he warm blood-sex that establishes the living and re-vitalizing connection between man and woman, how are we to get that back? I don't know. Yet get it back we must: or the younger ones must, or we are all lost. For the bridge to the future is the phallus, and there's the end of it. But not the poor, nervous counterfeit phallus of modern "nervous" love. Not that. . . . If England is to be regenerated . . . it will be a phallic rather than a sexual regeneration. For the phallus is only the great old symbol of godly vitality in a man, and of immediate contact.[16]

For Lawrence, then, his campaign about sex specifically pertained to saving England, healing England. But healing England of what? The ravages of the Great War, World War I, and the industrialization that had corrupted society and made possible in Europe the unprecedented horrors that defined that war? For Lawrence, the sexlessness of England was symptomatic of the degeneration of the nation and of the failure to recover a right relationship with the life force in the aftermath of the tragedy of the war and of the age.[17]

Let us look at the opening passage of *Lady Chatterley's Lover,* the short first chapter of this novel about an upper-class woman's relationship with her husband's gamekeeper, Mellor:

> Ours is essentially a tragic age, so we refuse to take it tragically. The cataclysm has happened, we are among the ruins, we start to build up new little habits, to have new little hopes. It is rather hard work: there is now no smooth road into the future: but we go round, or scramble over the obstacles. We've got to live, no matter how many skies have fallen.
>
> This was more or less Constance Chatterley's position. The war had brought the roof down over her head. And she had realized that one must live and learn.[18]

Then the reader is introduced to Lord Chatterley:

> She married Clifford Chatterley in 1917, when he was home for a month on leave. They had a month's honeymoon. Then he went back to Flanders: to be shipped over to England again six months later, more or less in bits. . . .
>
> The gay excitement had gone out of the war . . . dead. Too much death and horror. A man needed support and comfort. A man needed to have an anchor in the safe world. A man needed a wife. . . . But early in 1918 Clifford was shipped home smashed, and there was no child.[19]

For Lawrence, the idea of the body and sex as means of salvation from the ravages of modern warfare/mass death comes in the aftermath (immediate or not) of World War I. For readers in Japan, the trope of the impotent, war-wounded English lord and his wife, who seeks solace and meaning in beautiful and potent relations with men, resonated with gendered metaphors of Japan's defeat and recovery.

The defense team in the Tokyo trial correctly emphasized Lawrence's views of healthy sex as sacred and beautiful. In his 1929 essay, Lawrence makes grand claims about the power of sex: that it could cure England of its ills, make England's people whole again, and save them from the fall.[20] The defense also touched on what we can now see as Lawrence's rather idiosyncratic understanding of what constitutes sex: he viewed the phallus as sacred and, in a narrative of progress, as a means for England to move forward. Not only did Lawrence insist on the primacy of the heterosexual bond, but he even condemned masturbation, the "nervous" love, partly because of the secrecy it demanded and partly because the "gray" and puritanical establishment and older generation condoned masturbation because it could be made secret.[21] Regardless of the national and psychological specificities of Lawrence's claims about sex, his linking of the body, morality, and recovery from national trauma found a receptive audience in 1950s Japan, which was still reeling from the brutality of war and defeat. At the same time, the *Chatterley* case as an event spoke to much more than the citizens' spiritual war wounds.

Writing as Provocation

Itō Sei and Oyama Hisajirō's initial encounter with Lawrence's novel was in no way accidental, nor were they naïve about D. H. Lawrence's intent in writing such a provocative work. When Oyama selected the notorious novel for publication after the war, the Japanese publishing world was in very much a transitional phase: picking itself up after the devastation of the war, chafing under the Occupation's censorship system, and uncertain about the artistic and political tides of the times. Serious and upstanding, Oyama knew he wanted something better than the domestic pulp fiction many publishers were churning out, some profitably and others not. A small press, Oyama shoten also had to watch the bottom line and to hope for profits. Art and sex made money, but how much sex? What made art? And who would be judging the quality of each? In 1952 Japan, these questions were up for grabs. Itō and Oyama knew Lawrence as being on the forefront of elite modern British literature but also as being slightly dangerous, an author who not only represented sex but also tied it to larger social issues.

It is important to keep in mind that translator Itō was not simply a hired gun but an erudite writer and critic who aligned himself closely with Lawrence and other modernists. Like many aspiring novelists in the late 1920s, Itō fell under the spell of Freud, Proust, and especially Joyce and Lawrence, and he found inspiration for his own fiction in their writings.[22] Although he was an author of novels and short stories, Itō's most significant contributions may have been in other areas. For example, he was the editor of a literary journal that introduced readers to the works of Virginia Woolf and Aldous Huxley. He also undertook the daunting task of translating Joyce's *Ulysses* into Japanese during the early 1930s and published an expurgated translation of Lawrence's *Lady Chatterley's Lover* in the mid-1930s.

Whether we call Itō's fervently nationalistic wartime writings in the 1940s opportunistic, unprincipled, or blindly conformist, we are not surprised to find that the man of letters happily rekindled his love for British modernist literature after Japan's defeat.[23] Somehow—perhaps because of his Anglophilia—he escaped being at the center of the discourse on war responsibility and complicity. By 1950, Itō had already built a name for himself as a prolific and important postwar novelist and literary critic. Thanks to the mass media, the *Lady Chatterley* trials had the effect of propelling him to an even greater level of fame. After the 1951 trial ended and while the case was under appeal, Itō published a "documentary novel," *The Trial* (*Saiban*, 1958), which explained in a style accessible to a broad readership the workings of the legal process and also the court proceedings. By the mid-1950s, Itō had become one of the most frequently encountered voices in the literary world.[24]

Thus at the first *Chatterley* Trial in 1951/1952, Itō Sei certainly could speak with confidence not only about the novel under dispute but about Lawrence, too, and what we now call modernism.[25] The distinguished literary scholars and critics who came to the courtroom as special witnesses for the defense bolstered his authority as a critic. The modernist artists in whom Itō had found inspiration as a young man also harbored a conviction that literature could benefit society: "the belief that the publication of a poem or the exhibition of a painting can so triumphantly confirm the creator and so decisively serve the culture."[26] Finally, Itō found himself drawn to Lawrence's ideas about sex: "I want men and women to be able to think about sex, fully, completely, honestly, and cleanly."[27] Thus when

Oyama released the first edition of the *Chatterley* translation in 1950, the Japanese literary community was familiar with Lawrence's fiction and often dogmatic critical writings as well as with the broader discourse to which they belonged. Although the discourses of modernism arose earlier in the century, their significance in debates over sexuality and identity only increased in the postwar era.

In "A Propos of *Lady Chatterley's Lover*," about the controversy over his most recent novel, D. H. Lawrence explained his views of the importance of frankness in sexual matters, not only in the arts, but also in society:

> English publishers urge me to make an expurgated edition, promising large returns . . . and insisting that I should show the public that here is a fine novel, apart from all the "purple" and all "words." So I begin to be tempted and start in to expurgate. But impossible! I might as well try to clip my own nose into shape with scissors. The book bleeds. . . . And in spite of all antagonism, I put forth this novel as an honest, healthy book, necessary for us today. The words that shock so much at first don't shock at all after a while.[28]

Lawrence did not stand as a solitary advocate of open treatment of sexuality at that time—indeed, Freud and James Joyce come to mind as likeminded figures, and they, in turn, exemplify significant and widespread trends in twentieth-century culture. As we will see, Lawrence's outspokenness about sex and the novel eventually took discussion of the novel out of the relatively narrow realm of literary critical discourse and into courts of law, thus rendering public and political the debate on morality and art that surrounded the novel.

Along with other modernist writers such as Joyce, Lawrence's fiction enjoyed considerable media attention, and thus his books were "news that stayed news."[29] In legal venues around the world, Lawrence's opinions and his fiction, as well as his status as a high modernist novelist of "undoubted artistic integrity," came to be employed as a means of advocating for and legitimating sexual frankness in art.[30] Significantly, the several landmark trials concerning Lawrence's *Lady Chatterley's Lover*—all test cases for determining the parameters of obscenity after the war—took place in the United States and its allies England and Japan during the 1950s and early 1960s. This was at the height of the Cold War, when the United States was trying to strengthen consumer markets both at home and within its allies' borders, as well as offering evidence of a freedom superior to that of the Soviet foe.[31] With their new mass-market paper-backs, publishers and booksellers were a growing industry. Unlike cars, however, books can overtly express ideas, sometimes dangerous ones.

All the *Lady Chatterley's Lover* trials, whether in Japan, the United States, or England, showcased expert witnesses and defense attorneys who argued against classifying Lawrence's frank and detailed evocations of sexuality as obscene. Following the precedent set in the 1933 *Ulysses* obscenity trial in the United States, the defense in every case labored to "consecrate" the novel as a whole, and especially those passages deemed objectionable, by positioning them in the realm of art.[32] Judges provided legal confirmation of the sanctity of the unity of the work of art, thus making respectable the language in Joyce's novel that had previously been considered pornographic.[33] The work of naturalizing pornography took place partly in Joyce's novels and those of other high modernists and also in public and institutional contexts, such as the legal system, journalism, and academia.

Nonetheless, it took decades for *Lady Chatterley's Lover* to gain the same acceptance as proper literature as Joyce's work had achieved. The prolif-eration of expurgated versions of *Lady Chatterley* (many of them pirated) after the novel's initial publication in 1929 revealed that it was possible to remove the twelve "objectionable" passages and still have some sem-blance of a novel.[34] In contrast, in *Ulysses,* Joyce's highly unconventional and yet seamless narrative approach, as well as its allusive qualities, made it notoriously difficult to read and thus more easily categorized as artis-tic.[35] In other words, the artistic merit of Lawrence's novel was more diffi-cult to establish than was that of Joyce's work.

What does it mean for pornography to become art? In his praises of *Ulysses,* critic Edmund Wilson explained the process as one in which the artist attains mastery over something dangerous, with virtuosity as his weapon: "To have subdued all this material to the uses of a supremely fin-ished and disciplined work of art is a feat which has hardly been equalled in the literature of our time."[36] In contrast to the adulation accorded Joyce, a writer who could tame the obscene with his impressive formal control of language, critics varied widely in their estimation of Lawrence's talents as a writer, describing him as a genius one moment and a sloppy, repeti-tive writer the next. The figure of the Romantic artist, sincere, pure, and incapable of obscenity, figured prominently in the reputation of *Ulysses* as art. The novel's imagined reader also mattered: T. S. Eliot's influen-tial emphasis on the parallels to Homeric legend in his review of *Ulysses* assumed an elite reader with a classical education who would not be considered a threat to the social order. In contrast, Lawrence's novel might challenge some readers with its discussions of ideas about the ills of modern society, but because of the familiar elements of its plot structure (adultery, forbidden romance), it placed fewer demands on its readers. Indeed, "censorship advertised the work of Joyce and Lawrence far beyond the avant-garde audience," but it was Lawrence's novel that the untutored reader found more accessible.[37] In this way, both criticism and reader reception are essential to the transformation from obscenity to art.

The controversy over *Lady Chatterley's Lover*'s status continued for more than two decades after Lawrence's death in 1930. This lack of generic clarity arose partly because Lawrence had understood writing as a means of expressing his controversial ideas and was unwilling—and perhaps unable—to cloak himself with the mantle of pure Romantic genius and virtuosity. Lawrence's strong objections to many facets of contemporary British society and morality, as well as his desire to improve his country, fueled his conviction that he must produce a contentious novel, one that he felt certain the censors would clamp down on. That is, Lawrence regarded his art as efficacious, as having the potential to effect needed changes in society—not, perhaps, as solutions to specific social problems, but with the potential of healing grander maladies from which English civilization suffered.[38]

It was precisely this combination of Lawrence's optimism about sexuality and concern about the nation's future that Oyama, the publisher, and Itō, the translator, found attractive.[39] Having worked through the strict censorship system of imperial Japan and under contemporary Allied Occupation censors, Oyama was well aware of the risks inherent in issuing an unexpurgated version of a controversial novel. But Lawrence's message of hope for the future and the chaos of print culture as the Occupation was ending encouraged Oyama to take a chance. Itō had studied European modernism since the relatively open "Taishō democracy" era of the 1920s, and so he anticipated the safety offered by invoking the category of high art from the English-speaking world, now the language of the allies.

As it turned out, far from providing the hoped-for artistic safe haven, *Lady Chatterley* resulted in Oyama's becoming one of the principal figures in the first of several legal cases.[40] Several aspects of the Japanese trial foreshadowed the American and British trials of nearly a decade later. In all the cases, the publisher stood as the accused. All the trials received extensive coverage by the media and signified legal confirmation of trends in capitalist cultural production, particularly in print culture. In the end, though, the Japanese case took on a quite different meaning from the subsequent trials, one that only partly had to do with defining obscenity. Instead, the Tokyo *Lady Chatterley* trial was the first opportunity since Japan's defeat in the war for the literary community, publishers, government, and intellectuals to debate in a public forum the means of determining boundaries of respectability and morality, political authority, and the body. The political and cultural contexts of the Cold War held tremendous sway in the way that the trial unfolded as critical debate and as public spectacle under the media's watchful eyes.

Media, Democracy, Spectacle

As Lynn Hunt and Walter Kendrick pointed out, pornography is most fruitfully understood as naming "an argument, not a thing," an argument over the divisions between public and private, as well as which forces in society have the authority to regulate the boundaries of morality.[41] Furthermore, the idea of pornography has always been "historically shaped" because its definition hinges on a society's tolerance of the "physical, sexual reality of individual selfishness," which, in turn, foregrounds a subject separate from the "higher moral authority." In postwar Japan as elsewhere, the link between obscenity and the profound political implications of this understanding of the subject/citizen is complicated by the fact that sexually explicit materials also "provoke . . . commercial interest in the sense of profit."[42]

Not surprisingly, the Tokyo trial on sex and censorship became a darling of the media. Newspapers effortlessly garnered attention by splashing the "Obscenity or Art?" headline in large print—the more often, the better. And yet readers seeking titillation were not the only audience. Broad interest was shown by the diversity of spectators, defenders, journalists, and witnesses present. The nature and quantity of newspaper, radio, and newsreel coverage also confirmed the urgency of many themes explored over the course of the trial. The literally hundreds of articles about the *Chatterley* trial that appeared in national and regional newspapers often emphasized the "the ghost of the prewar censorship system," the "unfortunate bureaucratic spirit" of the police, the "broad implications" of the test case, the political and moral "responsibility of writers," and a new "political consciousness" engendered by the process.[43]

Chief defense attorney Masaki Hiroshi made it known publicly that he had agreed to represent Oyama and Itō because he realized the trial would be a public forum for him and for like-minded people to express their opinions about the value of the new constitution and freedom of speech. The trial, he announced with relish, would be a test case about obscenity, as well as an opportunity for the "citizen to judge the JUDGES."[44] Except for the translator, Itō, who was surprised at the full courtroom and the flashing cameras of the newspaper reporters on the first day, most participants were aware that the trial would permit them to be heard by the broad public, constituting a potentially significant stage in the building of Japan's new democratic capitalist culture and its articulation of new values. In postwar Japan, the trial marked the debut of writers as activists, the writers who saw themselves as "an elite with an ability to create a following among the influential literate sector of society in a way that was unsettlingly similar to the ambitions of the state itself," to borrow J. M. Coetzee's phrase.[45]

For the reading public, the *Lady Chatterley* trial came as a novelty, the first big postwar "culture trial" to focus on literature and politics. Whether the new postwar constitution would survive the post-Occupation era, given the weakening of progressive forces by the Reverse Course, the depurging of conservative forces by Supreme Allied Commander Douglas MacArthur, and Japan's impending independence, loomed as a major question. An open courtroom in which the judge did not simply dictate the state's will was in stark contrast to the pre-1945 system, when texts had been censored by administrative means and literary trials were extremely rare. Even when a censorship case did go to trial, it would inevitably conclude with a guilty verdict, a warning to the heedless.[46]

For most of the nine-month trial, spectators crowded the seats in the cramped courtroom in central Tokyo, with many famous men and women among their numbers: novelists Kawabata Yasunari (then head of the Japan PEN Club), Hirabayashi Taiko, Sakaguchi Ango, Funahashi Sei'ichi, Ooka Shōhei, and Niwa Fumio; critics Yoshida Ken'ichi (son of Prime Minister Yoshida Shigeru), Nakamura Mitsuo, and Usui Yoshimi, among others. The court permitted Oyama and Itō to form an unusually large defense team, headed by the idiosyncratic lawyer Masaki Hiroshi and including novelist Nakajima Kenzo (who was also the head of the Japan Copyright Council and a leader in the Japan Writers' Association); the Tamakis, two brothers who had become lawyers; and the English literature scholar Fukuda Tsuneari. Among those who eagerly participated as witnesses were social scientists, Christian activists, scholars, journalists, high-ranking police bureaucrats, critics, educators, professors, novelists, physicians, feminists, and grassroots activists. As if in direct fulfillment of Lawrence's wish that young people read his novel so they would learn correctly about sex, the defense also called a seventeen-year-old high-school girl named Sone Chiyoko, who spoke with great intelligence about Lawrence's novels.[47]

A surprising array of people rallied in *Chatterley*'s defense. Some, such as critic Aono Suekichi, had been persecuted by the militarists for their leftist or liberal political beliefs. In contrast, Itō had employed pro-imperial rhetoric during the war, and scholar Fukuda Tsuneari of the defense team, although known as a maverick intellectual, had publicly stated his critical views of leftists.[48] Perhaps some people secretly saw participation in the trial as a form of penitence for the literary community's lack of resistance during the Asia-Pacific War.[49] But for others, the Occupation's Reverse Course had blocked other avenues for activism.

Sex and Business Matters in the Free Market

A positive evaluation of the free circulation of sexually explicit texts and images, as well as the identification of the open representation of sexuality with a high level of freedom and democracy, depends on the framework of a free-market, consumer-oriented capitalist society. During the second half of the twentieth century, the increasing authority of publishers and their business practices in market economies, accompanied by a shift to fewer legal restrictions on freedom of speech (in cultural, if not political, realms), also contributed to the evolution of this new set of cultural values in the Western bloc. Even when lifted, the association of censorship with literary texts imparted an "aura" and increased their value as "symbolic capital."[50] A thriving literary marketplace fit in well with the Cold War goals of proving the free world's superiority through the vitality of consumerism. The worth of literary and artistic works, furthermore, went beyond mere market exchange value; art also represented a space beyond the reach of the state, thus asserting the importance of the private sphere to a liberal society.

In this context, the Japanese *Lady Chatterley* case differed from the later British and American cases because the publisher, Oyama, had no way of predicting the level of legal or financial risk involved or the outcome of the trial. Until 1949, the police had focused their censorship efforts almost exclusively on the *kasutori* magazines (the "dregs" or "pulp," cheaply produced popular magazines on sexual themes that flooded the market in the immediate postwar period). Oyama did know that the police had met with considerable opposition when they tried to ban texts outside the *kasutori* genre, specifically two best-selling novels: a popular contemporary comic novel by Ishizaka Yōjurō, and Norman Mailer's current U.S. hit about the war, *The Naked and the Dead*.[51] In contrast, *Lady Chatterley* offered several advantages as a test case: the author was both respectable and controversial but no longer vulnerable to direct attack. His novel concerned World War I, not the still-too-vivid World War II, and a genteel English world that was vaguely familiar yet not contemporary.

Oyama's decision to release *Lady Chatterley's Lover,* Lawrence's last novel, as the first book in a multivolume edition of Lawrence's selected works may have been motivated at least partly by a desire for publicity and profit. It is hard to condemn the Japanese publisher on these grounds owing to the financial and legal uncertainties that he faced, especially in comparison with the cases of American and British publishers.[52] The American publisher Grove Press proceeded with a complete and unexpurgated *Lady Chatterley's Lover* only *after* the U.S. Supreme Court's landmark *Roth* decision of 1957 had articulated the legal precedent that pornography and sexually explicit materials were, for the first time, protected under freedom of speech and the press. Similarly, the British Penguin publication followed closely on a change in obscenity laws in that country. Therefore, both the American and British publishers issued unexpurgated editions of *Lady Chatterley's Lover* with the clear understanding that they would emerge victorious in major test cases of recently altered legislation and that they furthermore would enjoy considerable profits as millions of readers were lured to the aura of the "freshly decensored," yet now perfectly respectable, text.

The literary marketplace and the growth of publishing in the postwar period also are important to *Chatterley*'s postwar fate. This novel is remarkable for the author's high degree of involvement in all stages of its production and marketing and his advocating for his works. In the 1910s and 1920s in Europe, a number of authors, such as Joyce and Eliot, sometimes used private publishers and had close relationships with their patrons/investors.[53] Precisely because Lawrence, anticipating a battle with British censors, published the book himself (privately in Italy), he had a relationship to his novel that many of his peers did not. As Richard Ellis pointed out, "Censorship confrontations in the United Kingdom and the United States are publishers' and booksellers' battles and . . . characteristically . . . publishers were the main courtroom protagonists."[54] Given the extent of Lawrence's involvement in the actual production of the physical book called *Lady Chatterley's Lover* and his personal and artistic belief in its importance, the novel's notoriety is not surprising, even after his death.[55] In the Tokyo trial, the understanding of the book as a commodity and a cultural product was made clear when the publisher of the Japanese translation was found guilty of marketing the Japanese version of *Lady Chatterley* as if it were salacious material.

Social Science Creating Art

The *Lady Chatterley* case offered an opportunity for the literary community to fashion a new identity, an essential project in the aftermath of the compulsory domestic turn inward that accompanied the expansionism and militarism abroad forced by the Asia Pacific War and World War II. In the courtroom, Oyama and Itō's defense team achieved this cosmopolitan redefinition partly by identifying the appreciation of Lawrence's fiction as a gauge of Japanese culture. No less than the nation's pride was at stake if Japan, in a public forum, exposed itself as unappreciative of a European literary masterpiece. It would be a mistake to read this approach as "a simple belated imitation of Western models."[56] Rather, this tactic deliberately echoed themes persistent in social discourse from the start of the project of building a modern nation-state in the mid-nineteenth century: the imperative of standing shoulder to shoulder with "civilized" nations and the anxiety over the hierarchy implicit in East–West relations. The defense team thoroughly understood the historical contexts of Lawrence's novel and, furthermore, knew full well that the critical reception of *Lady Chatterley* in the English-speaking world had been mixed but saw no advantage in making the prosecution aware of this small detail. Through the democratic forum that was the trial, a free press, and Itō's book *Saiban*, the defense promoted the appreciation of Lawrence's exalted art and thought to all citizens.

In a strikingly original move, the defense skillfully employed social science methods to distinguish Lawrence's text from pornography. Therefore, although the trial may have taught readers about democratic institutions in the broadest sense, Itō approached the proceedings and his own journalistic novel about the trial as means of introducing the people to a broad range of literary critical theories and their applications.[57] Even though he might have included Marxist criticism among the theoretical approaches, he did not. Not one who would ever be accused of being "Red," Itō's understanding of literary criticism was based on Western European and American schools of thought.

Furthermore, Itō stated that he imagined the "general reader" as his audience, and as proof, he stressed that even the pricing of the paperback edition of *Saiban* was intended to make the volume accessible to a mass audience, reaching as many fellow citizens as possible.[58] His readers would learn about European-influenced literary criticism and also "new, American-style approaches" of literary criticism (*bungaku hihyō*), based on the disciplines of psychology and mass communication studies.[59] Itō's claim here is a bit disingenuous because, although social scientific data and method are frequently presented as evidence during a trial, such evidence is not in relation to the literary critical endeavor per se. Rather, the defense's use of psychological method and mass communication studies had two purposes: (1) to align the defense with a rational, scientific worldview (in opposition to the prosecutor's subjectivity) and (2) to separate pornography from art.

The defense did not have to try hard to maintain this alignment with rational, scientific scholarship. As it turned out, the social scientists presented themselves to Oyama before anyone knew that the publication of *Lady Chatterley* would result in prosecution. Just as the second volume of the translation was going to press, a Tokyo University graduate student named Kido Kōtarō contacted Oyama to tell him that as part of his studies in social psychology, he was doing research on sexual attitudes. Specifically, Kido planned to study the extent to which *Lady Chatterley* influenced readers' attitudes, and to that end, he asked Oyama to include a reader's survey in the forthcoming book. Kido was working with the influential social psychologist Minami Hiroshi at Hitotsubashi University, who at the time was involved in a study of Japanese sexuality sponsored by the Democratic Scientists Association (Minshūshugi kagakusha kyōkai).[60]

Kido's survey postcard including the following questions:

1. What do you think someone in a marriage similar to that of Lady Chatterley should do?
   a. Stay married.

    b. Take a lover.

    c. Get divorced.

2. Do you think that romantic love can survive solely on the basis of a spiritual connection?

3. What did you think of the descriptions of sexual acts in the novel?

    a. Beautiful.

    b. Dirty.

    c. Obscene.

4. Did you feel sexually excited while you were reading the novel?

5. Do you think this book should be banned (or expurgated)?[61]

Although Oyama initially objected to the question about banning the novel, in the end he agreed to include survey postcards in thirty thousand copies of the second volume.[62] Readers also were asked for their age, occupation, and political party affiliation (both members of the conservative Jiyū Party and the Socialist and Communist parties numbered high among the respondents).

As the trial progressed, both the participants and the newspapers took frequent note of the survey as part of *Lady Chatterley*'s publication history. The vast majority of the three thousand respondents found Lawrence's description of sex "beautiful" and opposed banning the book. The defense consequently used the results of this survey of reader response as a means of distinguishing *Lady Chatterley* from the native *kasutori* pulp magazines and of positioning its clients on the side of science and rationality. For the most part, the media's coverage of the case also sided with the defense. Several newspapers, however, singled out the survey postcard as an instance of the publisher's attempting to "flatter" readers into thinking that he cared about their opinions. As a result of this upbraiding of Oyama as a greedy entrepreneur, one of the psychologists developing the survey wrote an article in which he defended Oyama and explained that the purpose of the survey was scientific research rather than financial gain.[63]

Despite the researcher's clarification, the prosecution took full advantage of the ambiguity surrounding the survey in order to criticize Oyama's motives for publishing the book in the first place and for his decision to include the survey. In the verdict, the judge also used the survey as evidence of Oyama's pornographic intent in marketing the book. The guilty verdict did little, however, to dampen enthusiasm for the aesthetic elevation of explicit representations of sex, a lasting legacy of Lawrence and other modernists.[64] The combination of data from scientists, along with cultural legitimization in the form of praise for Lawrence's art by prominent literary critics, had the effect of naturalizing sexual explicitness in elite art.

Throughout the trial, the defense relentlessly worked to disqualify the prosecution and the police from their assumed roles of cultural and moral arbiters. Masaki Hiroshi and his colleagues repeatedly portrayed the chief prosecutor, Nakagome Noriyori, as uncultured, unable to string together a grammatical sentence, and a sloppy, inaccurate reader of fine literature. In the public's mind, this strategy had the result of undercutting the prosecution's attacks while elevating the more literate and cultured defense, people capable of distinguishing art from dirt.

Battling the Feudal Mind-Set, Making Sex New

While the new constitution promised the salvation of Japan, D. H. Lawrence's novel—regarded by some as obscene—paradoxically suggested a means of redeeming the spirits and morals of the citizens. The defense team's Masaki Hiroshi praised both the publisher and the translator for their lofty goals in publishing a Japanese version of the Lawrence novel. According to Masaki, the publisher and translator had undertaken production of the unexpurgated translation because they were "overwhelmed by the decline in morality, the loss of the elevated human spirit, the self-destructive, decadent trends, all of which are symptomatic of—or perhaps causes of—the spiritual and material poverty of this nation in near ruins." As an antidote to this spiritual and decadent decline, Itō and Oyama offered a work of art to stimulate citizens to recognize that human sexuality is "full of mystery, like the life of a flower" and also "sacred."[65]

The defense team also placed considerable hope in the potential of the Japanese version of *Lady Chatterley's Lover* to help Japanese people "regard sexuality as a serious matter" and, consequently, to raise their country's cultural standards. In contrast to the prosecution's insistence that Japanese readers were not capable of reading the novel intelligently, the defense offered the novel, with its pursuit of "beauty and truth," as a means of elevating Japanese readers' outlook. The attraction of the similarly optimistic view of the power of sex held by Lawrence had been expressed by British critics in the early 1930s: "*Lady C.* was to state a cause for millions who search a solution of the world's problems through normal sex."[66]

How dare the prosecution accuse Lawrence of anything but noble intent, the defense angrily asked, when it had never bothered to raise charges of obscenity against the publishers of the wildly popular Japanese "entertainment novels" (kōdan), which featured explicit sex and emphasized mindless escapism?[67]

The defense's focus on Lawrence's linking of sex and the nation's fate found a receptive audience in Japan for several reasons. First, Lawrence's elevated vision of sexuality fitted with the aim of various constituents to seek a positive alternative to the lurid kasutori magazines and decadent and carnal literature (such as that of Sakaguchi Ango and Tamura Taijirō) that had dominated the market since the defeat.[68] Lawrence's linking of sex, tenderness, and subjectivity also reinforced the postwar revulsion at the memory of the imperial regime's conscription of bodies as well as its taboo on the senses. At a time when the old imperial values no longer presented a viable long-term model for sexuality, many trial participants referred to pressing contemporary social problems, such as prostitution, the lack of sex education, and the morality of youth. Although they were not brought up specifically during the trial, the gendered anxieties about the imposition of the Occupation's sexual desires and the mobilization of a segment of the female population as a "floodwall" to protect the chastity of Japan's women also loomed.[69]

It is tempting to view the trial as part of a linear narrative of modernity and progress, with the defense rejecting a feudal mind-set that represses sex and advocating instead an open and enlightened freedom of sexual expression that affirms democracy.[70] No one in the courtroom, however, advocated a libertarian, absolutely permissive print culture, and for good reason. Indeed, more than a half a century after the Tokyo trial, many of the questions raised about representation and sex remain controversial: What are the differences among pornography, obscenity, erotica, and art? Is there a cause-and-effect relationship between erotica/pornography and social behavior? Is pornography especially harmful to women? While it is clear that women in particular have long been victimized by many varieties of sexual exploitation and violence, feminists of different persuasions disagree on how much sexually frank texts and films should be censored.[71]

Even though Itō anticipated that some of the female witnesses would offer the sharpest condemnations of Lady Chatterley's Lover, none of them did. But they did raise important questions about sexuality and gender that most of the male witnesses did not. The testimony of Azuma

Masa, head of a reform school for girls, highlighted the significant class divisions among women. While praising the value of Lawrence's "beautiful ideas," Azuma confirmed that the delinquent girls at her school lacked the literary sophistication to read and appreciate *Lady Chatterley's Lover*. Their level of literacy limited them to women's magazines like *Romance*. The novel, therefore, was not within their grasp as either a civilizing or a corrupting force.[72] Even Etsuko Gantret, a Christian and head of an activist group that fought against prostitution and promoted prohibition, the purity of women, and world peace, refused to condemn Lawrence's novel as the prosecution had hoped (partly because she would not evaluate something that she had not read).

Most of all, Masaki, Itō, and the team welcomed the illuminating testimony of Kamichika Ichiko, a scholar of women's social movements and head of the publication *The Women's Times* (*Fujin taimuzu*). When asked whether she had read the novel, Kamichika responded that she had in fact borrowed the book from her daughter. She identified the ignorance of "more than half" of Japanese women about sex, as well as the imbalance between men's excessive desire and women's inadequate desire (born of this lack of knowledge), as impediments to women's liberation. Praising Lawrence for writing clearly about sex, she declared the novel suitable and beneficial for young women aged seventeen and older. Kamichika praised the use of "the power of literature" to promote a proper understanding of desire and sexuality. A forceful speaker, Kamichika came close to making the chief prosecutor, Nakagome Noriyori, admit that the entire case was based on his woefully mistaken readings of Lawrence's novel.[73]

Why were the police willing to place such great stakes in the *Lady Chatterley* trial? For the Japanese government officials and the police, SCAP's relatively loose policy on sexually explicit materials meant that the local authorities could stand as the "authorizer of discourse" for at least one facet of society—the regulation of sexual expression in cultural production—while the Occupation had chosen to control nearly every other area of print culture.[74] Lest their corner on power go unnoticed by the public, the police enlisted the media to publicize its efforts at banning books.[75] The police had employed the same legal statute (Article 175) to bring obscenity charges against *Lady Chatterley's Lover* as it had for the amorphous categories of *kasutori* magazines. Both the prosecution and the defense frequently offered the genre of the *kasutori* magazines as a negative domestic example of the representation of sexuality, even though the genre had started to decline by the time the *Chatterley* trials were under way.[76]

Before the trial, the police seemed not at all eager to invite debate about the standards for obscenity or the law itself. Instead, it handled all the obscenity accusations in a manner remarkably reminiscent of the imperial era—out of court. The police expected a direct admission of guilt and an apology from publishers and writers. When those in the *kasutori* business obliged, the matter was resolved. But when the police hauled in Oyama, he refused to agree with their definition of *Lady Chatterley's Lover* as obscene.[77]

The police thus presented itself in the media as morally righteous because it was working to rid society of morally degraded texts, even though it would allow no one to dispute its interpretation of propriety. The police's relationship with the *kasutori* industry, furthermore, proved to be more complicated than the rigorous enforcement of Article 175 suggested.[78] That is, during the trial, the defense managed to reveal that some police bureaucrats and prosecution witnesses had themselves published articles in *kasutori* magazines.[79]

The defense team followed a careful strategy of portraying the prosecution as ignorant heathens, offering as proof Nakagome's poor and incomprehensible writing, his mistaken readings of Lawrence's literature, and his undisciplined body (specifically, his inability to maintain a poker face during the proceedings). The prosecution could not even read *Lady Chatterley's Lover* as intelligently as did Sone Chiyoko, the seventeen-year-old high-school student who testified.

Building on this characterization, Masaki and Fukuda Tsuneari also painted the prosecution outlook as "sensual and subjective" (*kankakuteki, shukanteki*), in contrast to the defense's qualities of "seriousness, responsibility, and dignity." Even though some prominent men on the defense side had sold articles to the *kasutori* magazines, they did not have the same haze of sleaze hovering around them as the prosecution did.[80] Far from protecting the "public welfare" guaranteed by the constitution, the police, through the act of accusation, had rendered a fine work of literature "pornographic."[81] The worldview of the prosecution and its witnesses (identified with the Meiji constitution) posited sex as entertainment, dirty and obscene. To make matters worse, the prosecution resorted to witnesses who lacked the mental capacity to conceive of sex as an "idea" (*shisō*).[82] In his closing statement, Masaki dubbed the police's approach the "temptations of the devil that will destroy Japan for all eternity."[83]

In the late 1940s, political scientist and theorist Maruyama Masao envisioned the social sciences as the bearer of enlightenment to the people, as the "guide to the democratization of knowledge in postwar Japan."[84] During the *Lady Chatterley* trial, Masaki and his peers demonstrated their superior understanding of the novel's sexual morality by offering ample empirical evidence gathered by social scientists, thus positioning themselves to oppose the "sensual" and illogical argument of the prosecutors. Thanks to the influence of the social sciences, particularly sociology and social psychology, they were able to offer statistical analyses of the appearance of sexually explicit situations in *Lady Chatterley* and those found in the "pulp fiction" prevalent in the Occupation era. In addition, the defense included as evidence clinical studies comparing the quantifiable reactions of readers to such categories as "beauty of language," "frankness of sexual description," "value of the work as art," and "degree of sexual stimulation" in *Lady Chatterley* compared with those in contemporary Japanese erotic books.[85]

Although *Lady Chatterley's Lover* occasionally was compared with texts such as Boccaccio's *Decameron* and erotic books of the Edo period, most frequently it was the contemporary, native *kasutori* magazines against which the British novel was obsessively measured. Most often during the trial, the *kasutori* genre was offered as a monolithic entity, even when individual titles were given. The contemporary discourse on sexuality was much more diverse than this simple binarism suggests, however. The reading public could choose from *kasutori* that were pure porn but also had access to cheaply produced yet educational and progressive magazines.

They also could easily obtain the philosophical literary decadence of novelists Sakaguchi Ango and Dazai Osamu. Although Sakaguchi attended the trial as a spectator, his "carnal" writing was never specifically mentioned, perhaps because his harrowing tales show bodies rebelling against the memories of the traumas of war without offering positive visions for the future. Yet Sakaguchi's illuminating juxtaposition of the imperial notion of *kokutai* (national polity/body), by which the state brutally regulated the life of every body (as a soldier, as the mother and wife of a soldier, as a productive worker), with *nikutai* (carnal body) resonated strongly with the defense's arguments. But the latter also proposed an alternative, a new sexual morality to be part of the new democratic culture.

The Occupation authority's motives in placing the regulation of obscene and sexually explicit material in Japanese hands remain unclear. Certainly, it was not because SCAP regarded sex as unimportant. Rather, perhaps the puritanical Americans wished to avoid comment on the suppressed fact of extensive sexual relations between its personnel and the occupied people. Perhaps the strident and often hypocritical voices of the prewar U.S. antivice societies still rang in their ears, reminding them that far from being so trivial, representations of sex presented a clear and present danger.

To others, therefore, the Occupation authority's decision not to restrict obscene and sexually explicit material raised great concerns. Activist groups and publishers, whose motives were not necessarily regressive, also found alarming the flood of *kasutori*. Some women's groups grappled with the authorities' less than nuanced approach to monitoring publications pertaining to sexuality.[86] Early on, publishers' organizations registered with the authorities their concerns about the seemingly unchecked *kasutori* industry. They may have considered the high-volume *kasutori* business as a financial threat because it sold hundreds of thousands of copies with low overhead. And as Oyama Hisajirō himself demonstrated, many publishers also wished for higher ethical and cultural standards for the industry.[87]

What exactly did the defense wish readers to learn about sexuality from *Lady Chatterley's Lover*? We noted Itō's praise of Lawrence's consecration of sex and Masaki's regard for Lawrence's desire to defeat the pornographic imagination, which sees sex as dirty, taboo. Lawrence wrote, "The right sort of sex stimulus is invaluable to human daily life. Without it the world is grey. . . . But even I would censor genuine pornography . . . you can recognize it by the insult it offers, invariably, to sex, and to the human spirit. Pornography is an attempt to insult sex, to do dirt on it. This is unpardonable."[88]

Creating Democratic Discourse in the Courtroom

If the government regulation of obscenity only partly concerns sex and can be more productively understood as a process of negotiating the locus of authority, as well as the boundaries of public and private, citizen and state, then the Japanese *Lady Chatterley* case was an instance of that very process made transparent. The terms of the definition resided soundly within the framework of liberal democracy and the free market. As if to emphasize that the trial participants were democratic citizens, newspaper photographs of the trial showed close-ups not of book covers but of Itō and Oyama sitting on the wooden courtroom chairs or crowded shots of spectators. As further evidence of the centrality of the *process* of the trial and its employment of the topic of pornography as a means of voicing many urgent national concerns unrelated to sexuality, I reiterate the fact that the verdict (guilty) ultimately did *not* have the effect of suppressing the representation of sexuality in subsequent literature, film, and art.[89] In addition, public opinion was highly critical of the verdict.

As Jay Rubin eloquently demonstrated, the defense was determined to "portray the prosecution as representative of the feudal, authoritarian, class-bound, anti-individualist, anti-human mentality that had suppressed thought and speech and the pursuit of individual happiness in prewar Japan and which had been, as they saw it, ultimately responsible for leading Japan into war."[90] Not only did the prosecution seek to deprive Itō and his publisher, Oyama shoten, of their rights, the defense asserted, but the authorities exposed themselves as particularly authoritarian by expecting "the people to tremble with fear in their presence. . . . Itō protested that under the new Constitution a defendant was to be presumed innocent until proven guilty, not presumed guilty because he failed to go along with the prosecutor" as defendants often "fearfully did in the prewar days . . . certain of the retribution if they did not confess 'guilt for a crime they had no intention of committing.'"[91] The defense questioned whether those involved in the prosecution were, as people, capable of defending the newly guaranteed rights and whether they adhered too strongly to the ways of the past.[92] Those advocating for Itō and Oyama held up the postwar constitution as the sole means of saving "this ruined nation" (*bōkoku*). In the 1950s during the Cold War, the anxieties provoked by the possibility of a reprisal of fascism would have resonated (consciously or not) with the free world's panic over the authoritarianism of the Eastern bloc.

In the later American and British trials, new legislation may have served as a catalyst for bringing *Lady Chatterley's Lover* to court, but neither the political systems nor the relationship between the authorities and constituencies—those who made the decisions about boundaries—had changed radically. In Japan, in contrast, the *Lady Chatterley* case stands clearly as the first postwar literary trial conducted under an entirely new system of government, one imposed by occupiers whose departure was imminent.[93] To understand the extent to which Japanese democracy was then in a very early stage of "self-definition," it is helpful to recall that Maruyama Masao wrote bitterly in 1950 that at present there was "no democracy worth defending in Japan."[94]

The trial therefore was a significant early opportunity for the diverse participants to present, in a public forum, their views on the major distinctions between public and private and human rights and to define concepts that, until Japan's recent past, had been a distinct political *other*. These ideas included the sovereignty of the people, the sanctity of the citizen apart from a national family, the individual's ability to control the fate of his or her body, sexuality as private and personal rather than in the service of strengthening the nation, an unrestricted press, and an open marketplace. Those assembled also extolled the intellectual's responsibility in setting moral standards for all of society. The new constitution had already established the institutional framework for democracy. Democratic culture, however, took time to develop. In the early 1950s, the "normative core" of democratic culture was "formed by social mobilization and broad political criticism." After 1955, with Japan's economic miracle, the stabilization of the Liberal Democratic Party, and the ongoing Cold War, this "normative core" instead involved "consumer participation in an expanding GNP."[95] The *Chatterley* trials spanned this transitional period in the history of democratic values.

The best-known Japanese text associated with the trial, Itō's *Saiban*, states at the very beginning that the author wished to provide "easy-to-understand explanations of the functioning of the law in postwar democracy" and to clarify to the reader the many ways that the law affected their everyday lives.[96] Itō himself had gone through this same process of reeducation at the start of the trial when his knowledgeable defense team explained to him in detail the differences between the pre-1945 legal system and the present one and the new roles of the prosecutors and the defense. Not insignificantly, Itō attributed some of his knowledge of the democratic courtroom to an American movie in which a lawyer paces restlessly around the courtroom as he cross-examines a witness.[97]

In this trial, the defense admitted to only two possible political persuasions: on the defense's side proudly stood the advocates of the new constitution, happy to have sacrificed during the war to receive this gift from God (the postwar constitution), and supporters of human rights, hopeful for a new elevated morality and culture for Japan. Only a few short years after the Tokyo War Crimes Trials, Itō and others who in their writing had supported the imperial cause were doubtless relieved to be included without question in the enlightened camp. Itō even rhetorically aligned himself with those who had been politically persecuted by the imperial government by comparing the present trial with those that had been conducted in the "name of the emperor." How had the leftist writers felt when on trial, he wondered. He regretted that he had never attended a trial of a leftist writer but not that he had never taken an oppositional stance himself.[98]

On the opposite side were the prosecution and the bureaucracy, still wallowing in the imperial mind-set and ignorantly and blindly looking at the world through the lens of the Meiji constitution. Masaki leaped gleefully at the opportunity to cross-examine Watanabe Tetsuzō, the one witness who showed no shame as he praised the Imperial Rescript on Education and further extolled the democratic virtues of the Meiji constitution.[99] A Diet member who served on multiple influential boards and committees, the reactionary Watanabe seemed positioned to influence many aspects of government policy and practice, a prospect that alarmed Masaki.

In his closing statement, Masaki took the opportunity to blast the police by linking them with a name that was an easy symbol of the evils of the militarized state and the shame of Japan, former Prime Minister Tōjō Hideki (who was executed during the war crimes tribunals, before MacArthur pardoned many others accused of class-A war crimes in 1949). The police, he said, had the same primitive ways of thinking as "that cruel Tōjō," who had "whipped the Japanese people to the brink of extinction" and who was regarded as a "barbarian by people the world over." Even more insidious was the police's desire to bind the Japanese people to propriety and custom in order to keep them in a "primitive spiritual state."[100]

Masaki took it upon himself to remind the prosecutors, with their outdated thought, that Article 21 of the new constitution stated: "No censorship shall be maintained."[101] In the defense team's eyes, however, the prosecution's worst crime was not its willingness to ignore those parts of the new constitution that did not suit its purposes. Rather, the police and the prosecution suffered from the "sensual" mode of thought that resisted rationality in political matters and, as we have seen, was disinterested in aesthetic matters.

This distinction between the rational and the sensual and potentially fascistic was one that had been made in the recent past by political scientist Maruyama Masao. In his essay "From Carnal Literature to Carnal Politics" (1949), Maruyama warned against the dangers of connecting desire with politics and art:

Most of the writers who grind out carnal or sex-obsessed brands of literature do so knowing full well that what they write doesn't spring from everyday events in the lives of ordinary people. And it's the same for the reader. Isn't it precisely because the circumstances depicted are remote from his actual life that he's so attracted? In other words, literature constitutes a kind of "symbol" of something he longs for.[102]

As a prominent public intellectual, Maruyama's despair over the future of Japan's postwar democracy ("If we don't control carnal literature and carnal politics in one way or another, then it's senseless to talk about Japan as a democratic and cultured nation") emanates from his reading of an unhealthy balance of the culture/nature binarism.[103] For Maruyama, the postwar grounding of literature in desire, the body, and sensuality was potentially fertile ground for a fascist revival and would prevent Japanese writers from creativity based on "free flight of imagination," which would be the appropriate creative basis for a literature of democracy: "It's just that such literature takes the most sordid moments of our sensual experience, multiplies the number, and, in doing so, magnifies them out of all proportion. An imagination capable of such exaggeration appeared to be soaring away in unhampered freedom, but actually it's grubbing around on its hands and knees in quite a commonplace world."[104]

Maruyama's influential articulation of anxiety about the tyranny of the sensual and the body in Japanese literature helps us understand why the defense of the *Chatterley* case might place considerable hope in the potential of the Japanese version of *Lady Chatterley's Lover* to raise the moral standards of the Japanese people. Not only could they see "sexuality as a serious matter," but they also might separate it from the sensuality (*kankaku*) in which fascism finds its basis and with which, as we have seen, they associated the prosecution. The determination of whether the translated novel should be regarded as "art or pornography" thus is related to the goals of "civilizing" a nation bereft by defeat.

Maruyama also expressed the centrality of literature in society by linking literature with political practice. Along with labor unions and other voluntary associations, however, the literary realm was still dominated by patterns of thought and social relations that Maruyama defined as premodern. Such an emphasis on carnality would hamper the "founding of a [proper] new civic society on the ruins of the old order."[105]

One outcome of the Tokyo trial was the revelation of constituencies and individuals who had interest in obtaining the authority needed to participate in defining a new morality in the framework of a representative democracy. Beginning in 1949, intellectuals and activists watched as the Occupation, with the help of conservative Japanese forces, pursued its anticommunist Reverse Course and purged labor activists, politicians, journalists, and others. The trial thus became a safe venue for intellectuals and journalists who wanted to voice their political views but who also feared a resurgent authoritarianism, especially given the "depurging" of people accused of war crimes that accompanied the Red purge.[106] With the economy finally rallying as Japan benefited from the Korean War, publishers found paper more accessible and a larger potential audience for their publications. As the "dregs" erotic magazines had shown, sex sells, but not all publishers shared the revelatory celebration of decadence evident in those titillating rags. Another outcome was the clarification of the means by which to participate in the public sphere in the new liberal democracy, and here we see that the media spectacle was one means.

In conclusion, the Tokyo *Lady Chatterley's Lover* obscenity trial was one of the first postwar public forums in which writers and citizens could openly debate political, literary, and sexual values. Although the trial did not result in definitive visions of what constituted the literary community's postwar identity, the debate that took place in the courtroom and in the media mobilized rational thought and social scientific method as means of battling the subjectivity, carnality, and lack of critical faculties of those representing the state. Despite the guilty verdict, the defense effectively confirmed the high modernist assumptions that aesthetic response should encompass sexuality and rejected the state's unilateral attempt to posit subjectivity divorced from sex. In the realm of sexuality, the defense rejected the police's cynical regard for sex as a dirty open secret, as well as the Occupation's use of sex as a distraction from the Reverse Course and instead advocated a dignified, informed approach to sex. Finally, in political terms, the defense team struggled to pull Japan out of the chaotic decadence and carnal politics on which the regressive, recently depurged leaders might base their power. Instead, Masaki and others who participated in the trial tried to demonstrate democracy as lived democratic values and an evolving "political culture, not only as imposed institutions."[107]

Regardless of the extensive media coverage garnered by the *Lady Chatterley* trial and the involvement of many literary figures during the 1950s, not all writers then became absorbed in the spectacle and the debate. Novelist and poet Hara Tamiki, for one, grew obsessed with yet another facet of the Cold War: the eerie specter of nuclear annihilation. If the Korean War encouraged recovery and brought a measure of prosperity to some in early 1950s Japan, the conflict also revived the threat of deployment of the atom bomb in warfare, by no less than President Harry Truman. As a survivor of the 1945 Hiroshima atomic bombing and witness to the start of the nuclear arms race, Hara was living with mounting anxiety about nuclear apocalypse. Hara's writings and life epitomized the peculiar Cold War fears and imagination engendered by the invisible threat, even as he worked to realize the promise of participatory democracy guaranteed by the new age.

The true artist, in my opinion, with his insight into life, and his sense of humanity, knows that the situation cannot be as hopeless as an Atomic cloud would indicate. His regard for humanity should provide a passionate confidence in his fellow man.   —Paul Hogarth

3   Hara Tamiki *First Witness to the Cold War*

In 1955, British critic John Berger insisted that "it is criminally irresponsible for any intellectual today not to consider his and every subject in relation to the threat of the H-bombs!"[1] Although Berger's claim may now seem nothing more than panic or wild exaggeration, it does serve to remind us of the public concern in the 1950s about the seemingly unlimited and deadly nuclear arms race. For readers in many countries, the American writer John Hersey put a human face on the suffering and hell of the world's first nuclear attacks in his book *Hiroshima* (1946). In Japan, Hara Tamiki (1905–1951) was one of the first professional writers to describe the experience of the Hiroshima bombing and its aftermath.

Many critics in Japan credit Hara with prescience because he wrote about the atomic bombings with great urgency and purpose, as if in anticipation of the events that would later lead to Berger's pronouncement.[2] Hara's novella *Summer Flowers* (*Natsu no hana*, 1947) became one of the most highly praised and influential A-bomb narratives in Japan, one that informed all subsequent retellings and remembrances of the first use of a nuclear weapon on a city.[3] Even the publication of *Summer Flowers* seems something of a miracle, given that Hara was determined to see his story into print despite the Allied Occupation's ban on depictions of the bombing. He also faced the resistance of many Japanese people, for whom the hibakusha and the bombings of Hiroshima and Nagasaki marked not only Japan's defeat in a world war but also its dubious status as the only nation chosen for attack using nuclear weapons.[4]

As an artist, Hara accepted the moral mission of speaking out against such weapons. The political polarization of Cold War Japan weighed heavily on him, although his antinuclear writings and activism never included a larger analysis of political and social factors contributing to the arms race. The path that Hara ultimately chose demonstrates that the Cold War had a profound effect on the writer's ability to believe in the utility of his own testimony. Then, in 1951, the same year that British painter Paul Hogarth exhorted artists to resist hopelessness in the face of an "atomic cloud," Hara chose to end his own life.

Despite the pessimism implied by Hara's final act, many prominent writers and critics found him the most compelling of the many hibakusha writers. In particular, the Nobel Prize–winning novelist Ōe Kenzaburō became one of Hara's strongest advocates. The affinity that Ōe felt for Hara came partly from his admiration for Summer Flowers, but perhaps even more from Ōe's conviction that Hara's oeuvre expressed the spirit of the Cold War age. Ōe found meaning in Hara's later writings and death and extolled Hara as the first victim of the Cold War.

After Summer Flowers, Hara did not remain content with his role as a primary witness to the atomic bombing but instead experimented with different modes of writing in an effort to make sense of the new and menacing guerre de nerfs. In contrast to his realist approach in Summer Flowers, he tried alternative modes of nonrealist writing about the bomb in his later works. That Hara's writings encompassed both realist and naturalist modes and experimental and nonrealist narrative strategies is itself characteristic of an emerging Cold War age in the Western bloc, which espoused a "healthy pluralism" rather than rigid adherence to orthodoxy as a positive environment for cultural production.[5] Rather than validating a single mode of narrative over another, we should look at the complementary nature of the experimental and realist approaches to these emerging Cold War liberal democracies.[6] Hara's career does not exhibit a linear progression from realist to surrealist and Romantic writing. Although he found realism and documentary appropriate to writing about the bombing and its immediate aftermath, when he sought to evoke the Cold War battlefield that he perceived Tokyo to be, he chose nonrealist approaches.

Before the Soviets' possession and the demonstration of thermonuclear weapons, many people in the Allied nations and Asia approved of

the United States's use of A-bombs in Japan. Consequently, the antinuclear movement constituted a distinct minority in the Western bloc during the first decades after the war. In this atmosphere, Hara was prescient
in his conviction that the use of nuclear weapons would lead to extreme
consequences for the world, and he also was notable for his articulation of
his place as a battlefield in the Cold War.

Politically, the gradual process through which Japan embraced a victim
consciousness based on the atomic bombings and the repression of the
country's militarist past are well-known aspects of postwar society. Decades later, the tenacity of the victimhood discourse has created the false
impression that the 1950s culture was inward looking and resistant to the
profound influences of the highly unstable Cold War world. In this book,
I discuss Hiroshima as a center where artists and activists worked in response to Cold War realities. Despite the talk of peace there, the 1950s
in Japan was, as in many other nations, a "period characterized by metaphors of battle," a place implicated by the "Cold War polarization between
Washington and Moscow."[7]

Several signs that artists and cultural production at this time were
embroiled in larger currents of the Cold War include the dispute over
the meanings of peace, the conflict over the designation of Hiroshima
and Nagasaki as cities of peace, and the urgency that fueled the effort
to create knowledge about the bomb. Literature, film, and painting contributed to this transformation of the local experience of atomic bombing in Hiroshima and Nagasaki into a national and universal discourse of
atomic anxiety and Cold War culture. One thread that runs through this
discourse is the process of acquiring knowledge about the bomb in an age
dominated by a clash of extreme fear and rationality.

A-bomb literature arose not only in relation to the literary establishment but also in interaction with visual evocations of the bombings and
their aftermaths and with the social conditions and processes that affected
the circulation and reception of these works. The various artistic media
and the work of artists should also be seen in relation to the overarching
dynamics of the antinuclear and peace activism, for which all these media had utility (as didactic tools, as moral inspiration, as cautionary tales).
Like the A-bomb murals of Maruki Iri and Maruki Toshi, Hara's prose
and poetry and Kamei Fumio's films had different social lives and a variety of uses within the broad field of high Cold War culture, well before
A-bomb literature and art earned canonical status through works such as
Ibuse Masuji's novel *Black Rain* (*Kuroi ame*, 1966).

Hara Tamiki, Creativity, and the Bomb

Cultural evocations of the bomb often treat the weapon as the work of the devil or as human creativity contaminated by evil and madness. At the same time, some artists and scientists have regarded the bomb as a seed of moral transformation. Hara Tamiki's *Summer Flowers* describes a horrific scene in Hiroshima of maimed and suffering bodies and piles of burned corpses, but the text also expresses wonder at the transformative, positive power of the weapon. At 8:15 A.M. on August 15, 1945, Hara comes tumbling nearly naked, sightless, and screaming out of the bathroom, where he experienced the moment of the bomb's detonation. For Hara, the blast does not bring injury or death but instead an unexpected rebirth, a new life in which he has a moral purpose for his writing: acting as a witness to the destructive potential of the new weapon.

One does not have to experience the bomb directly to be changed by it. Hearing or reading testimonials of *hibakusha* or seeing images of the aftermath also have the power to transform. The first frame of an *Asahi Graph* magazine cartoon from 1952 shows a family bickering on their way to see an exhibition of Hiroshima photographs. In the next frame, we see them clinging to one another for comfort as they emerge from the exhibition.[8]

Cold War culture arose from the newly finessed technology that was the atomic bomb and also from the evolution of a discourse that privileged nuclear weapons as novel and exceptional in their psychological and cultural meanings. This exceptionalist discourse depended on the production of texts and images, commemorative practices and spaces, and representational processes that adhered to the concept of nuclear power as simultaneously fearsome and productive and as a sign of scientific triumph over the forces of nature. The discourse was, furthermore, classically modernist in its configuration of the age as an entirely new period in the history of humanity and of the earth. The bipolar nature of the Cold War's political and military struggle meant that the exact profile of atomic exceptionalism varied, depending on one's political belief. Notably, atomic exceptionalism was part of American triumphalism. The Soviet Union did not initially glorify atom bombs in its official discourse but instead boasted of its future use of nuclear power for constructive purposes. In contrast, many in China and Korea regarded the use of the atomic bomb against Japan as justified punishment and necessary for their liberation from Japan's imperialism.[9]

A family visits an exhibition of A-bomb photographs. (Cartoon from *Asahi Graph*, May 21, 1952, 20, Courtesy of Asahi shinbunsha and Nemoto Susumu)

The process of constructing the dominant modernist discourse about nuclear weapons took place during the 1940s and 1950s. Just as nuclear technology and international relations during this period changed rapidly and often hazardously, cultural production relating to nuclear weapons was in a state of considerable flux as well. The literature, art, film, and criticism of Hiroshima and Nagasaki figured prominently in the development of the rhetoric of the bomb and of Cold War culture, in both Japan and other countries.

In our effort to understand the emerging discourse of the Cold War, we must keep in mind several unusual features of what we are calling a war: that the Cold War was waged mainly through discursive fields and not primarily on a geographical, spatial battlefield. Thus it was made up of narrative, visual, and diplomatic culture. As an imagined war, it compared two ideological systems—that is, if we define ideology as the cultural and social understandings of our relationship to the material world. Paradoxically, the nuclear weapons usually considered a defining characteristic of the Cold War were weapons only in a symbolic, even abstract, sense.

Hara Tamiki: First Victim of the Cold War

Among the many significant cultural figures who contributed to the corpus of A-bomb literature, Hara Tamiki arguably claims the longest-lasting appeal among a broad readership and the least controversial place in the modern literary canon. His novella *Summer Flowers* is frequently anthologized in Japan and has been translated into many languages.[10] His poetry about the bombing, such as "Give Me Water" (Mizu o kudasai), remains among the best-known A-bomb verse. Influential writers such as Ōe Kenzaburō praised Hara as one of the most gifted of the A-bomb writers, which had the effect of stabilizing Hara's place in the literary canon.

Numerous authors have described the bombings of Hiroshima and Nagasaki, so what distinguished Hara's work? Part of the answer lies in Hara's reputation as a man acutely sensitive to his times and to the central dilemma of the nuclear age. A case in point, Ōe championed Hara as the "first person to experience the Cold War" and as the writer best able to communicate the horrors of nuclear weapons to younger generations, even many years after Hara's death.[11] In Ōe's opinion, Hara speaks to all readers in the world who share the universal antinuclear consciousness, and his writings have the power to awaken younger generations of Japanese readers and foreign audiences to the evils of nuclear weapons. In a lecture to scientists, Ōe asserted that literary writers had an important role in the struggle against nuclear weapons. Drawing on Kurt Vonnegut's comparison of writers to the canary in the coal mine, Ōe described writers as more sensitive to the dangers of the age and thus able to warn others. Hara did not succumb to external forces but instead chose to end his own life, some say as a means of protesting the nuclear peril.

But what is the nature of Hara's protest or, more accurately, of his plea? For the most part, his stories and poems vividly communicate the aftermath of Hiroshima's bomb as hell on earth and offer a compelling portrait of the physical and emotional suffering of people whose everyday life and rituals had been destroyed.[12] Hara was not alone in telling this story but was joined by many amateur *hibakusha* and some important professional authors. Hara's works are distinctive because they describe not only the bombing but also the times, the early Cold War and its culture, in a way that few other writers did.

Hara's timely suicide took place at a high point in Cold War tensions. His life, death, and oeuvre resonate with the central tropes of the Cold War discourse, such as hope and fear, madness, the contaminated body, fear of an invisible, "eternally absent" enemy, and the transformative power of the bomb. Hara's narration of nuclear trauma had the moral purpose of protesting the violence of atomic weapons, but it also aimed at affirming the imagined salvation of aesthetics and art. Hara's image as the "Cold War's first victim" stemmed, furthermore, from his ambiguous political stance as an advocate of peace and antinuclearism divorced from ideology.[13]

Hara's critics and readers responded to his writings in ways that contributed to the building of the Cold War discourse of the bomb. I chose Hara—from the many writers who took the A-bomb as their topic—as the focus of this chapter partly because the ambiguity in his life and works has allowed for a diverse reception. This contrasts with other well-known A-bomb writers such as Toge Sankichi and Kurihara Sadako, whose political commitments and activism are clearly defined by their biographies. Granted, Hara's early A-bomb prose and poetry, as well as his suicide, function as potent symbols for antinuclear activism. At the same time, even in the 1950s, the critic Hara Kenchū mourned Hara's lack of politics even as he praised *Summer Flowers* and other works.[14] This "lack" doubtless was meant to indicate Hara's absence of specific ideological convictions and distance from party politics. It is Hara's ambivalence— poised between aestheticism and progressive politics—that made him the quintessential Cold War A-bomb writer. The marked absence of a clear political stance in Hara's work and life contributed to the canonization of his work in a Cold War literary establishment that increasingly eschewed overtly "political" (that is, progressive or leftist) art.

The single political event most often linked to Hara's suicide is President Truman's public announcement in 1951 that he would not rule out the use of nuclear weapons in the Korean War. The two events that dominate the image of Hara, therefore, are the August 6, 1945, bombing of Hiroshima, preserved forever in his *Summer Flowers,* and the Cold War threat of using nuclear bombs again. Given such a framework for his life, it is difficult to disregard Ōe's vision of Hara as the "first Cold War victim." But we will consider more carefully why and how Ōe conceived of Hara, of all the many *hibakusha* of Hiroshima and Nagasaki, in this manner. Ōe understood Hara as having made an existential choice of death as a means of resisting the insanity of the arms race, a choice similar to that of the *Hiroshima-teki ningen* (Hiroshima-style person) whom he lauds in his *Hiroshima Notes* (*Hiroshima nooto,* 1954). For Ōe, Hara's death also resonated with a very personal incident: the early 1960s suicide of a friend in Paris who, it seems, also killed himself for reasons of nuclear anxiety.

Triumph of Technological Violence and Rebirth

Among the countless stories about the bombing, *Summer Flowers* has an auratic presence, for several reasons.[15] On one level, Hara Tamiki's text has much in common with other compelling modern narratives of extreme trauma, especially in its attempt to "convert trauma into the occasion for sublimity, to transvalue it into a test of the self or the group and an entry into the extraordinary."[16] At the same time, the author's attitude toward his work and the history of this particular text distinguish *Summer Flowers* from the numerous other accounts (fictive or not) of surviving destruction and mass death in Hiroshima. Not only is it one of the very first accounts to appear in print, but the author depicts his own survival as exceptional. Hara himself uses the word "rare" to describe his ability to write such an account so soon after the traumatic incident took place. He also presents the story as an urgent matter and his own voice as one that needs to be heard. This attitude differs from his passivity in promoting his own writings before the death of his wife in 1944 and the bombing in 1945. Contributing to the aura of this story was its ability to circumvent the Occupation censors, who banned all texts and images regarding the atomic bombings.

When *Summer Flowers* first appeared in June 1947, it represented one of the extremely few published accounts of the experience of Japanese urban air war, much less of an atomic bombing. Of the many subsequent narratives about Hiroshima and Nagasaki and the relatively few narratives of the vast death and destruction caused by the firebombings of dozens of Japanese cities, certainly none have been as carefully shepherded and admired as *Summer Flowers*. Literary critics and writers such as Yamamoto Kenkichi and Sasaki Kiichi helped Hara identify an appropriate venue for the story, one that would likely escape the notice of the Occupation censors, because they felt a sense of urgency about Hara's evocation of Hiroshima. As another means of evading the Allied censors, Hara's colleagues even contemplated having the story translated into English and then retranslated back into Japanese in order to make it appear as if the original story were not Japanese. Although Hara originally sent the piece with the title "Atomic Bomb" to the prominent literary journal *Kindai bungaku*, the editors quickly realized that it would be difficult to obtain the Allied censor's approval for the story.[17] Not only would the title amount to a confession that the piece concerned one of the Occupation's taboo subjects, but the journal also was mainstream. They thus concluded that a smaller university press journal such as *Mita bungaku* (of Keio University) would draw less attention from the SCAP censors. Hara had attended Keio and had published numerous poems and stories in *Mita bungaku* since the mid-1930s and so was well known to its editors.[18]

Thus the public appearance of *Summer Flowers* was something of a miracle. Hara fashions a distinctive narrative voice in the work, one characterized by unusual powers of observation and compassion. Like his poems about the bombing, *Summer Flowers* has an immediacy that readers find compelling. The narrator employs tropes of ritual and mourning, in addition to references to artistic genre, as a means of orienting readers to the chaotic, hellish aftermath of the bombing. Hara helps the reader comprehend the mass destruction by first introducing the narrator's sorrow for his wife, who died of natural causes roughly a year before the bombing. Only after this man's ritual of mourning for an individual does the narrative shift to the day of the bombing and the countless deaths it caused. The novella's three-part structure introduces the reader to the protagonist's family life in Hiroshima during the months before the bombing, thus evoking the social structures and daily life of wartime Japan.

After Hara committed suicide, no one could read *Summer Flowers* without wondering whether his repeated encounters with natural and unnatural death had led to his self-destruction. Whatever the case, Hara seemed intent on *managing* death, whether by validating his wife's death through means of ritual mourning or by choosing suicide himself. In turn, Hara's

validation of mourning (in the form of sorrow for his wife) offered readers an opportunity to relive their grief over their own wartime experiences
with death.

During the late 1940s and 1950s, when mourning for the war dead was
far from an unambiguous task, a narrative expression of the dedication of
the living to the dead could only be called exceptional. For Hara, grieving
for the A-bomb victims was not only an acceptable but also an imperative emotional state. In one of the novella's most famous passages, he
insists, "I kept telling myself again and again—don't live for yourself; live
only to lament those who have died."[19] This assertion can be understood
as possessing psychological and historical weight. As Dominick LeCapra
notes, psychologically a traumatized person's "bond with the dead, and especially with dead intimates, may invest trauma with value and make its
reliving it a painful but necessary commemoration or memorial to which
one remains dedicated."[20] For a nation recently confronted with massive
violence and death during war, Hara provides the reader with the means
by which to lament the death of family and friends and also the countless
deaths at Hiroshima.

Whether or not Hara's choice of suicide was directly linked to the news
of the American president's refusal to rule out the repeated use of the
bomb and to the resulting fear of impending nuclear war is uncertain.
His writings make it clear that he had an idealized vision of death, partly
because he imagined it as a realm where he could join his beloved wife.
The protagonist in Hara's work further confirms that Hara imagined a
fearful, hostile present. Death therefore seemed like a positive alternative to the displaced, wandering Hara, who found no comfort in Cold
War Tokyo. He also felt alienated from the recovering city of Hiroshima,
which was neither the wartime city that he and his wife had known nor
the smoldering ruins that he remembered from 1945.

In contrast to many accounts of the bombings, *Summer Flowers* establishes an inversion of what, for most people, was the end of the war and
the start of the relatively peaceful postwar period. For Hara, the war began
with the August 6 bombing, for the event disrupted what for him had
been an orderly existence, despite the ongoing war. For example, the well-
known beginning of the first part of the novella describes the ritual of observing the first anniversary of his wife's death, when the narrator goes to
purchase flowers for his wife's grave. For influential readers like Ōe, the
war that commences, the world that comes into existence on August 6, is
the Cold War.[21]

We also can understand Hara's story as itself contributing to the development of the discourse of a changed world, the realm born of the new weapon. Hara's use of the trope of the August 6 bombing as a rebirth, as generating a new world, resonates with the Cold War theme of a new age of progress. On one level, *Summer Flowers* guides the reader through the hell and destructiveness of the bomb. However, the emphasis on the metaphors of rebirth and new life resulting from that same event paradoxically evokes the bombing as a positive, transformational occurrence. The experience of the bomb gives the narrator new reason to live, even though he had been determined to follow his wife in death.

As further evidence of the bomb as a paradoxical source of life, the trope of rebirth appears in other works as well. Hara elaborates on the idea of the bomb creating new life: "That atomic bomb had moved him intensely, awakening in him a new passion and interest in other people."[22] In the short work "Feet of Fire," the protagonist, deranged by the lack of proper diet and haunting memories of Hiroshima, imagines that he has a new companion, whom he names "New Adam." This phoenix-like rise from the flames, albeit in one sense intensely personal, also has something in common with nuclear universalism and the understanding that the moral crisis occasioned by the bomb affects everyone, not just the Japanese. Richard Minear explains this ethical transformation as the realization that the bomb has "exploded in our moral universe."[23]

In retrospect, we recognize Hara's impulses as resonating with the ethical stance embraced by many citizens of the world who abhor nuclear weapons and the potential environmental and biological disaster they threaten but who also succumb to the atom's utopian technological allure. On a broader geopolitical level in Hara's own time, however, the newly developing discourse that equated the leveled, irradiated, and rebuilt Hiroshima with a new age of peace for all humankind was easily recognizable as a particularism that thought "of itself as universalism" and not as a viewpoint shared universally.[24] In other words, the United States's agenda of refashioning its own image as a lover of peace and the sudden shock over the loss of its nuclear monopoly were motivating forces behind the emphasis on the development of a supposedly universalist concept of nuclear power in the Western bloc during the early 1950s. It was not until the early 1960s that generals and heads of states on all sides shared something like an antinuclear worldview, as demonstrated by with the Test Ban Treaty of 1963. Not surprisingly, it was in this post-treaty era when Ōe Kenzaburō visited Hiroshima and wrote his famous *Hiroshima*

Notes. Hara's emphasis on the redemptive powers of the bomb thus survived these different frameworks of nuclear universalism.

Literature as Testimonial

One of the major scientific and medical projects of the 1940s and 1950s
was the compilation and analysis of data on the effects of atomic and hydrogen bombs on living creatures and the earth. This type of scientific,
empirical knowledge is one type of knowledge about the bomb. Another
type was based on witnessing the experiences of Hiroshima and Nagasaki. Most often, this witnessing took the form of written memoirs, oral
narration, and pictures created by *hibakusha* and others.

The aims of the witnessing and testimony of the survivors of the Hiroshima and Nagasaki bombings stemmed from both a universal basis
and a local impetus. Specific stories served a therapeutic function for the
hibakusha themselves and were an opportunity to remember and honor
the dead, who were regarded as sacrificial victims. Storytellers thus might
underscore to their audiences the "critical differences within the community of universal victimhood," such as their individual opposition to or
difference from the hegemonic ideology that gave rise to the war and the
order that it sustained.[25] In universalist terms, survivors told their stories
in order to prove the terrors and immorality of air war, in the hope of pre-
venting future generations from suffering a similar fate. Thus the stories
emphasized individual and community suffering, as well as the horror of
death, trauma, injury, and destruction at the hand of an unseen, mecha-
nized attack. In narrative, writers most often underscore the anonymity
of the bombers with the simple description of a tiny B-29 bomber flying
high in the blue sky over Hiroshima on a hot summer day, followed by
the flash (*pika*) and roar (*don*) of the explosion.

The imagined audience for these stories included members of the
same community, the same nation, as well as readers in distant countries. The universalist assumption of a global audience is either that people everywhere, regardless of culture and political belief, will reaffirm
their moral opposition to the use of weapons of mass destruction or that,
after learning from the story of the evils of weapons of mass destruction,
they will experience an ethical transformation. The majority of A-bomb
survivors did not have training as professional writers or visual artists,
yet the assumed authenticity of their experience and their ability to wit-

ness trumped conventional demands that their work meet established aesthetic standards.

The valorization of moral content and the act of witnessing itself carried over into the reception of the works by survivors who also were trained artists.[26] When the A-bomb paintings of Maruki Toshi and Maruki Iri toured England in 1955, for example, the influential critic John Berger praised the panels but predicated his "recognition of the significance of the work" on "the suspension of normal aesthetic judgments."[27] And as Kozawa Setsuko demonstrated, the initial scorn of some Japanese critics for the Marukis' paintings did not prevent them from becoming the best-known visual evocations of the 1945 bombings in Japan, even though—or perhaps because—they ceased being objects of critical and aesthetic evaluation.[28] In contrast, critics have consistently praised the formal and aesthetic features of Hara's postwar writings.[29] This uncontroversial critical acceptance facilitated the gradual canonization of his work and was enjoyed by few other A-bomb artists. As they became central to the cultural discourse, Hara's writings influenced the conception of generations of readers of the meanings of the atomic bombings and of the Cold War.

Experience as Knowledge

In his writings, Hara Tamiki described the experience of the bombing and also the repeated experience of remembering that day. During his remaining years on earth, Hara often found himself overwhelmed with memories of the bombing, his mind swirling with images that he repeatedly compared with paintings of hell, with hot flames and naked, suffering bodies. Some readers have found Hara's evocative style so moving that his works have become the main lens through which they understand their visits to Hiroshima. Critic Sasaki Ki'ichi described his first visit to Hiroshima: "As I sat on the same riverbank, I heard the voices—I need some water; Help me! When will morning come? Water, water, give me water. . . . Oh, Mother, Sister. . . . I heard the cries of the students, the young girls. . . . I saw them praying." Although Sasaki only imagined the ghastly scene, he sensed a spiritual, almost magical presence: "I felt that Hara Tamiki was walking with me and that I was seeing the things that Hara Tamiki had seen and that I was feeling what Hara Tamiki had felt. It was like walking through a dream. That day, I was bewitched by *Summer Flowers,* just as one is bewitched by a fox."[30] In this way, the novella has functioned as the prototype of the A-bomb memoir and, because of its canonization, has defined the experiences of many who seek to experience the bombing vicariously as they imagine themselves becoming *hibakusha.*

Hara's work thus provides one type of knowledge, if we can call empathy a type of knowing. Specifically, Hara taught that the bombing resulted in the suffering of ordinary people and that the experience and ruins left by the bombing were best understood in relation to the netherworld rather than in terms of this earth. For many *hibakusha,* the act of witnessing was cathartic, ridding them of overwhelming memories and negative emotions so that they could carry on with everyday life. One other goal of talking or writing about such an experience is to teach others by evoking an empathetic connection with those who suffered. Such testimony promotes a moral or political end, such as the abolition of nuclear weapons. Accordingly, Hara, encouraged by activist writers such as Sasaki Kiichi and Yamamoto Kenkichi, shared the political aim of demanding an end to the atomic bomb. Yet he could not emerge from the narration cleansed and full of hope because the Cold War present never released him from the fear of nuclear annihilation.

Critics John Treat and Nogami Gen described *Summer Flowers* as a realist narrative, and within the broader category of realist prose. They found similarities between *Summer Flowers* and documentary writings and war memoirs, respectively.[31] Notably, *Summer Flowers* shares this quality of realism with most other *hibakusha* narratives. Even Ibuse Masuji's novel *Black Rain,* perhaps the most structurally complex and narratively sophisticated evocation of the bombing, uses a somber realist approach. Ibuse employs a multiplicity of first-person narratives, while the larger narrative frame is a novel of manners told in the third person. In this way, the novelist emphasizes the reintegration of the *hibakusha* into the community and naturalizes the maimed space of Hiroshima as a recognizable Japanese city.

Hara, however, did not retain realism as his main narrative approach in his later prose works about the bombing, because his background as a poet and his prewar interest in surrealism surfaced not long after he wrote the predominantly realist *Summer Flowers.* Instead, Hara started to work with more fantastic and experimental modes of prose narrative. These stories complement *Summer Flowers* and reveal the Hara Tamiki who is not only a *hibakusha* of Hiroshima but also a man who is acutely aware of the tense and eerie atmosphere of the contemporary world.

Departing from Politics and Realism

Hara Tamiki's postwar work encompasses both the moment of the bombing and its most anxious Cold War aftermath. In the mid-1950s, the Marxist critic Hanada Kiyoteru judged Hara as more modern and relevant than A-bomb artists like Ōta Yōko and Maruki (Akamatsu) Toshi, describing Hara's works as "a very contemporary version of our inner worlds."[32] A consideration of Hara's prose collection *After the Bombing* (*Genbaku igo*) and other works will clarify the ways that his writing resonates strongly with Cold War culture.[33]

All A-bomb art is inherently political, whether overtly or not. But a defining aspect of Hara's career and writings is the indistinctness of his political stance. The biographies of many artists and intellectuals of Hara's generation often reveal a pattern of political interest or activism, followed by *tenkō* ("turning away," that is, a renunciation of leftist or progressive beliefs under government pressure during the militarist era).[34] Hara's life featured just such a prewar "flirtation" with leftist politics. During the 1920s, Hara was involved in Moppuru, a trial support organization connected to the Communist International, and he was arrested twice for political activities and his association with the leftist movement.[35] After that, he ceased his overt political activity, and after the war, Hara did not join the Japan Communist Party, as did many in his cohort. Instead, he seemed content with protesting the horrors of war in general and the atom bomb in particular, without addressing the exact causes of the bombing or the arms race.

Despite the Occupation's purge of communists, socialists, and leftists, such a single-mindedly *non*ideological antinuclear, antiwar stance was by no means typical. If anything, a polarized political climate dominated the late 1940s, 1950s, and even 1960s, so a nonaligned peace movement was only a goal during that era, not a reality. Perhaps because of Hara's dedication to aesthetic ideals rather than specific political goals, he revealed his leftist sympathies only with the greatest reluctance. For example, in the story "Ice Flowers" (Hyōka, 1947) the protagonist heads for Tokyo, inspired by a friend's claim that one can encounter "new people" in the city.[36] Once in the metropolis, he carefully observes a group of people as they post political placards around the train. A fellow passenger, despite being dressed in a business suit, finds inspiration in the activist messages and starts to sing the "International." As a cool breeze blows through the train car, the narrator wonders whether "new people" are among the group of activists. But he is not, remarkably enough, moved to action or a deeper consideration of the political situation.

Similarly, in his book reviews and essays, Hara extolled the efforts of others protesting the immorality of the atomic bomb. Unlike his fellow writers and friends Abe Tomoji and Sasaki Kiichi, Hara did not propose concrete solutions for the current unsettling dilemma of world affairs, which included the growing antagonism between East and West and the arms race, nor did he espouse a particular ideological stance. Instead, Hara's most specific pronouncements about contemporary activism took the form of public support for the Appeal for Peace antinuclear petition drive.[37]

The Bomb as Fear and Madness

"When confronted with the threat of such expressions of concentrated violence as A-bombs and H-bombs, the only people who can remain optimistic are madmen, idiots, and fascists," wrote Hanada Kiyoteru.[38] Hara Tamiki's choice of suicide made it clear that he was anything but an optimist. Ōta Yōko, a fellow *hibakusha* and writer about the A-bomb, bemoaned his choice of death as old-fashioned because it suggested pessimism and acquiescence to the threatened violence. Yet Hara did exhibit optimism of a sort. Part of his hope came from a conviction that his post-bomb writings would live after him and function as testimony against the use of nuclear arms. Realist works like *Summer Flowers* and poems like "Give Me Water" fit firmly in this testimonial tradition. Hara also left behind a body of works that departed from the documentary impulse, such as "Land of My Heart's Desire" (Shingan no kuni, 1951) and *After the Bombing* (*Genbaku igo*, 1947–1951). It is in these works that Hara narrates the consciousness of the Cold War, rather than Hiroshima, using tropes of madness, hallucinations, fear, and transformation of the contaminated body.

Before the bombing, Hara was associated with avant-garde artistic movements, such as Dadaism, surrealism, and experimental poetry, and he was also drawn to Romanticism. Although his pre-1945 writings are not highly regarded, they provided a basis for his work after the war. Indeed, his literary and artistic sensibilities helped him transform the trauma of the bomb into something compelling. Just as post–World War I artists created Dadaism, surrealism, cubism, and other modes as a means of making sense of the unprecedented violence and technologies of war, Hara made use of the nonrealist modes of narrative to evoke the aftermath of the bombing, as well as his vision of the Cold War world. Hara's later works thus depart from the realism of *Summer Flowers,* as their narrative vantage point hovers on the edge of reality and sanity. Most of these experimental works are in a series of short prose texts collected under the title *After the Bombing.* Some of the parts feature first-person narrators, and others are in the third-person. Ōe Kenzaburō urges readers to regard *After the Bombing* as a single longer work, a novel of sorts.

The link between Hara and madness is certainly one reason for his association with the Cold War. The theme of insanity arises from both his writings and his public persona. Because of Hara's sometimes odd behavior in social situations, his publisher Maruoka Akira concluded that "it was not at all surprising that Hara seemed somehow strange to others [*doko ka iyoo ni mieru*]."[39] Many people who knew Hara personally described him as taciturn, socially awkward, and under stress. He would visit friends' homes, only to sit in silence, and he obsessively focused on his late wife and on literature, to the exclusion of almost everything else.[40] In his memoirist work, Hara describes living penniless in a rented room in Tokyo, without so much as a match to light a cigarette. One day, he goes out into the street and tries to light his cigarette using a lens and the sun, only to have his landlady scold him, "Other people will think you are crazy." He sees himself as different and is moved to tears when some Tokyo friends invite him into their home for dinner, surprised that anyone would want to associate with someone "like me."

While many critics tactfully skirted the issue of his odd deportment, Sasaki Kiichi actively promoted the link between Hara's mental hypersensitivity and the concept of madness as a means of illustrating that Hara's temperament was suited to the atomic "age of fear." Even when his wife was alive, Sasaki tells us, Hara had a delicate constitution (*shinkeishitsu*). For example, the mere prospect of a short trip would make him so nervous that he would throw up his breakfast.[41] According to Sasaki, Hara had always feared other people and suffered from anxiety, and even when he was a boy, Hara was full of

> pathological anxiety and fear. He was a child who would turn pale and flee upon hearing the sound of the flute announcing the lion dance [at a festival]. Reading one of his early poems called "Terror" reveals that, for the young Hara, anything and everything was

a source of fear, from the ceiling boards to the toilet to the potted plants in the garden to girls . . . everything in the external world made him afraid.

Sasaki compared Hara with Michelangelo, who fled his hometown of Florence when there were rumors of war, and to Erasmus, who packed up and leaped into a carriage when he heard of the plague coming within a hundred miles of his home. It was this same nervous condition that plagued Hara in adulthood. Sasaki addresses readers: "Healthy people, please rest assured. He is the one who is a madman, plagued by delusions."[42]

Similarly, Maruoka paints a vivid picture of a delicate Hara, who leaps up in fear and trembles at a flash of lightning, even years after the war is over.[43] That this level of anxiety was not regarded as normal even in the 1950s is illustrated by a scene in Kurosawa Akira's film *Record of a Living Being* (*Ikimono no kiroku*, 1955). During a ferocious thunderstorm, only one of the characters in the movie cowers in fear—certain that the flash of light is from a bomb. He is the man whose extreme fear of a nuclear war has driven him so far over the edge that the man's family is able to persuade the court to declare him incompetent. Clearly, though, one of Kurosawa's aims is to question the sanity of those who are not afraid of the bomb.

Like Kurosawa, Sasaki Ki'ichi places a high value on the insights offered by Hara and describes him as a man who "possessed a clear memory of something that most people have forgotten, something that we should not forget. He is awake while normal people are sleeping, and has a premonition of future danger before the rest of us do." Despite the association of Hara with madness, Sasaki emphasizes that Hara's "recent fears were definitely not mere delusions. They were realistic fears. He was pushed to a state of extreme fear by something that exists in reality, something to which we must pay attention."[44]

This madness that was sometimes part of Hara, sometimes part of the people he created on paper, and sometimes the tenor of the times becomes clear in an essay he wrote in answer to the scholar Watanabe Kazuo's *Essays on Man* (originally published in 1948 in *Mita bungaku*). Hara focuses on Watanabe's view that madness is not necessary for great creativity because it inevitably results in pain and sacrifice. For this reason, according to Watanabe, humanists must avoid madness. There is no room for madness in a period of human history threatened by a new type of apocalyptic war, a fight to the death between "two systems and two worldviews." No victor will emerge from such a war, a war waged with the "new weapons."[45]

Indeed, we should not underestimate the level of fear and anxiety concerning the bombs during the decade after the end of the war or the extent of Hara's horror. Abe Tomoji criticizes those who cynically belittle the fear and anxiety expressed in Hara's work and condemns those who say that the Japanese should submit to the United States because it has a bigger stockpile of weapons.[46] One reason that Ōe Kenzaburō and Nogami Gen praise Hara is his prescience, his prediction of the age of fear, before most people truly realized the apocalyptic potential of the weapons and even before scientists had even created the most fearsome warheads. Through art, Hara predicted the psychological breadth of the geopolitical and cultural conflict known as the Cold War.

Hara believed in the idea of nuclear apocalypse before it was commonly accepted. Since 1945, the general public has been able to read reports of the apocalyptic potential of nuclear war with atomic weapons. But at that time, such devices were relatively small and primitive. The initial July 1945 test at Alamogordo, New Mexico, had not made the atmosphere explode, as scientists feared, and the destruction from the August 1945 bombs in Japan remained localized. Perhaps for these reasons, in the bomb's infancy some military planners and politicians stubbornly believed that atomic bombs could be deployed in a manner analogous to that of conventional bombs, in which bombers drop bombs on individual cities, resulting in containable, local collateral damage. Until the first U.S. hydrogen bomb test took place on November 1, 1952, therefore, the destructive potential of nuclear weapons remained largely hypothetical, and this was more than a year after Hara's death.[47] The Soviet Union tested its first thermonuclear device (hydrogen bomb) in August 1953.

The public came to understand the difference between the atomic bombs and the destructive magnitude of thermonuclear weapons by several means. First, the media disseminated stories about the possible effects of the new weapons. On November 16, 1952, the *Chūgoku shinbun* (the Hiroshima newspaper) quoted Japanese physicists to the effect that the H-bombs were five hundred to one thousand times more powerful than the Hiroshima and Nagasaki bombs. Readers also learned that these newly tested weapons could destroy not only cities but eventually all life on earth.

Hara therefore never knew how horrific the H-bomb really was, since he died before the initial tests. He also did not live to see the 1954 Test

Bravo at Bikini, which surpassed all prior explosions in terms of destructive force and release of radiation. Even so, Ōe and others have credited Hara with prescient visions of apocalypse and the Cold War. They did so not solely because Hara wrote that in the future "wars will destroy all nations and all people equally" but also because of his evocation of the central values of the Cold War, especially his private fear of the bomb and his desire to control his body against all odds.[48] Separate from his witness of Hiroshima, Hara made glamorous the "terrifying banality of the bomb" and the "absolute indifference of the Epicenter" by imagining that its potential victims had the power to resist its profound violence through aesthetics or suicide.[49]

Reinventing the Bomb, or Madness and the Invisible Body

In his writing, Hara Tamiki invented various ways of controlling the chaotic and destructive experience of the bombing. The contrast between the *Summer Flowers* metaphor of rebirth and Hara's other evocations of the weapon's transformative power makes clear that the bomb does more than give life and take it away. In a classic Cold War fashion, Hara also engaged in several unexpected activities: he became a bomb maker; he discovered the Cold War front in Tokyo; and he had a vision of an extraordinary bomb capable of creating a mad, fantastic man: the Glass Man.

If Hara were one of the bombed, he also invented his own bomb. His invention may make readers uncomfortable because the notion of a *hibakusha* creating a bomb contradicts the moral purpose of witnessing, the solemn project of the survivor working through past trauma and warning the world. Why would a witness to the only nuclear war engage in such fantasy? For Hara, these imaginary moves are strategies that "maintain the tension between the overwhelming reality of the remembered events and the tenuous, always elusive status of memory itself."[50] At the same time, Hara's rewriting of past trauma can be seen as part of a psychological "working through of the past in a manner that enables survival or a reengagement in life" experienced similarly by other witnesses of mass trauma.[51]

Hara wants his bomb to explode with the same intensity as the A-bomb, but with productive results rather than a terror of death and destruction. In "Feet of Fire" (Hi no kakato, 1948), a short piece included in

After the Bombing, he uses the notion of a music bomb, one that "explodes in my head." Not coincidentally, the new bomb is born amid the material conditions of Tokyo soon after the war:

> A music bomb.
>
> These words released a flash of light in one corner of his mind, and he stopped in his tracks on the crowded street, steadying himself from the shock. In his pocket, he had the thousand yen that he had at last been able to withdraw, despite his frozen bank account, by showing proof of unemployment. A thousand yen was not enough to get him through the month, and one could never tell when even that amount of money might be transformed into utterly worthless paper. He felt quite certain that the new yen in his pocket were plummeting in value even as he stood there, still in the street. It occurred to him that somewhere, in a place unknown to him, there were people making preparations to rob men like him of their very existence. This realization flowed down through his body, all the way to his heels; the clamor to the left and right of him threatened to crush him as sound echoed around him.
>
> A music bomb . . .
>
> . . . His body started to move again, two steps and then three. But the flash of light that had cut through his head traveled far beyond him and seemed to spread without limit. He could not stand the thought; his head burned hot. His entire body seemed about to split apart from the heat and the light. "No, I can't give in to this," he thought. Making a conscious effort to calm himself, he continued to walk through the crowd. Even as he did so, the thing threatening to explode ran throughout his body, to the tips of his fingers. . . .
>
> With those words, countless fragments of chains of ideas floated into his head. The first thought that flickered through his mind when the words *music bomb* came into his head was the proposition that all organic matter could be affected by music. Therefore, inorganic matter would also change freely in response to a special music device. The special music emitted from the device would also arrange and rearrange the nuclei of atoms. The magical power produced as a result of this method would be extraordinary, beyond human imagination.
>
> Consequently . . . therefore . . . and then . . . Along with this odd idea, he imagined that the mystical power had already begun to af-

fect his body, and then the experience of Hiroshima, which never left his brain, seeped into his premonition of the music bomb, and he yelled out in agony.

. . . Adam

This single name sprang from him, as if a divine inspiration. . . . That name came back to him like some kind of salvation.

"So that's it. It's Adam. . . . I am putting you in charge of the idea of the music bomb."[52]

In this way, Hara describes the process of creating a new persona, one separate from the man who experienced the August 6 bombing and whose identity is inextricably bound up with representing that experience in a realist, mimetic mode. He achieves this separation of identity through several means, of which the use of the third-person narrative is the most obvious. The narrator of *Summer Flowers* emphasizes to the reader that when the Hiroshima bomb burst, he did not see the flash of light that everyone else saw. In contrast, the bomb inventor in "Feet of Fire" witnesses the flash of light and feels it in his being. It is that light that brings him to the sober realization of his financial condition and then inspires him to invent a fantastic machine.

Hara can authenticate the past experience of the Hiroshima bomb, and he shares in the spirit of the Cold War. He even goes so far as to participate in the proliferation of whimsical, imaginary bombs (in an imaginary war). Proliferation during the Cold War entailed not only the production of material bombs but also images, abstractions, demonstration models.

For Hara, bomb production was inspired by the Manhattan Project and by art, particularly Kajii Motojirō's brilliant short story "Lemon" (Remon, 1925). In "Lemon," a desperately poor and dying man uses what little money he has to buy a lemon, only to leave the fruit on top of a stack of books in a bookshop. He imagines a moment of power from his placement of the lemon: "What a peculiar villain I was, to leave a glittering gold bomb ticking on the shelves of Maruzen [bookstore]. If the bomb did in fact violently explode . . . how exciting it would be . . . and then nothing would be left of that oppressive place but a heap of sawdust."[53]

After 1945, A-bombs terrorized by their mere existence, not by their use.[54] Since no bombs were used for military purposes after 1945 and the United States kept the bomb design secret, invention (or, more accurately, reinvention) and proliferation became central tropes in Cold War discourse. The first instance of this reinvention can be found in the Soviet

Union's 1949 bomb, based, of course, on espionage, as the Rosenberg case revealed. The abstraction of bombs encouraged the use of metaphors of a Cold War fought with propaganda and the media. Thus Marshall McLuhan described the Cold War as "an electric battle of information and of images" and suggested the idea of information bombs, media bombs.[55]

Tokyo as a Cold War Front

Critic Nogami Gen attempted to wrest Hara's *Summer Flowers* from the grips of the *hibaku bungaku* (A-bomb literature) by reframing the novella as a "report from the battlefront." In other words, Nogami tried to classify Hara's Hiroshima piece as part of the preexisting genre of firsthand accounts of soldiers at war, in resistance to the notions of the novelty of the atomic age and the periodization of post-1945 Japan as an exclusively *postwar* age. Following Nogami's logic, we can read one of Hara's most unsettling works, "Ice Flowers," as an evocation of Tokyo as the front in the Cold War rather than as a postwar city in recovery. In his use of the third-person narrative, Hara departs from his familiar realist mode and tells the story of a Hiroshima *hibakusha* who goes to Tokyo in order to escape the ruins of the A-bombed city. Once in Tokyo, though, he is still starving and feels, if anything, even more alienated from his surroundings than he had in his decimated hometown. Despite the destruction of Hiroshima and the huge loss of life, he still has some family there, and some family property remains as well. But in Tokyo, he has to use introductions from friends and colleagues in order to find rooms to rent.

Most Tokyoites are going about their business, seemingly having forgotten about the war and the bombing. In contrast, the protagonist's extreme alienation becomes clear at several points. He identifies most with a homeless woman and her baby, whom he sees sitting on the street. He guesses from her blank expression that she, too, has experienced sudden displacement. At that moment, despite his feeling of displacement, the narrator senses something familiar in his surroundings. He wonders, "This is a strange and rare season. Am I the only one who encounters dazzlingly beautiful visions and pure atmosphere as I walk through the burned-out ruins, starving, and pushed nearly to the precipice of life and death?" The tone of this passage is characteristically dramatic, and the scene is familiar to readers who know his Hiroshima stories. They therefore have to ask themselves which bombed city is he describing? It might be the Hiroshima of Hara's memory, the Tokyo where the writer spent his final years, or even the imagined post-Truman-bomb Korean Peninsula. Wherever the ruins and our solitary hero might be, the scene definitely suggests the Cold War vision of a home front in the imaginary war. There are no soldiers in uniform, no trenches, no guns. The violence at this front is so abstract and invisible that the imagination of death does not include bodily harm.

The theme of displacement is central in much of Hara's postwar work and career. Along with the literal displacement and wandering caused by the widespread destruction of cities during the war, the sense of lost home and alienation become familiar tropes. As Ōta Yōko did, Hara left Hiroshima soon after the bombing and moved to Tokyo. Why did he do this? Possibly the devastation of the bomb forced him to leave, and he also had encountered the scorn of villagers toward evacuees from Hiroshima. They look coldly at the *hibakusha* and ask whether they all will starve to death in the end. Even in metropolitan Tokyo, his landlady shuns him and criticizes his seemingly odd behavior. For readers, Hara's wandering provided yet another reason for interpreting him as a figure of universal suffering and displacement.

Because Hiroshima was Hara's hometown and an atomic bomb exploded there first, it would seem natural for Hiroshima, rather than Tokyo, to occupy a central position in his work. In *Summer Flowers*, at least, it does. Hara's literary friends in Tokyo, furthermore, continued to associate him with Hiroshima even after he moved to the capital, but not just because of his experience there on August 6, 1945. They found his speech charming and enjoyed hearing his Hiroshima dialect when he came to visit. And yet Hara himself did not feel part of the postwar Hiroshima and chose not to return there to live, despite his family's urging. Each time he went back to Hiroshima, he found it rebuilt a bit more, but not necessarily to his liking. Two years after the bombing, he took the long train journey from Tokyo to Hiroshima, only to find the city covered with hastily built wooden shacks and young people wearing cheap yet fashionable clothing. He arrived to find his brother in the midst of clearing away what remained of his home and carpenters stoking a bonfire with logs from the charred trees on his property. Hiroshima was not the city it had been before August 6, 1945, and its recovery had not reached a stage that would encourage him to forget the flattened houses, ruined buildings, and piles of corpses that he had seen in the months after that date. When Hara traveled to Hiroshima again in April 1950, he attended

Hara Tamiki speaking at the Japan PEN Club meeting, Hiroshima, April 1950. (Courtesy of *Chūgoku shinbun*)

a peace symposium sponsored by the PEN Club. As one of the prominent Tokyo writers invited to speak at the symposium, Hara found the city "utterly changed from the ruins of five years ago." Nothing remained in Hiroshima to "directly convey the horrific remains," and he could not "feel from the land of contemporary Hiroshima . . . things such as the spirits of the dead that lurk beneath the earth."[56]

Hara chose to die in Tokyo, hundreds of miles from his family home and, perhaps more significantly, his wife's grave in Hiroshima. Hara never felt at home in Tokyo, either, and became a wanderer, renting out rooms in near strangers' houses, unable to find sustenance for his body or soul. His extreme alienation from place also encourages an understanding of universal significance of Hara's death.

Because of the moral and political authority of the Hiroshima experience, Hara spent the last years of his life writing about bombed-out cities. Hara noticed evidence of the firebomb destruction in Tokyo and mentioned areas that had escaped the incendiary bombings. His colleagues who had survived the firebombings of Tokyo rarely mentioned what had happened to them because those fires had been eclipsed by the atomic events. Their silence did not mean a lack of trauma or loss, however. The arrival of the manuscript of Hara's *Summer Flowers* at the *Mita bungaku* editorial office prompted Maruoka Akira, one of the editors, to reflect on the condition of the building in Tokyo where he worked. He sat in "a burned-out building in Tokyo, window glass cracked from the flames, and parts were covered with boards, where the glass had broken away. I could feel the wind that swept over the burned-out ruins."[57] As with the Marukis' atomic-bomb murals, reading or viewing an account of the atomic bombing was an opportunity for people in other parts of Japan to learn of the rare events in faraway Hiroshima or Nagasaki. Accounts of the destruction caused by the "new weapon" also prompted memories of their own experiences with strategic bombing and with the war in general.

Much of the destruction, injury, and death in *Summer Flowers* may have been recognizable to Hara's compatriots who had lived through the fire-bombings in Tokyo and other cities. In that sense, one of the first steps in the universalization of Hiroshima and Nagasaki experiences was people in other Japanese cities—in conventionally bombed cities—comparing their own experiences with those of the *hibakusha*. Despite the initial discrimination against the *hibakusha*, people in other cities also came to understand that Hara's stories bore special moral and political significance. In other words, they regarded his writings on Hiroshima as of interest to a broad audience, not as the narrative of a local problem. This realization also accompanied the spread of knowledge about the characteristics of nuclear weapons through testing, as the next chapter discusses, as well as through the diplomatic and military process of the arms race.

Just Another Japanese Writer's Suicide?

The authority of Hara Tamiki's works also stems from its canonization. Unlike most other *hibakusha* writers, Hara had deep links with the male literary establishment that helped canonize his work. Agonizing as the move may have been for him, Hara's decision to live and then to die in Tokyo encouraged the view of his writing and his suicide as belonging to the nation (if Tokyo is the center of the nation). The timing of his death, moreover, seemed to exemplify the global nuclear despair. The critical response to Hara's oeuvre and death led to the understanding that he possessed universal significance. Indeed, so compelling was the symbolism of Hara's suicide that Nogami Gen regarded Hara as an "event" (*dekigoto*).

The conventional reading of Hara's suicide is that nuclear war had again become a possibility, and the fear of violence comparable to that of Hiroshima drove Hara to take his own life. Both Hara's suicide and his published testimonials served as a warning to subsequent generations about the dangers of nuclear weapons. To Ōe Kenzaburō, Hara was the perfect sensitive victim, both physically and artistically. His dramatic end also seemed to demonstrate that writers had a role to play in nuclear politics.

In 1951, not everyone attributed Hara's suicide primarily to either the trauma of the bombing or the growing arms race. Some regarded Hara's death as signaling something important about the times or even about the century. Hotta Yoshie defined Hara as a "witness to the twentieth century."[58] Likewise, Nakamura Shin'ichirō depicted Hara's encounter with Japan's chaotic postwar period as being one of the most tragic.[59] These statements combine a certainty that Hara's suicide marked a challenge to current affairs with a vague sense about the precise significance of Hara's defining experience, Hiroshima. The confusion arises not from a lack of information, for by the end of the Occupation and especially after 1949, the strict ban on A-bomb–related texts and images had gradually eased. Japanese readers could obtain translations of John Hersey's *Hiroshima,* as well as photographs of the bombed cities.

In contrast to these vague interpretations of Hara's suicide, two admirers at the time made a pointed attempt to understand his death as signifying something other than merely personal misery or general alienation. Sasaki Kiichi and Maruoka Akira saw a direct connection between Hara's demise and atomic weapons. The first to link Hara's suicide with Truman's announcement was his brother-in-law, the writer Sasaki Kiichi, who wondered whether it was

> sheer coincidence that the day before Hara . . . laid down his body on the railroad tracks, the following headlines appeared in the newspapers: "Use of A-Bomb Will Lead to US Victory over Soviets, Road to Peace and Self-Defense" and "USA–Bomb Use Necessary to Beat Russians." . . . Was it a coincidence that Hara Tamiki experienced the A-bomb? Is it coincidence that the horrible experience would not leave his mind?[60]

The perception of merely local significance, however, remains strong in both Hara's writings and his suicide. The critic Itō Sei, for example, offered words of praise for *Summer Flowers,* but ultimately regretted that

Hara's account of August 6 lacked a truly universal appeal. If Hara had been more ambitious, Itō lamented, he would have employed the most current journalistic style. Itō's comparison doubtless alluded to Hersey's *Hiroshima,* which became the most prominently featured work on the bomb in the Western-bloc media from the time of its publication in the *New Yorker* in 1947.[61] Itō weighed the formal aspects of *Summer Flowers*— such as the framing of the bombing with the narrator's attempt to mourn his wife's recent death, the narration of family life in the months leading up to the bombing, and the lyrical style—against Hersey's omniscient narrative stance and economical style.[62] In retrospect, it also is clear that a text's capacity for universal appeal derives not only from stylistic or formal qualities but also from networks of power that dictate the material and social fate of those texts, especially their circulation and distribution.

Nonetheless, Itō's judgment of *Summer Flowers* suggests more than a formal evaluation of a text alone and instead reminds us of the constellation of cultural meanings, the ideological values of the local literary field that promoted Hara's work in 1940s and 1950s Japan. What kind of writer would begin a story about the atomic bomb with a memory of the lovely yellow flowers he bought for his late wife several days before the bombing? Granted his kinship to poets of many other places and times, Hara, we should remember, also belonged to a well-established lineage of sensitive Japanese literary antiheroes, including canonical writers like Akutagawa Ryūnosuke and Dazai Osamu, whom I will discuss later. As was the case with Ōe, many writers and critics were heartened by the idea that a kindred spirit could have political and moral influence through both art and death.

Some of his contemporaries described Hara primarily as a poet; he was pure (*junsui*), hypersensitive, and childlike.[63] Clearly, such qualities can be used to describe either a certain cultural type or the model sacrificial victim of the bomb. Many later exemplary *hibakusha* have been portrayed as young women (such as the Hiroshima Maidens, Sadako and the thousand origami cranes, and Yasuko in Ibuse's novel *Black Rain* and, particularly, in the film adaptation). Hara could be physically weak, childlike, and sensitive, but he was still a man. His masculinity shared little with the soldier (brave or defeated) or the family man of the postwar fiction or the seething violence of Ishihara Shintarō's solitary manhood (described in chapter 5). Hara was a poet and a man.

The writer Kaiko Ken, however, rejected the frequent description of Hara's death and his literature as pure (*junsui*). Hara was no angel, Kaiko reminded readers: in his younger years, he had attempted suicide with a

woman and had even bought out a geisha's contract. Kaiko was not pull-
ing dirty linen out of the closet in order to besmirch Hara's good name.
Rather, Kaiko's comment reminds us of the extent to which Hara's literary persona dovetails with the image of the archetypical masculine
literary hero, one exceedingly familiar to readers of modern Japanese literature. As with Akutagawa and Dazai, Hara fostered a particular masculine artistic self. Like the *nimaime* character type so popular in prose,
theater, and the stage, this persona is characterized by emotional delicacy,
hyper-self-awareness, weakness, adoration of women, a desire to be loved
by women, and a disposition for love suicide. Such sensitive writers, in the
modern era at least, also chose European poets and novelists as their spiritual and artistic mentors. The life course of such a man dictated a tragic
and dramatic end, and thus Akutagawa's and Dazai's suicides stand as
major events in twentieth-century literary culture. So powerful and loved
was the persona of literary youth that Hara himself recognized, "Even if
I disappear, there will be other young men just like me sitting blankly in
some corner of the world."[64]

The different explanations that friends and colleagues offered for
Hara's death shows the pull between Hara as local antihero and Hara as
poet turned consummate A-bomb witness. Many of the early tributes to
Hara make clear the currency of his personal and public identities as the
antihero and artist. Like Dazai's and Akutagawa's, his version of masculinity was inextricably linked to women with whom he was romantically
involved, as well as to self-destructive behavior. Unlike Akutagawa and
Dazai, though, Hara did not repeatedly implicate the women in his suicidal plans. When reconstructing the events of the evening of his suicide,
more than one colleague described Hara's visit to a bar where he drank
heavily and spoke cheerfully with the bartender and other customers.
Hara even left suicide notes for many of his friends and associates. In
one, he declared his desire to make his parting from others "nonchalant"
(*sarigenaku wakaretai*).

Over the years, critics have downplayed the fact that Hara's behavior
followed a pattern of devotion to art and romance, self-destructive behavior, and dramatic suicide in ways that were quite similar to those of
Akutagawa and Dazai. Perhaps this is because the Romantic, somewhat
dissolute literary persona does not fit well with the image of a virtuous
A-bomb survivor necessary for a narrative that transcends boundaries.

At the time of his death, Hara was famous enough for a prominent literary journal to dedicate most of an issue to memorial essays on his life and

works, and encomiums appeared in other journals as well. Most Japanese writers who paid tribute to Hara after his death were quite familiar with some of the extremely personal reasons that may have led to his suicide. One was that after his wife's death from tuberculosis on September 29, 1944, Hara decided that he would live for only one more year.

To others who knew him, Hara's death had nothing to do with celebrity suicides or literary archetypes but instead could be explained by the distinctly local material conditions of postwar Japan. Along with millions of others, Hara suffered from poverty, a lack of food, and social isolation. Yet Hara's suffering was exacerbated by choices he himself made. In contrast to his siblings, Hara had disassociated himself from attempts to rebuild a life in his native Hiroshima. He refused to consider remarrying and instead struck out on his own in Tokyo, where he moved from one rented room to another. No one in Tokyo had much food to share in those days, and the near strangers who were Hara's landlords offered him little or no sustenance, materially or emotionally. Anyone who had been around him since the end of the war could easily observe his fragile grip on life, and so his suicide did not come as a total surprise. As Suzuki Shigeo observed, Hara had nothing to look forward to or to give him hope, since he steadfastly refused to "be baptized, join the Communist Party, or get married."[65]

Yet Hara's links with Akutagawa and Dazai remain crucial in other ways. Specifically, they helped establish a precedent of suicide as a form of artistic/political statement. Although both Akutagawa's and Dazai's determination to commit suicide had deep roots in their individual psychology and personal angst, both writers also have been understood as acutely sensitive to the contradictions of modernity. Akutagawa wrote in his famous suicide note of his "vague uneasiness" (bonyari to shita fuan). We will never know whether he was driven to suicide by the anxieties of political modernity, despair over the limitations of representation and narrative, mental illness, or a combination of these factors.[66] When contrasted with the deaths of leftist writers like Kobayashi Takiji and Ōsugi Sakai, who were killed by the thought police, suicides like Dazai's seem exceedingly limited in their political efficacy. Hara's suicide shared a sense of inevitability with those of Dazai and Akutagawa, but Hara alone also could claim a direct link to an exceptional historical event, one defined by unfathomable violence and death.

Dazai protested the oppression of modernity and the defeat by embracing dissipation, and in the end he turned to suicide defined by decadence and excess. Akutagawa's vision of modernity boiled up in a fusion of madness and creativity, and Hara was clearly drawn to Akutagawa's strategic evocations of madness. If he were ever in a frame of mind similar to Akutagawa's when he wrote "Cogwheel" (Haguruma, 1927), Hara commented, he certainly would take his own life, too. In his brilliant "Cogwheel," Akutagawa wrote about a man whose daily existence is an obstacle course littered with paranoia and hallucinations, an allegory for the fractures of the individual and modern society.[67] When considering the motives for Akutagawa's suicide—a clash of the "modern spirit" and "dark fatalism"—Hara modestly concluded that he himself was so lacking in fatalism that a suicide on his part would be more like an "accident."[68] Even Hara did not anticipate a politically significant suicide for himself. Ōta Yōko, another prominent *hibakusha* writer, saw Hara's suicide in particular as "old-fashioned and lacking in modern spirit."[69] Nonetheless, Hara's demise has attained considerable symbolic currency by making Hara a martyr of the age of fear and the first man to succumb to the full force of the Cold War.

The Nuclear Sublime

Hara Tamiki's writings and those of people who knew him confirm that he had long been obsessed with death and also harbored an especially romantic, idealized understanding of death. His prose work "On the Shore of a Beautiful Death" (Utsukushiki shi no kishi ni, 1950) offers an example: "Even when death did visit his wife, perhaps she would bring to herself another death, a beautiful death, one beyond the agony that she faces now."[70] This aesthetic conception of death was something that Hara shared with one of his favorite poets, Rainer Maria Rilke. In Rilke's novel *Titie* (1910), a man leaves his home to spend time in Paris, which he comes to perceive not as a city where people move to in order to live but as a place where they come to die: a beautiful city and a beautiful death. Rilke wrote the novel before World War I and thus in an age when the rhetoric of aestheticized death, even on the battlefield, still had credence. Even after Hara had seen the mutilated bodies and pain of Hiroshima, he still clung to the romantic notions of death.

During the six years after the bombing, Hara suffered from both the haunting memories of August 1945 and from the inhospitable Cold War present. He used the discourse of art and aesthetics in order to evoke his experiences in Hiroshima and to control the horrifying memories. In *Summer Flowers* and other works, Hara repeatedly compares the ruins of the city and the human suffering with scenes in movies and paintings of hell. Strikingly, his ideal of beautiful death served as an alternative to the memories of the bomb and to the inhospitable Cold War present. By Hara's own admission, he sought refuge from the "anxiety and chaos" of the postwar period by "constructing a solid world within." The best-known image related to that "world within" is the beautiful "phantom flower" (*maboroshi no hana*) evoked in one of his poems as an alternative to the ugliness without.[71] Part of that interior space included a vision of death "not as a horrific picture of hell, but as calm and harmonious."[72]

Hara stressed the provisional nature of his own survival: "The tragedy of Hiroshima seemed like a painting of the Last Judgment. Although I escaped from there, the god of death has not let me out of his sight." Strikingly, the memories are mainly visual, not emotional, and even those images are controlled through transformation into static paintings:

> I think that, somewhere inside me I am still affected by that scroll painting of the inferno, by that cluster of naked bodies crazed with death, those images that were burned onto my eyes. I suppose that I appear to my landlady as an unfortunate creature who is fleeing from the final judgment. It cannot be helped that the smell of death clings to me, as I have been living day to day with starvation and humiliation.[73]

A Contemporary Version of Our Inner Worlds

If we consider works other than *Summer Flowers,* such as the collection *After the Bombing,* we will find a remarkable synthesis of Hara's fear, madness, anxiety, and sense of displacement. Hara transforms the persona of this collection of short prose pieces into a "Man of Glass" (Bidōro gakushi), a character inspired by Cervantes's novella about a Man of Glass (*El licenciado vidriera,* 1613; also translated as *Glass Graduate*), who loses his mind after drinking a poisoned love potion and then becomes convinced that his body is made of glass. In the reception of Hara's work, this image of the Glass Man and the associated tropes of transparency and vanishing have dominated the creation of an image of Hara as a Hiroshima *hibakusha* and as an artist with a message about the Cold War world.

As in the case of Akutagawa's later work, Hara associates insanity with insight and bursts of creativity. In Cervantes's story, the Man of Glass is different because his delusional perception of his body allows him extraordinary insight into the contradictions of society and morality, whereas Hara brings the delicate creature into the postwar world:

It occurred to him that he might write a novel with the title *The New Glass Graduate*, inspired by a novella by Cervantes that he had read recently. Cervantes's Glass Graduate, convinced that his own body is made of glass, lives in fear of being touched by others. Because of the very sensitivity and precision of the material that makes up his body, however, his mind also becomes active and astute. He is able to respond to all questions in an instant, and his answers never fail to demonstrate profound insight. For example, a man asked him how to prevent himself from being envious of others. The Glass Graduate responded, "Sleep, for while [you are] sleeping, you will be the equal of those whom you envy." On another occasion, though, the unfortunate Glass Graduate made the following pronouncement: "My lord, you offer encouragement to violent boors even as you dash the hopes of the weak and virtuous. You nourish shameless tricksters while you let starve the modest and meek."

He found these words quite compelling and tried to imagine what would happen if a man like this were to appear in present-day Tokyo. In his own tale, he would have the new Glass Graduate be born of the shock of the atom bomb. As he stood among the crush of people on the train, he pictured to himself a man made entirely of glass. The broken glass of one of the train doors caught his eye. In an instant he could describe the agitation of the Glass Graduate.[74]

Not only was Hara's mind plagued by horrifying pictures and memories, but his body also was wracked by invisible ghosts of radiation and the hunger of the age. Imagination of the Glass Man functions as a way of disassociating himself from his contaminated body and creating, through art, a new body. Despite Hara's exposure to the bomb and its invisible radioactive rays, the doctor who examined him diagnosed him with a case of radiation sickness so mild that it could be treated just with rest and a nutritious diet. Nonetheless, the desire to make his body transparent, to purify his body, indicates that Hara understood himself to be contaminated. For the Glass Man, transparency signified insight, and the transparent body transformed flesh into something beautiful, exceedingly fragile, and thus untouchable and safe, not made of flesh and blood and nerves and not of this world. Hara is clearly drawn to this vision of transparency as a source of insight, but he also connects transparency with becoming clear and vanishing—in other words, with his poetic notion of death.

Paradoxically, starvation is another trope that Hara uses to suggest mastery of the body. The trope associates the age with spiritual hunger. If death can be beautiful and extreme, so can the deprived body. That food was scarce in late 1940s Tokyo is undeniable. Hara, however, employs the figure of starvation both literally and figuratively. In "Ice Flowers," he earns money from his job but starves anyway; he goes to see a doctor, who is surprised at how skinny he is:

> One day, he visited the hospital in Shinanomachi. Once again, from within him, the Glass Graduate opened his eyes and inspected everything around him. . . . Suddenly, he was overcome by memories of his late wife, who had died of TB. It made him unbearably sad. When his turn came to see the doctor, he had once again become the Glass Graduate.
>
> "Have you always been so thin?" the doctor asked as he probed his body.
>
> "I lost weight because I had nothing to eat," he replied. Though a seemingly matter-of-fact response, it came out sounding like a rationalization. Indeed, he noticed that the doctor who was examining him looked robust and healthy, though he too had no rations to speak of.[75]

Cold War Tokyo offers him no sustenance, no nourishment. The trope of starvation also links Hara with another expression of supreme artistic and social alienation: Franz Kafka's short story "The Hunger Artist" (1922). Kafka describes a man who practices the "art" of fasting as he sits on display in a cage. The hunger artist confesses to his impresario that he would end his fast if only there were a food that he liked to eat.

Hanada Kiyoteru found Hara's Man of Glass relevant to the Cold War mind-set. To him, the Glass Man was a "very contemporary version of our inner worlds" and prescient of a "sweet pure world" and a "world of sweet, pure things." For Hanada, then, this image of the Glass Man was an appropriate ghost (yūrei) and a prototype for the inner worlds of "A-bomb literature" (genbaku bungaku). What is behind Hanada's evaluation of the Glass Man? He mentions, first, Kafka's "The Metamorphosis" (1915), a story about a man who changes into a giant beetle and feels extreme alienation from human beings. In addition, Hanada writes,

> The Glass Man might be an attempt to cleanse and redeem the body contaminated by radiation, but it is also an entity created by the bomb. In the atomic age, nuclear technology is imagined not only as a destructive power but also as the unleashing of energy for positive ends, whether power generation, earth-moving projects, or transformation. Godzilla is one obvious contemporaneous example of atomic power imagined as transformational, or mutational.[76]

Hara's fascination with the transformational potential of the bomb, as opposed to its destructive capacity, thus finds expression in the figure of the Glass Man.

In conclusion, one canonized version of Hara Tamiki represents him as a poet sensitive to human suffering and pathos, who was fated to sacrifice himself in order to warn humankind about the evil manifest in nuclear weapons. His spatial analogue is the city of peace, Hiroshima (or Nagasaki). This version of Hara's persona encompasses elements of the common man, one whose personal grief takes precedence over the national project of total war. Narrating his own story, this man mentions first—and as most significant—his young wife, who died from natural causes. All his fellow citizens are serving in the military; he is the only man "walking through the city with a bouquet of flowers"; the scent of the incense that he had carried with him as an offering at her grave "still lingered in his jacket pocket" only days before the bomb was dropped.[77] Only after highlighting this small act of poetic resistance on a very personal level does Hara describe the devastation of the entire city of Hiroshima. This powerful and, in one sense, well-established narrative strategy fits perfectly with the worthy message of peace that has evolved in Hiroshima and Nagasaki over many decades. It is partly this aesthetic and moral vision of Hiroshima that Ōe Kenzaburō found so appealing in Hara, among the many *hibakusha* writers. This chapter also explored the reception of other after-the-bomb writings by Hara, works that have little utility in the ahistorical, beautiful vision of Hiroshima as a city of peace. Hara decided to move away from Hiroshima and to live in Tokyo, the center of the nation that was being drawn into a new, polarized world order, a metropolis slowly recovering from devastation by military technologies, the morality of which would not be discussed fully until decades later, during the Vietnam War.

Theoretically, the framework of the Cold War helps us understand why Hara's contemporaries and someone from an admiring younger generation, like Ōe, were drawn to the Hara who invented bombs and lived in Tokyo, a city that made him think only of the apocalypse. Sasaki, and later Ōe, succeeded in making Hara's extreme anxieties, surreal imagination, and art—and even his final leap—seem natural because they characterized them in relation to the imagination of their age. The outlines of the Cold War age took the form of a particular cluster of cultural and political values that dominated the 1950s. Many facets of the spirit of Hara's age appear clear in retrospect: the hesitation to express political convictions; the tropes of anxiety and insanity; the search to gain control, through narrative, of both the apocalyptical and the constructive potential of nuclear technology; and the imagination of Japan as implicated in the unstable and volatile contemporary world. We have also seen that four years after Hara's death, at a time when weapons testing forced the majority of the public to acknowledge the implication of the arms race, director Kurosawa Akira drew (consciously or not) on Hara's hypersensitivity to create the memorable character Nakajima in *Record of a Living Being*. Hara's life on the edge and his anxious, fertile imagination became a voice for the complexity and urgency of this moment in the Cold War.

Not all of Hara Tamiki's contemporaries agreed with his vision of the atomic age. Filmmaker Kamei Fumio's encounter with the antinuclear movement encouraged him to become directly involved with political activism and also resulted in extensive research on the effects of the new types of nuclear devices that were developed after Hara's death. Kamei's prolific filmmaking and his desire to produce new kinds of knowledge and an awareness of radiation and fallout contrast sharply with Hara's involvement with the same social issue.

The debate about the proper or correct Holocaust representation, while perhaps never irrelevant, can be bracketed and the criteria of judgment shifted. If mimetic approximation, drawing on a variety of knowledges (historical, autobiographic, testimonial, literary, museal), were to emerge as a key concern, then one could look at other Holocaust representations through this prism rather than trying to construct a Holocaust canon based on narrow aesthetic categories pitting the unrepresentable against aestheticization, or modernism against mass culture, memory against forgetting.
—Andreas Huyssen, "Of Mice and Mimesis"

4   "The World Lives in Fear" *Kamei Fumio's*
Nuclear Films

In the mid-1950s, filmmaker Kamei Fumio (1908–1987) arrived in Hiroshima with plans to make a documentary about the anti–nuclear protest movement. Unlike Alain Resnais, director of *Hiroshima Mon Amour* (1959), Kamei did not focus in his films on the dissonance between the public imagination of a demolished, radiated city and the sometimes strikingly modern, sometimes shockingly mundane, reconstructed Hiroshima. Nor was Kamei surprised when he witnessed conflict in the city of peace, such as the clash of police and protesters and the clamor of activists debating among themselves. For Kamei did not understand Hiroshima primarily as a site of memory or as a small peaceful oasis in the midst of the tense, unsettled Cold War world. In contrast to the discourse of peace and victimization advanced by some grassroots activists (an image quickly co-opted by both the Japanese government and Japan's most powerful ally, the United States), Kamei viewed the city as the principal battlefield in the Cold War.[1] He likewise saw the millions of people who made the journey to Hiroshima as fighters in the struggle over words and images, hearts and minds, in a conflict dominated by the superpowers but manifest within the borders of each of their allies as well.

Between 1955 and 1961, with the arms race heating up and Cold War tensions rising, Kamei made documentaries on three topics: the antinuclear movement, the dangers of radiation, and the movement against the U.S. military bases. In this chapter, I explore the antinuclear and radiation documentaries in depth and consider their connection to Kamei's military base films. His Cold War documentaries and their reception contradict the image of 1950s Hiroshima—and, by extension, 1950s Japan—as a culture fully enthralled with the myth of Japan as a victim and a wholly willing partner in the project of "universal peace" promulgated under the Pax Americana. From this perspective, we can see the dramatic protests against the United States–Japan Security Treaty of 1960 not as a drastic shift away from post–Allied Occupation culture and politics but as the culmination of the dynamism of 1950s culture. The story of the conception of Kamei's antinuclear films and their reception cannot be fully understood without an appreciation of the shifting discourse on social activism, nuclear weapons, science, and democracy.

Long before Kamei set foot in Hiroshima, he had gained a reputation as a man with an uncanny sense of the key issues of his times. Kamei knew the risks of antagonizing the authorities, as by the 1950s he had already earned the distinction of being the only Japanese filmmaker to end up in jail during the fifteen years of war. His arrest resulted directly from the documentaries that the imperial military had commissioned him to make at the front. Then during the Occupation, Kamei became famous as the filmmaker who condemned Japanese capitalists for leading the country toward militarism and imperialism, in *A Japanese Tragedy* (*Nihon no higeki,* also known by the English title *The Tragedy of Japan,* 1946). The Occupation's censorship system and Prime Minister Yoshida Shigeru's anger resulted in the removal of the film from theaters. *A Japanese Tragedy* lives on in the writings of historians like John Dower, Kyoko Hirano, and Abé Mark Nornes.[2] Although few critics have acknowledged the significance and uses of Kamei's antinuclear films, generations of viewers have watched uncredited segments of Kamei's antinuclear documentary work in Resnais's classic *Hiroshima Mon Amour.*[3] In them, Kamei fully realized the relationship of the genre of documentary to subjectivity, ideology, and power.

Kamei's nuclear films include *Still, It's Good to Live* (*Ikite ite yokatta,* 1956), *The World Is Terrified: The Reality of the "Ashes of Death"* (*Sekai wa kyōfu suru: "Shi no hai" no shōtai,* 1957), *Fluttering Pigeons* (*Hato wa habataku,* 1958), *Voice of Hiroshima* (*Hiroshima no koe,* 1959), and *Toward a World Without Arms* (*Gunbi naki sekai o,* 1961). *The World Is Terrified* is a science film; the other four document the second, fourth, fifth, and seventh World Conferences Against Atomic and Hydrogen Bombs. The dates of production fall between the alarming Bikini (*Lucky Dragon*) H-bomb test incident in 1954 and the Limited Test Ban Treaty of 1963.[4] Kamei's nuclear films and their reception are compelling in the ways that they draw attention to the dynamic interaction of culture, political activism, and science characteristic of the high Cold War.

In the four World Conference documentaries, Kamei represented the developing mass antinuclear movement, a groundswell defined by the ideological differences in a dramatically polarized world and, momentarily, seemingly capable of transcending those divisions. Kamei's film evocations of the ban-the-bomb movement differ radically from images that would later dominate, such as Ōe Kenzaburō's portrait of what he saw as a hopelessly fractured, pathological activism in the early 1960s. To a certain degree, the gap in understandings of the peace movement was generational. Starting in the 1960s, young generations of social activists accused the established antinuclear movement of emphasizing nuclear issues at the expense of other, more immediate social issues. They also blamed the "peace" movement, and especially the Left, for promoting discourses of victim consciousness. In retrospect, however, it is difficult to disentangle the conservative government's eager co-optation of the Japan-as-victim narrative, the straightforward pacifism of the depoliticized mass peace movement, and the Left's approach. While the antinuclear stance of the state may have had its basis in the country's strong antinuclear sentiments, the advocacy of peace also offered practical financial and security advantages for government and industry. Just as the Japanese government's reverence for the peace of Hiroshima emerged from a complex set of motives and goals, so the Left's views on peace and the bomb grew out of a larger dialogue among Marxists and progressives in Japan and links with the Eastern bloc and independent progressives in other parts of the world.

In only one of the four films, *The World Is Terrified*, did Kamei chose to focus exclusively on the science of the bomb. Here he disseminates the evolving knowledge about nuclear technology, whereas the other films focus on experiential accounts of Hiroshima and Nagasaki and the protest movement. In making the radiation documentary, Kamei acknowledged science's centrality in the public discourse of the bomb at the height of the Cold War. The film also is a critique of the relationship among science, nationalism, and power.

In the rapidly changing political atmosphere of the Cold War, Kamei's approach to representation differed according to his imagined audience, which included a variety of local audiences within Japan as well as international audiences—especially, he hoped, those in the nuclear nations. One of the key points of contention in the international Cold War battle of words and images was which bloc would lead its people to peace—the capitalists or the communists. Beginning in the 1940s, the Soviet Union offered peace as one of the nation's highest ideals. During the 1950s, President Dwight D. Eisenhower pledged that the United States would "wage peace."[5] The contradiction between the astronomical military expenditures in both nations and the stated goal of peace did not diminish the value of the idea of peace or peace as a national goal. Few people in the 1950s regarded Hiroshima as exempt from this debate.

Why Journey to Hiroshima?

What does one learn from visiting Hiroshima and Nagasaki? Does the visitor go in order to acquire knowledge, to feel and to mourn, or to recall other tragedies? Or to pray for peace? Half a century or more after the fact, tourists encounter a well-managed Hiroshima, with its appropriately solemn and monumental Peace Park. Although visitors arrive at the Genbaku (A-bomb) Dome and the park with a variety of motives in mind, they are sure to note the proximity of a bustling business district and the Hiroshima Carps baseball stadium (until 2009).

When Kamei Fumio first went to Hiroshima about a decade after the war's end, the project of constructing a city of peace was in its infancy. There was no consensus among visitors as to the significance of the journey or the meaning of peace. During the 1950s, French director Alain Resnais made a film that questioned whether visitors could see anything at all in Hiroshima or feel empathy for the trauma of the other: "Tu n'a rien vu à Hiroshima. Tu ne sais rien [You saw nothing in Hiroshima. You know nothing]." During the same period, Kamei filmed Hiroshima as a Cold War front where important ideological and cultural battles were being fought.

In the 1930s, Kamei and his production crews traveled with the Japanese Imperial Army to the front; in the 1940s, they went to the coal mines and rice fields of rural Japan and to the Imperial Palace of the postwar emperor; and in the 1950s, they visited U.S. military bases encroaching on farming and fishing villages. As Abé Mark Nornes pointed out, many of Kamei's films about war, industry, and rural society were utterly conventional.[6] Yet in other works, Kamei took what in retrospect appear to be extraordinary risks. In films like *Fighting Soldiers* (*Tatakau heitai*, 1939), he represented a subtle but clearly critical stance on the political status quo at a time when such criticism was strictly forbidden.[7] Nornes identified Kamei's participation in "hidden discourses" at times when all opposition seemed to have been quashed. Again, during the Occupation when freedom of expression was the slogan of the day, Kamei made the astonishing *A Japanese Tragedy*, only to be struck down again, this time by both the U.S. Occupation and the Japanese prime minister, Yoshida Shigeru.

In contrast, the post-Occupation atmosphere would seem to have been the first opportunity for Kamei to create films that he believed in and in the style he wished, without fear of censorship. He showed peace marches to Hiroshima and huge masses of people gathered from around the world at the World Conferences Against Atomic and Hydrogen Bombs to protest the arms race and bomb testing. Yet are we to read these journeys to Hiroshima as demonstrations of a peace-loving people, a nonaligned movement advocating for the sad victims of technology gone wild, expressing a universal yearning for peace? Many decades of Japan under the peace constitution, as well as memorial meetings each August 6 and 9, have solidified such an image of the antibomb movement in Hiroshima and Nagasaki. That is not, however, what the journey meant to Kamei or to others who traveled there in the 1950s.

An Eternal City of Peace

A common narrative of Japan's antinuclear movement describes a unified nonaligned movement based on the peace of Hiroshima, a peace without boundaries and divorced from ideology and history. This single-minded movement is said to have fractured and lost its momentum in the early 1960s as a result of a destructive and fractured Left. In fact, from its inception in the late 1940s, the antinuclear movement itself was never united around a single definition of peace, nuclear weapons, or Hiroshima or Nagasaki. This is because the movement always embodied the polarized ideology of the Cold War. Readers of the left-wing Japanese press were encouraged to view the Soviet Union as a bastion of peace, with its offer to lead the world away from the bellicose capitalists and toward a socialist society in which war would be unnecessary. This image of the Soviet Union seemed to have some validity before 1949, the year when Moscow

developed its first bomb, but also remained an integral part of leftist rhetoric throughout the 1950s. In contrast, the mainstream Japanese press
tended to promote the so-called universalist vision of peace. This vision
was articulated in one version of the city of Hiroshima, which laid claim
to universal values, but only under the peculiarly American notion of capitalism and the free world as font of all peace.

The divided vision of peace sprang from ideological differences and
the bitter experiences of the recent past. As Lisa Yoneyama observed,
many people from the former colonies of Asia did not share the vision of
Hiroshima's transcendent peace. The proceedings of the World Conferences Against Atomic and Hydrogen Bombs also reveal the ideological
and ethnic diversity of the activists gathered in Japan.

The so-called universalist vision of peace, it should be noted, evolved
in civil society and not primarily from the state. Some postwar intellectuals subscribed to a belief in Japan's moral responsibility to teach peace,
particularly in the efficacy of Hiroshima as a "city of peace" and in the
discourse of an "internationalist peace consciousness" engendered by a
visit to the center, with its "intimate experience of suffering in the recent
war." The transformative power of this journey (whether spatial, textual,
visual, or auditory) ideally expands to the "outer rings of a national and
ultimately international outlook."[8]

Different nationalist concepts of universal nuclear peace arose in the
Eastern and Western blocs. From soon after the end of World War II, the
Soviet Union advanced the goal of a peace, which, it claimed, only a communist society could deliver. Soviet rhetoric contrasted its own social and
economic goals with capitalism's thirst for war and offered as evidence
the United States's development and use of nuclear arms as well as American belligerence in the Korean War. During the first half of the twentieth
century, interaction among capitalist states was characterized by war. In
contrast, the United States credited American atomic bombs with the creation of peace in the postwar period. This ideological battle became even
more pitched, but also more abstract, as the United States and the Soviet
Union engaged in a fierce arms buildup.

As the early Sino-Soviet alliance raised American anxieties and spurred
the U.S. strategy of containment, the Western bloc's definition of peace
increasingly stressed the concept of economic prosperity and liberalism
under the nuclear umbrella. During his presidential campaign in 1952,
Dwight D. Eisenhower articulated this "free-world" vision of peace: "Our
aim in 'cold war' is not conquest of territory or subjugation by force. Our

aim is more subtle, more pervasive, more complete. We are trying to get the world, by peaceful means, to believe the truth. That truth is that Americans want a world at peace, a world in which all peoples shall have opportunity for maximum individual development."[9] The United States sought to minimize its bellicose image through this type of rhetorical emphasis on peace.

In this polarized atmosphere, Kamei drew on a variety of "knowledges" in order to represent the protesters' march to Hiroshima and the effects of the bomb. What threads of knowledge and discursive fields were prominent in the 1950s? From the Left came the understanding of the United States as "atomic imperialist," and from the popular media, the image of an America in active pursuit of nuclear war.[10] Other pressing issues and concerns included the potential for nonalignment in a polarized world, the science of the bomb, the utopian and destructive atom, and the powerful myth of scientific progress and modernity as embodied in the bomb. Kamei's documentaries on Hiroshima, Nagasaki, and Bikini and his many journeys there highlight the various culturally and ideologically bound uses of peace in Cold War Japan.

The lack of consensus concerning the 1950s discourses surrounding Hiroshima can also be seen in the contrasting reactions to the city by filmmakers Kamei Fumio and Alain Resnais. Although Resnais and Kamei worked in Hiroshima during roughly the same period of time, the two men came away with entirely different visions of its meaning. Resnais's journey to Hiroshima in 1958 made him want to tell a story, but not one about Japan or really even about the bombing. The core themes in Resnais's film are France's trauma under the Nazi regime, romance, and memories of World War II Europe. Although the French director made Hiroshima into a site of memory (*lieu de memoire*), it was a memory of other places.

Not long after he had completed *Night and Fog* (1955), the acclaimed film about the Holocaust, Resnais was commissioned to make another documentary, this time about the effects of the atomic bombings in Japan. But he ultimately rejected that assignment. In his thinking, Japanese filmmakers had already produced excellent documentaries about the bombings. Indeed, so impressed was Resnais by the Japanese films that he borrowed clips from them to use in the film that he eventually did make: the prize-winning *Hiroshima Mon Amour*.[11]

In contrast to Kamei's activist agenda, Resnais was interested in modernist themes of isolation, the memory of trauma, and romance amid the ruins. The Japanese lover (Okada Eiji) of Resnais's French heroine (an actress played by Emmanuelle Riva) denies that she could have seen, learned, or understood anything during her visit to Hiroshima. "You have seen nothing in Hiroshima," he tells his lover. Indeed, in her mind's eye, she sees her own wartime past in the Nazi-occupied French town of Nevers rather than in the revived city before her or in the radiated ruins of his memory. In 1960, the year after Resnais's film was released, the French tested their first atomic bomb.

In *Hiroshima Mon Amour,* the heroine has come to Hiroshima to star in a "film about peace," but the groups of antinuclear activists who march and carry placards only clutter the screen. They appear in crowd scenes in which they impede the lovers' progress. Resnais's protesters are, in any case, mere cinematic activists, extras hired to appear in the French woman's peace movie. In contrast, Kamei's films focus almost entirely on the activists. For Kamei, Hiroshima has no time for romance, nihilism, or individuals isolated by their memories. Instead, he reads the city as a place where the groups of activists can display their vitality, diversity, and hope. Kamei does not offer the audience the collective hero of proletarian art, however, but invokes many different individual activists and leaders.

It is easy to read Kamei's ban-the-bomb films simply as early expressions of the myth of Japanese victimhood that subsequently became fully entrenched in the state and media. It is true that Kamei chose not to emphasize Japan's imperialist militarist past in the documentaries and that in *Still, It's Good to Live,* he focused on female *hibakusha*. It would be a mistake, however, to portray Kamei simply as an aging leftist seeking refuge from the anticommunist present in an apolitical oasis of peace. In his own career, Kamei had already felt the full brunt of the militarist past as he sought to analyze and represent the empire in both wartime and during the Occupation. In a medium as public, commercial, and visual as film, furthermore, he did not have the luxury of extended debates on war responsibility that continued to transpire in the print media. Through the medium of film and the press, Kamei described his immediate contemporary concerns: the lasting effects of the Red purge, the arms race, Korea, the presence of the U.S. military in Japan, the Bikini incident. For him, such Cold War issues needed to be taken up in Hiroshima, as well. My purpose here is not to redeem Kamei but to show that he, along with many others, wished to take an active role in the diverse and complex discourse on Hiroshima and the bomb as part of the Cold War culture, and not only as part of Japan's domestic debates on the past.

There are many famous news photos of Americans who traveled to Hiroshima during the 1940s and 1950s, including Norman Cousins, Eleanor Roosevelt, and the Occupation authorities. But these images give the false impression of a consensus on the meaning of the designation city of peace, which had been Hiroshima's since 1949. Their visits seem to confirm that the city had become the spiritual center of the Pax Americana. As the contrast between the 1950s Hiroshima films of Resnais and Kamei illustrates, however, nuclear anxiety and a desire for peace did not eliminate national concerns, local imaginations, or ideological commitment.

Kamei's documentation of the annual meetings of the World Conference Against Atomic and Hydrogen Bombs reminds us that in an ideologically polarized world, the meaning of peace varied greatly depending on political convictions. Indeed the meanings of Hiroshima continued to shift greatly for more than a decade, for several reasons. With the astonishingly rapid changes in military technology, knowledge of the bomb was no simple matter. By 1949, Fat Man and Little Boy, the types of bombs that the United States had dropped on Hiroshima and Nagasaki, were obsolete. In addition, the superpowers continued to vie for control of the dominant notion of progress as symbolized by humankind's imagined control over the atom. In turn, this new relationship between scientists and the atom appeared to create a new atomic age, an era separate from the barbarian violence of the world war. Maintaining these myths depended on suppressing knowledge about radiation, as well as severing the link between conventional and nuclear air war. The growing nuclear club therefore used propaganda to control scientific and public understanding of the bomb.[12] The rocky social and cultural processes that resulted in the myth of a unique atomic age and a new peace unfolded during the late 1940s and 1950s. The reactions of several other visitors to Hiroshima further illustrate the unsettled discursive field surrounding this city.

A Unique Site of Nuclear War, a Singular Epoch

Both the Western and Eastern blocs' narratives of peace depended on a belief in the singularity of the atomic age. Detaching the apocalyptic violence of the atomic bomb (and later the hydrogen bomb) from the conventional violence of World War II constituted a central value of Cold War discourse, one that arose through various discursive strategies. One strategy centered on imaginations of space: Hiroshima as decimated, only to be resurrected as the city of peace, and journeys to Hiroshima as essential to understanding the bomb. Another discourse subscribed to the belief in progress and used metaphors to identify the work of scientists with sacred power, and the fission and fusion of atoms with the revelation of the secrets of the universe.

Another significant Cold War dynamic involved the United States's and the Soviet Union's pattern of denying the harmful effects of radioactivity. Propaganda and the suppression of information were essential tools in this effort. Propaganda campaigns in the media depended on textual explanations to shape the public's understanding of radioactivity. They also required the establishment of specific visual representations of the new weapon. Accordingly, the ubiquitous aerial images of the mushroom cloud encouraged the viewer to conceive of the Hiroshima and Nagasaki bombs mainly as huge and visible in their destructive power. As the controversy in the mid-1990s over the Smithsonian Institution's display of the *Enola Gay* (the airplane that dropped the A-bomb on Hiroshima) illustrated, the mushroom cloud has often been used as part of America's triumphalist narrative to hide the human costs of nuclear weapons and the human faces of the *hibakusha*.[13] In addition, images of mushroom clouds give the viewers the false impression that they have seen the destructive power of the bomb. The clouds are not the explosion but are instead the aftermath, the debris of pulverized and now radioactive matter and bodies and heat swept up toward the sky.[14] It was nearly a decade after the Hiroshima and Nagasaki bombings before most of the public even began to acquire a rudimentary appreciation of the grave threat of high- and low-level radiation.

Some of the many accounts of Hiroshima contradicted the dominant scientific and historical narratives that viewed the bombings as the triumphal moment of twentieth-century warfare and technology. Other accounts encouraged empathy for the human suffering while also emphasizing Hiroshima and Nagasaki as unique places separate from the violence and destruction of war before the bombs were dropped. The contrast between the Hiroshima visits by the writer Hara Tamiki and Dr. Kusano Nobuo, for example, shows two such radically different conceptions of the bombed cities. On his first visit to Tokyo shortly after the end of the war, Hara was surprised to find a bombed city where buildings still stood amid the ruins after the extensive aerial attacks in the spring of 1945. He had just arrived in the capital from the only other bombed city he had ever seen: Hiroshima. Hara had been living in Hiroshima on August 6, 1945, the day of the bombing, and remembered the city as completely flattened to the ground, full of charred corpses, a place resembling nothing other than paintings of hell.

Traveling in the opposite direction—from Tokyo to Hiroshima—physician Kusano Nobuo initially did not perceive the A-bombed ruins as radically different from those in other destroyed Japanese cities. In dozens of Japanese cities, one could see the same collapsed buildings, mile after mile of wooden homes reduced to ashes, metal beams warped by extreme heat, and charred stones. Many of the patients whom Kusano examined while in Hiroshima had the same varieties of injuries found in victims of conventional ordinance, such as napalm and TNT. The only thing about Hiroshima that genuinely shocked Kusano was what he discovered while performing autopsies. He learned firsthand, and for the first time, about the harmful effects of massive doses of radiation on the human body, about the reasons that so many apparently uninjured people died an excruciating death during the days and weeks after the explosion. In his groundbreaking article "The Corpses Resist" (Shikabane wa kōgi suru, 1952), Kusano wrote, "Photographs of the rubble of buildings and burned flesh do not convey the true destructive power of the atom bomb."[15] It was not the doctor's intention to challenge Hara's representation of the Hiroshima bombing as a unique living hell, nor was he calling into question the possibility of properly or correctly representing the experience and the trauma of the bomb, as have critics of art and literature. Rather, he was trying to bring attention to what made the A-bomb unique: its release into the atmosphere of high levels of radiation.

Since 1945, millions of people have made the journey to and from Hiroshima. Hours and days after the bombing, residents went to search for relatives and friends, and journalists, photographers, and filmmakers came from other parts of Japan to investigate and record what was promised to be a high-profile story. Weeks and months afterward, scientists from the Manhattan Project visited to gather data about the results of the bomb. Occupation personnel marched in. Physicians came to examine patients at the behest of the Atomic Bomb Casualty Commission (ABCC). The Hiroshima painters Maruki Toshi and Maruki Iri left and returned many times with their murals of the atomic bombings. Three years later, Hara visited again and was surprised to find that the city was no longer a wasteland.

On the first anniversary of the bombing, relatives, friends, and neighbors gathered to mourn the dead and dying, and many strangers appeared too.[16] Starting in the late 1940s, the antinuclear activists came, by train, by bus, and on foot. In the early 1960s, the novelist Ōe Kenzaburō reflected on the failures of the antinuclear movement as he looked down at Hiroshima from an airplane bound for Tokyo. Groups of schoolchildren visited as part of their peace education. The pope, the Dalai Lama, Mother Teresa, prime ministers, and presidents all paid homage in Hiroshima.

Unlike Hara and Kusano, most of these travelers were spared the agony of seeing with their own eyes the unusual corpses or the usual injuries, familiar types of damage, or the new, apocalyptic ruins. Some were surprised at the lush green trees, grass, and shrubs that flourished despite the U.S. prediction that plants would not grow in Hiroshima or Nagasaki for seventy years. Remarkably, though, the United States had not, at the time, foretold long-term harm to the human body.[17]

Decades after the bombings, most readers and visitors find Hara's account of the A-bombed city more familiar than Kusano's because Hara uses conventional tropes of war writing in order to evoke Hiroshima's destruction. Hara could safely assume that readers could imagine pictures of hell, of the battlefield, and even of corpses. His writings also express the dominant trope of the singularity and wonder of the nuclear age. In contrast, most readers do not know how to imagine the damage to the inside of the body to which Kusano refers. Only his authority as a physician persuades us to accept his shock at the types and extent of injury to internal organs and tissues. Most readers also find exceptional the doctor's identification of the destruction in conventionally bombed cities with that in the cities that we have learned to understand as unique sites of a new type of war, spaces that witnessed the birth of a new epoch.

While both accounts of the bomb's destruction help readers grasp the threat of nuclear weapons, first-person accounts by *hibakusha* like Hara gained over time tremendous prominence in the discourse about Hiroshima and Nagasaki. During the decade following Hara's death in 1951, however, the testimony of the *hibakusha* did not occupy a central place in antinuclear activism and cultural production. Instead, it was the global antinuclear movement, artists, and scientists who were at the forefront of defying and defining the bomb.[18]

When Kamei and his crew were filming in Hiroshima more than a decade after the bombing, they met many people who were more interested in talking about the fortunes of the Hiroshima Carps baseball team than about the effects of radiation.[19] Some residents of the bombed cities were "drunk on baseball," Kamei later recalled, as if that would exempt them from both the dark memories of the past and the daily dose of radioactive ash from H-bomb tests. The disjuncture between the seeming vigor of the antibomb movement, on the one hand, and the all-consuming business of daily life under prospering capitalism, on the other, can also be understood as the vast distance between the historical moment of Hiroshima and Nagasaki and the precarious dilemma of the Cold War.

Empirical data on the effects and dangers of radiation and the ideological messages of activists who marched to Hiroshima formed two important kinds of knowledge about the bomb in Cold War Japan. Kamei Fumio made nuclear films related to other cultural products that centered on the bomb. His cinematic representations of a citizen activist antinuclear movement embody the ideological tensions inherent in the polarized Cold War world. His scientific documentary about radiation, *The World Is Terrified,* and the story of its reception remind us of other channels through which the Cold War battle of words and images was being fought in Japan, though in a more subtle way than in other parts of the world.

Kamei Fumio created the atomic documentaries with a diverse group of viewers in mind: the two dominant strands within the antinuclear movement—that is, the Left and the advocates of the Western bloc. He also wanted to include in his audience the great majority of viewers who had been indoctrinated by the anticommunist legacy of the Occupation as well as by the conservative Japanese state.[20]

Local Audiences, Universal Audiences

In the 1950s, after many years of working under powerful centralized authorities—first the imperial Japanese government and then the Allied Occupation—Kamei Fumio was able to produce films without concern for the censor's pen or the possibility of arrest. He kept in mind his audience and the aims of the organizations that commissioned his films. Despite the General Headquarters' purge of communists from 1949 and the residual prewar anticommunist sentiments that reemerged in the Japanese government, pro-Marxist, progressive figures like Kamei had great influence on the cultural production and activism of the 1950s.

After the Occupation, certain dominant ideological discourses affected Kamei's conception of his audiences and his approach to filmmaking. In addition to his own progressive ideals, a philosophy of nuclear universalism appeared, particularly in regard to the development of antibomb organizations and in official government ritual and policy. Kamei's 1950s documentary films show the complexity of issues facing those who might participate in progressive cultural productions, especially on the atomic issue.

A study of the reception of Kamei's mid-1950s documentaries allows us a fresh perspective on the evolution of the Cold War distinction between what constituted universal and local issues. The director made three anti–U.S. military base protest films in 1955 and 1956 and five atomic documentaries between 1956 and 1961. His willingness to undertake these projects in such rapid succession and over a relatively short period of time suggests the urgency of both political issues and the vigor of the social activists who were the heroes of his films. Why, then, did critics and viewers draw a sharp distinction between the local and the universal relevance of the Kamei's A-bomb documentaries, on the one hand, and his anti–U.S. base films, on the other?

Both contemporary commentators and subsequent critics have tended to define the atomic problem as universal in nature and the antibase controversy as a local matter. For example, in 1954, the writer and critic Fukuda Tsuneari criticized activists for confusing the "local" issue of U.S. bases in Japan with national and global problems like the bomb. For Fukuda, the bases mattered only to people who objected to having them next door but not to the nation as a whole.[21] Fukuda, who visited the United States at the height of the Cold War hysteria and when civil defense programs were in full swing, recognized that Americans also were worried about the destructiveness of nuclear weapons. In contrast, Fukuda remarked, Americans did not rise up in opposition to the military bases that had been established in foreign countries in their name. Following Fukuda's logic, James Orr labeled the 1950s opposition to the U.S. military presence in Japan as one of the "divisive political issues" that the supposedly nonpartisan ban-the-bomb movement attempted to avoid under the leadership of Yasui Kaoru (1907–1980). But the rigid definition of the antibase movement as local and partisan, in contrast to the bomb movement, is misleading.

Kamei's interest in the antimilitary base protest was comparable to his devotion to antinuclear activism. The extensive network of U.S. bases in Japan had been an important social issue since the early 1950s. During the Cold War, overseas military bases constituted a crucial part of American strategy, as the United States's policy of containment dictated,

The 1955 anti–U.S. military base protest, as depicted in Nakamura Hiroshi, *5th Sunagawa*, oil on panel (1955). (Museum of Contemporary Art, Tokyo. Courtesy of Nakamura Hiroshi)

among other things, the positioning of a string of military bases around the perimeters of the Soviet Union and China. Moreover, these U.S. facilities were not static entities. During the 1950s, the U.S. military extended many of the air bases' runways in Japan in order to accommodate heavier, larger bombers, whose payload might be either nuclear or conventional bombs.[22] Communities on the bases' perimeters were most immediately affected by the roar of the considerably larger jet engines and by airfields that expanded to cover farmland. Yet, as demonstrated at the time of the Korean War, the United States–Japan Security Treaty of 1960, and, later, the Vietnam War, many citizens had political and moral concerns that went beyond their own communities, such as opposition to the use of Japan as a base for U.S. bombing sorties to other Asian countries. Between the Korean and Vietnam wars, there were no actual destinations for American bombers, only the eternal preparation for thermonuclear attack on the Soviet Union, in a war imagined by the nuclear strategists.[23]

Kamei's involvement in the antinuclear conference films grew directly out of his work on documenting the antimilitary base protests in the town of Sunagawa. While filming in Sunagawa, Kamei met Yasui Kaoru, the head of the Japan Council Against Atomic and Hydrogen Bombs (Gensuikyō [Gensuibaku kinshi Nihon kyōgikai]), the umbrella organization for the antibomb movement, who was there to observe the demonstrations by local residents and labor unionists. Yasui had emerged as a key leader in the effort to form a united antinuclear movement, a struggle that finally bore fruit in August 1955 when the first World Conference

Against Atomic and Hydrogen Bombs was held in Japan. At Yasui's request, Kamei took charge of filming the proceedings of the World Conferences and other related antinuclear social activist events.[24] The "Declaration" (sengen) of the first antibomb conference specifically stated that "the possession and stockpiling of warheads and the expansion of military bases all are linked to nuclear war. Preparation for nuclear war at military bases throughout the world, not only in Japan and Okinawa, continues. This is the reason that the struggle against bases is fought along with the antinuclear movement."[25]

Political motives clearly lay behind the differing classification of Kamei's two documentary series. To progressive forces especially, both the American military presence and the threat of nuclear weapons were considered part of the U.S. aim of global hegemony. Some backers of the Soviet Union identified atomic imperialism (genbaku teikokushugi) only with the United States, whereas others on the Left perceived the possession of nuclear weapons as unacceptable for either opponent in the Cold War rivalry. The appeal of Marxist antinuclear thinking is evident in the speed of the Japanese translation of Atomic Imperialism, a book by the American Communist James S. Allen. The book was originally published in the United States in 1952, and the Japanese translation appeared the next year.[26]

Style and technique also contributed to the divergent classification of Kamei's Sunagawa and atomic films. Recognized and revered by subsequent generations of filmmakers, such as Ogawa Shinsuke, the Sunagawa trilogy stands out for its technique and visual achievement and is further proof of the importance of the U.S. military presence as a political issue.[27]

Kamei's formal approaches and thematic emphases in the antibase films are reminiscent of his wartime documentaries banned by the imperial government because of their failure to idealize Japan's militarism. As in his films Fighting Soldiers and Kobayashi Issa (1941), the Sunagawa films exhibit extraordinary compassion for the women and men who labor on the land and valorize their connection to the earth. In Fighting Soldiers, for example, Kamei offers an admiring glimpse of some Chinese peasants who return to plow the fields that the Japanese Imperial Army had trampled through and temporarily occupied. The Japanese military had hired Kamei to make a film about the bravery of Japanese soldiers. But after the unit decamped, Kamei and his crew did not follow along but instead shot footage of the Chinese peasants. He included this footage in the film, portraying the Chinese as hardier and more admirable than the exhausted, shabby Japanese men marching toward the front. In a similar way, Kamei employed a variety of techniques to create a stunning portrait of the brave and determined Sunagawa farmers, who were loath to hand over their fields and villages to the Americans, and other villagers who conducted sit-ins as a means of protesting U.S. military plans to test weapons on a local beach. Viewer can see the influence of Kamei's commitment to humanism and Marxism in the formal approaches to the Sunagawa films.

The English-language literature has frequently framed the antibase movement as an expression of xenophobia and specifically as anti-American. In contrast to the simplistic and negative portrait of the movement, this variety of social activism should be regarded as a more complex phenomenon, with diverse roots in progressive, pacifist, and leftist thought. Cold War dynamics certainly meant that at some levels, East-bloc policies influenced the movement. Despite the strong leftist ties, though, the antibase groups were not merely acting on orders from Moscow or Beijing or Cominform. In other words, we should allow for the possibility of independent Marxist and progressive activists and intellectuals whose motives were more complicated than mere nationalism or obedience to international communism. Even the prominent communist Miyamoto Kenji advocated a multipartisan, nonaligned stance for the antinuclear movement.[28] Miyamoto furthermore urged the movement to remain aware of the many people in Japan and the United States who advocated rearmament despite the postwar peace constitution. The post-Occupation period was thus a new political climate for the peace movement. One could be antinuclear without being a pacifist and leftist without strictly adhering to the Soviet line.

For people on the Left, the Marxist narrative of history offered a plausible view of peace as possible only under socialism or communism. The Korean War seemed proof of the theory that capitalism inevitably led to warmongering and profiteering. Indeed, economic determinism alone could not adequately account for ethnic and nationalist causes of war. By the same token, reducing the Left's negative view of the United States to purely nationalistic terms (as shallow xenophobia), ignored the powerful global spread of progressive thought in the 1950s (in contrast to significant trends of rabid anticommunism in the United States). Any sound critique of the U.S. aim of hegemony through a policy of containment and its willing participation in the nuclear arms race had to consider the complex interrelationship of capitalist ideology, expansionism, and nationalism.

It was not only the Left that subscribed to the idea that the U.S. bases were evidence of America's master plans for a nuclear war. Military bases abroad, along with a rapid buildup of nuclear weapons, formed two key components of the U.S. policy of containing the Eastern bloc. During the 1950s, the U.S. military declared its doctrine of "massive retaliation" and also laid plans for a possible American first strike with H-bombs on thousands of Russian cities and towns. Although the Soviet Union was actively engaged in the arms race by the mid-1950s, its nuclear arsenal paled in comparison with that of the United States.[29] The Japanese anti–U.S. military movement may have had leftist roots, but the expression of antibase sentiment was not confined to radicals. Criticism of the injustice of the nuclear club's treating "Japanese as guinea pigs" was based on both the ABCC's treatment of the *hibakusha* and the Bikini tests. A photo in a mainstream journal showed a *Lucky Dragon* crewman who declared, "I will not be a guinea pig [*morumotto*] for the Americans." Thus the antipathy toward the U.S. military presence arose from the Left and within the evolving mainstream discourse of the Japanese peace movement.

The Japanese antinuclear movement also had strong ties with European progressives and leftists, who in certain parts of Western Europe included many politically and culturally authoritative figures and organizations. In late 1940s and 1950s France, in particular, both the Communist Party and Marxist thought retained considerable credibility, especially in contrast with McCarthy-era American society. It therefore is an oversimplification to label the organizers of the World Convention for Peace held in Paris in 1947 as simply a "communist-sponsored committee," as the communist participants included distinguished scientists such as Pierre Joliet-Curie and the famous artist Pablo Picasso.[30] In the United States, the Stockholm Appeal's antinuclear petition drive, which also originated in the European antinuclear movement, won the support of W. E. B. DuBois, who was threatened with a jail term for his antinuclear activities and pronouncements.[31]

Antinuclear Activism and Universal Ideology?

When Kamei Fumio made his nuclear films, he had to take into account a complex domestic antinuclear movement that traced its history back to the 1940s. This type of social activism in Japan did not develop in isolation but instead was related to larger domestic and international organizations and philosophies. Next we examine some of the roots of the early antibomb movement.

Histories of the antinuclear movement and even the cultural histories of the period emphasize two aspects of the Japanese ban-the-bomb movement: the centrality of the March 1954 Bikini, or *Lucky Dragon*, incident (*Bikini jiken*) in inspiring widespread antibomb sentiment, and the prominence of women—especially "ordinary homemakers"—in spearheading a mass antinuclear movement.[32] Undeniably, the heavy media coverage of the damage caused by the U.S. thermonuclear Test Bravo to the crew of the *Lucky Dragon* and other fishing boats and to Japan's food and water supply brought home the dangers posed by atmospheric nuclear testing in a way that the Hiroshima and Nagasaki events had not for most people in Japan. The fear that radiation could contaminate their rice and water seemed to have been the only thing that would propel citizens into activism. For some, the fallout from the Bikini test marked bomb testing as a threat to consumption in an increasingly consumer-oriented society.[33] For others, the concern over fallout and the effects of radiation gave rise to an early environmental awareness. For increasingly hegemonic conservative political parties, the suffering *Lucky Dragon* crew transformed Test Bravo into Japan's third nuclear event after Hiroshima and Nagasaki. Accordingly, a September 1954 *Asahi News* newsreel named Kuboyama Ai, the *Lucky Dragon* crew member who died, the world's very "first victim of hydrogen bombs."[34] In turn, the evolution of a seamless Hiroshima-Nagasaki-Bikini narrative enforced the discourse of Japanese victimization by absolving the nation and its citizens from responsibility in major world conflicts and global violence while enhancing the worthy message of Japan as separate from the bipolarized and increasingly tense Cold War.

The dominant image of the Japanese antinuclear movement as first and foremost a self-serving, easily co-opted movement arose partly because of the need of certain Cold War constituencies to project an image of Japan's transformation into a capitalist free-world workshop. Essential to the articulation of the myth that harmless and well-meaning housewives started an apolitical peace movement was the erasure of the many diverse and often left-oriented peace groups that already existed all over Japan.[35]

In Kamei's documentaries, the viewer watches large crowds of protesters filling the screen, only some of whom appear to be ordinary homemakers. Kamei shows an extraordinarily diverse group of participants at the World Conferences, which include students and labor activists, Buddhist priests and Christians, *hibakusha* and doctors, women and men, young and old, urban and rural dwellers, and Japanese and people from abroad.[36] These films, along with contemporary texts about antinuclear politics, show an energized and growing movement and a discourse distinct from the "ordinary homemaker" activism that dominates current understandings.

Precisely because of this diversity, Gensuikyō faced the formidable task of offering a solution to local concerns (how to get rid of fallout in our/my backyard) and of creating a positive goal that a wide range of groups in a highly polarized political climate would find acceptable.[37] The chosen goal was peace. Nor was its ideology always so vulnerable to co-optation by conservative politicians, Soviet policy, or the American ally. After all, Gensuikyō was principally an umbrella organization that brought together many existing local antinuclear and activist groups, which themselves represented a broad range of political viewpoints and stances. Not surprisingly, the Japanese antinuclear movement never agreed on a single definition of peace.

While it is true that the left-oriented groups spoke with the loudest voice, the pre-1954 movement did not depend solely on a Soviet affiliation. One can see the diversity of the movement in the proceedings of the first World Conference Against Atomic and Hydrogen Bombs in 1955. Some voices are stridently anti-imperialist (that is, anti-American and pro-Soviet), but many others show the search for a third way separate from the U.S.–Soviet rivalry, inspired variously by Marxism, humanism, or liberalism. The Japanese umbrella organization Gensuikyō included not only grassroots citizens' organizations both radical and moderate, but also labor unions, regional organizations, and even politicians from conservative political parties, such as the newly founded Liberal Democratic Party.[38]

That few historians fully acknowledge the leftist origins of antinuclear activism in Japan is perhaps not surprising given the anticommunist legacy of the Cold War. English-language histories of the antinuclear movement often characterize the Left as sick and fractured and blame the failures of the antinuclear movement on a pathologically divided leftist movement. It also is common to attribute Kamei's decision to quit filmmaking in the 1960s to divisions within the Japanese Left. Kamei was purged from the Japan Communist Party, as were the Marukis and many other artists and intellectuals. The eventual splintering of the Left was perhaps symptomatic of an increasingly ineffectual political stance, as well as of the divisions in the larger communist world. Yet a consideration of leftist involvement in the early ban-the-bomb activism reveals that it was essential to launching the movement. Marxist thought also meant a great deal to the intellectual and creative lives of people like Kamei.

Gensuikyō's principle of nonpartisan unity in opposition to the bomb found inspiration in the progressive Partisans of Peace movement in Europe. Beginning in 1949, European activists had advocated an ideal of nonalignment. Evidence of the inspiration of progressive European activism and, more specifically, Marxism in Japan can be found in progressive cultural journals like *Shin Nihon bungaku* (*New Japanese Literature*) and *Jinmin bungaku* (*The People's Literature*) in the 1940s and 1950s. As dedicated to a hard-core pro-Soviet line and the methods of socialist realism as *Jinmin bungaku* was, the magazine's editors extolled the European activists' call for a nonaligned antinuclear movement, one exemplified by the Stockholm Appeal petition drive.[39] The less dogmatic *Shin Nihon bungaku* similarly affirmed the Partisans' goal of transcending ideological and national borders in the common aim of abolishing nuclear weapons and war. Many writers and intellectuals were attracted to the Partisans' call for the establishment of local antinuclear groups, which in Japan were called Japan Associations to Maintain Peace (Nihon heiwa o mamoru kai).[40]

In the European case, many prominent activists, including scientists like Pierre and Irène Joliet-Curie and artists like Louis Aragon and Picasso, were themselves communists or socialists. As a precedent for a nonaligned peace movement, the European Left could look back to the recent examples of the pre–World War II Popular Front and the wartime Resistance, which advocated nonpartisan unity in the battle against fascism. It also is important to note that, for example, Communist parties in postwar France and Italy operated as powerful and effective political forces at the local and national levels.[41]

The prominence of Europe's communists contrasts with the marginalization of Japan's communists and socialists. Anticommunism in Japan gained momentum during the repressive years of the empire, only to be resurrected during the Occupation's anticommunist purges and strengthened in the post-Occupation era by the American-allied, Liberal Democratic Party–led conservative hegemony. Despite this negative atmosphere, the Japan Communist Party and the Japan Socialist Party continued to hold seats in the Diet and to play an active role in domestic party politics.[42]

During the 1950s, despite the stigma attached to the Japan Communist Party and Marxism by General Headquarters' Reverse Course and the Japanese authorities' collusion with the powerful American McCarthyist agenda, the Japan Communist Party as a party and individuals devoted to Marxism still remained at the core of antinuclear activism.

During the 1950s, the Stockholm Appeal and peace activists were often branded in Japan as "Red" or anti-American. Anticommunist conservative forces in Japan, in tandem with the United States, Japan's occupier and ally, even identified the term "peace" specifically with Marxism and Soviet ideology. One of the demands in the Stockholm petition states that any nation engaging in the first use of nuclear weapons will be defined as breaking international law, and this first-use declaration has frequently been interpreted as anti-American. But the ambivalence of the appeal's wording reveals the willingness of the Partisans' movement to be non-aligned. If the United States were branded as a villain and excluded, then the aim of a worldwide, multipartisan antinuclear organization would not be realized.[43] Although a rigid clash of ideology characterized the Cold War rivalry among nation-states, many individuals and groups in civil society sought an ideological basis separate from official state discourses.

An important event in the history of the antinuclear movement was the April 1949 Parisian Peace Congress (Congrès mondial des partisans de la paix), which Japanese readers would have found notice of in the June 1949 issue of Shin Nihon bungaku and in newspapers. The literary magazine included a copy of the telegram from Pierre Joliot-Curie in which the scientist, as one of the organizers of the meeting, asked the Japanese delegates to confirm their participation.[44] The Paris congress advocated the establishment of activist groups in each region, as well as an international petition drive, and the resulting local organizations that made up the Japan Associations to Maintain Peace became significant sites of activism. The June 1950 issue of Shin Nihon bungaku contained the responses to a survey about the growing threat of world war as the arms race heated up and also about the increasingly conservative political climate in Japan. To the question, "How have you participated in the movement to prevent war and to protect peace?" a number of writers mentioned their participation in the Stockholm Appeal and the Japan Associations to Maintain Peace.

Soon after the war, many cultural figures in Japan—such as the writer Abe Kōbō, the artist Okamoto Tarō, and Kamei—enthusiastically joined the Communist Party. During the 1950s, however, the repercussions of anti-Stalinism in the Soviet Union and Sino-Soviet rancor, compounded by United States's anticommunism, destabilized Japan's Communist and Socialist parties.[45] Given this unsettling political context, it is not surprising that Kamei and other individuals dedicated to Marxist thought and practice would find Gensuikyō's nonpartisan message appealing. Although Kamei's antinuclear movement films cloak his ideological roots, we can find much in these works in common with his overtly political antibase documentaries.

For many of the most committed antinuclear activists and leftists (including Kamei), the goal of peace was linked to notions of broader social and economic change, ideas based on progressive and Marxist thought. For many of the newer members of Gensuikyō and Kamei's potential audience, however, the Marxist notion of peace was too "political" and seemed tainted by "Red" thought. By the same token, the huge influx of moderate and conservative elements under the Gensuikyō umbrella brought pre-Bikini progressive activists into the mainstream. One man from Nagano Prefecture who participated in the first World Conference in Hiroshima was glad for the legitimacy that the nonaligned organization afforded the cause: "It used to be that when ten of us got together and sang the 'No More Nukes Song' [Genbaku no uta], they would label us 'dirty communists' [aka]. But we won't have to put up with that kind of taunting anymore."[46]

Yasui Kaoru, chair of the Gensuikyō conference, was central to setting the organization's goal of nonpartisan (not based on a specific ideological stance) and nonaligned (not aligned with the Western or Eastern bloc) vision of peace.[47] Yasui was inspired by the European activists. In his foreword to the first conference proceedings, for example, he cites Jean-Paul Sartre, who had declared at a recent antinuclear meeting in Helsinki, "What will bring us peace is neither the maintenance of the status quo, nor a retreat to the past, but unlimited progress."[48]

Filming Protest, Filming a Human Face

When tailoring the World Conference films for a broad audience, Kamei Fumio had to take into account both the nonpartisan rhetoric of Gensuikyō and the political climate of the day. Kamei visited the office of Gensuikyō first when starting to make Still, It's Good to Live. He wrote that

> it turned out to be a small, dirty place. . . . The public had little if any interest in the anti–H-bomb petition drive. Once we were filming

a farmer who was soliciting signatures for the peace petition in the city of Hiroshima. He was the elder brother of a *hibakusha* who had died [of radiation sickness]. We aimed the camera at him as he stood with the petition ballots. He looked so uncomfortable in his necktie, for he had never worn one before, and was very restless. Whenever someone walked by, he would bow deeply, but no one agreed to sign his petition. We continuing shooting, certain that the next passerby would sign, but each one would just walk right by him. Time after time, we wasted film with this same scene. That, however, was the reality. In other words, even in Hiroshima, the fact was that people cared nothing about anti–H-bomb petitions or government support for the medical expenses of the *hibakusha*. That is why it took such tremendous effort to develop the anti–H-bomb movement. If anyone and everyone were willing to sign the petition, there would have been no need for activism. So we decided to use the film of the man as is. Personally, I felt grave doubts about my fellow Japanese when I realized that there were no demonstrations in the wake of the Bikini test fallout in Japan (the very country where the A-bombs had been dropped). [In contrast] in India, people in the streets were protesting against the testing.[49]

Despite the willingness of millions of Japanese people to sign the Stockholm Appeal's antinuclear petitions, Kamei did not perceive other significant signs of widespread consensus or meaningful political action in opposition to nuclear weapons.

Yet Kamei's World Conference films do not give the viewer the slightest hint of the small dirty Gensuikyō office, and they also downplay the public apathy that he emphasizes in his writings. In visual and narrative terms, all the documentaries share a focus on movement and place. Kamei fills the screen with scenes of large crowds of people applauding enthusiastically as they listen to the passionate words of speakers in the vast hall and energetically engaging in discussions. Kamei also highlights the peace marches (*heiwa kōshin*), which started in villages and towns all over Japan and headed for Hiroshima or Tokyo. The peace-march scenes link the nuclear films to the Sunagawa films, in which the camera often focuses on the movement of masses of resisters (but not, significantly, on the Japan Communist Party or the Sōhyō labor unionists). These are not the anonymous masses: Kamei includes many extreme close-ups of the faces of protesters and marchers in order to emphasize the individuality of each one.

In *Still, It's Good to Live*, Kamei carefully excluded direct references to the classic Marxist narrative of history, thus fashioning the film in the hope that a general audience would be receptive to its message. Abé Mark Nornes described Kamei as an active cultural producer who worked in "hidden discursive fields" during the imperial era and the Allied Occupation. This characterization also is relevant to the social and ideological discourses of the 1950s. Kamei's veiling of the ideological message is not surprising when one considers that he was working after the Occupation's Red purge and in the context of the increasingly conservative Japanese government. A case in point, *Still, It's Good to Live* received attention in the mass media and reached a general audience.

In this film, Kamei employed conventional narrative strategies partly in response to Gensuikyō's aim of building a broad, nonpartisan nuclear movement. *Still, It's Good to Live* consists mostly of a series of vignettes about individual *hibakusha* and their struggles with illness, depression, and despair. Told in the form of melodrama, each portrait also contains a glimmer of hope for the future. Kamei believed that he would reach the greatest number of viewers with the film's antinuclear message if he used "old" means of expression, which he defined as conventional modes of representation familiar to the audience.

In later decades of the Cold War, the *hibakusha* and their stories of suffering, survival, and hope formed the core of the Hiroshima journey. Kamei's main goal in the mid-1950s, however, was not to document the psychological, social, and medical plight of the *hibakusha*. Rather, he included the portraits of them to bring a human face to the relatively new movement. In this sense, his approach is similar to John Hersey's narrative strategy in *Hiroshima* (1946), in which he sought to humanize the former enemy for the American reader.

All but one of the six *hibakusha* featured in Kamei's *Still, It's Good to Live* are women, and their portraits differ in an important sense from those in Kamei's overtly Marxist early-postwar feature films and documentaries. Instead of striving for liberation and justice for workers and farmers, the *hibakusha* in *Still, It's Good to Live* are shown as trying to lead modest, ordinary lives. Echoing the interests of the well-intentioned yet misdirected American rescue mission of the so-called Hiroshima Maidens, the voiceover narrator mourns the fact that the A-bomb destroyed the young women's feminine beauty. Some of the "keloid girls" undergo plastic surgery on their faces; others work with orphan children who are blind and thus cannot see their scars.

Kamei Fumio and Watanabe Chieko on a hilltop overlooking Nagasaki. (Courtesy of Japan Documentary Film)

Yet Kamei was not satisfied with a narrow portrait of the female *hibakusha* whose only goal was beauty or, perhaps, marriage. His film instead emphasizes the ways in which the women have made themselves useful members of society despite their physical disabilities and trauma.[50] Most of them found work, making clothing or caring for others; only one of them became an antinuclear activist.

Watanabe Chieko had not left her home in Nagasaki in the ten years since the bombing because she had lost the use of her legs. Kamei and his crew take her out on her first tour of the rebuilt hometown. The camera shows Kamei himself carrying Watanabe to a hilltop, from which she can look out over Nagasaki. She appears again later in the film at the World Conference Against Atomic and Hydrogen Bombs, this time dressed nicely in a fashionable cotton dress and carried by her mother. It is her urgent testimony about the evils of nuclear weapons that prompted the title of the film, *Still, It's Good to Live*. Watanabe's psychological and social isolation as a *hibakusha*, as well as her broken body, had made her despair, and she considered suicide. However, when she tells her story of the bombing before the assembled at the World Conference, the welcoming applause makes her realize that she, too, has a contribution to make.[51]

For some activists and certainly for the conservative government, the image of the female *hibakusha* was a useful tool in constructing a gendered discourse of Japanese "innocence, victimhood, and perserverance."[52] The suffering female could also work to counter the debate over the responsibility for the war (*sensō sekinin*), by erasing memories of noncombatants' cooperation in the total war of empire.[53]

In Kamei's case, however, the focus on women was not entirely inconsistent with his films up to that time. He often featured heroic women, such as the coal miner played by the well-known actress Yamada Isuzu in his feature film *A Woman Walking Alone on the Earth* (*Onna hitori daichi o iku*, 1953). Especially in his antibase documentaries, Kamei portrays strong and vital women who work on the land and protest shoulder to shoulder with men. Furthermore, Kamei's 1940s feature films position women in a Marxist revolutionary framework.

In *Hiroshima Notes* (*Hiroshima nōto*, 1965), Ōe Kenzaburō created a view of the *hibakusha* as noble Others and Hiroshima as "inspiration," a space whose tragedy would inspire "the genesis of a 'human renaissance.'"[54] Kamei, in contrast, showed the *hibakusha* as ordinary people who had suffered but, like millions of their compatriots, had tried to carry on in the instability of the postwar period. For many in Kamei's domestic audience, Hiroshima was an unfamiliar space, the ruins of which they had seen in the popular press for the first time only a few years earlier. In order to normalize the *hibakusha* for the domestic audience, therefore, Kamei portrayed them in familiar quotidian settings, where they enjoyed the support of their families and others around them. The film presents an optimistic and decidedly rosy view of *hibakusha* leading purposeful lives in a society that cared for them.[55]

In making the film on the first World Conference, Gensuikyō and Kamei had in mind both a domestic and an international audience. An English version of the film (narrated by Yamada Isuzu) was released simultaneously. Like John Hersey in *Hiroshima*, Kamei selected *hibakusha* whom American audiences would find familiar and nonthreatening. Gender was an important criterion. The many women in *Still, It's Good to Live* reminded U.S. audiences of the Hiroshima Maidens project spearheaded by Norman Cousins, editor of the *Saturday Review of Literature*. The maidens, a group of twenty-five *hibakusha* who traveled to New York for restorative surgery in 1955, were widely covered in *Time* magazine and other U.S. media. In addition, the camera often focuses on foreign delegates at the conference, who are greeted with enthusiastic applause from the audience. At the end of *Still, It's Good to Live,* Kamei features an American of European descent visiting the Peace Museum who comments in English, "It is a shame that something like this had to happen." Kamei does not challenge the woman's understanding that the A-bombing was inevitable. It is enough for foreign (Western-bloc) audiences to have someone with whom to identify, someone who has made the journey to Hiroshima for them.

Finding a receptive American audience during the 1950s was no easy task, given the marginality of the antibomb movement in the United States. Literary critic Honda Shūgo described the perceived lack of understanding of Japan's Cold War dilemma:

> Many people in other countries have no idea why we feel compelled to back the antinuclear movement. For example, [if one mentioned radioactive *maguro* (tuna)] people in other countries had no idea what kind of fish *maguro* was. They even asked whether it was a fish that Japanese eat a lot and how we cook it. [My friend who had traveled in the West] was asked about the number of deaths resulting from the Bikini test. [Crew member] Kuboyama was still alive at that point, so his answer was none. They also asked my friend, "So what have Japanese people done to oppose the H-bomb?" He told them that the Diet had passed a resolution, and they wanted to know what else the Japanese had done. Even after my friend explained that local governments had issued antinuclear resolutions, too, and that there had been an enormous petition drive, they still weren't satisfied.[56]

Honda's story reveals as much about the challenge of finding a language and set of images in common with audiences in other countries as about the extent of sympathy for the antibomb movement.

The boom in antinuclear activism in Japan after Test Bravo was linked to the media and the movement's skillful manipulation of a set of familiar images: foods that most people eat regularly and the bodies of ordinary people, all contaminated by radioactive fallout. Newspapers and newsreels repeatedly showed pictures of radiated tuna that made Geiger counters click, *Lucky Dragon* crew member Kuboyama Ai in his hospital bed, and his weeping elderly mother, wife, and small daughters. The lack of empathy by the foreigner in Honda's story reminds us that this particular cluster of images, as basic as they may seem, resonated with

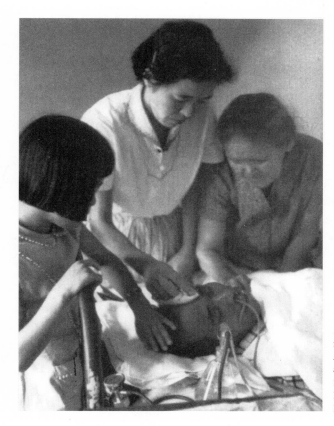

Lucky Dragon crew member Kuboyama Ai and his family at a Tokyo hospital, 1954. (Courtesy of Daigo Fukuryūmaru Foundation)

Japanese audiences in ways that it likely would not have in other cultural contexts. It also highlights the Japanese media's and the movement's success in molding a certain understanding by Japanese audiences of what constituted the dangers of fallout. Under the gaze of an approving Japanese government, the media mobilized citizens by emphasizing the personal, individual risks caused by the fallout, although the larger economic cost could have been highlighted as well. In fact, the fishing and shipping industries, food establishments, and the transport system suffered huge financial losses.[57] Contemporary American audiences had similar concerns: strontium 90 in milk and bomb shelters. The antinuclear movement took advantage of the public's self-interest.

In order to reach a broad international audience with Gensuikyō's test-ban message, Kamei could not rely solely on the local discourse. His five antinuclear documentaries thus show him trying to find a common ground between Japanese and international (especially Western-bloc) au-

diences. Soviet and Chinese audiences could look to their own government for antinuclear texts and images.

Kamei Fumio, Radiation, and the Secrecy
of the Nuclear Complex

As demonstrated in Dresden, Osaka, and dozens of other cities, conventional ordinance was capable of causing destruction comparable to that
of atomic bombs, although it required a far greater commitment of time,
equipment, and men. What distinguished the atomic bomb was its massive release of radioactive rays into the atmosphere, which resulted from
its core of radioactive materials such as uranium and plutonium. Radioactivity can travel through concrete and steel, flesh and bones, stealthily
without being seen or felt. High levels of radiation destroy healthy tissue,
and even low levels over extended periods can wreak havoc on the human
body. It was precisely this toxic aspect of the device that possessor countries were unwilling or unable to acknowledge and that the United States
and the Soviet Union tried the hardest to hide.

When Kamei Fumio made *The World Is Terrified*, the difficulty inherent in using a visual medium to communicate the dangers of invisible radioactivity was only one of his challenges. Despite Japan's alleged nuclear
allergy, Kamei turned out to be one of the handful of prominent cultural
figures who worked with extraordinary energy during the 1950s to bring
attention to the complex implications of the nuclear arms race. Doubtless, the "political terror" of the Cold War contributed to the reluctance of
many to protest openly and to educate the public.[58]

Kamei was a progressive filmmaker at the height of the United States's
and Japan's anticommunist project. He also was a Marxist during an era
when anti-Stalinism, factionalism, and Sino-Soviet tensions gave rise to
tremendous discord among the Japan Communist Party, the Japan Socialist Party, and their members. He wanted his films to reach the broadest possible audience. What assumptions might he have made about his
audiences' political commitments, their imaginations of the bomb, and
their knowledge of its radioactivity?

The media's continuing revelations about Hiroshima, Nagasaki, and
bomb testing, as well as popular cultural representations of the bomb,
were integral to what general readers and viewers might have known and
understood about nuclear weapons and peace at the height of the Cold

War. Audiences had seen the well-known August 1952 issue of *Asahi Graph,* purported to be the first mass-circulation publication to show the devastation of Hiroshima and Nagasaki.[59] Many had seen the Marukis' monochrome A-bomb paintings of hellish scenes centering on the injured, suffering people of Hiroshima and Nagasaki, and the movie *Godzilla* (*Gojira,* 1954) included the flash (*pika*) of the nuclear test that awoke the monster.

Audiences around the world were genuinely alarmed at what seemed like the real possibility of impending nuclear war. And the public had good reason to fear: they heard the radio reports and read in the newspapers about the United States's cavalier threats to use big bombs, subsequent diplomatic failures to ban nuclear weapons, and the naïve and dangerous atmospheric testing of increasingly powerful devices by all members of the new nuclear club. During this period of flux in the Cold War, cultural figures and the private sector became extremely active in bomb-related events and research, a level of widespread cultural and social involvement not seen since.

Kamei's cinematic intervention into the scientific debate over radiation or, rather, his insistent reintroduction of scientific and empirical perspectives into the raging popular discourse about nuclear weapons came not long after the public in Japan had been slapped in the face with the dangers of radioactive fallout. This happened in the wake of the U.S. thermonuclear bomb test Bravo. The explosion of a thermonuclear device of unprecedented proportions in March 1954 attracted extensive media coverage initially because the Japanese fishing boat *Lucky Dragon Number Five* (*Daigo Fukuryūmaru*) was exposed to extensive fallout in the South Pacific, resulting in radiation disease in the entire crew and, in September, the death of one of them, Kuboyama Ai.

Many cultural histories of Japan suggest that Occupation-period censorship had kept the Japanese public completely ignorant of the atomic bomb and nuclear technology. The *Asahi Graph's* (circulation 70,000) publication of photographs of Hiroshima and Nagasaki in 1952, followed by the *Lucky Dragon* incident two years later, are often cited as the extent of the public's exposure to nuclear news.

In fact, the Japanese public was not completely in the dark about the science of the atom. Science enjoyed considerable status in culture and the media during these decades. The cultural emphasis on science was manifested in several ways. Some leaders attributed the American victory in the war partly to its scientific strengths and, conversely, Japan's defeat to its lack of scientific advancement.[60] The press made celebrities of physicists such as Albert Einstein, Pierre and Irène Joliet-Curie, Robert Oppenheimer, and Nobel Prize winner Yukawa Hideki. In contrast to its strict censorship of texts and images concerning the atomic bombs that the United States dropped in 1945, the Allied Occupation encouraged publicity of future positive applications of nuclear technology, such as medical uses and power generation. Even after the Occupation ended, the mainstream media (often encouraged by state agendas) continued to offer the Japanese reading public the utopian promise of nuclear technology. This was a topic frequently featured in the U.S. and Soviet media as well. Japan's first test reactor began operating in 1955.[61]

Under the pressure of international diplomacy during the Cold War, the complex technology of weaponry changed constantly and rapidly during the 1950s. In their daily newspaper, readers learned about atmospheric tests of increasing enormous and destructive types of bombs, about radioactive fallout, and about the evolution of delivery systems that could launch missiles across oceans.

During the 1950s, the cultural, scientific, and diplomatic discourses on the bomb were in their formative stages and had not yet become the exclusive purview of a small group of nuclear strategists and experts whose mind-set and language excluded outsiders. This close link between knowledge and power was embodied in Dwight D. Eisenhower, who began his presidential term in 1953 "with a more thorough knowledge of nuclear weapons than any president before or since" because of his military and National Security Council experience during the bomb's formative years.[62] Conversely, the careers of physicists such as Oppenheimer and Pierre Joliet-Curie, both pioneers in nuclear physics but later excluded from the nuclear establishment because of their political convictions, illustrate the fragile hold that even scientists had on the course of the atomic age.

Other than a general acquaintance with nuclear technologies, what knowledge about radioactivity might Japanese audiences have brought to Kamei's atomic documentaries? The mass media's emphasis on Japan's three major nuclear events—Hiroshima, Nagasaki, and Bikini—suggests a widespread understanding of the reasons that nuclear weapons were said to constitute a threat to life on earth. Indeed, by 1957, Japanese audiences knew the terms radioactivity (hōshanō) and radiation/radioactive rays (hōshasen) and had seen many images of the Geiger counter. Scientists like Dr. Kusano Nobuo singled out high-level radioactivity as the quality that set the A-bomb apart from conventional weapons.

A passing acquaintance with relevant terms and the machines mea-suring levels of radiation, however, is not the same as understanding the workings of radioactivity. Indeed, the very characteristics of radioactive rays, such as invisibility, discourage easy understanding. Furthermore, the damage done by other types of energy released by nuclear weapons is easily conflated with the harmful effects of radiation. Considering that at the time American "scientists did not know the answers to many impor-tant questions about the health effects of low-level exposure" to radiation, it is hardly surprising that general viewers had only a superficial under-standing of the invisible rays that made the Geiger counters tick.[63] Ac-cording to Samuel Walker, although the scientific community had been aware since the early twentieth century of the dangers of overexposure to radiation, "empirical evidence was sparse" regarding the low-level radia-tion in known substances such as X-rays and radium. Because the nuclear fission used in weapons "created many radioactive isotopes that did not exist in nature," scientists and medical personnel after Hiroshima "had to consider the potential hazards of new radioactive substances about which even less was known."[64]

Governments had secrets to keep, but they themselves were also ac-quiring what must be called basic knowledge about the effects of radia-tion on the human body and the environment. The controversial Atomic Bomb Casualty Commission was the most obvious instance of state-sponsored information gathering. Such large-scale research was neces-sary, it must be remembered, because Hiroshima and Nagasaki were the very first large-scale nuclear events that had significant health effects on a large population of people. In other words, scientists themselves in 1945 did not have a sophisticated understanding of the effects of massive doses of radiation on the human body. Before this time, the only observed in-stances of radiation sickness had been scientists and researchers, such as Marie and Pierre Curie, the Manhattan Project staff, and factory workers who worked extensively with uranium and other radioactive materials, but usually at low levels of exposure. Doses of radioactivity not only are invisi-ble but also can destroy the human body from the inside at a microscopic level. It therefore was in the best interest of the U.S. and Soviet govern-ments, locked in an arms race, to keep such information under wraps as it slowly emerged. Politics dominated the dissemination of knowledge about radiation.[65]

Although people around the world feared nuclear weapons as a de-structive force, the most common descriptions of the bomb employed metaphors associated with large-scale natural phenomena (Ōe's floods, the sun exploding), wrathful deities (Oppenheimer's reference to Shiva and the *Bhagavad Gita*), or monsters (Godzilla), rather than rational, scientific description. Thus audiences in the 1950s had little scientific understanding of the ways that this type of energy might affect life on earth.

Not one single method can convey the significance and threat of a scientific and cultural phenomenon as complex as nuclear weapons. Yet precisely because the Cold War discourse on the bomb was riddled with alarmist, anxiety-provoking rhetoric and secrecy, Kamei sought to arm his viewers with at least some of the knowledge that gave scientists, the ABCC, and governments such great power. Indeed, the publicists for Kamei's *World Is Terrified* posed the question: "What will we find when we pull back the veils that cloak the secrets of radioactivity [*hōshanō no himitsu*]?"[66]

Suppression of the Atomic Secret

The association of the bomb with secrets and secrecy encompassed much more than the mysteries of the invisible rays and atomic structure. The massive Manhattan Project, which was said to have unleashed the secrets of the universe itself, had remarkably been kept a huge secret—despite the enormous mobilization of workers, federal funds, and industrial resources—from both the American public and the United States's wartime allies, including the Soviet Union. During the 1950s, Japanese newspapers and magazines covered in detail the trials and executions of Julius and Ethel Rosenberg, who had been accused of spying—that is, revealing atomic secrets to the Soviet Union.[67] In contrast to the efforts of doctors and scientists like Kusano Nobuo and of antinuclear activists to make the public aware of the dangers unique to nuclear weapons, the official discourse concerning atomic and hydrogen bombs depended on keeping secret the knowledge of radioactivity. Among members of the nuclear club, this active denial continued for more than a decade after August 1945. We can clearly discern the government's pattern of suppression of information, which took the form of initial denial of the radioactive damage by a nuclear event, followed by a begrudging admission to most major nuclear events, including Hiroshima and Nagasaki, Test Bravo, and Chelyabinsk.[68]

An atomic device was first detonated during the top-secret Manhattan Project in July 1945, and Hiroshima was the first event revealed to the public. The active suppression of facts concerning radioactivity, then, started immediately after the August 1945 bombings. When British journalist Wilfred Burchett reported on the radiation sickness he had seen in Hiroshima, the U.S. military initially denied the negative effects of residual radiation.[69] This denial may have been based partly on ignorance, for the officers making the statement had not set foot in Hiroshima or Nagasaki. But even after scientific and medical evidence of radiation disease and death became available, the two largest possessor nations (the United States and the Soviet Union) continued to downplay the danger. After all, governments had invested huge amounts of money and faith in "the paramount instrument of victory," as Senator Brien McMahon (D-Conn.) optimistically called nuclear arms. It was in their interest to keep the weapons' reputation clean.

Secrecy about nuclear weapons and the hazards of radiation arose partly from the controversy over the bomb's ethical dimensions and partly for security and strategic reasons. Challenges to the morality of nuclear weapons had appeared as early as August 1945. Upon hearing the news of the atomic bombings, Bertrand Russell summed up the dilemma inherent in the bomb's development: "It is impossible to imagine a more dramatic and horrifying combination of scientific triumph with political and moral failure than has been shown to the world in the destruction of Hiroshima."[70]

With the U.S. government's desire to maintain a monopoly on atomic weapons for as long as possible, it is not surprising that secrecy remained top priority. After 1949, with the confirmation of the Soviets' possession, however, the reasons for keeping secrets about the bomb seemed to have disappeared, yet this was clearly not the case. In the aftermath of the Rosenbergs' atomic espionage trial, even the mainstream American media continued to justify the government's aim of secrecy. The *Chicago Daily News,* for example, editorialized that U.S. efforts to maintain confidentiality about the hydrogen bomb had been "foiled" by revelations in the Japanese press and Japanese scientific community concerning H-bomb tests in the South Pacific after the Bikini incident.[71] Even so, during the 1950s, Japanese scientists tended to defer to the United States in the interpretation and release of its findings about the effects of radiation.

In order to justify the escalating arms race and to quell questions about the morality of the Hiroshima and Nagasaki bombings, the United States and the Soviet Union therefore found it necessary to pull a veil of secrecy over the realities of radiation. Numerous incidents of public denial and cover-ups of dangerous radioactive release continued among the nuclear nations through the 1980s.

The American government, among others, did not want to admit to the public that its nuclear weapons were anything but very destructive versions of the same big old bombs they had been employing all along. For example, in 1954, when the crew of the *Lucky Dragon* fishing boat showed signs of radiation poisoning following Test Bravo, the United States made light of Japanese complaints and claimed that fallout from the mammoth test could not possibly have affected a boat so far away. Members of Congress even labeled the *Lucky Dragon* a communist spy boat that spouted spurious lies.[72] But when photos and medical reports of the crew circulated, the United States eventually backed down and agreed to compensate the victims.

The extensive American civil defense campaigns during the 1950s and 1960s similarly understated the dangers of radiation by suggesting to mass audiences that one could fend off the deadly effects by simple measures, such as keeping windows and curtains closed. In 1959, the quintessential Cold Warrior Edward Teller and other scientists involved in a proposed atomic earth-moving project in Alaska denied that nuclear blasts would result in significant amounts of radioactive pollution in the environment.[73] In the United States, as well, cavalier attitudes toward radioactivity and the lack of safety culture resulted in extensive radioactive pollution in the land and water around the nuclear production facilities at Hanford, Washington, as well as in the near misses at the Three Mile Island plant in Pennsylvania in 1979 and at the Davis-Besse plant in Ohio in 1998.[74] Similarly, in the Soviet Union, storage facilities and reactors built with seemingly no awareness of the potential dangers of chain reactions and high-level releases of radiation led to extensive environmental pollution and to catastrophic accidents such as the long hushed-up explosion at Chelyabinsk near the Ural Mountains in 1957 and the better-known Chernobyl disaster in 1986.

Fire-Breathing Monster: The Bomb in Popular Culture

Popular culture tended to mystify, rather than clarify, the danger of nuclear weapons. In the absence of an extensive government civil defense campaign like that in the America, popular culture and the press in Japan played even larger roles in molding public images and understandings of the bomb. Even in the classic movie *Godzilla*, doubtless the most famous Cold War Japanese film, a Japanese fishing boat is sailing across the calm waters of the Pacific when suddenly a brilliant flash of light and violent winds appear to sink the vessel. The powerful explosion angers Godzilla, a giant fire-breathing creature that rises from the depths of the ocean and rampages through Tokyo. Inspired in part by the *Lucky Dragon* incident, *Godzilla* is full of Geiger counters clicking away and expressions of alarm about the dangers of testing hydrogen bombs.[75] Yet, even though Dr. Serizawa and Dr. Yamane repeatedly tell the audience that radioactivity threatens life on earth, we see no evidence of its harmful force. The only types of destructive energy shown in the film are the shock blast from the test at the beginning of the movie and the trampling and crunching of the fire-breathing monster Godzilla.

In *Godzilla*, then, scientists promote the dissemination of knowledge about nuclear weapons in only the most general terms. Through a combination of the scientific acumen and self-sacrifice of the brilliant Dr. Serizawa, the soothing tones of a children's choir that sings of mourning and peace, rituals in rural villages, and the crowd-controlling savvy of Japan's nascent Self-Defense Forces, humans ultimately triumph over the destructive monster and, by extension, nuclear weapons. Even more than other films of its genre featuring atomic creatures, huge or mutant, *Godzilla's* ability to quell anxiety about nuclear weapons contributed to the film's huge popularity both at home and abroad. Nonetheless, knowing about a dubious device such as Dr. Serizawa's oxygen destroyer did not arm the viewer with the type of knowledge necessary for understanding thermonuclear weapons' dire threat to the earth.

As discussed in chapter 1, another prominent mid-1950s film representation of nuclear anxiety is Kurosawa Akira's controversial *Record of a Living Being* (*Ikimono no kiroku*, 1955). Following in the wake of the *Lucky Dragon* incident, the movie dwells on Cold War concerns and nuclear fears strictly on familial and psychological levels. Kurosawa's protagonist, an industrialist obsessed with nuclear war, plans to find refuge from radioactive weapons and fallout by moving his entire extended family to South America. In contrast to Kamei, though, Kurosawa never hints at the existence of an antinuclear movement, nor does he valorize knowledge as ameliorative.

The Science Film: Knowledge as Power

Since 1945, the testimonies of those who experienced the Hiroshima and Nagasaki bombings have come to constitute one valuable type of knowledge. Owing to the ethical authority of testimonial as a genre, these narratives have frequently been employed for ideological purposes, including the creation of a conservative discourse of Japan-as-righteous-victim and the old leftist narrative of the people's struggle against capitalism. The prominence of *hibakusha* in Kamei Fumio's first nuclear film, *Still, It's Good to Live*, suggests that the director valorized the experiential narrative. However, in his other four films he decenters the *hibakusha* and instead calls his audience's attention to the science of radioactive rays or to the antinuclear movement. These focuses contrast greatly with popular cultural images seen in *Godzilla* or *Record of a Living Being* and suggest the widespread concerns expressed in the journalistic media.

By making *The World Is Terrified*, therefore, Kamei created a means by which his audience could acquire another type of knowledge about nuclear weapons: scientific knowledge. In defiance of the United States's and the Soviet Union's aim of discouraging this type of learning, reviewers of Kamei's film pleaded that the documentary "must be seen widely." A Tokyo University professor affirmed that because of its emphasis on science, *The World Is Terrified* presented the "reality" (*jijitsu*) of nuclear weapons, which must be made accessible to the layperson. Everyone in Japan had read about or seen images of the so-called ashes of death (*shi no hai*), but who knew much beyond those buzzwords and stock images? The reviews vividly suggest the dynamics of the public discourse on testing. Photographer Kimura Ihei praised Kamei's film for its accessible explanations of "things we worry about on a daily basis," such as high radiation levels in water and the food chain.[76] Antinuclear activist Shimizu Keiko dates the awareness of the "ashes of death" to Test Bravo and the Bikini incident. It was then that people began to "fear the rain, stopped buying tuna, and became neurotic about milk and [vegetables that we eat regularly such as] spinach."

The Bikini incident of March 1, 1954, dominated the newspapers and newsreels that year, first with coverage of the injured crew and the Japanese–U.S. negotiations over compensation and, finally, in the autumn, with the death of crewman Kuboyama Ai. Newsreels, the radio, and newspapers, which were at the time the most common sources of news for the majority of people, frequently showed or narrated scenes of

Murakami Yoshio, *A-Bomb Tuna*, woodblock print (1955): (*left*) "Fish Shop: Tuna Sold Here Not Radioactive" and (*right*) "Tuna Demands 'No More Nukes!'" (Courtesy of Daigo Fukuryūmaru Foundation)

scientists passing a Geiger counter wand over the exposed crew members' bodies. The cameras also show scientists waving their equipment over the so-called A-bomb tuna (*genbaku maguro*), which had to be buried in deep pits because of toxic levels of radioactivity. In addition to the telltale click of the Geiger counter, the swollen, raw faces, necks, and hands of the *Lucky Dragon* crew members became familiar images in the media. In the case of radiation disease, however, external wounds are not the cause of death and illness but merely symptoms of damage deeper in the body. As Susan Lindee wrote, exposure to high doses of radiation resulted in "the slow and invisible pathologies of those bodies over the decades."[77]

In the aftermath of the *Lucky Dragon* incident, viewing audiences also heard of the research efforts of Japanese scientists to bring to light the effects of strontium 90 and other radioactive substances in the atmosphere, food supply, and water. The media also extensively covered the research efforts of the crew of a boat called the *Shunkotsumaru* as it sailed the Pacific and measured levels of radioactivity in ocean animals and plants.

This research helped alert the public to the widespread contamination of food and drinking water supply by radioactive fallout. During the mid-1950s, literally millions of people from all walks of life signed antinuclear petitions, although the groundswell of opposition was soon followed by a widespread attitude of resignation. Shimizu Keiko summed up the public's attitudes:

Over the past six years, the superpowers have detonated more than one hundred nuclear bombs. . . . Every single day, the newspapers contain one frightening article after another about radiation: "Cesium Detected in Powdered Milk," "Cesium in Rice Too," "Levels of Strontium in Air Rising." After this barrage of terrifying stories, one becomes psychologically numb to the danger. We all know that the "ashes of death" are a threat to human beings, yet the negative effects do not appear immediately. . . . The United States, England, and the Soviet Union always try to convince us they are doing all they can to protect us from those dangers.[78]

Even before Test Bravo, writer Hara Tamiki, among others, took note of the Occupation's use of the "Three S's" (sports, sex, and speed) for the purpose of mollifying and distracting an alarmed public from politics and the arms race. For a moment, though, it seemed that the United States and the Soviet Union had lost control over Cold War propaganda owing to the unforeseen outcomes of the massive H-bomb tests. Indeed, these cracks and inconsistencies in propaganda about the bomb created spaces for the antibomb movement to have its message heard.

The dangers of fallout seemed immediate and pressing, but they also were abstract. Even though the threat loomed in the rain and the food supply, people did not become ill immediately because of the relatively low levels of radiation. Luckily for the nuclear nations, news reports of the increasing levels of dangerous fallout (the unintended consequence of testing) were sufficiently abstract that the public at first had little reason to challenge the absurd claims of safety. Nuclear domination and the deterrence regime depended on the coexistence of two things: the intimidation of the public through relentless reminders of the threat of nuclear war and ensuing apocalypse, and the abstractness and invisibility of radioactivity. In this ideological context, Kamei's film *The World Is Terrified* not only had a didactic function, but it also encouraged activism by the many people who "did not know the facts [about radioactivity] in the first place, who had chosen to ignore the realities of fallout, or who had simply grown accustomed to living with the terrifying reality" of the Cold War.[79]

Many contemporary reviewers of Kamei's radiation film found his choice of topic and approach convincing and the treatment compelling. In contrast to his overtly antinuclear films, the scientific topic of this documentary suggested a nonaligned political stance. Conversely, Kamei's approach communicated subtle yet clear ideological underpinnings. Historian Matsushima Eiichi viewed the film's presentation of data about radiation (and particularly Tokugawa Musei's voiceover narration) as far more convincing than the scenes of antinuclear protest in the streets.

Since it was Kamei who produced the only documentary film about the antinuclear movement to date, Matsushima was not necessarily rejecting political activism. Rather, he was affirming the urgent need to disseminate scientific knowledge about the effects of radiation on the body.

Kamei commented on the restraint he had exercised when expressing an ideological message in *The World Is Terrified:*

> I could have urged a political solution to the threat of nuclear weapons by showing scenes of antibomb petition drives or the annual peace conferences or the testimonials of the *hibakusha*. But I consciously chose not to include shots [of antinuclear activism]. I had the sense that a gap has developed between the lives of the people and politics. I believe that an issue affecting people everywhere cannot be resolved exclusively through the political [system].[80]

In order for Kamei to engage in scientific discourse, he felt he had to exclude overt references to politics, whether that be the ambiguous stance of the state or the straightforward yet divided Left.

Domesticating Science

What Cold War battle was Kamei Fumio fighting in *The World Is Terrified?* One of his aims was establishing an oppositional Japanese scientific point of view distinct from the hegemonic American or Soviet perspective. This stance, furthermore, differed from the attitude of many in the Japanese scientific community who were cooperating with the dominant U.S. agenda. The origins of Kamei's awareness of the scientific gaze that views the *hibakusha* as guinea pigs necessary for the project of developing nuclear weapons can be found in his *Still, It's Good to Live*. For some of his own portraits of the *hibakusha*, Kamei borrowed or cannibalized images from the documentary *The Effects of the Atomic Bomb on Hiroshima and Nagasaki (Genshi bakudan no kōka: Hiroshima-Nagasaki, 1946)* in order to show the bodies of the injured soon after the bombing.[81] Although shot by Japanese filmmakers, the documentary imposed an "explicit point of view" through both the introduction of scientists and physicians who examine the *hibakusha* and the city and the use of a narrator who speaks for the foreign scientists "in the strange, unnervingly technical language of specialists." Abé Mark Nornes remarked on the positioning of "the epicenter as the ultimate reference point" in the 1946 film. A decade later, Kamei borrowed clips of that same film to introduce the perspective of the bombed, the *hibakusha*, in *Still, It's Good to Live*.[82]

In 1957, with the Occupation long over and nuclear testing a part of daily life, Kamei made an entire film from the point of view of the Japanese scientists. Kamei's predecessors had been commissioned by the Allied Occupation forces to document the aftermath of the Hiroshima and Nagasaki bombings. The "mug shots" of the injured and dying would become data for the U.S. military about the impact of their new weapons. The stance of cold objectivity in *The Effects of the Atomic Bomb* paralleled the outlook of the ABCC, which examined the *hibakusha* but did not provide medical treatment for them. Despite its attitude of authority, the U.S. government had no prior experience in treating large numbers of patients with radiation sickness. So as part of the Occupation, many scientists and medical personnel, Japanese and foreign, were swept up in this American research project.

In contrast, Kamei's mid-1950s film features Japanese scientists who were deeply troubled by the moral questions surrounding the ABCC and subsequently motivated by the alarming effects of thermonuclear tests. These men and women were engaged in research on the effects of radiation on animals and humans, the food chain, the earth, the atmosphere, and bodies of water. Their activities, however, did not represent the attitudes of the entire Japanese scientific community.

Despite its scary title and the sensationalist approach to publicity, *The World Is Terrified* is not a horror movie per se. Rather, it belongs to the longstanding genre of science film (*kagaku eiga*), which makes "the direct, scientific representation of reality an uncompromising value."[83] *The Effects of the Atomic Bomb* also belongs to this genre. Yet Kamei himself had a keen awareness of the subjectivity even of documentary and science films.[84]

Although he observes many conventions of the science film, Kamei's subjectivity manifests itself in a variety of ways throughout the film. Several times, the narrator subtly editorializes in the film. In addition, the director's confidence that the viewers will be interested in genetics and radioactivity communicates an attitude of respect for his audience's intelligence. Another manifestation of subjectivity comes through in the film's positive presentation of the Japanese scientists who devote themselves to researching radioactivity, despite the lack of funding.

Only at the very end of *The World Is Terrified* does Kamei directly state his own stance. Distinguished from the rest of the film by the handwritten title "Author's Note" and the voice-over narrator, this statement by Kamei reads as follows: nuclear weapons are not natural phenomena, and therefore we humans possess the ability to abolish them "if only we put our minds to it [*sono ki ni sae nareba*]." This seemingly innocuous statement caused considerable controversy at the time. For nuclear advocates, the idea of abolishing nuclear weapons was a pipe dream and, even more heinously, constituted a stance critical of the United States or the Soviet Union, committed as both nations were to a world order based on nuclear might and domination. For those on the Left, Kamei's words failed to identify the enemies of peace (that is, either the United States or all possessor nations, depending on one's party loyalties). Kamei's own explanation for including this statement is revealing: "This film shows in detail the dangerous contamination by the ashes of death [that we all face], and this might make timid people [*ki no yowaii hito*] neurotic. I worried that the film [without the "Author's Note"] might cause people to give up or contribute to a loss of confidence among people in the antibomb movement, such as those in the petition drives."[85] Typically in tune with his times, Kamei reveals here more than just a solicitous attitude toward his audience. He also reminds us that Cold War ideology depended precisely on nuclear nihilism and emotions of fear and powerlessness about the existence of the nuclear world order.

Kamei and his crew made every effort to produce a science documentary that would not intimidate or alienate the audience. They worked to lower the viewer's affective filter by several means, one of which was sound. Kamei made the strategic choice of the former *benshi* (silent film narrator) Tokugawa Musei for the voice-over narration. Because the screenplay consists largely of descriptions of scientific procedures and findings, it could easily have been either intimidating or deadly boring, and the rapid rhythms of an anonymous newsreel announcer's speech would only have increased the audience's anxiety about the alarming news of the "ashes of death." To viewers accustomed to such urgent, staccato types of narration common in 1950s newsreels and science films, Tokugawa's calm voice had the effect of narrowing the gap between daily life and the scientific laboratory. Kamei clearly wanted to maintain the calm of the audience in order to prepare them for the task of acquiring a detailed understanding of the invisible threat. His sparing use of ominous orchestral music creates an atmosphere of foreboding, not panic. The loud ticking of clocks that mark the time elapsed between exposure to radiation and death in animal experiments also serves as a reminder of the doomsday clock, which indicated with its second hand the world's proximity to nuclear war.[86]

Given the legacy of the ABCC, Kamei also had the challenge of making the work of scientists palatable to a general audience. He knew that his audience could easily be intimidated by the abundance of shots of graphs, charts, robotic arms, equipment, and researchers in white lab coats and protective gear. Yet Kamei evokes a sense of admiration for the dedicated scientists whose mission is to tear away the veil of secrecy over radiation. Kamei shows us researchers carrying out various types of studies: from high-tech laboratories with thick walls and "magic hands" to poorly funded sites that must use recycled materials in order to gather data. Kamei portrays the scientists as nonthreatening by showing them conducting experiments with animal subjects (rather than human) or gathering data about the soil, air, and water. When he does include shots of human fetuses deformed by exposure in utero or of *hibakusha,* we never see scientists in proximity.

Because of the Cold War's political climate, it took courage for the scientists to appear in Kamei's documentary, as many in the scientific community had downplayed the unique dangers of the bomb and especially of radiation, "out of deference to the U.S."[87] It also would have been easy for Kamei and the scientists to succumb to nuclear nihilism, especially in light of the political "terror" conspicuous in the Cold War. Thermonuclear weapons could destroy the world many times over. No one would survive, so why worry about genetics? *The World Is Terrified* was Kamei's way of creating knowledge: "Even if we are powerless, it is better at least to be aware."[88]

Spreading Knowledge

Kamei Fumio was also fascinated by the processes by which knowledge is shared and moves. The World Conference documentaries communicate the spread of ideological and moral understandings of nuclear arms from Hiroshima to other cities in Japan and from Japan to the world as delegates from other countries join in the meetings and peace marches. Similarly, in *The World Is Terrified,* Kamei focuses on place and movement in order to highlight the spread of knowledge about radiation throughout the country.

Kamei and his crew move from the laboratory of one Japanese scientist to another, from rural locations to research sites in the city. At one point he takes us from Tokyo to a Hiroshima hospital. For the most part, how-ever, the viewer sees numerous other locations: urban and rural, earth and atmosphere, land and sea, rooftops and city streets, a park near the Impe-rial Palace, and ordinary village roads all over Japan. Remarkably, Kamei dethrones Hiroshima and Nagasaki as the main sites of nuclear contami-nation. In other words, the sanctified journey to Hiroshima and Nagasaki, the cities of peace, does not constitute the core of the documentary.

By deemphasizing the 1945 bombing sites, moreover, the film encour-ages the viewer to conceive of radioactivity separately from wartime his-tory. In that sense, *The World Is Terrified* might be described as a science film about massive environmental pollution. Or it may be best seen as one of the quintessential films of the Cold War, a documentary concern-ing a battle fought with propaganda, secrecy, deterrence, and terror, in which the entire earth and the molecules of living creatures are made into battlefields.

The director employed several structural techniques in order to make difficult material more palatable to the audience. The intertitles introduc-ing the subsections of *The World Is Terrified* offer broad, immediate cate-gories such as "The Joy of Life" and "Destruction of Life." They also high-light all the sites of daily life affected by the fallout: Food; Living Creatures (Ingestion, Inhalation), Medical Issues, Birth, Children, Blood, Air, the Earth. The start date for this contamination was an event in everyone's recent memory: the March 1954 Bikini incident.

Kamei draws in the audience by delaying the gruesome visual evidence of the harm of radiation on the human body until more than halfway through the film. Near the beginning and the end of *The World Is Terri-fied*, we see, at close range, two easily understood scientific experiments. Although they vividly demonstrate the dangers of high doses of radioac-tivity, the experiments would be only mildly upsetting to most viewers because the subjects are small animals and the cause of death is invisible. The earlier montage presents two birds in a cage who have been exposed to a high dose of radiation. As the narrator counts the passing minutes, "Nine, ten, eleven . . . ," the birds struggle and then, at the twelve-minute mark, die. The narrator then offers the brief comment, "This is radia-tion." Similarly, near the end of the film, the finder focuses on a mouse that has been zapped with radiation as it writhes in pain and then dies. The camera lingers on the motionless body of the mouse, and the voice-over narrator notes soberly, "The mouse is dead." As filmmaker Honma Naoya commented,

There were people who claimed that it wasn't necessary for the narrator to say that the mouse is dead, because the visuals showed you that already. They criticized this voice-over as a violation of the basic tenants of film. It would have been more effective to play peaceful music with the image of the dead mouse and leave it up to the viewer's emotions. At the time I agreed with these criticisms, but now I see that it was typical Kamei. It was his way of forcing the viewers to think about the problems [of fallout].[89]

Yet Kamei does not stop at such obvious examples of harmful radiation, examples that, presented in isolation, might give rise to skepticism. Who is to say that it was radioactivity that killed the birds and the mouse? The audience cannot see the radioactivity but instead must trust the scientific devices designed to detect radioactivity: the ubiquitous click of the Geiger counter, the streaks of light on a screen that measures the rays. The camera lingers as it peers through a microscope focused on cancerous cells taken from a *hibakusha*. The microscope shows us the wonders of birth as tiny fish burst forth from eggs, but we also see creatures deformed by high doses of radiation. A diagram illustrates the effects of radioactivity on the chromosomes of multiple generations of flies and fish.

Kamei strategically juxtaposes the scientific studies with well-known cultural references and shots of daily life in order to make the scientific findings seem more familiar to the audience. For example, one sequence commences with a close-up of a two-headed creature, which turns out to be a newborn fish deformed by radiation, and then cuts to a shot of a H-bomb mushroom cloud, followed by a glimpse of a painting of a pregnant woman, recognizable to the audience as a detail from an A-bomb panel by Maruki Toshi and Maruki Iri. As a way of linking the fish with human beings, the narrator comments, "This is reminiscent of the hell scenes depicted in the Marukis' A-bomb paintings." As mournful orchestral music plays, the film shifts to a shot of another two-headed creature, which the narrator announces is not a fish, as was the mutant creature in the opening shot, but a human.

In a similar manner, Kamei juxtaposes a medium shot of healthy children playing happily outdoors with the extremely disturbing shots of deformed fetuses in jars of formaldehyde (some provided by doctors in Nagasaki, others from Hiroshima, and even some data provided by the ABCC). Interspersed between these alarming images, we briefly see the image of the cenotaph at the Hiroshima Peace Park. The narrator reads the inscription "May they rest in peace. The mistake will not be repeated" and then comments, "Indeed, we too are compelled to say this same prayer [*Mattaku soo inorazu ni wa irarenai kimochi desu*]." In other words, the visual shock of these scenes encourages Cold War viewers to find new meaning for the Hiroshima prayer. Rather than the images of injured bodies and dripping flesh made familiar by the Marukis' panels and the *hibakusha* testimonials from wartime, we see the surprising and nightmarish effects of radioactive fallout from H-bomb testing. These are new images that even the Cold War warriors may never have imagined and would certainly want to hide. This montage is followed by a long shot of a formaldehyde jar containing a radiation-ravaged fetus that rests on the podium of an otherwise empty lecture hall as Christian hymns swell in the background and then concludes with a long shot of the Genbaku Dome. The steel frame of the building destroyed in the 1945 bombing seems mundane in comparison to the mutant creatures produced by radiation.

Given the heightened anxieties about fallout and testing during the 1950s, one might expect that other filmmakers and authors might have made similar efforts to promote understanding of the cause of widespread fear and panic. But as it turns out, Kamei was one of the few cultural figures who at the time attempted an exposé of the unique dangers of the bomb. Before Kamei's documentaries, the handful of documentary films on the topic included the ABCC-commissioned *Effects of the Atomic Bomb on Hiroshima and Nagasaki,* and a short by Asahi News called *A-Bomb Nagasaki* (*Genbaku no Nagasaki*). There also were a few feature films on the A-bombing, including Shindō Kaneto's well-known *Children of the A-Bomb* (*Genbaku no ko*, 1952, also known as *Children of Hiroshima*), which was heavily promoted in the leftist press. Feature films included Kurosawa Akira's *Record of a Living Being* and, of course, *Godzilla*.[90] For an issue of widespread concern, the number of films is quite modest. Many political forces worked against investigating and disseminating knowledge about radiation.

Reception: Critics and Social Responsibility

For a documentary film, *The World Is Terrified* received a fair amount of attention in the press. True to form, Kamei Fumio had chosen a timely, well-publicized topic. In addition to the specialized—and often politically progressive—literary or film journals in which Kamei's work was usually reviewed, news and culture magazines targeted at a mass audience, including *Geijutsu shinchō* and *Chūō kōron*, presented prominent articles about *The World Is Terrified*. Kamei hoped for the broadest possible audience for his documentary and therefore tapped into the new and rapidly expanding genre of inexpensive weekly magazines like *Shūkan yomiuri* and *Heibon*. With coverage of *Still, It's Good to Live* in the mainstream mass media the year before, Kamei's documentaries started to gain a broader reputation among the general viewing public.

As the title of the film *The World Is Terrified* suggests, Kamei and company did not shrink from appealing to potential viewers' desire for entertainment. The publicity for the movie is downright sensationalist, describing the films as "erotic-grotesque-shocking" (*ero-guro-shokkingu no dokyumento*) and stating that "the film contains extremely shocking scenes. Pregnant women and children under twelve not admitted." The largely positive reviews by scholars, artists, critics, and scientists confirm the film's educational value. No one complained that the film's serious, objective approach did not live up to the sensationalist full-page ads that appeared in the press.[91]

Kamei viewed these postwar documentaries as instruments of social change. In his work about activism—both his acclaimed anti–military base Sunagawa films and the World Conference documentaries—Kamei sought to instill in his audiences a sense of admiration for the people and their political struggles in the new participatory democracy. In contrast, the director seemed less certain about the effect of *The World Is Terrified* on his newly broadened audiences. The incident that freed him from his concern that the film might cause his viewers to despair, rather than to learn, involved the mass-market magazine *Heibon* (the title means "ordinary" or even "mediocre"). Two young women, who were fans of *Heibon* and had recently been hired by the magazine, previewed *The World Is Terrified*. Rather than falling into despair, they both said that they had learned a great deal from the film and affirmed the director's conviction that everyone must know about the terrible effects of radiation. Hearing their response, Kamei regretted his own arrogance. Previously, he had seen himself as standing in a position of "bestowing" knowledge on others, and he modestly admitted that he had underestimated the "intelligence" of his viewers.[92]

Even though Kamei had taken care to exclude the rhetoric and style of the Left (influenced by socialist realism) from this science documentary, someone in high-up places did not take kindly to his attempt to educate the public about radioactivity. It was surely no coincidence that a scathing review of *The World Is Terrified* was printed in the evening edition of the national *Asahi* newspaper on the same day (November 12, 1957) that the film opened in Tokyo. A negative review had appeared in the local *Tokyo* newspaper on November 9.

That such a review in the national press could have a disastrous effect on the reception of a film was not lost on Ogura Mami, who took it upon herself to respond in detail to the *Asahi* review. Some of the *Asahi* writer's (whose pen name was Tetsu) criticisms were related to the clarity of explanation: Kamei does not offer an in-depth explanation of chromosomes or genetics, for example. Echoing the words of the scientist who wrote the *Tokyo* newspaper review, Tetsu also complained that the audience of *The World Is Terrified* would not come away with a clear understanding of permissible doses of radiation; in other words, how much radiation could the human body be exposed to before things would start to go wrong? Finally, the film did not explain the unit used to measure radioactivity, the micromicrocurie (*maikuro maikuro kyurii*). Ogura responded that Kamei's point was not to prescribe exact dosages or to give the audience an in-depth lesson on genetics but to alert people that exposure to excessive radiation could lead to genetic mutations in later generations.[93] Ogura also easily refuted the critic's complaints about film technique and editing.

The *Asahi* review had little to say about the fate of the small animals and fetuses that had been exposed to radiation. In *The World Is Terrified*, Kamei invokes the point of view of the scientist, and most of the action takes place in scientific laboratories and research sites. The director begins his study of the effects of radioactivity by showing scientists measuring levels of radiation in fallout and the water. He also includes experiments in which scientists expose birds and rabbits to massive dosages of radiation. The animals quickly develop tumors or die. We also peer through the microscope at genetically mutated fish and see disturbing shots of deformed fetuses.

The *Asahi* reviewer, however, did not complain about these disturbing images but instead focused on the inclusion of adult humans whose moral and physical world has or will be shaken by the A-bomb or fallout from H-bomb testing.[94] For example, Tetsu condemned as "too cruel" Kamei's portraits of parents of Hiroshima and Nagasaki children who were born with physical and mental handicaps. The critic's focus, however, reveals more about the common prejudice against the *hibakusha* that arose from a combination of ignorance about what ailed them and shame (or perhaps anger) at Hiroshima's and Nagasaki's symbolic role in Japan's defeat. It was well known that Kamei took great care to ask permission before he filmed or interviewed *hibakusha* and that he respected the wishes of those who declined his request. In contrast, shortly after the bombing, as part of its fact-finding mission, the ABCC commissioned still photos and films of *hibakusha* as they lay recovering or dying in hospital, but it did not ask permission.

It is little wonder, then, that Kamei had a difficult time finding people who would agree to be interviewed, much less expose their scars to the camera. One of Kamei's biographers described the process by which the filmmaker sought to earn the trust of potential interviewees:

> The *hibakusha* had been living as inconspicuously as possible, staying at home, out of public notice, so they wouldn't be seen by others. They had "closed up the doors of their hearts." So Kamei had to get them to open up and to agree to appear in front of the camera. Therefore, when he first visited them, he would leave the camera outside and just take in a tape recorder. He conducted more than fifteen hours of interviews. Eventually some *hibakusha* agreed to be filmed, perhaps having come to the understanding that Kamei and crew were sympathetic allies.[95]

Even after acquiescing to Kamei's request, however, some resisted the camera's gaze. When Kamei asked one interviewee to show the keloids on her face to the camera, she instead turned the unscarred side of her face to the lens.[96] Ogura commends the parents who had the "courage to appear in the film in order to speak out against nuclear weapons."[97]

Kamei deprived his potential detractors of the opportunity to challenge his ideological stance by purposely omitting overt political references and also by adopting the formal conventions of the science film. Given that, the *Asahi* reviewer attempted to discredit Kamei's morality. He almost accuses Kamei of voyeurism for his use of scenes of young lovers embracing on a grassy lawn in Hibiya, near the Imperial Palace. Kamei's goal in filming the lovers, Ogura points out, was to highlight their innocence of the invisible threat that filled the air and covered the grass and the serious implications for human genetics. Notably, Tetsu does not bother to challenge the empirical data presented or the authority of the many scientists who appear. Instead he attacks an easy target: Kamei Fumio.

Although the *Asahi* review was largely spurious, it had the power to shake the faith of many potential viewers because it appeared in a widely distributed national newspaper. In her response, Ogura demanded that the critic with the pen name Tetsu take responsibility for damaging the reputation of a documentary with laudatory aims, a film that surely would contribute to the betterment of society. Without question, someone powerful did not like Kamei's antinuclear message. Mighty nations like the United States looked askance at the antinuclear movement, as opposed to the peace movement, for the moral and political questions it raised about the status quo of the Cold War.[98]

Certain factions of the Left also offered negative criticisms of the film. In 1953, the Japan Communist Party had demanded that Kamei, along with many other cultural figures, engage in self-criticism. Kamei declined to do so, repelled by the growing dogmatism of the party and troubled by the rapidly changing face of international communism. Despite Kamei's central role in documenting the World Conferences Against Atomic Bombs and Hydrogen Bombs before and after *The World Is Terrified,* he was criticized for the science film. The latter contrasts markedly with the director's approach in *A Japanese Tragedy,* in his early postwar feature films, and in the anti–U.S. military base films. In all these films, Kamei followed a classic Marxist narrative of history, valorizing the struggles of the people and condemning capitalism and imperialism. In contrast, in the radioactive documentary, he largely maintains the objective point of view of the science film. Problematic was the concluding intertitle (people can solve the issue of nuclear weapons "if only they put their minds to it"). From the party's position, emphasizing individual agency and discounting the social and economic processes that lead to the arms race was reactionary.[99]

To Ogura, as to critics on all points of the political spectrum, the question of audience was significant. The world tour of the A-bomb paintings by Maruki Toshi and Maruki Iri demonstrated that international audiences were receptive to Hiroshima and Nagasaki, cities with the authority to act as witnesses to nuclear war. Ogura worried that the bad press would jeopardize *The World Is Terrified*'s chance to be shown abroad. Not surprisingly, though, she was able to find a Russian scientist who praised Kamei's film.

As had been the case with the Marukis' murals, the Soviet government favored antinuclear messages because they could be used to criticize the

United States. From the Japan Communist Party's point of view, however, Cominform might find Kamei's approach to be problematic, for the film failed to condemn the imperialist American aims. More seriously, the documentary made folly of the "any and all country" (*ikanaru kuni*) debate. Some on the Left condoned nuclear possession and testing by socialist countries while condemning America's possession, because the United States was considered the enemy of peace and thus would certainly use the bombs to nefarious ends. The exact nature of the danger of ashes of death caused by U.S. and Soviet testing was one of the "secrets" that Kamei attempted to show in this film.

During the late 1950s and early 1960s when Kamei's nuclear films appeared, a younger generation of activists and filmmakers criticized him and other adherents of the Old Left. Makino Mamoru pointed out that some filmmakers who were alienated by the dogmatism of the Communist and Socialist parties regarded Kamei's adherence to a classical Marxist narrative as "the utopic illusion of an aging revolutionary."[100] Caught in the rapidly changing ideological landscape of the anti-Stalinism of Khrushchev's Russia and the anticommunism of the Japanese–U.S. security regime, progressive cultural figures struggled to articulate a viable political vision. Kamei was remarkable for his willingness to work for the establishment (the imperial military in wartime and Mitsubishi in the postwar period) while at the same time articulating the "hidden discourse" of progressive politics in his atomic documentaries.

Worlds away from Kamei Fumio in conception and spirit, the young novelist Ishihara Shintarō was creating influential cultural products during the same years that Kamei was working on his atomic-bomb documentaries. Ishihara, still a college student in the mid-1950s, rode the crest of a youth culture boom with his fantastically popular Sun Tribe novels, popular music, and films. This wave signaled a new articulation of urban middle-class culture in tune with Japan's transformation into a model capitalist liberal democracy that was a fundamental articulation of the Cold War.

5   The Aesthetics of Speed and the Illogicality of Politics *Ishihara Shintarō*

as a Cold War Youth

The much adored and much despised rebellious youth of 1950s Japan put in a cameo appearance in Kurosawa Akira's quintessential Cold War film *Record of a Living Being* (*Ikimono no kiroku*, 1955) in the form of the illegitimate teenage son of Nakajima, the patriarch intent on escaping the nuclear threat.[1] The adolescent distinguishes himself not only by his insolent rejection of his father's anxieties and authority but also by his cutting-edge sense of style: he appears in a fashionable aloha shirt and sports a trendy haircut. In one scene in the movie, Nakajima appears at his son's apartment and pressures the boy to hand over the passbook for his savings account, from which Nakajima intends to withdraw money needed to fund his mad scheme to flee the bomb. The boy refuses his father's request and then, slowly and deliberately, turns his back on his father. Calmly, the youth drowns out his father's frantic demands by raising the volume on his record player. In this boy, the audience catches a glimpse of the generation who knew the war only as young children and, of equal significance, who have grown up with expectations of prosperity and individual choice. Unlike their parents or older siblings who were the agents of total war, they do not assume material privation or scarcity. The teenager in the aloha shirt constructs his identity through a sense of individualism based on his choice of styles that signal resistance to older modes through the assertion of narcissistic vitality, carefree hedonism, and boundless energy. This style and mode of being bore intimate connections to consumerism and the burgeoning mass culture of the mid-1950s.

Movie audiences in 1955 would have identified the teenager's fashion sense, his attitude, and his love of popular music with the figure of novelist and screenplay writer Ishihara Shintarō (b. 1932). Ishihara and his ilk (the Sun Tribe) represented an extremely significant current in culture: rebellious youth accustomed to prosperity, a new and vital force suitable to a Japan now on the road to creating a model version of liberal capitalist democracy in East Asia. While we can find many antecedents to Ishihara's rebel figure in Japan and beyond its borders, Ishihara was undoubtedly the most successful cultural and commercial exploiter of the iconic status of rebel youth, an image both alluring and threatening to society during the 1950s. One of the remarkable things about Ishihara's novels and films is that the literary establishment also paid attention to them and attempted to relate them to preexisting modes of narrative.

Ishihara was born only a year after James Dean (1931–1955). Despite their similar iconic values in mid-1950s culture, Ishihara never engaged in the kind of high-risk behavior that led to Dean's premature death. Instead, he established himself as a verbally provocative but socially and politically conservative force in Japanese society. Not long after winning Japan's most prestigious literary prize with his first novel in 1954, Ishihara declared in a public interview, "I want to drown in youth." As if that statement were not sufficiently provocative, Ishihara added that given the chance, he would like to "commit murder."[2] One might expect such outrageous public statements to bring his career as a novelist to an abrupt end. Instead, Ishihara rose to even greater fame as a writer of fiction and nonfiction, an actor and a screenplay writer, all the while using shock as an integral part of his public persona. His "long history of aggressive provocation" also contributed to his success as one of Japan's best-known and most controversial politicians (most recently, the governor of Tokyo and a rumored candidate for prime minister).[3] So long and varied was his career that during his second term as governor, Ishihara sought to jog the public's memory of his debut in the form of a 2004 television program about his biography of his famous brother, Ishihara Yūjirō.

Contemporaneous with Dean's film *Rebel Without a Cause* (1955), Ishihara's brash appearance as a novelist and film director signaled the mass media's engagement with a new type of postwar rebellious and alienated youth.[4] In both the United States and Japan, the new focus on youth culture in the 1950s exposed profound anxieties about morality and the family in a new age characterized by the threat of atomic warfare, the specter of communism, and the threat of fascism evoked by mass society.

The 1950s also witnessed a tremendous boom in movies and novels about adolescence. Mass cultural producers began to recognize youth culture as a popular theme and a symptom of the demographic changes that were giving rise to potential new audiences. As in Hollywood, Japanese publishers and film companies faced the challenge of producing "stories *about* teenagers" and also shifting "their operations so that their productions were more explicitly created *for* teenage markets increasingly understood as active and profitable."[5] In the interwar era, Japanese publishers had adopted some production and marketing strategies that targeted specific audiences, as the popular magazines for adolescent boys and girls demonstrate. From the time of Ishihara's first novel, *Season of the Sun* (*Taiyō no kisetsu*, 1954), however, the mass marketers found themselves offering cultural products that promoted a new kind of rebellious, individualistic image of youth rather than the healthy, conformist young people common before 1945.

When Ishihara's novels about prosperous, fast-living, and often violent youth first appeared, they enjoyed tremendous commercial success, and many prominent literary critics and writers of the day deemed them worthy of serious critical consideration. Although Ishihara's first novel won two high-profile literary prizes, some readers found the amorality of his fiction repellent. Screenplay writer Wada Natto, for example, saw merit in Ishihara's novel but also asserted that "like mothers everywhere, I was shocked." Novelist Satō Haruo reacted to young Ishihara's *Season of the Sun* and *The Punishment Room* (*Shokei no heya*, 1956) with outrage and advocated censorship of "juvenile delinquent literature." Yet shock value alone cannot account for the attention that Ishihara's work attracted. Nor would even Ishihara's most ardent fans claim that he had extraordinary talents as a literary stylist.

Instead, the reading public and critics alike sensed something different about Ishihara's fiction. His writings from the 1950s and his public persona generated new categories of aesthetic evaluation: a previously unknown youthful freshness as well as a feeling of speed toward a bright future.[6] The allure of freshness enabled readers and critics to tolerate Ishihara's fantasies of violence, his love of hyperbole, and his apparent flirtation with fast, high-risk behavior. At the same time, Ishihara's early career and the public's wildly diverse responses to all that he stood for and all that he touched (literature, film, television, journalism, fashion, sports, politics) indicate the proliferation of Cold War sensibilities in Ishihara's time. We should not dismiss his outrageous remarks about youth and ho-micide as the naïve wildness of youth, nor should we slight his popularity as a trivial incident, a lapse in aesthetic judgment by an otherwise so-phisticated reading public. Rather, the attention that Ishihara garnered resulted from his status as both catalyst and symptom of Japan's tremen-dous cultural change.

When interpreting Ishihara's impact, students of the 1950s frequently invoked the hyperbolic claim by critic Togaeri Hajime that the reception of Ishihara's novel *Season of the Sun* marked the veritable "death of the literary establishment" and thus the demise of elite art and aesthetics.[7] Despite Togaeri's anxieties, however, the literary establishment survived Ishihara's perceived assault. We should therefore consider other indica-tors of *Season of the Sun*'s value as both a work of literature and a cultural artifact. This chapter examines Ishihara's debut as a significant cultural event that illuminates the parameters of culture in the 1950s, a pivotal time of cultural change in Cold War Japan. By looking carefully at Ishi-hara's novel and the simultaneously popular and critical reception of it and the college student-turned-star, we can better understand the extent to which Japan must be regarded culturally as part of the Cold War's evolving "free world."[8]

The massive student movements surrounding the revision of the 1960 United States–Japan Security Treaty dominate the popular imagination as the first flowering of a youth culture in Japan. The young Ishihara's overwhelming presence in popular culture during the 1950s and his sur-prising political activism, though, demonstrate that he also led another current of youth culture, one fostered by an emerging stable capitalist culture deemed essential to America's strategy of containment. In Ishi-hara's work, tropes of youth, speed, and a new masculinity and freshness are closely linked to a privileged culture of rebellious youth predomi-nant in Japan and its postwar allies. Reminiscent of the American star James Dean's dominant iconographic presence, Ishihara raced away from a present made doubly anxious by news of H-bomb testing and fallout and embraced speed as a pleasure distinct from the values prescribed by older generations. Far from representing a passing fad of youth culture, Ishihara and his *Season of the Sun* foreshadowed what became the main-stream of culture in the post-Occupation era. In addition, because of the promise of a new political potential for Japanese citizens during the first decade of its postwar sovereignty, Ishihara ultimately resisted the anomie and apathy of a James Dean and, only a few years after *Season of the Sun*'s release, became enmeshed in politics.

Ishihara Shintarō Courts Controversy

Even though most of the Japanese public identifies Ishihara Shintarō as a politician, and people around the world know him as the neonationalist coauthor of *The Japan That Can Say "No,"* Ishihara wishes to identify himself as a successful novelist.[9] With no fewer than five best-selling books to his name and a number of literary prizes, his claim may seem justified. Yet after the 1970s, most literary critics and scholars disdained his novels and generally refused even to critique them.

Ishihara's prominence as a public figure throughout the postwar period can be traced back to his literary debut in 1955 when he captured the coveted Akutagawa Prize with his first novel, *Season of the Sun*. Still a college student at the time, Ishihara became an instant celebrity, and with amazing speed, a cinematic adaptation of his novel appeared in movie theaters throughout Japan. Nonetheless, many commentators treat Ishihara's flashy and youthful debut as merely a colorful, yet ultimately minor, episode in his long career as a provocative politician and writer.

Ishihara later presented himself as a man with an uncanny ability to read the times, a novelist who "sleeps with the age." The very stages of his life reflect perfectly those of postwar society: he claims that his own adolescence coincided with that of Japan (the mid-1950s) and, furthermore, that "the decline of post-bubble Japan resonates with my physical decline."[10] His self-promotion aside, Ishihara did indeed exhibit sensitivity to the aesthetics of speed and youthful rebellion that created a gendered ideal of virility in the unsettled early decades after the war. Ishihara's version of masculinity promised a swift escape from the malaise of Japan's defeat, but paradoxically, this masculine rebellion did not entail a vision of social change. Instead, it confirmed the breakneck pace at which Japan embraced mass culture, consumerism, and high capitalism and espoused a regressive conception of gender.

In political terms, it was Ishihara who rejected Mishima Yukio's playacting with politics and formulated his own forceful definition of the relationship between politics and art. Throughout his career, Ishihara fashioned a provocative and radically violent masculinist realm in his novels. At the same time, he affirmed a new relationship between art and politics that came about under the conservative, hegemonic, so-called 1955 political system, as I will discuss here. Even those who rejected Ishihara's early novels and his youthful celebrity during the 1950s could not help but take notice of his promise of newness and his offer of a renewed masculinity. Even those who disagreed with his conservative ideology found remarkable his activism in both the artistic and political spheres.

The Vitality of the 1950s

Roughly a decade after Japan's materially and spiritually devastating defeat, the Korean War had fueled its economic recovery sufficiently that Ishihara Shintarō's fictional portraits of prosperous youth did not strike readers as complete fantasy. Thus Ishihara tempted his audience with the prospect of a materially abundant lifestyle worth aspiring to (though likely not yet within reach for most), as well as with visions of a new generation that was innocent of war and subscribed to moral and social obligations different from those of their parents.

Ishihara distinguished himself from other pop culture stars by both his uncanny ability to sense the needs of the time and his entry into politics. Only a few years after appearing on the front pages of dozens of newspapers and magazines as a college student writer and in the crucial moment just before the massive grassroots protests against the renewal of the United States–Japan Security Treaty, Ishihara again claimed the limelight, this time as a man with political awareness and ambitions.[11] Ishihara first made his presence known at meetings of the Young Japan League (Wakai Nihon no kai), a short-lived coalition of socially conscious novelists, critics, and artists. Around the same time, Ishihara involved himself in the Liberal Democratic Party's power structure and was later elected as a Diet member on its ticket.[12] Ishihara thus initially articulated his idiosyncratic understanding of the proper relationship between literature and politics and between writers and political authority in a way that was anathema to most of his fellow artists. In contrast to many artists and writers of his generation, Ishihara expressed skepticism about the viability of grassroots activism, the type of citizen involvement made possible by the defeat and the postwar constitution. He instead subscribed to a political establishment that by the 1960s security treaty fully exhibited its contradictory, perhaps illogical nature: observing the constitution as representing liberal democratic ideals yet tending to rule by oligarchy. In retrospect, both moments—Ishihara's stunning literary debut, a time that signaled his affirmation of the aesthetics of mass culture, and the period when he embraced the possibilities of political office and a new understanding of the peculiar logic (or lack thereof) of postwar political authority—color our understanding of Ishihara's career and of Japan's postwar culture.

Not Just a Novel

Ishihara Shintarō's *Season of the Sun* reads like a rather conventional novel about heterosexual romance: college student Tatsuya meets Eiko, and they fall in love, although their relationship hovers ambiguously between lust and romance. Tatsuya is an athletic type who loves sailing and is also a boxer. Eiko admires Tatsuya in the boxing ring. From his vantage point, "Eiko fascinated Tatsuya in the same way that boxing did. She caused him the same mixture of shock and pleasure that he felt whenever he was knocked down in the ring."[13] They make love (or, perhaps more to the point, have sex) on Tatsuya's sailboat one moonlit night. They get involved with other people (one of whom is Tatsuya's own brother, Michihisa); they feel jealous. Eiko becomes pregnant. Tatsuya emerges from his confusion over the slightly tempting possibility of fatherhood and ultimately tells her that he does not want to have anything to do with the baby. Eiko dies from complications of an abortion. In an outburst at Eiko's funeral, Tatsuya cries out, "None of you understands!" to the assembled adult mourners.

Complicating Ishihara's desired identity as a novelist is the fact that he never was *just* a novelist but was always involved in cultural production in a variety of interesting and provocative ways. Cultural history points to his influence principally as the author of novels on which popular Japanese films were based. The renowned film director Oshima Nagisa attributes his own inspiration for Japanese New Wave cinema to a film adaptation of Ishihara's novel *Crazed Fruit* (*Kurutta kajitsu*, 1956): "In the rip of a woman's skirt and the buzz of a motorboat, sensitive people heard the heralding of a new generation of Japanese film."[14] This reaction to the cinematic version of an Ishihara novel sounds remarkably like the excitement of French filmmakers upon viewing *Rebel Without a Cause* at around the same time. Up-and-coming directors like François Truffaut and Jean-Luc

Godard regarded the movie as "a model for their own quest for a fresh and unspoiled contemporary cinema in which adolescents' complex 'vision du monde' could play a major part."[15]

Well known in studies of post-Occupation cinema is the mid-1950s appearance of the "Sun Tribe" films based on Ishihara's novels *Season of the Sun, The Punishment Room,* and *Crazed Fruit.* Critics like Satō Tadao, David Desser, and Michael Raine deemed these films as important for several reasons. First, as with the director Oshima Nagisa, their evocation of a new type of hero/antihero who is rebellious, violent, and sexually potent sparked the development of Japanese New Wave cinema. These films glorified youth culture, an emphasis that became a central cultural value in the post-Occupation age. The films also forged a cultural link between Japan and the free-world iconography of the juvenile rebellion exemplified by James Dean and *Rebel Without a Cause.* The medium of film played a major part in evoking the new antihero, and films had great popular appeal (that is, they enjoyed huge tickets sales) with audiences. Finally, the Taiyōzoku (Sun Tribe) film phenomenon spurred citizen protests and ultimately resulted in the post-Occupation reorganization of Eirin (the film censorship board).[16]

The Taiyōzoku movies also represent the beginning of the flashy career of actor/"multimedia star" Ishihara Yūjirō (1934–1987). Yūjirō, the younger brother of Shintarō, "epitomized the sensitive tough guy" and was easily the most popular male film star in Japan during the 1950s and 1960s.[17] Although the elder Ishihara entered the public eye first and thus introduced his fast-living brother to audiences by featuring him in film adaptations of his novels, it was the more approachable Yūjirō who soon became the movie idol, a regular on long-running television action programs and the adored singer of pop songs. Ishihara Shintarō loved to forefront his affiliation with his popular younger brother. Even when he was a mayoral candidate, he repeatedly reminded the voting public of his affection for his late brother, Yūjirō. Ishihara's *My Little Brother (Otōto,* 1996), a memoir about his relationship with Yūjirō, rose to the top of the best-seller lists.

Now that we have ascertained the importance of film in the greater cultural moment of *Season of the Sun,* let us turn to the place of Ishihara's novel in literary history. The majority of film studies scholars view Ishihara's novels as if they, though controversial, somehow fit neatly into literary history.[18] But to students of modern Japanese literature, Ishihara's centrality in film studies—and on the cultural scene in the 1950s—may come as a surprise.[19] Even though the novel *Season of the Sun* won the

Ishihara Yūjirō (*center*) in *Season of the Sun*. (Courtesy of Mainichi shinbunsha)

Akutagawa Prize in 1955, most critics ignore Ishihara's work in canonical studies of postwar literature. Instead, critiques of mid-twentieth-century literature concentrate on the more "serious" literary writers who came to the forefront during those years, like Mishima Yukio, Ariyoshi Sawako, Sono Ayako, Kōda Aya, and Ōe Kenzaburō, or the Daisan no shinjin authors Yasuoka Shōtarō, Kojima Nobuo, and Endō Shūsaku, as well as the twilight careers of many respected older novelists.[20] At most, critics mention in passing Ishihara's audacity, "his iconoclastic, self-centered style and his eager association with the journalistic media."[21]

The Diverse Reception of a Prize-Winning Novel

Looking back at the reactions in the 1950s to the novel *Season of the Sun*, it is evident that much of the outcry and acclaim came from journalistic sources, which fanned the flames of outrage against a supposedly rebellious generation portrayed in the films based on Ishihara Shintarō's novels. The images of the Sun Tribe youth dressed in aloha shirts and sporting stylish short haircuts were visible everywhere, thanks to the movies, advertisements, television, and posters. For the film studios and, in turn, the publishing houses, this sensational approach resulted in packed movie theaters and even higher sales of the prize-winning novel.[22]

Although some members of the public lapped up the Sun Tribe cultural products, others, such as the Parent Teachers Association, turned out on the streets to protest what they perceived as the immorality of *Season of the Sun*, *The Punishment Room*, and *Crazed Fruit*.[23] But not everyone rejected the novels out of hand and instead were determined to make sense of Ishihara's seemingly new type of fiction. For example, Wada Natto, a screenplay writer for director Ichikawa Kon's cinematic adaptation of *The Punishment Room*, initially disdained the novels when viewing the book from a parent's point of view.[24] In her capacity as a writer, however, she could see the merit in Ishihara's work: "Once I had decided to produce a script based on one of Ishihara's books, shock alone was insufficient."[25] Others, however, would not stand for what they perceived as a decline in morality.[26] The lively public debates over the movies resonate with the "moral panics" stirred up when *Rebel Without a Cause* and other juvenile delinquency films appeared in America and Western Europe around the same period.[27]

Central to our understanding of the cultural meanings of *Season of the Sun* are the diverse literary critical reactions to the novel and its points of intersection with mass culture, the marketplace, and the literary establishment. Fortunately, we have ample evidence of the critical views of the novel because Ishihara won two literary prizes for his first novel.

Ishihara and the Prize for New Writers

The contemporary literary critical establishment (and publishers) was radically divided in its evaluations of Ishihara Shintarō's early Sun Tribe novels.[28] The contemporary reception of his early works can be gauged in several ways: by looking at the awarding of literary prizes and the pronouncements of the selection committee judges, the critical judgments of other writers and critics, and journalistic performances such as *zadankai* (roundtable discussions) that serve to promote the works and authors in the marketplace and also to generate critical judgments. All of these became part of the reception and consumption of Ishihara's novels and contributed to their cultural significance.

When Ishihara won his first literary prize for *Season of the Sun*, the Bungakukai shinjinshō (the journal *Bungakukai*'s New Writers Prize), in 1955, the judges on the prize committee did not lambaste Ishihara's work.

Instead, the Bungakukai selection committee members (all male novelists and critics, mostly in their forties or fifties and thus adults during
the war) evaluated the novel as fresh and entertaining and therefore an
appropriate choice for a new writers' literary prize.[29] Notably, the term
shinjin (in this context, "new writer") became one of the key terms employed throughout the debate over *Season of the Sun*. In 1955, some deni-
zens of the literary establishment, particularly its commercial promot-
ers and publishers, longed for a *shinjin* who exuded "freshness."[30] These
new writers would inevitably be young people, not the older people who
smelled of the wartime. Too many members of the wartime generations
were grappling with guilt and complicity, even as the myth of victimization grew and the possibilities of democracy were embraced in the new
postwar, post-Occupation age. As Japan became increasingly implicated
in the world as it was refigured by Cold War politics and emerged as a
"profiteer" during the U.S. involvement in the Korean War, "one gray,
mundane day followed another, and it was against this stagnant age and
society that some in the younger generation rebelled."[31]

Perhaps more accurately, certain members of the generations that had
experienced the war as adults saw fit to celebrate youth who, although
alive during the war, did not have to shoulder its heavy moral legacy.
These young people frolicked in recreational sex and sports and behaved
as if oblivious to the material privations suffered by so many fellow citizens in the early postwar decades. Conventional literary histories label
early postwar writers in relation to the war and its end as the "wartime
writers" (*senchū-ha*) and the "first generation of postwar writers" (*dai-
ichiji sengo-ha*). Only the *shinjin* (literally, "new person") designation did
not refer specifically to the war. Ishihara was thirteen years old at the time
of the defeat (too young to have served in the army or even in the national
mobilization) and thus qualified as a *shinjin*.

Obviously, Ishihara belonged to a much younger generation than
the judges, and he displayed the proper degree of "mannered anomie,"
though in many ways different from that of James Dean.[32] The ideas of
youthful rebellion and of "angry youth" resonated in the Bungakukai
award committee's explanations of why it had chosen *Season of the Sun*.
In Japan, as in other Cold War capitalist countries, the phenomenon of
rebellious youth had become a preoccupation of the media and society.
American movies like *The Wild One* (1953), which were distributed widely
in Japan and Europe, similarly evoke the youthful and speed-driven aesthetic of youth gangs: "We're just gonna go. . . . You just go. . . . The idea

is to have a ball."[33] Popular culture representations of youth culture and juvenile delinquency coincided with a scholarly shift in the understanding of the psychological and social significance of youth.[34] Rather than regard the problems of youth as pathological and even criminal, influential psychologists like Erik Erikson defined the rebelliousness of postwar youth as a "natural, if not healthy response to the turmoil of modern adolescence."[35] Opinions were radically divided, moreover, about the responsibility of the mass media in promoting or even causing the youth rebellion. Although Japan shared these views of youth culture with the United States and Western Europe, the Ishihara phenomenon was different because it located the causes of rebellious youth in the postwar period, as opposed to the wartime. In the United States, in contrast, the James Dean film *Rebel Without a Cause,* while seemingly a quintessential postwar youth film, was inspired by a nonfiction book about disturbed youth written by a psychologist during World War II.[36] The violence prevalent in juvenile culture was attributed to the war or to its lingering effects, along with the arms race.

By the mid-1950s, fiction concerning *après-guerre* youth and their problems was a familiar genre in Japan, with many such youth "everywhere on the streets." Inoue Yasushi, a member of the prize committee, singled out Ishihara's achievement as portraying with "utter casualness" these delinquent youths as well as the amorality of the main character.[37] The judges did not trace the rise of rebellious youth to wartime, to the Occupation forces, or even to American or European culture. Indeed, they accepted rebellion as a global *"après-guerre"* phenomenon and identified the rebels in visual terms (by their style on the streets) rather than in terms of political protest or social alienation.

For all its flaws, though, the Bungakukai judges decided that the novel did deserve the prize. Not one of the Bungakukai readers expressed shock at (or even commented on) the sexual relations depicted in the novel— such as the fact that both Tatsuya and Eiko had sex with multiple partners (Eiko's partners included Tatsuya's own brother). And none of them bothered to mention the subsequently controversial "erection thrust through the shoji paper screen" passage. Yoshida Ken'ichi insisted that "morality" was an inappropriate evaluative category for *Season of the Sun,* because generically the novel does not concern such matters. Rather, Yoshida wrote, *Season of the Sun* should be considered a hard-boiled novel about sporting youth, of the genre one often encountered in British or American fiction.[38] Similarly, to Hirano Ken, it was the exotic setting and props that distinguished the novel. He put it this way: "this decrepit old-fashioned student" has never seen wrestling or boxing and has never ridden on a sailboat, so the novel "opened up a new world for me."[39]

Audacious Youth Wins Elite Prize

Perhaps it should not be surprising that when the same novel by Ishihara won the Akutagawa Prize in the following year, it caused a huge controversy.[40] Although the Akutagawa Prize, like the New Writers Prize, was intended to highlight the accomplishments of a newcomer, it had a much longer history and greater prestige than the Bungakukai prize, so the stakes were much higher. From its inception in the mid-1930s, the Akutagawa Prize also had been closely linked with the literary establishment and its project of canon formation.[41] Consequently, the awarding of the prize to a work that some committee members regarded as deeply flawed and culturally tainted led the novelist Nakano Shigeharu to proclaim that the committee's majority decision to select *Season of the Sun* for its award in 1956 had resulted in corrupting the Akutagawa Prize itself.[42] Still others declared that the award signified the death of the literary establishment.[43] But neither of these hyperbolic claims helps us understand what really caused the ruckus over *Season of the Sun*. For better clues, it is instructive to look at what else was happening at the time to Ishihara's career and his book, specifically the mass cultural contexts of their fame and reception that damned them in the eyes of some critics. Also, to the judges of the Akutagawa Prize, Ishihara's focus on manhood and a new variety of youth seemed crucial because the prize had considerable influence in the world of Japanese letters.

The Akutagawa judges' strong reactions to *Season of the Sun* also coincided with the appearance in 1956 of the film version of the novel. For the Akutagawa selection committee, it was not only the linking of an often lurid popular culture medium (film) that tainted the novel but also the involvement of the *shūkanshi* (weekly magazines/tabloids) in codifying the Taiyōzoku aesthetic and in publicizing—or perhaps creating—the Taiyōzoku phenomenon/boom.[44] For Nakano Shigeharu, even the mainstream media were complicit in advancing Ishihara's dubious cause. In a 1956 article ostensibly about his memories of the Akutagawa Prize, he lambasted Ishihara not only for his bad novel but also for his audacity in writing an article about literature for a mainstream newspaper. The proper involvement in journalism for a boy of his age, Nakano pointed out, would be interviews about college life in popular magazines. More than anything, Nakano railed against the mass media's ability and willingness to manipulate readers. Notably, Nakano's argument has in much in common with Theodor Adorno's and Max Horkheimer's critiques of the culture industry, which were influenced by experiences in a fascist state and its manipulation of the mass media for repressive ends. The *shūkanshi* convinced "youth who know nothing about art" that *Season of the Sun* had merit and that the novel was a "social phenomenon."[45]

Other judges, such as Uno Kōji and Satō Haruo, found reasons other than the culture industry and the specter of authoritarianism to condemn Ishihara's work. They also raised the issue of morality in regard to both the Akutagawa Prize procedures and the contents of Ishihara's novel. Uno exposed what he viewed as the publisher's skewing of the voting so that the prize would go to *Season of the Sun* (perhaps in order to compete with television). He also took note of Ishihara's selection of "unusual topics" such as boxing. In contrast to Hirano Ken, Uno condemned this focus, as well as Ishihara's inclusion of "sexually graphic passages," as mere "pandering to the age and to journalism."[46] Although Satō insisted that he did not reject the amorality (*hanrinri*) of *Season of the Sun*, he concluded that Ishihara's "aggressive stance in the novel is lowly."[47]

In hindsight, it is a bit difficult to comprehend Satō's and Uno's repulsion at *Season of the Sun*'s sexual explicitness because the novel is, in the end, rather tame. Readers, furthermore, can find much more graphic descriptions in many prewar and Occupation-period Japanese novels and a greater focus on the body (*nikutai*) and sexual obsession. Uno found no need to place the novel in this literary context because the potential corruption of contemporary morals seemed more urgent. In *Season of the Sun*, the famous "erection thrust through the shoji" is the only genitalia mentioned, and the sex/love scene on the sailboat is extremely cinematic in style, with lips reaching for lips and saltwater streaming down foreheads:

> Soon they scrambled back on board and lay down panting on the sails which covered the deck. Still breathing hard, their lips came together and they could taste the salt water that ran down their cheeks as they kissed over and over again. Automatically their hands went to each other's wet bathing suits, but their garments would not come off easily. Wild with impatience, they finally pulled them off, their lips still touching.

The boat rocked violently before regaining its balance. It had been the cradle for a passionate and intoxicating pleasure which neither Eiko nor Tatsuya had known before.[48]

Although the "erection thrust through the shoji" passage earned fame, Ishihara could not even claim it as his own innovation. Novelist Takeda Taijun, famous for his "carnal literature" (*nikutai bungaku*) of the immediate postwar period, had previously featured a similar episode in *Ikei no mono* (*Deformed Thing*, 1950).[49] For the Akutagawa judges, however, Takeda's novels would be understood as part of the immediate postwar embrace of decadence (as liberation) and of the view of degraded sex as linked inextricably to wartime abuses of the body.[50] As a member of the Sun Tribe, Tatsuya's sexual/romantic fantasy life had little in common with the prostitute-tied-up-and-whipped sordidness typical of Takeda's "carnal" books. If anything, Ishihara's love scenes are reminiscent of a D. H. Lawrence novel, though much less explicit: "His only notion of [love] was limited to an image of himself and a woman in the forest somewhere, where they played about naked among the trees."[51] Ishihara's allusion to Lawrence resonates with a broader discourse on the elevation of Japanese culture through more meaningful depictions of sex that took place during the 1950s as part of the legal case concerning Lawrence's *Lady Chatterley's Lover* (discussed in chapter 2). The judges who rejected the casual extramarital sex in *Season of the Sun* also must have had in mind Maruyama Masao's rejection of "carnal literature" as something that degraded the body, the spirit, and, in turn, all of Japanese culture.

Even Kawabata Yasunari, one of the four decidedly ambivalent Akutagawa judges, was disturbed by the mass media's radically increased emphasis on the Akutagawa Prize and concluded that the prize had become "too powerful."[52] Kawabata the critic recognized that *Season of the Sun*'s many flaws as a novel were "only too obvious." In his own novels, he had explored the complexities of sexuality, desire, and obsession, but in much more profound and explicit ways than the young Ishihara could have imagined. Kawabata thus identified with much greater precision and clarity one of the reasons for the anxiety about the potential co-optation of the closed world of pure literature by the exploding mass culture of the mid-1950s. Rather than condemning Ishihara in moral, generational, or aesthetic terms, as did many of the Akutagawa judges, Kawabata indirectly suggested that the problem stemmed from the economic system and the culture industries that were making possible the instant fame of a "spoiled youth," one who had barely read any of the canonical works of modern Japanese literature. To add insult to injury, Ishihara had not served the requisite "ten years of suffering" as an apprentice to the literary establishment.

A New Aesthetic

If the 1956 Akutagawa Prize committee members agreed on anything, it was that *Season of the Sun* exuded an aesthetic quality that they all labeled "fresh" (*shinsen*). Partly, the work's freshness derived from the identity of the author as a *shinjin*, although certainly not all works by *shinjin* considered over the years were fresh. Other descriptive terms paired with "fresh" included "moist" (*mizumizushii*), "youthful," and "energetic." Accordingly, the term "energy" became a code word for the athleticism and heterosexual verve of the male characters. The judges consistently applied the term "freshness" as a means of positive evaluation. Later readers can only guess that perhaps *Season of the Sun*'s preoccupation with recreational pastimes such as boxing and sailing, or novel things like aloha shirts and ukuleles, which seemed unfamiliar to some of the older judges, contributed to its novelty. In the end, though, these motifs alone seem insufficient to explain the judges' assertion that Ishihara had created a text that was somehow new, despite its stylistic conventionality and lack of innovation in plot and character.

In retrospect, *Season of the Sun* also articulated a cultural style that became an important aesthetic in the post-Occupation culture: the cultural style of speed, deliberate speed, a speed that accompanied "the excitements of electronic speed, [the rush to] face down nuclear anxiety, and incorporate newly aggressive demands and examples from . . . youth culture."[53] In the novel, Tatsuya rushes away from basketball to take up boxing; the boys and girls fall into bed with each other almost instantly. We learn that Eiko's former boyfriend died in a car accident on the way to a rendezvous with her: "He had sped along in his car and then crashed into a train."[54] Tatsuya and Eiko and their age-mates are always on the move, fast in their cars and boats and trains. On Tatsuya's sailboat, Eiko switches on her portable transistor radio to instantly create a mood, though it turned out to be "a slow dance perfect for lovers."[55] Even the dynamic of Tatsuya and Eiko's relationship is described with the term *supiido* ("he lost his own pace in her speed and intensity").[56] This love for speed certainly characterizes the postwar period's modernity. As W. T. Lhamon describes this aesthetic: "Each of the several reasons for the new deliberate speed in culture is deeply connected to the illusion of what came to be known as 'post-scarcity state' energy and the arrogance of its consumption. The implicit aesthetic of a deliberately speedy style matches the consumer economics of the period."[57]

In Ishihara's novel, Tatsuya and his brother Michihisa become embroiled in a fast and furious betting match, a buying and selling scheme over whom Eiko will sleep with, and then Eiko starts trading, too, anxiously laying forth money to buy herself the man she wants. The novel itself rushes forward at a fast pace. One of the Akutagawa selection committee members, Funahashi Seiichi, identifies the desirable quality of speed in relation to fast carnal pleasure rather than fast financial transactions. He uses the term *kairaku,* or pleasure or, perhaps, instant gratification in order to explain the force driving the Taiyōzoku: "The *kairaku* that Ishihara depicts is different from that of the early postwar writers who glorified decadence. *Kairaku* is not something you can buy with money. You don't need money to buy the pleasurable sensation of ripping through shoji paper with a youthful erect penis. The purer the pleasure, the farther it is from money."[58] Whether we find this image compelling or pathetic, Ishihara and readers like Funahashi regarded it as an image that conveyed perfectly the amoral pursuit of instant gratification, of speed.

What Class Rebels?

Other provocative aspects of Ishihara Shintarō's novels appear at the intersections of *Season of the Sun* and *Rebel Without a Cause* (a film well known then in Japan). Lurking beneath the surface of the debate over *Season of the Sun* is the question of socioeconomic class. Nakamura Mitsuo identifies Tatsuya and his group as spoiled kids (*amattareta seinen*).[59] The novel focuses exclusively on the moneyed class of people to which Tatsuya and Eiko belong: a extremely small segment of the population at a time that would prove to be the takeoff of Japan's high-speed economic growth. Although Tatsuya mouths off about his disagreements with the older generation, he is ultimately connected to them by what has been termed the "golden umbilical cord."

In the classic American youth film *Rebel Without a Cause*, hypocritical middle-class parents mistake materialism for love, and that in part leads to the rebellion of Jim Stark (the James Dean character). Nicholas Ray's film, then, proposes a "renewed commitment to the family" and parental responsibility and love as remedies for the social problem of troubled youth.[60] In contrast, the motives for rebellion and the pursuit of amorality are less clear in *Season of the Sun*. Both Tatsuya and Eiko come from fairly well-to-do families: Tatsuya's father buys him a sailboat, and Eiko has a "big car." Both have a ready supply of cash. Tatsuya, at least, gets lots of attention from his parents. But significantly, it is not the money itself that has steered these kids from respectable homes in the wrong direction; it is something suggested only abstractly and in passing by the narrator as the emptiness of postwar society ("barren soil"):

> If the adult world feared them as a dangerous force, second only to communism, this fear was groundless. A new generation brought forth new sentiments and a new code of morals. . . . They stood erect, like cactus, without looking down to see that they were blooming in barren soil. . . . The youth unconsciously tried to destroy the morals of their elders. . . . The young looked for something bold and fresh to build on. And besides, who started measuring naked human feelings in terms of material things?[61]

Initially, the general public understood juvenile delinquency as a social problem in their communities and also as one portrayed in the media in Western-bloc countries. Troubled youth had also attracted considerable academic interest from sociologists and other social scientists.[62] In order for rebel youth to become culturally acceptable and marketable figures, the mass culture industry first had to mask the class and social origins of juvenile delinquency and then to turn a social issue into a matter of style palatable to the middle and upper-middle classes. The iconic status of rebel youth arose from the Hollywood evocations such as Marlon Brando as a member of a motorcycle gang in *The Wild One* and James Dean in *Rebel Without a Cause*, partly as a reaction to the widespread social panic expressed in the media about the problem of juvenile delinquency.

Audiences in free-world societies across both the Pacific and the Atlantic were drawn to Hollywood imports such as *Rebel Without a Cause* because of the suggestion of rebellion as a style, rather than delinquency based primarily on socioeconomic causes.[63] Although researchers identified juvenile delinquency primarily with working-class youth, the rejection of conformity and embrace of rebellion and hedonism gradually changed from values associated with a single social class into an experience "encoded in leisure styles."[64] Contemporary audiences of the James Dean film would understand the rebellious behavior of the teenagers in the film as the contamination of the middle class by lower-class "slum youth."[65] In a somewhat different manner, *Season of the Sun* links the alienation of youth exclusively to the wealthy. Furthermore, Ishihara's work excludes any mention of the fact that the majority of the population was still recovering from the material devastation of war. Nor does the novel or film mention that well-heeled youth were an anomaly in mid-1950s Japan.

While *Rebel Without a Cause* finds fault with the neuroses and materialism of individual parents, Ishihara's novel highlights the problematic behavior and attitudes of the children rather than of the older generation. Tatsuya and his buddies behave like spoiled children with their mothers, but around their fathers, they show a very different face.[66] In a key passage, Tatsuya happens to run into his father on the train on his way home and joins him in the first-class seats. Tatsuya mutters,

> "I think I'll get a first class train pass during training [for boxing]. It's so much more comfortable." His father heard him and lowered his paper noisily.
>
> "What's that? Where did you get such silly ideas? You're still in college, you know. If your training tires you so much, you'd better give it up. In any case I haven't got money to waste on a train pass for you."
>
> "Money to waste?"
>
> For a moment, Tatsuya felt nothing but hatred for his father. [*Daiichi, papa wa sonna kanemochi janai zo. Kane mochi ja nai? Kare wa sono shunkan chichi o kokoro kara nikunda.*][67]

Why does Tatsuya feel hatred for his father at this point? Not only has the family dynamic gone awry, but also the youth is denied the materialism to which he assumes he should aspire. The novel remains ambiguous in its stance on materialism and consumerism.

Readers and critics in 1955 may have found Tatsuya's attitude "spoiled" but also attractive: this lust for prosperity, a consumeristic promiscuity that could negate the dire scarcity of earlier postwar years.[68] In addition, Tatsuya's desire to ignore his father's selective frugality and his proper place as a student resonated with the logic of postwar consumer society around the world. As W. T. Lhamon noted, many adults in 1950s America saw Elvis Presley and other promiscuous and emphatically materialistic expressions of youth culture as threatening, but their disapproval masked those qualities of the 1950s youth culture that made up a part of the cultural fabric. As Japan was drawn into the values of the capitalist free world, such views of youth culture were powerful.

The fear and anxiety provoked by the Cold War also contributed to fueling the idealization of the energy of youth. Just a year or so earlier, a horrified public had learned about H-bomb testing in the Bikini atoll and the resulting 1954 *Lucky Dragon* contaminated fishing boat incident, as well as the widespread radioactive fallout. Ten years had passed since Hiroshima and Nagasaki were bombed, but it was only several years earlier, with the end of the Occupation, that the public learned more about what had happened in those cities and of the apocalyptic imagination linked with the arms race. Thus in 1956, the writer Aoshima Yukio wondered whether "social anxiety brought on by hydrogen bombs has become a threat to young people and has prompted their desire for instant gratification."[69] Again, about U.S. society in this same era, Lhamon wrote, "Clearly this perceived threat militated against calm appraisal. Otherwise, critics would have seen that a culture living under the fear of nuclear annihilation could be expected to fetishize cartoons of vitality. A consumer society without precedent could be expected to celebrate among its members those with the readiest energy for fulfilling its values."[70] The characters in Ishihara's *Season of the Sun* exemplify such "cartoons of vitality." (Note that "cartoon" refers to easily read representation, not parody.)

In addition, Ishihara's novel elides mention of the war and defeat and omits any reference to A-bomb anxiety. This contrasts with the focus of the media and popular culture on nuclear weapons and testing evident in the contemporaneous *Godzilla* (*Gojira*, 1954), Kamei Fumio's atomic films, and Kurosawa Akira's *Record of a Living Being*. Notably, allusions to atomic anxiety and the end of the world figure much more prominently in *Rebel Without a Cause*. Indeed, Mick Broderick sees *Rebel Without a Cause* as being "at the vanguard of modern American cinema in its exploration of . . . the psychic schism created by the Cold War and its association of nuclear Armageddon."[71]

Mixed in with these pointed criticisms of *Season of the Sun* as being about "wild boys from good homes," one can detect a tinge of envy. Ishikawa Tatsuzō, one of the prize judges, hinted at this: "Perhaps the danger is what makes him a new face [*kiken dakara koso shinjin da to ieru kamoshirenai*]."[72] The ambivalent view of rebellious youth as both dangerous and as standing for a robust, voluptuous, promiscuously democratic time can be found in the culture of other Western-bloc allies as well. In Japan of this era, the articulation of the freshness and vigor of well-fed youth such as those evoked in *Season of the Sun* signified a desire for revitalized masculinity.

Dynamics of Rebellion and Conformity

The portrait of masculinity in the novel makes it attractive to certain segments of the reading audience. The family dynamic in *Season of the Sun* strikes a familiar chord as an archetypal pattern found in modern literature in Japan. The young male Tatsuya longs for union with and dependence on the maternal and shows resistance against the paternal. He also enjoys promiscuity and, to the end, remains resistant to monogamy. In contrast, the ill-fated young heroine, Eiko, experiments with recreational sex but acquiesces to Tatsuya's demand that she terminate her pregnancy rather than making the choice herself (thus appearing to refute the role of nurturing mother). The novel ends with Eiko's death, thus confirming the validity of Tatsuya's regressive model of family and gender. The simplicity of plot and flatness of character encourage the following reading of *Season of the Sun:* the woman character's sexuality, desire, and freedom of choice are punished, whereas the promiscuous, emotionally immature male characters are validated.

The character of Tatsuya furthermore confirms the homosocial yet strappingly heterosexual virile male, as opposed to the emasculated masculine images prominent in the Occupation-period fiction about which Sharalyn Orbaugh and Michael Molasky have written and even in contrast to the confused *daisan no shinjin,* still enmeshed in wartime or downtrodden by the family.[73] Tatsuya clearly values only recreational sex, as we can see by his refusal to take responsibility for Eiko's pregnancy. He furthermore rejects fatherhood because of its potential to tarnish the solitary masculinity of the idealized, powerful boxer:

> "I'm not telling you definitely to have the child. It's entirely up to you. All I said was that it wouldn't be a bad thing to have a baby of our own." . . . Then one morning he saw a newspaper picture of a champion boxer holding a baby in his arms. This finally decided him. The sight of the boxer smiling foolishly, with his gown open at

the front, annoyed him. In the ring he would have been a completely different man. Tatsuya made up his mind that Eiko should have an abortion. The child would not live because of his father's vanity as a sportsman.[74]

Readers of the novel find the narrator's moral stance ambiguous. While the final sentence of this passage seems to criticize Tatsuya's narcissism, little in the plot of the novel or in the development of character (such as it is) confirms such a critique. Despite exhibiting a modicum of conscience, Tatsuya ultimately resists a heterosexual, compromised existence as a man, and the novella ends with the teenager flailing away at a punching bag, which seems to him haunted by Eiko's smiling face: "As if in a dream, Tatsuya struck it again and again."[75]

Thus *Season of the Sun* challenges preexisting conceptions of gender only insofar as it offers an idiosyncratic remedy for Occupation-era notions of masculinity as enervated and ineffectual. Although the men valorized in *Season of the Sun* are clearly heterosexual, their primary links are to sports, the male body, and the homosocial realm of boxing. Viewers may recall a similar emphasis on the homosocial bonds embodied by the James Dean and Sal Mineo characters in *Rebel Without a Cause*, whose affection coexists with the idealized heterosexual bonding between Dean and Natalie Wood. Ishihara, in contrast, evokes a peculiar siege mentality of the imagined masculine realm by evoking Tatsuya in violent encounter with an encroaching feminine force. Specifically, Tatsuya pummels a punching bag that he imagines as Eiko. In contrast to the vision of a renewed dedication to the nuclear family offered in *Rebel Without a Cause*, Tatsuya also rejects the opportunity to become a father and partner in a heterosexual marriage.

Formats of Mass Culture

Although Ishihara Shintarō's novel itself appeared in well-established elite cultural magazines such as *Bungei shunjū* and *Bungakukai*, the *shūkanshi*'s (weekly magazine/tabloid) extensive focus on the films and the Ishihara brothers themselves forged a further link between the novel *Season of the Sun* and mass culture. Conversely, Ishihara himself sought to maintain a high-profile connection between the *Season of the Sun* narrative and the elite literary culture. He did so partly by quickly turning the novella into a single-volume book format, which lent legitimacy to the work by separating it from the ephemeral journal format and also by creating a hard-copy identity for the text distinct from film. According to his publisher, Shinchōsha, the enterprising Ishihara pressed the editor to put out a single-volume version of the novel before the film was released.[76] In this way, Ishihara skillfully manipulated the publishing world with the goal of speedily obtaining an elevated position in the cultural hierarchy, which had previously been attainable only through slow ascendance up the ranks of the literary establishment.

Was it his age or lack of experience that allowed Ishihara to participate willingly in the type of culture industry that alarmed Nakano Shigeharu, resonating as it did with the dangers of the mass media and cultural production under fascist regimes? Far from finding mass culture repulsive and alien to his idea of art, Ishihara reveled in the multimedia mass presentations of his novel in movies, posters, songs, television, and magazines both elite and kitsch. In addition, he easily assumed the role of celebrity as commodity, but at the same time, Ishihara craved the legitimacy afforded by ties with the literary establishment.

As we have seen, the comments by the member of the Akutagawa selection committee indicate the polarization in the literary elites' attitudes toward the mass media and popular culture. Satō Haruo, for one, despised Ishihara's juvenile novel as "the lowest type of literary art" (*bungei*), and even though he acknowledged Ishihara's "astute grasp of the times," he complained that his sensitivity was "no greater than that of journalists and entertainers." *Season of the Sun* was not, Satō asserted, "something written by a literary man."[77]

Although he was not an Akutagawa judge, the novelist, translator, and literary historian Itō Sei also singled out journalism as a significant component of Ishihara's popularity. He emphasized the active role of journalists in generating contemporary culture and did not denigrate their writing as inferior to that of literary men:

> Of late, many of the fictional works that won literary prizes were confessions or exposes about growing up during the war. . . . Journalists have a great interest in what younger people [who came to age after the war] have to say. So Ishihara [who wrote about something other than youth during the war] came in like a ball of fire just when they were waiting for someone like him. . . . But young people around the age of twenty have a very narrow set of interests . . . and

so the novel holds the readers' attention as an expression of youthful angst [*wakamono no sakebi*].[78]

Doubtless, Itō's positive experiences with publicity in the *Lady Chatterley's Love* trial only a few years earlier encouraged this optimistic view of
journalism.

Paradoxically, the advertising strategy of the journal *Bungei shunjū*,
which featured the Akutagawa Prize–winning novel and the committee's
evaluation, reveals the influence that such mass media consumerism had
on the very judges who feared it the most. A newspaper advertisement for
the March 1956 issue of *Bungei shunjū* wooed potential customers with
the claim that "never before has an Akutagawa Prize novel stirred up such
a storm! A fresh breeze brought for the first time to postwar literature
by a youthful 23-year-old talent!! A controversial work." The ad copy also
quotes the judges' own liberal use of terms such as *shinjin*, "moistness,"
"newness," "youth," "energy," and "pleasure" in order to evoke the desirable quality of "freshness." As a means of suggesting the rebelliousness of
Ishihara and his novel, the ad further includes the selectively edited negative judgments of the older writers: "Uno Kōji: 'I can't bear to watch this
one win the prize.' Satō Haruo: 'I'm repulsed by the aesthetic flaws in this
work.' Ishikawa Tatsuzō: 'It's dangerous but exactly what we want from a
shinjin.'"[79] In other words, the judges resisted certain moral and aesthetic
aspects of *Season of the Sun* that they regarded as signs of capitulation to
the mass culture emphases of journalism. At the same time, in the act of
awarding the prize to Ishihara's novel, they embraced the aesthetic quality
of freshness/newness that was becoming an influential cultural value of
the Cold War age. *Season of the Sun*'s quality of freshness resonates with
an aesthetic that critics have identified retrospectively as "speed," a quality associated with modernity and loved in much of the writing, film, and
music of the 1950s in many of the free-world nations.

Ishihara as a Public Figure in 1950s Japan

It pleased Ishihara Shintarō to be showered with scathing criticism from
the older generation, as their barbs also served to confirm his rebellion.
He claimed not to care about the establishment's opinion. Because he had
earned the prize, though, he did take the time to read seriously their criticisms, and he may even have learned something about the establishment

of which he was now a part. From his most pointed critic, Satō Haruo, Ishihara knew that *Season of the Sun*'s prize resulted from politics (*seiji*). As Nakano explained, "The choice of this novel was a 'political' and not a literary one. [Only illogical politics could dictate that] it is a bad novel, therefore we should award it the Akutagawa Prize. . . . In contemporary Japanese politics, at the point when intellectuals have come to a general consensus [on a course of action], the exact opposite course is put into effect."[80] Not many years later, the understanding that Japanese politics could be illogical and/or contradictory changed Ishihara's life forever.

In venues other than the prize committees, critics continued trying to determine whether Ishihara's fictional works and his public presence presented a danger to society with their glorification of hedonism and representation of playing fast and loose with life and morality.[81] In contrast to his more prudent contemporaries, like Etō Jun (1932–1999) and Oda Makoto (1932–2007), Ishihara adored hyperbole and even pretended to aspire to murder, as we have seen. Discussing a high-risk behavior familiar from the silver screen—the game of "chicken" in the movie *Rebel Without a Cause*—Ishihara declared that he would be willing to try the game, if only given the chance. True to form, he also felt it necessary to add that he (like James Dean) had no particular reason for wanting to drive in cars toward sheer cliffs.[82] In this way, he clearly identified himself with the iconic "rebel without a cause" figure that suited the tense Cold War culture so perfectly.

Ishihara's constant appearance in the print media, on the movie screen, and on television meant that he had a high public profile. From another point of view, Ishihara "was the first example of a writer who had completely capitulated—in the view of the old guard—to the temptations of the popular media."[83] Characteristically, he consciously manipulated those media opportunities in order to mold his image. In addition to his outrageous and seemingly impulsive pronouncements about his reckless desire, Ishihara loved to play into the controversial categories that journalists would set out for him. Thus in a roundtable discussion labeled "Angry Youth," up-and-coming critic Etō Jun dispelled the notion that the assembled young writers were angry and recognized that the "angry generation" was merely a label assigned to them by the media. Of those assembled, Ishihara alone refused to distance himself from this identity and instead willingly played up to his reputation as an angry young man.[84] Similarly, Ishihara actively sought to foster his reputation as a rebel by denouncing the very "postwar" (*sengo-ha*) writers who derided his sudden appearance in prominent and powerful literary circles and by boasting that their criticisms did not concern him in the least. But his contemporaries Oda Makoto and Kobayashi Katsu called him on this: "Ishihara can act like he doesn't care about the *bundan* [literary establishment] because he's part of it."[85]

Strange Bedfellows: The Young Japan League

Throughout the Occupation and especially in the decades following it, people struggled to create a viable means of participation under the new postwar constitution and political system. Contrary to Ishihara Shintarō's maverick public persona, he shared intellectually with other writers of his generation the conviction that art can influence society and political culture. Ishihara, however, came to a strikingly conformist definition of his proper political role, whether as artist or citizen. While the turbulent and widespread political protests of the security treaty era suggest that grassroots individual and group activism dominated, Ishihara early on perceived the option of party politics, even with its contradictions, as a promising avenue for political participation.

Even if Ishihara initially earned his reputation in 1955 as an angry young man riding the crest of the global youthful rebellion wave, he very soon seized on other opportunities to expand his role as a public figure. Rather than rebellion without a cause, Ishihara's topics of concern rapidly broadened to encompass politics, morality, and society. This happened even before he successfully ran for election to the Diet or became the governor of Tokyo.

Even in the mid-1950s, when Ishihara would not hesitate in the least about publicly trashing established literary figures, the literary establishment, and the values of "adults," he was concerned about the opinions of his contemporaries, and especially those of serious writers of fiction. This was apparent when conversation turned to the connection between literature and politics. In a 1956 roundtable discussion, the novelist and activist Oda Makoto condemned young people who recklessly claimed that they had the right to "create their own values." Oda singled out as particularly repellant those people who regarded war as "something like pro wrestling" (and therefore acceptable or perhaps even cool) and who therefore refused to participate in the peace movement. Even though Oda named no names, Ishihara immediately retorted, "I've never compared war to pro wrestling. . . . Anyone who would do so is reckless and has little regard for human life." Then Oda took Ishihara to task: "Then why don't you write novels that won't give children the impression that [war is just a sport like wrestling]?"[86]

Once the Kishi regime came to power in early 1957, Ishihara and his cohort could no longer mull over politics in such broad and abstract terms. Kishi Nobusuke, who had been purged by the Allied Occupation because of his key role in economic planning for the Japanese Empire in the 1930s and his subsequent position as "vice minister of munitions under Prime Minister Tōjō Hideki in 1943–44," somewhat surprisingly rose to office of the prime minister only a little more than a decade after having been arrested for war crimes.[87]

In 1959 in a series of roundtable discussions in which Ishihara participated, the talk soon turned to the pressing issue of the proposed revision of a law defining the limits of police duties (keishoku-hō).[88] The government's proposal of broadening the police's authority to conduct searches reminded many people of the tyranny visited on them under the name of the prewar and wartime Peace Preservation Laws (Chian iji hō), which had allowed the police, unchecked, to arrest those who criticized the government and to carry out other repressive and brutal measures.[89] Wesley Sasaki-Uemura explains that because the police duties bill, introduced in the Diet on October 8, 1958, coincided with the beginning of negotiations regarding the renewal of the security treaty, "people also suspected that Kishi would use the police to ensure the treaty's passage or even to revise the constitution."[90]

At this moment in history, even Ishihara felt compelled to join a grassroots oppositional political movement. In 1958, he attended meetings of the newly formed Young Japan League (Wakai Nihon no kai), composed of about fifty up-and-coming young writers, musicians, painters, critics, and theater people. The group's immediate goal was publicly expressing the members' organized opposition to the proposed revisions of the Police Duties Law (Keishoku-hō kaisei-an hantai). In retrospect, it is difficult to think of an odder assembly of writers: Ishihara Shintarō, a future right-wing politician and nationalist; Ōe Kenzaburō, a future Nobel Prize winner and progressive; Etō Jun, a future prominent literary critic and neonationalist; Sono Ayako, a future prominent novelist, Christian, and neoconservative; and Abe Kōbō, a future prominent avant-garde writer, Marxist, and playwright, among other artists in their twenties and thirties.[91]

Although the scale of the citizens' opposition to proposed revisions of the Police Duties Law did not rival the demonstrations against the United

States–Japan Security Treaty that commenced later in 1959, millions of people put their names on petitions and participated in strikes and demonstrations. Among writers, those who had experienced wartime oppression spoke out first, warning that the proposed revisions would lead to the government's repression of freedom of speech and possibly even a revival of the abuses of power on a scale comparable to that during the 1930s and 1940s. More than six hundred writers who were members of the Japan PEN Club and the Japan Writers Association (Nihon bungeika kyōkai) signed a petition against the Kishi government's plans. The PEN Club writers included such prominent novelists as Kawabata Yasunari, Ōka Shōhei, Funahashi Sei'ichi, and Takami Jun.[92] The Young Japan League was one of the first political coalitions of young artists in the post-Occupation period. Although its members united in the common goal of expressing their opposition to a particular domestic issue, they showed great diversity in their opinions about the relationship between art and politics.

Ōe Kenzaburō, Abe Kōbō, Etō Jun, Sono Ayako, and Ishihara Shintarō—the most outspoken of the participants—extolled the virtues of grassroots political involvement as an essential and valid part of participatory democracy. Ōe furthermore believed that citizen participation in protest would influence the course of mainstream politics. In contrast, the leftist Abe quoted Lu Xun, who said that while soldiers lead the revolution, writers merely bring up the rear. Ishihara took an even more extreme view of the efficacy of citizen participation: politics, he insisted, worked less logically than that.[93] Part of Ishihara's understanding that the real reins of power often lie far from the normal citizen/artist's reach came from his contact with Liberal Democratic Party politicians. But even as Ishihara set his aim on party politics, he maintained his identity as a novelist.

In contrast to the popular angry young rebel image, in the roundtable discussion Ishihara revealed that he, like his fellow writers, was grappling seriously with the meanings of the relatively new system of postwar democracy:

> During the war, the relationship between the state [kokka] and the self/individual [jibun] was very close, to the extent that people willingly gave their lives for the state. . . . Now, because of postwar democratic education, the state and individual are supposed to be connected democratically, but even if there are student protests, before they can come to any real resolution, there is another problem to deal with. Even if some changes subsequently occur, one cannot

tell exactly what brought about that change. In fact, I have a strong sense that things are not decided according to logic. Conceptually, politics, the state, and the individual are close, but in reality they are far apart. Increasingly, the individual is getting further away from the reality of politics.[94]

Ōe viewed artists' political activism as effective only in coalition with a wide variety of other citizens' groups. He saw clearly, as Ishihara must have, that citizens did not regard the members of the Young Japan League as righteous "artists" or "writers" per se but rather as celebrities. Repeatedly, Ishihara and Ōe disagreed about the latter's idealism about the power of literature to influence politics and the importance of artist's political activism.[95] Ultimately, it was Ishihara's skepticism about the value of grassroots citizen participation that steered him toward elected office, in which he could wield an authority that he did not believe the written word or protest alone would afford him. Accordingly, he cast his lot with the recently established Liberal Democratic Party, correctly perceiving the strength and stability of the so-called 1955 system, which relied on the conservative hegemony manifest in that political party. In turn, the party was key to maintaining Japan's status as a key Western-bloc ally in Asia. Although Ishihara eventually criticized Japan's subservience to the United States and broke with the party, early in his career he took advantage of the powerful political orthodoxy.

Precisely a decade after Japan's surrender in World War II, Ishihara's debut as a novelist echoed the rapid rate of change in postwar culture prompted by a rapidly growing economy and a heightened commitment to the Western bloc's vision of Japan as a model capitalist liberal democracy. Rather than apprenticing himself to the literary establishment and working his way up to the big time, Ishihara rose almost instantly from being a college student who dabbled in literature to a media celebrity-writer. His novels found their way onto the silver screen with impressive speed. He sped onto the new media of television and quickly embraced every opportunity to model the fashion codes of rebellious youth for magazines and newspapers. Ishihara even raced around on motorboats: in short, he moved and worked with great speed.

In Kurosawa's *Record of a Living Being*, the teenager in the aloha shirt is a relatively minor character but at the same time a type that the director felt compelled to represent in a film that was very much a portrait of its times. In mid-1950s Japan, Ishihara was in no way a minor cultural figure but instead a person who had his finger on the pulse of multiple currents of contemporary society and whose influence on how people conceived of youth and consumerism was considerable. In league with *Rebel Without a Cause* and other imported cultural products, the Sun Tribe novels and films and their interpretive communities and consumers gave rise to a shift in the perception of generations, consumerism, and identity. In other words, it was "through youth that postwar consumer society of the 1950s discovered itself."[96] The project of containing communism and stabilizing capitalism required a conceptual change: Ishihara presented youth as a "privileged Cold War trope, as a healthy sign of domestic culture and economy, rather than as a looming threat from without."[97]

Ishihara Shintarō brought together the elite culture with mass cultural forms, foreshadowing the postmodern leveling of these diverse yet related cultural spheres. His aggressive self-promotion embodied the promise of a prosperous, "unspoiled," and vigorous society and a bright future. Ishihara and his forays into novel writing and filmmaking created a point of intersection between Japan's evolving contemporary culture and that of its Cold War allies, as well as new directions for the stagnating post-Occupation Japan.

Conclusion *Cold War as Culture*

By most accounts, the Cold War began during the administration of President Harry S. Truman, so it is only fitting that the Truman Presidential Museum and Library in Independence, Missouri, explores many aspects of the international conflict. Visitors discover detailed exhibits on subjects such as the formation of NATO (North Atlantic Treaty Organization) and the Marshall Plan, the significance of the Truman Doctrine, McCarthyism, civil defense in America, the success of the Berlin airlifts, and the East–West divide in Europe. A detailed display offers a balanced presentation of Truman's decision to drop atomic bombs on Japan. In contrast, the Cold War in Asia is represented in only a single small area: a cleverly installed domed ceiling in one corner that shows a multihued map of the earth as seen from the North Pole, with the Asian continent dominating the center and Japan and other islands arrayed along the eastern and southern coastlines. Spotlights illuminate relevant regions on the map as a recorded voice explains the origins and course of the hot war on the Korean Peninsula. A row of miniature lightbulbs flashes on the line of friction: the thirty-eighth parallel. The museum's brochure explains the extent of the Cold War in Asia as "the rescue of South Korea from communist aggression." In American public memory and academic histories, military conflicts dominated Asia's Cold War. We

204 COLD WAR AS CULTURE

therefore know little, if anything, about the social and cultural ramifications of this half century of social and ideological conflict in East Asia, much less about the Cold War as a lived experience.

Similarly, popular culture offers only limited insights into Japan's early Cold War. I do not know whether Harry Truman saw the movie *Godzilla* (*Gojira*, 1954), but millions of Japanese and Americans in his day certainly did. In retrospect, it is easy to understand the film's appeal to contemporary Japanese and American audiences, even without the skillful cutting in of the Raymond Burr character. *Godzilla* depicts a stable, prosperous society with a smoothly functioning infrastructure (the government, the police, the scientific community, the media) populated by ordinary, well-nourished people who believe in myth (Godzilla) but who are scientifically advanced (the oxygen destroyer). War memories are selectively and briefly included. In the person of Dr. Serizawa, a war veteran with a scar to prove it, Japan does the right thing. He sacrifices himself in order to eliminate the threat of Godzilla and thereby returns the realm to stability. Nuclear events are not attributed to any nation. No one is to blame but the bomb itself. We all are potential victims. In this sense, *Godzilla* fits well with the United States's 1950s understanding of itself and with Japan's wishes for recovery and moral rectification, but it does not tell us a great deal about Japan in that era other than a few fears and many aspirations.

The disconnect between the Cold War and Japan's history is not limited to the United States. When Japanese scholar Marukawa Tetsushi met with intellectuals in China, Korea, and Taiwan, he was taken aback by how often they brought up the topic of the 1959/1960 Japanese protest movement against the United States–Japan Security Treaty. Finally, Marukawa realized that his Asian counterparts were bringing up the protests as a means of including Japan in a broader issue about which they were deeply concerned: the Cold War and its influence on Asia.[1] These dialogues opened his eyes to the centrality of the Cold War in the Koreas', Taiwan's, and China's cultural and national identities and, conversely, to the willful silencing of this framework in the analysis of Japan's post-1945 culture.

The word "war" in the Cold War encourages us to focus on bombs, battlefronts, and mushroom clouds. In contrast, however, this book has emphasized the complex cultural histories of the Cold War. Indeed, the image of the Cold War as a thriller at the highest diplomatic levels dominating academic studies and media coverage—as well as in popular cultural representations from Ian Fleming's James Bond to John le Carré's George Smiley—constitutes only part of the story.

Without doubting the significance of the diplomatic and military history of the Cold War, I have chosen to pose a different set of questions, ones that encourage an understanding of the Cold War as a complex social and cultural, mostly nonmilitary, process. What did people and societies experience on a cultural level? How did the Cold War affect cultural production? What institutional and economic structures influenced the articulation of the Cold War in the cultural realm? This book aims at enhancing our knowledge about the complex connections of global geopolitics, domestic discourse, and cultural production in other parts of the world, where the Cold War may have seemed less thrilling. Locally, the spirited resistance, both radical and regressive, of the Japanese artists and critics discussed here suggests the vitality of the Cold War's cultural aspects. As Marukawa theorized, "The Cold War cast its shadow between the lines of texts [and films] produced in Japan," owing to the fact that Japan, though in one sense swept up in the Cold War, was also "complicit [in the process] and in some ways played a leading role."[2] On a political and economic level, Japan took a "leading role" in stabilizing the capitalist bloc in Asia. That is, Japanese artists and intellectuals were not passive recipients of a wave of geopolitical tension or the dominance of the Western bloc. We have seen the myriad ways that individuals seized the opportunities created by the strange tension and openness of the early Cold War.

I have tried to show how Japan's culture flourished intellectually, artistically, and morally during the first decades of the Cold War, based on the understanding that artists and critics have a vital role to play in building society. Cultural rather than martial in nature, these projects included the challenge (and excitement, paradoxical as that may seem) of contributing to the atomic discourse and even to the nuclear sublime; the enthralling process of negotiating new or renewed interactions with a wide range of cultural forms, artists, and activists from around the world; and the project of forging new domestic understandings of what democracy means. Just as the Pacific War and World War II profoundly affected Japan's culture, so did the Cold War.

One important dynamic that defines the Cold War experience is the increased interaction with texts and ideas from allies and enemies in a culture already known for its cosmopolitanism and openness to the world outside its borders. We have explored Japan's cultural Cold War from one of several possible angles: the story of artists and intellectuals in contact with art, ideas, and forms from the Western bloc, and the cultural frictions that arose from Japan's incorporation into the American alliance, beginning with the inception of the Cold War-as-process. But this is not the only vantage point or the only group of individuals or cultural events relevant to Japan's Cold War.

A few scholars like Marukawa have told the story of the "forgotten, ambiguous war and its relevance to today" from the perspective of Japan's intersections with other parts of East Asia. Some of the people he describes, such as Takeuchi Yoshimi (1910–1977), had deep ties with continental culture as a scholar of Chinese literature and the translator of Lu Xun. Therefore, the key events of this era, such as the founding of the People's Republic of China and China's involvement in the Korean War, had vastly different meanings for Takeuchi than for an Anglophile critic like Itō Sei. Even so, in the early 1950s Takeuchi and Itō, along with Shakespeare scholar Fukuda Tsuneari, who also took an active role in the *Lady Chatterley* trial, participated in a vigorous debate over the potential for a literature of the people (*kokumin bungaku*) in Japan. Takeuchi may have had in mind a Marxist notion of the people, while Itō's idea of the people likely related to the spread of progressive liberalism in the early Occupation. Takeuchi later wrote laudatory articles about Mao Zedong, a heroic figure at the time on the Left, and participated in the political protest surrounding the United States–Japan Security Treaty in 1959/1960, whereas Itō's shining moment of political activism, though perhaps unintended, was during the *Lady Chatterley* trial. Although their paths later diverged, during the 1950s Takeuchi and conservatives like Itō had in common the vision of activist artists in a new liberal democracy.[3] That democracy, furthermore, was briefly in a state of flux and relative openness, as I have demonstrated, precisely because of the process of establishing a Cold War global order and the steep learning curve that this entailed.

The shock of one Taiwanese novelist, Chen Yingzhen (b. 1937), upon seeing a Japan Communist Party billboard, large and out in the open, from a train window in Tokyo, helped Marukawa understand the extent to which Japan's Cold War had differed from that of neighboring Asian countries. Japanese writers and activists had been sheltered from the most blatant practices of authoritarian anticommunist regimes. While Japan was fully implicated in the Cold War system, most Japanese artists and intellectuals lived in what Marukawa calls an "air pocket" that cushioned them from the political hot spots and also encouraged a state of amnesia about the Cold War itself.[4] In telling Takeuchi's and Chen's stories, Marukawa evokes yet a different dimension of the cultural process of this Cold War in Japan, one that we are beginning to understand only now.

In the post–Cold War world, international affairs and local culture are still enmeshed in structures and discourses established during the decades-long conflict. The lingering influence of the Cold War is evident in a variety of ways: antagonism toward the United States despite the dominance of capitalism, the revival of bipolar hostility, and the nuclear regime and deterrence.

A fundamental assumption of this book is that cultural artifacts must be understood as part of a broader cultural history and not in isolation. Although my textual analysis may seem too brief to some readers, I have tried to strike a balance between close readings of individual works and events and an exploration of the historical, social, and political contexts of creativity and reception. I also have examined the central intellectual and political currents that coexisted with the discourses of war responsibility and subjectivity (*shutaisei*) and that in turn were stimulated by domestic and international events and discourses.

Prominent among these approaches are the distinction between Marxism as a system of thought and the political practices of totalitarian communism in the Soviet Union and its relationship to other revolutionary states such as the People's Republic of China. Another significant trend was the public's fear of a fascist resurgence during the postwar period that was expressed in both the *Lady Chatterley* trials and the opposition to the Police Duties Law in which Ishihara Shintarō participated. As Harry Harootunian pointed out, modernism and fascism were "contemporary to each other in the first half of the twentieth century." Whether they would revive, entangled or separated, in the postwar period or be replaced by other discourses was not, as we have seen, clear to most people in the 1950s. There were economic reasons for this caution. Because there was "no normal state of capitalism," after 1945 people regarded with anxiety the potential for further crises in capitalism and the accompanying possibility of another world war.[5] The revelation of Stalin's brutal authoritarianism presented another reason for the need for vigilance. The progressive idealism of the early Occupation forces intermingled with the anticommunism of the Reverse Course and with the dominance of Marxist thought among artists and intellectuals. Etō Jun and others argued that the Allied Occupation resulted in a "closed linguistic space" that warped Japanese literature and writing. Granted, the Occupation's censorship and the U.S.–Japanese alliance forbade the discussion of topics such as patriotism and nationalism. Pride in military history and nation was not part of mainstream discourse. Nonetheless, I have explored the many ways in which Japan at this time engaged in open discourse and Japanese writers and filmmakers dealt productively with censorship and political pressure.

In the post–Cold War era, we see a conflation of high- and lowbrow culture, of art and commercial design, a process that began during the early Cold War. In this context, a number of artists revisited Japan's atomic events, resulting in an ahistorical linking of Japan's bomb with all cultural and commercial production in visual media. In an interesting contrast with the lonely quest of the *hibakusha* Hara Tamiki to reimagine the bomb creatively, Murakami Takashi's highly publicized edited volume *Little Boy: The Arts of Japan's Exploding Subculture* (2005) traces the many representations, cultural and aesthetic sensibilities, commodities, and media in contemporary Japan back to Hiroshima and Nagasaki.[6] In other words, Murakami fetishizes the bomb and attempts a masculine mastery of the bomb by representing it as generating every conceivable "exploding" art form (to borrow Okamoto Tarō's famous phrase) and medium in contemporary Japan. However problematic the linear concept of history may be, Murakami's cynical collapsing of time and history into his superflat conception is arresting, to say the least: "These monotonous ruins of a nation-state, which arrived on the heels of an American puppet government, have been perfectly realized in the name of capitalism. . . . We Japanese still embody 'Little Boy,' nicknamed like the atomic bomb itself, after a nasty childhood taunt." Murakami elaborates: "Whatever true intentions underlie 'Little Boy,' the nickname for Hiroshima's atomic bomb, we Japanese are truly, deeply, pampered children."[7]

This postmodern, superflat style exemplifies the collapsing of aesthetic, commercial, and political categories all into one. According to Murakami, the popular subculture and commercial aesthetic of cuteness (*kawaii*) and looseness (*yurui*) have their roots in the bomb, which emasculated and infantilized Japan. Murakami asks his readers first to realize that the Japanese have been made into a pathetic, febrile version of their beautiful, virile authentic selves, as has the nation as a whole: "Postwar Japan was given life and nurtured by America. We were shown that the true meaning of life is meaninglessness, and we were thought to live without thought. Our society and hierarchies were dismantled. We were forced into a system that does not produce 'adults.'"[8]

Murakami sustains the periodization of Japan as postwar when he states that Japan's postwar will end only when the current United States–Japan Security Treaty is dismantled. For him, Japan danced with only one partner: America. His effort to articulate a Japanese identity and to con-template the potential for new versions of that identity in the post–Cold War world is hampered by adherence to the understanding of Japan only in relationship to the defeat, the bomb, and war guilt. While I credit Mu-rakami and his coauthors for keeping the issue of nuclear weapons in the public eye, the specifically gendered and exceptionalist approach taken in *Little Boy* is a matter of concern. As in America, the bomb and Truman's decision are only one part of a much larger complex of social and cultural forces. Accordingly, placing contemporary Japan in the broader and more complex framework of the Cold War will encourage a fuller understand-ing of its place in the post–Cold War world and thus in the international cultural community.

In this way, the financially successful Murakami prepares us for the logical next step in the agenda of some in Japan: a revitalization of the country's virility, making the superflat moral and the infantilized places muscular. During his third term as Tokyo governor, Ishihara Shintarō responded as if to Murakami's manifesto (which Ishihara himself had articulated numerous times earlier) with another high-profile national-ist statement in his big-budget feature film, *For Those We Love* (*Ore wa kimi no tame ni koso shini iku*, 2007, directed by Shinjo Taku). The movie portrays in a positive and romanticized light the kamikaze suicide pilots at the end of World War II. The unstated goal is reviving the real, mas-culine, beautiful Japan. Precisely because of the waning American au-thority in the post–Cold War era and Japan's interest in forging a new national identity and refashioning its relations with other East Asian na-tions, these submerged currents of gendered nationalism have reemerged in the mainstream. The rise of neonationalism and fundamentalism around the globe may in part be attributed to the United States's unwa-vering support, during the Cold War and after, of anticommunist govern-ments, some that have changed into liberal democracies but others that persist as fundamentalist, authoritarian regimes.

In the post–Cold War period, as in the high-tension stages of the Cold War, Ishihara Shintarō's voice may be loud, but he most definitely does not speak for all of Japan's cultural and intellectual communities or for the broader public, for that matter. Indeed, as I have shown, Kamei Fu-mio, Odagiri Hideo, Maruki Toshi and Maruki Iri, and many others con-tributed in innumerable ways to Japan's creation of a diverse and vibrant cultural production and public sphere.

Notes

Introduction: The Strange Tension of the Cold War

1. A large literature exists on Gojira (Godzilla). See, for example, Yoshikuni Igarashi, *Bodies of Memory: Narratives of War in Postwar Japanese Culture, 1945–1970* (Princeton, N.J.: Princeton University Press, 2000); and William Tsutui and Michiko Ito, eds., *In Godzilla's Footsteps: Japanese Pop Culture Icons on the Global Stage* (New York: Palgrave Macmillan, 2006).

2. The major monograph on Cold War culture in East Asia to date is Rana Mitter and Patrick Major, eds., *Across the Blocs: Cold War Cultural and Social History* (Portland, Ore.: Frank Cass, 2004). The foremost work of Japanese scholarship that uses Cold War culture as an analytical framework is Marukawa Tetsushi, *Reisen bunka ron: Wasurerareta aimaina sensō no genzaisei* (Tokyo: Sofūsha, 2005). Well-known examples of the Cold War's influence on Anglo-European art and culture include Thomas Hill Schaub, *American Fiction in the Cold War* (Madison: University of Wisconsin Press, 1991); Robert J. Corber, *In the Name of National Security: Hitchcock, Homophobia, and the Political Construction of Gender in Postwar America* (Durham, N.C.: Duke University Press, 1993); Alan M. Wald, *The New York Intellectuals: The Rise and Decline of the Anti-Stalinist Left from the 1930s to the 1980s* (Chapel Hill: University of North Carolina Press, 1987); Paul Lauter, *From Walden Pond to Jurassic Park: Activism, Culture and American Studies* (Durham, N.C.: Duke University Press, 2001); Frances Stonor Saunders, *The Cultural Cold War: The CIA and the World of Arts and Letters* (New York: New Press, 1999); Stephen J. Whitfield, *The Culture of the Cold War,* 2nd ed. (Baltimore: Johns

Hopkins University Press, 1996); Joel Kotek, *Students and the Cold War,* trans. Ralph Blumenau (New York: St. Martin's Press, 1996); Gary D. Rawnsley, ed., *Cold War Propaganda in the 1950s* (New York: St. Martin's Press, 1999); and Serge Guilbaut, *How New York Stole the Idea of Modern Art: Abstract Expressionism, Freedom, and the Cold War,* trans. Arthur Goldhammer (Chicago: University of Chicago Press, 1983). For a succinct introduction to the history of the Cold War, see David S. Painter, *The Cold War: An International History* (New York: Routledge, 1999). Richard Saull offers a fascinating analysis of the Cold War from a Marxist viewpoint in *The Cold War and After: Capitalism, Revolution and Superpower Politics* (Ann Arbor, Mich.: Pluto Press, 2007). Other important works on the history of the Cold War and international relations include the many by John Lewis Gaddis, such as *We Now Know: Rethinking Cold War History* (New York: Oxford University Press, 1997); and Odd Arne Westad, ed., *Reviewing the Cold War: Approaches, Interpretations, Theory* (Portland, Ore.: Frank Cass, 2000). For the social sciences in Cold War America, see Ellen Herman, *The Romance of American Psychology: Political Culture in the Age of Experts* (Berkeley: University of California Press, 1995).

3. Part of Japan's imagined insularity stems from its geographical separation from its neighbors, in contrast to Germany, whose proximity to both the Soviet Union and Western Europe presented an immediate security threat. See Painter, *Cold War,* 26. Geographically, Japan never was divided as Germany, Korea, and Vietnam were, all of which bordered the Eastern bloc. Japan, in contrast, was a demilitarized zone floating in the Pacific Ocean.

4. The discourse of domesticity developed partially as an antidote to the all-consuming state of total war integral to Japan's empire and also in tandem with the vision of capitalist modernity encouraged by the West's approach to the Cold War.

5. Donald Richie analyzes Kurosawa's use of heat in this and other movies in *The Films of Akira Kurosawa,* 3rd ed. (Berkeley: University of California Press, 1984), 111.

6. Quoted in Richie, *Films of Akira Kurosawa,* 112.

7. From the late 1930s through the 1950s, five of Abe Tomoji's novels were adapted as feature films by well-known directors.

8. Abe Tomoji was a prolific scholar and writer. During the 1930s, he was at the forefront of literary modernism and was the founder of Herman Melville studies in Japan. Conscripted by the imperial military, Abe served in Java during the war and wrote about his experiences in semicolonial China. During the war, a translation of one of his short stories was published in the English-language Soviet journal *XXth Century,* published in Shanghai, available at libweb.Hawaii.edu/libdept/Russian/xx/toc_vol_7.html. In the early postwar period, Abe traveled again to China and translated Agnes Smedley's writings on China into Japanese. See Shu-Mei Shih, *The Lure of the Modern: Writing Modernism in Semi-Colonial China, 1917–1937* (Berkeley: University of California Press, 2001); and Mizukami Isao, "Abe Tomoji to Jaba chōyō taiken," *Bulletin of Tezukayama University* 23 (1986): 34–54. For Abe's involvement in the literary debates of the 1930s, see Kyoko Omori, "Detecting Japanese Vernacular Modernism: *Shinseinen* Magazine

and the Development of the *Tantei Shōsetsu* Genre, 1920–1931" (Ph.D. diss., Ohio State University, 2003), 37, 139, 140. On modernism in Japan, see William J. Tyler, ed., *Modanizumu in Japanese Fiction: An Anthology of Modernist Prose from Japan, 1914–1938* (Honolulu: University of Hawai'i Press, 2008).

9. A photograph of Abe at the E. H. Norman Memorial can be found in the E. Herbert Norman Papers, box 5, BC2124–170, www.library.ubc.ca/spcoll/AZ/PDF/N/Norman_E_Herbert.pdf.

10. In Japanese, *Kono reisen no bukimina kinchō no naka de*. Abe Tomoji, *Genshiryoku to bungaku* [*Atomic Power and Literature*], ed. Odagiri Hideo (Tokyo: Kōdansha, 1955), third page of unpaginated introduction.

11. John W. Dower describes the phases of the U.S. strategic policy toward Japan during the Occupation as (1) "demilitarization and democratization" (end of the war to mid-1947); (2) a "soft" Cold War policy, with primary emphasis on "denying Japan to the Soviet sphere" (mid-1947 to 1949); (3) a "hard" Cold War policy, in which Japan was assigned a positive, active role in U.S. anticommunism (1949–September 1951); and (4) an "integrated" Cold War policy when a regional approach was employed (with a "trilateral nexus" of the United States, Japan, and Southeast Asia) and the peace treaties concluded in late 1951/1952) (*Japan in War and Peace: Selected Essays* [New York: New Press, 1993], 160–86).

12. In his important *Reisen bunka ron*, Marukawa raises the question of whether Japan was a mere observer of the Cold War.

13. The discourse of peace-loving, war-renouncing Japan was contradicted in practice by the buildup of its Self-Defense Forces (SDF) and military expenditures and the continued occupation of military bases by the United States in accordance with the U.S.–Japanese security arrangement. As Andrew Gordon points out, however, as "officially sanctioned goals or ideals" the postwar constitution's "ambitious provisions have framed and continued to frame postwar discourse and shape institutions in important ways" ("Transwar Through Postwar Japan," in *Historical Perspectives on Contemporary East Asia*, ed. Merle Goldman and Andrew Gordon [Cambridge, Mass.: Harvard University Press, 2000], 278). A significant shift away from the ideals of Article 9 of the constitution did not begin until the Koizumi administration.

14. For an incisive study of juvenile delinquency in Japan from 1868 to 1945, see David R. Ambaras, *Bad Youth: Juvenile Delinquency and the Politics of Everyday Life in Modern Japan* (Berkeley: University of California Press, 2006).

15. Leerom Medovoi points out that the idea of the rebel youth (such as James Dean and Elvis Presley) "emerged at the dawn of the Cold War era because the ideological production of the United States as leader of the 'free world' required figures who could represent America's emancipatory potential" (*Rebels: Youth and the Cold War Origins of Identity* [Durham, N.C.: Duke University Press, 2005], 1). For President Eisenhower, the "bad boy" rebels "demonstrated that Cold War America, . . . remained a free nation whose people decided their own futures rather than being inserted, as in totalitarian societies, into predetermined positions in preexisting social structures" (211).

16. Kristen Ross, *Fast Cars, Clean Bodies: Decolonization and the Reordering of*

214 THE STRANGE TENSION OF THE COLD WAR

French Culture (Cambridge, Mass.: MIT Press, 1999), 138. Ross was writing about France during the same era. The rise of the middle class and rapid urbanization have been well documented in, for example, William W. Kelly, "Finding a Place in Metropolitan Japan: Ideologies, Institutions, and Everyday Life," in *Postwar Japan as History,* ed. Andrew Gordon (Berkeley: University of California Press, 1993), 189–216.

17. Medovoi uses the term "three worlds concept" to describe the triangular dynamic of the United States, the Soviet Union and the "more than a quarter of the world's population at that time" who fought to become independent from the colonizers (*Rebels,* 10–11). While decolonialization is a crucial dynamic of the Cold War and Japan, it is not the focus of this study.

18. In Japanese, *kono kyōfu no jidai no tsugi ni kuru mono.* Abe, *Genshiryoku to bungaku,* first page of unpaginated introduction.

19. Marukawa, *Reisen bunka ron,* 7–9. Marukawa traces his awareness of the issue of Cold War culture to his experiences with post–Cold War Taiwan and Korea, where popular prodemocracy movements in the 1970s and 1980s clearly were critiques of the Cold War regime. I first encountered Marukawa's book when I was in the final stages of this project. As a Japanese scholar interested in colonialism and regionalism, Marukawa chooses a different set of events, cultural figures, and texts than do I, an American scholar. Perhaps not surprisingly, I emphasize the atomic aspect of the Cold War much more. Marukawa looks for traces of the Cold War in intellectuals' and writers' encounters with China and Korea and in the cultural history of Okinawa as a site of American neocolonial occupation.

20. Marukawa also cites 1945 as the starting point in his study of the Cold War in Japan. Histories focusing on the Cold War in Europe, however, often regard the Berlin blockade in 1948 as the start. Others trace it back to the Allies' meeting in Yalta in February 1945. American journalist Walter Lippmann is credited with coining the term "Cold War" in 1947. The mainstream Japanese media publicly acknowledged the link between the atomic bombings and the Cold War soon after the Occupation, but the leftist press noted it earlier. Headlines in the August 6, 1952, issue of *Asahi Graph* read: "When did the Cold War, the stand-off between the US–USSR start? On August 6, 1945" (quoted in Marukawa, *Reisen bunka ron,* 12).

21. James G. Hershberg, "The Crisis Years, 1958–1963," in *Reviewing the Cold War,* ed. Westad, 303.

22. Melvyn P. Leffler, "Bringing It Together: The Parts and the Whole," in *Reviewing the Cold War,* ed. Westad, 56. By "anarchic," Leffler is likely referring to the unsettled nature of the global order before the 1962 Cuban missile crisis, owing to the rapid decolonization, the inevitable shifting of power relations among the major powers due to the outcome of World War II, and the novelty of the notion of nuclear weapons and deterrence. According to Hershberg, after the "near-hit with catastrophe" in 1962, "both sides took steps to moderate the intensity of their rivalry, and to try to ensure that subsequent direct tests of strength, especially in the vital arena of Europe, would be limited to political, economic, and ideological struggle, while military battles would be shunted off to Third World proxies

and the nuclear race kept within predictable, negotiable channels" ("Crisis Years," 304). Hershberg calls the period from 1945 to 1963 the "first, virulent stage of the Cold War" (319).

23. Quoted in Herman, *Romance of American Psychology*, 135.

24. Herman, *Romance of American Psychology*, 135.

25. Joseph Masco describes the bomb as a national fetish because "it takes a nation-state to build it and maintain it, and because the national hierarchy of nation-states is mediated through possession of the bomb. Nuclear weapons therefore maintain a magical hold on people's thinking, and in doing so, energize very specific national-cultural imaginaries" (*The Nuclear Borderlands: The Manhattan Project in Post–Cold War New Mexico* [Princeton, N.J.: Princeton University Press, 2006], 22).

26. Bruce Cummings quotes Secretary of State Dean Acheson's coining of the phrase "great crescent." Cummings also notes that although "containment was thought to be preeminently a security strategy against communist expansion, in East Asia the policy mingled power and plenty" ("Japan's Position in the World System," in *Postwar Japan as History*, ed. Gordon, 37–38). Laura Hein points out that the economic growth brought by the Korean War, along with the U.S. government's efforts to create an export market for the still-fragile Japanese economy, meant that the start of the Korean War in June 1950 was "certainly more important to Japanese economic history than was the political milestone of independence in April 1952" ("Growth Versus Success: Japan's Economic Policy in Historical Perspective," in *Postwar Japan as History*, ed. Gordon, 110).

27. Remember, however, that the course of Japan's economic development was in no way natural or inevitable. Rather, Japan's recovery and financial magnificence were an outcome of contentious domestic processes and of a "particular international environment and was thus very much part of the global development of advanced capitalism in the twentieth century" (Hein, "Growth Versus Success," 107).

1. The Meanings of War and Peace After 1945

1. Patrick Major and Rana Mitter, "East Is East and West Is West? Towards a Comparative Socio-Cultural History of the Cold War," in *Across the Blocs: Cold War Cultural and Social History*, ed. Rana Mitter and Patrick Major (Portland, Ore.: Frank Cass, 2004), 1–2. An important impetus to my book was the journal *Cold War History*. In this study, I do not address the Soviet cultural Cold War.

2. I have been inspired by studies of Japan's postwar culture, such as the work of Susan Napier, Davinder Bowmik, and John W. Dower; Lisa Yoneyama, *Hiroshima Traces: Time, Space, and the Dialectics of Memory* (Berkeley: University of California Press, 1999); John Treat, *Writing Ground Zero: Japanese Literature and the Atomic Bomb* (Chicago: University of Chicago Press, 1995); Michael Molasky, *The American Occupation of Japan and Okinawa: Literature and Memory* (New York: Routledge, 1999); Sharalyn Orbaugh, "The Body in Contemporary Japanese

Women's Fiction," in *The Woman's Hand: Gender and Theory in Japanese Women's Writing*, ed. Paul G. Schalow and Janet A. Walker (Stanford, Calif.: Stanford University Press, 1996); and James J. Orr, *The Victim as Hero: Ideologies of Peace and National Identity in Postwar Japan* (Honolulu: University of Hawai'i Press, 2001). Here I look at some of the same writers that Treat addresses in *Writing Ground Zero*, a groundbreaking study of Japanese literature and the bomb, in which he critiques large questions of art, modernity, trauma, and catastrophe. My study takes a different approach by shifting the focus to the social and ideological contexts and processes of writing, film, and art in 1950s Japan, with an emphasis on Cold War cultural history.

3. On civil defense, see, for example, Guy Oakes, *The Imaginary War: Civil Defense and American Cold War Culture* (New York: Oxford University Press, 1994); and Tracy C. Davis, *Stages of Emergency: Cold War Nuclear Civil Defense* (Durham, N.C.: Duke University Press, 2007). See also Bill Geerhart and Ken Sitz, *Atomic Platters: Cold War Music from the Golden Age of Homeland Security* (Hamburg: Bear Family Records, 2005), a book and compact discs.

4. Major and Mitter use the term "armed truce" ("East Is East and West Is West?" 4).

5. Such a focus on Europe in Cold War studies can be seen in the definition of the Cold War by the prominent scholar Melvyn P. Leffler, in which he never mentions Asia: "Historians define the Cold War as a complex phenomenon characterized by a rivalry between two powerful states with universalizing ideologies and conflicting systems of political economy. The rivalry led to the division of Germany and Europe, competition on the periphery, and a strategic arms race" ("Bringing It Together: The Parts and the Whole," in *Reviewing the Cold War: Approaches, Interpretations, Theory*, ed. Odd Arne Westad [Portland, Ore.: Frank Cass, 2000], 56).

6. Some notable studies of culture during the height of the Cold War in the Soviet Union include Vera Dunham, *In Stalin's Time: Middleclass Values in Soviet Fiction* (Cambridge: Cambridge University Press, 1976); and Deborah Field, "Irreconcilable Differences: Divorce and Conceptions of Private Life in the Khrushchev Era," *Russian Review* 57, no. 4 (1998): 599–613. See also Richard Stites, "Heaven and Hell: Soviet Propaganda Constructs the World," in *Cold War Propaganda in the 1950s*, ed. Gary D. Rawnsley (New York: St. Martin's Press, 1999), 85–104. My thanks to Heather Hogan for her insights. Another excellent resource is the Cold War International History Project at the Woodrow Wilson International Center for Scholars in Washington, D.C.

7. Charles Armstrong's insightful work focuses on the direct propaganda and reorientation efforts of the United States on the Korean Peninsula, in "The Cultural Cold War in Korea, 1945–1950," *Journal of Asian Studies* 62, no. 1 (2003): 71.

8. Major and Mitter, "East Is East and West Is West?" 8.

9. Andrew Gordon, "Transwar Through Postwar Japan," in *Historical Perspectives on Contemporary East Asia*, ed. Merle Goldman and Andrew Gordon (Cambridge, Mass.: Harvard University Press, 2000). See also Lisle Rose, *The Cold War Comes to Main Street* (Lawrence: University Press of Kansas, 1999), 64–119.

10. Foremost among the studies of the Occupation is John W. Dower, *Embracing Defeat: Japan in the Wake of World War II* (New York: Norton / New Press, 1999).

11. Gordon, "Transwar Through Postwar Japan," 283.

12. J. Victor Koschmann discusses both the debates among Japanese intellectuals and the Japan Communist Party in "Intellectuals and Politics," in *Postwar Japan as History*, ed. Andrew Gordon (Berkeley: University of California Press, 1993), esp. 395–413.

13. Harry D. Harootunian, "The Black Cat in the Dark Room," *positions* 13, no. 1 (2005): 140. Similarly, David S. Painter comments that in Western Europe, U.S. "covert-action programs undermined communist influence in trade unions and other institutions. The overall impact of U.S. aid policies was to narrow the scope of acceptable debate and facilitate the ascendancy of centrist parties" (*The Cold War: An International History* [New York: Routledge, 1999], 21).

14. Melvyn P. Leffler, "New Approaches, Old Interpretations, and Prospective Reconfigurations," in *America in the World: The Historiography of American Foreign Relations Since 1941* (Cambridge: Cambridge University Press, 1995), 81–84, quoted in John Lewis Gaddis, "On Starting Over Again: A Naïve Approach to the Study of the Cold War," in *Reviewing the Cold War*, ed. Westad, 42.

15. John W. Dower, *Japan in War and Peace: Selected Essays* (New York: New Press, 1993), 4; Wesley Sasaki-Uemura, *Organizing the Spontaneous: Citizen Protest in Postwar Japan* (Honolulu: University of Hawai'i Press, 2001), 25. Richard J. Samuels describes the founding of the LDP in November 1955 as "one of the most overdetermined events in Japanese political history. . . . Kishi had been maneuvering for it for half a decade, the business community and the U.S. Secretary of State John Foster Dulles each openly demanded it. . . . [The Japan Socialist Party's] consolidation in October led to formation of the Liberal Democratic Party one month later" (*Machiavelli's Children: Leaders and Their Legacies in Italy and Japan* [Ithaca, N.Y.: Cornell University Press, 2003], 231).

16. Gordon, "Transwar Through Postwar Japan," 284.

17. Sasaki-Uemura, *Organizing the Spontaneous*, 25; Samuels, *Machiavelli's Children*, 232.

18. Samuels, *Machiavelli's Children*, 186.

19. Marilyn Ivy further comments that "mass culture in this general sense arose together with industrial capitalism itself, for its very possibility is predicated on those technologies of both material and social production that emerged with the development of capitalism . . . in the postwar period the ascendancy of the electronic media, particularly television, has added new dimensions to this dynamic" ("Formations of Mass Culture," in *Postwar Japan as History*, ed. Gordon, 240). See also William W. Kelly, "Finding a Place in Metropolitan Japan: Ideologies, Institutions, and Everyday Life," in *Postwar Japan as History*, ed. Gordon, 195; and Koschmann, "Intellectuals and Politics," 404.

20. Ivy notes that the "creation of a large-scale consumption society as early as the 1910s and 1920s paralleled developments in the United States, as much of an emergent global culture of consumption was patterned on American

developments. . . . In many respects Japan was a full-blown mass society at least by the mid-1920s" ("Formations of Mass Culture," 240). Togaeri Hajime emphasizes the differences in the scale of mass culture in the interwar and postwar periods and the resulting absorption of the smaller literary and critical journals that managed to survive into mass media, in "Taiyō bungaku ronsō no yukue," in *Togaeri Hajime chosaku shū* (Tokyo: Kōdansha, 1969), 1:285, 287, 288. See also William Gardner, *Advertising Tower: Japanese Modernism and Modernity in the 1920s* (Cambridge, Mass.: Harvard University Asia Center, 2006).

21. As one source for this understanding of 1955, Ivy offers Kurihara Akira's *Kanri shakai to minshū risei: Nichijō ishiki no seiji shakaigaku* (Tokyo: Shin'yōsha, 1982) ("Formations of Mass Culture," 247). See also Dower, *Japan in War and Peace*, 17. During the 1950s, many other industrialized countries also witnessed this new type of mass culture and consumerism.

22. In many ways, postwar mass culture can be said to find its basis in the highly articulated and widespread prewar culture. However, a number of differences distinguish the two: (1) new technologies; (2) historical circumstances, if we regard postwar mass culture as part of a global capitalist project of recovery from wartime, wary of the links between fascism and mass culture, and also a buildup-up of strong capitalist nation-states; (3) the major postwar population shifts from rural to urban areas and concomitant changes in class affiliation (specifically, the growth of an urban middle class); and (4) the definition of post-Occupation mass culture as an indigenous mass culture, even as the "American Interlude" continued.

23. See http://www.cnn.com/SPECIALS/cold.war/episodes/14/documents/debate/.

24. Detailed critiques of *Record of a Living Being* can be found in, for example, Donald Richie, *The Films of Akira Kurosawa*, 3rd ed. (Berkeley: University of California Press, 1996), 109–114; Stephen Prince, *The Warrior's Camera: The Cinema of Akira Kurosawa*, rev. and expanded ed. (Princeton, N.J.: Princeton University Press, 1991), 159–71; Tsuzuki Masaaki, *Kurosawa Akira: "Issaku isshō" zensaku jissakuhin* (Tokyo: Kōdansha, 1998), 165–71; Yamada Kazuo, *Kurosawa Akira: Hito to geijutsu* (Tokyo: Shin Nihon shuppansha, 1999), 124–29; Mitsuhiro Yoshimoto, *Kurosawa: Film Studies and Japanese Cinema* (Durham, N.C.: Duke University Press, 2000), 246–49; Stuart Galbraith IV, *The Emperor and the Wolf: The Lives and Films of Akira Kurosawa and Toshiro Mifune* (New York: Faber & Faber, 2001), 214–23; and James Maxfield, "'The Earth Is Burning': Kurosawa's *Record of a Living Being*," *Literature/Film Quarterly* 26, no. 2 (1998), available at http://findarticles.com/p/articles/mi-qu3768. Because of the atomic theme, *Record of a Living Being* is often grouped with Kurosawa's *Dreams* (1990) and *Rhapsody in August* (1991).

25. The subtitles of *Record of a Living Being* use "fear" as an equivalent for *fuan*, but the term can also mean "anxiety," "unease," and "angst."

26. Richie, *Films of Akira Kurosawa*, 112.

27. Richie, *Films of Akira Kurosawa*, 110.

28. As Maxfield comments, "The sullen, silent response of the majority of the family to his begging of them crushes Nakajima" ("Earth Is Burning").

29. The boy's haircut is in the same style as the popular Shintarō-*gari,* or Shintarō cut, made popular by novelist Ishihara Shintarō, who is discussed later and in chapter 5.

30. Employees at the foundry appear frequently in the film, but mostly as background characters.

31. Richie and others note that Kurosawa was devastated by the death of his collaborator Hayasaka Fumio, who died before the foundry fire was filmed. Richie states that Kurosawa regarded this scene as a failure because, after his friend's death, he could not focus properly (*Films of Akira Kurosawa,* 112–13). This personal circumstance may well have affected the film, but the political climate should also be taken into account.

32. Kurosawa and Hayasaka initially considered making the film as a satire. Stanley Kubrick made an atomic satire with *Dr. Strangelove* nine years later.

33. Yoneyama discusses the use of Hiroshima as a city of peace for Cold War purposes and the predominance of "nuclear universalism" in constructing the meanings of Hiroshima, in *Hiroshima Traces,* 15–21.

34. Yoneyama discusses the "spatial division of labor" between Hiroshima and neighboring Kure, where both Japanese Self-Defense Force and U.S. military bases are located, in *Hiroshima Traces,* 124–25.

35. On antibase and antinuclear movements, leftism, and women's involvement, see Christopher Gerteis, "Japanese Women, Their Unions and the Security Treaty Struggle, 1945–1960" (Ph.D. diss., University of Iowa, 2001).

36. Yoneyama, *Hiroshima Traces,* 20, and on Hiroshima as a "Peace Memorial City," 18–21.

37. Kido Shigeru, Yanagisawa Jirō, and Murakami Kimitoshi, *Sekai heiwa undō-shi* (Tokyo: San'ichi shobō, 1961), 49–50.

38. For a more recent challenge to the notion of Hiroshima as a city of peace by a local activist, see Yuasa Ichirō, *"Heiwa toshi Hiroshima" o tou: Hiroshima to kaku, kichi, sensō* (Tokyo: Gijutsu to ningen, 1995).

39. Not coincidentally, the origins of the Non-Aligned Movement (NAM) also date to 1955. An organization of Asian and African nations formed in reaction to the threat of war between the two power blocs of the Soviet Union and the United States, NAM espoused an anticolonialist and anti-imperialist stance. In his 1955 speech in Bandung, Indonesia, Prime Minister Jawaharlal Nehru of India focused on the central role of atomic and hydrogen weapons in the relations of the two "power blocs." To Nehru, the "moral force of Asia and Africa" must also "count" in an era when the world faced possible nuclear war. My gratitude to Wendy Kozol for this point.

40. Major and Mitter, "East Is East and West Is West?" 7–8.

41. During the 1950s, conservative forces in Japan worked for the elimination of Article 9.

42. Yoneyama discusses Tange in *Hiroshima Traces,* 1–3, 70. On submissions for the Peace Park design by Isamu Noguchi and others, see Bert Winther-Tamaki, *Art in the Encounter of Nations: Japanese and American Artists in the Early Postwar Years* (Honolulu: University of Hawai'i Press, 2001), 7.

43. Painter, *Cold War*, 7.

44. Joseph Masco, *The Nuclear Borderlands: The Manhattan Project in Post–Cold War New Mexico* (Princeton, N.J.: Princeton University Press, 2006), 9.

45. Thomas Doherty, *Cold War, Cool Medium: Television, McCarthyism, and American Culture* (New York: Columbia University Press, 2003), 11.

46. Major and Mitter offer a viable explanation for the high-profile civil defense effort in the United States, which also helps us understand why such projects were not launched in most other countries. They note that the United States was "keen to maintain the momentum of public mobilization achieved during the Second World War, but even before 1945, stateside Americans had not experienced directly any of the horrors of the European or East Asian home fronts" ("East Is East and West Is West?" 3–4).

47. Watanabe Kazuo, *"Tachidokoro ni taiyō wa kieru de aroo" Bikini suibaku hisai shiryō shū* (Tokyo: Tōdai shuppan kai, 1976), 599–603.

48. According to Paul Boyer, "Within hours of Truman's announcement [of the bombing of Hiroshima], newspapers and magazines were offering detailed explanations of nuclear physics . . . and euphoric discussions of an atomic-energy utopia of limitless power, atomic cars and planes, medical wonders, boundless leisure, and revolutions in agriculture" (*Fallout: A Historian Reflects on America's Half-Century Encounter with Nuclear Weapons* [Columbus: Ohio State University Press, 1998], 13).

49. A military spokesman commenting on the "world's fourth atomic bomb" (that is, the nuclear device detonated after Alamogordo, Hiroshima, and Nagasaki) in the Marshall Islands. See *Washington Post*, July 1, 1946, 8.

50. On the history, politics, and morality of air war, see the foundational work by Michael S. Sherry, *The Rise of American Air Power: The Creation of Armageddon* (New Haven, Conn.: Yale University Press, 1987). An essay that highlights East Asia is Mark Selden, "The Logic of Mass Destruction," in *Hiroshima's Shadow: Writings on the Denial of History and the Smithsonian Controversy*, ed. Kai Bird and Lawrence Lifschultz (Stony Creek, Conn.: Pamphleteer's Press, 1998), 51–62. Also notable is the exceptional essay by the Nobel Prize–winning physicist P. M. S. Blackett, "The Decision to Use the Bombs" (1947), in *Hiroshima's Shadow*, ed. Bird and Lifschultz, 78–89. Blackett recognizes the Cold War dynamics of the decision by the United States to employ atomic bombs, long before Gar Alperovitz's so-called revisionist interpretation of Truman's motivation for choosing nuclear weapons over invasion.

51. Watanabe, *"Tachidokoro ni taiyō wa kieru de aroo,"* 600.

52. Miyake Yasuo, *Kaere Bikini e: Gensuibaku kinshi undō no genten o kangaeru* (Tokyo: Suiyōsha, 1984), 43–78 (on the *Shunkotsumaru*), 113–79 (on Japanese scientists, nuclear research, and political activism).

53. I am indebted to Wendy Kozol for her insights on testing.

54. Takada Jun, *Sekai hōshasen hibakuchi chōsa* (Tokyo: Kōdansha, 2002), 46.

55. Orr, *Victim as Hero*.

56. Sherry, *Rise of American Air Power*, x.

57. Marshall McLuhan, *Understanding Media: The Extensions of Man* (New York: Signet Books, 1964), 298.

58. Even literary magazines like *Kindai bungaku* had articles about Einstein and modern physics.

59. Dower, *Embracing Defeat*, 195.

60. The notable exception is Kurt Vonnegut. Descriptions and memorialization of the firebombings of Dresden, London, and Tokyo have become much more common since the 1990s, in the aftermath of the Cold War.

61. Naitō Makoto, *Shōwa eigashi nōto: Goraku eiga to sensō no kage* (Tokyo: Heibonsha, 2001), 156. Naitō also calls Russian filmmaker Andrei Tarkovski, who was also a college student then and inspired by the Voice of America and Hemingway, a Russian version of Taiyōzoku (172).

62. Kristin Ross, *Fast Cars, Clean Bodies: Decolonization and the Reordering of French Culture* (Cambridge, Mass.: MIT Press, 1999), 11. In her study of the French transition from empire and the rise of the middle class after the war, Ross refers to the work of Henri Lefebvre, Edgar Morin, and others on "privatization."

63. Seiji Lippit writes about notions of speed in the 1920s in *Topographies of Japanese Modernism* (New York: Columbia University Press, 2002).

64. Ross, *Fast Cars, Clean Bodies*, 186.

65. Ross, *Fast Cars, Clean Bodies*, 186. In Ross's view, the flourishing of American social sciences was a "kind of Marshall plan for intellectuals" in France after the war.

66. Ross, *Fast Cars, Clean Bodies*, 185–90; Frances Stonor Saunders, *The Cultural Cold War: The CIA and the World of Arts and Letters* (New York: New Press, 1999).

67. Andrew E. Barshay, *The Social Sciences and Modern Japan: The Marxian and Modernist Traditions* (Berkeley: University of California Press, 2004), 59.

68. Ellen Herman, *The Romance of American Psychology: Political Culture in the Age of Experts* (Berkeley: University of California Press, 1995), 134.

69. Herman, *Romance of American Psychology*, 134. All nations engaged in total war during the 1930s and 1940s mobilized their citizens and maintained their loyalties partly through cultural means.

70. The quotation concerning peace as "simply a period of less violent war" is from Department of the Army, "Psychological Operations," in *U.S. Department of the Army Field Manual*, FM 33–5 (Washington, D.C.: Department of the Army, 1962), 345n.2, quoted in Herman, *Romance of American Psychology*, 124.

71. Herman, *Romance of American Psychology*, 130.

72. Herman, *Romance of American Psychology*, 5.

73. Armstrong, "Cultural Cold War in Korea," 73–74. Armstrong borrows the term "reorientation" directly from the wording of U.S. cultural policymakers in the early Cold War.

74. The United States established the Office of War Information and, in 1951, the Psychological Strategy Board. The Soviets created Cominform in the same period. See Armstrong, "Cultural Cold War in Korea," 78.

75. Saunders describes the congress's extensive activities: it "employed dozens of personnel, published over twenty prestige magazines, held art exhibitions, owned a news and features service, organized high-profile international

conferences and rewarded musicians and artists with prizes and public performances. Its mission was to nudge the intelligentsia of western Europe away from its lingering fascination with Marxism and Communism towards a view more accommodating of the 'American Way'" (*Cultural Cold War*, 1–2).

76. Saunders, *Cultural Cold War*, 230, 246. Saunders calls it the "CIA's Asia Foundation." Joel Kotek also mentions the foundation's CIA connections and points out that it gained legitimacy and authority partly from its distinguished board, which included business leaders, foundation heads, scholars, writers, and the famous writer James Michener (*Students and the Cold War*, trans. Ralph Blumenau [New York: St. Martin's Press, 1996], 210, 265). My point here is not to demonize the Asia Foundation but to urge further studies of its activities and possible influence in Asia. I recognize that contemporary attitudes toward the CIA have been colored by the revelation of far less benign "dirty deeds" in Latin America and Southeast Asia. Much of the CIA-funded cultural exchange was far less nefarious.

77. Painter, *Cold War*, 14.

78. David R. Ambaras analyzes the place in society of "consciously outrageous youth" in both the early modern and the modern period (1868–1945), in *Bad Youth: Juvenile Delinquency and the Politics of Everyday Life in Modern Japan* (Berkeley: University of California Press, 2006), 9. While juvenile delinquency was not new, Ishihara's particular engagement with the media and the historical context distinguish his articulation of wild youth from earlier versions.

79. Armstrong, "Cultural Cold War in Korea," 72. Similarly, Major and Mitter point out that East Asia, "as a faultline region in the era, would repay much closer examination of its sociocultural history through a Cold War paradigm. A few topics, such as the importation of the nuclear theme into Japanese popular culture . . . have already received critical attention" ("East Is East and West Is West?" 8).

80. A few newspaper articles and photos of the bombed Hiroshima and Nagasaki appeared in Japanese newspapers before the Occupation censorship commenced. During the Occupation, several books about nuclear weapons were published in Japan, including one by the University of Tokyo physics professor Sagano Ryokichi, *Genshi bakudan no hanashi* (Tokyo: Kōdansha, 1949), and the Japanese translation of it by David Bradley, *No Place to Hide* (*Kakureru beki basho nashi*) (Tokyo: Kodansha, 1949). Bradley's nonfiction book describes the danger caused by the 1946 atomic bomb tests named Operation Crossroads.

81. Kozawa Setsuko, *"Genbaku no zu" egakareta "kioku," katarareta "kaiga"* (Tokyo: Iwanami shoten, 2002), 188.

82. In the 1950s, the exhibitions in and experiences of Hiroshima and Nagasaki were still largely considered local events, but they gradually were transformed into national and then universal experiences. On the evolution of this discourse in the media, see Fukuma Yoshiaki, *Hansen no medeia shi: Sengo Nihon ni okeru seron to yoron no kikkō* (Kyoto: Sekai shisōsha, 2006), chap. 4, 199–208.

83. Etō Jun, "Dazai Osamu," in *Hōkai kara no sōzō* (Tokyo: Keisō shobō, 1969), 214.

84. Miriam Silverberg, "War Responsibility Revisited: Auschwitz in Japan,"

2007, available at Japan Forum.org; Odagiri Hideo, *Watashi no mita Shōwa no shisō to bungaku no gojūnen*, 2 vols. (Tokyo: Shūeisha, 1988).

85. Painter notes that "by the end of World War II, the future of capitalism as an organizing principle for society was anything but secure" (*Cold War*, 8). In contrast, others regarded the war as a vindication of capitalism.

86. The notion of "atomic imperialism" appears in James S. Allen, *Atomic Imperialism: The State, Monopoly, and the Bomb* (New York: International Publishers, 1952). The Japanese translation of Allen's book appeared almost immediately in 1953. Allen was a writer, Marxist intellectual, activist, and political organizer in the American South and from 1962 to 1972 was the director of International Publishers, which was affiliated with the Communist Party U.S.A. Despite the Red purge during the Occupation and the maintenance of anticommunism by the increasingly powerful domestic conservative forces, the Japan Communist Party still had a small but viable presence in both party politics and the public at large.

87. Odagiri's essay is considered to be the foundational critical essay on *genbaku bungaku* (atomic bomb literature) by Kurihara Sadako; Kuroko Kazuo, *Genbaku to kotoba (shō): Hara Tamiki kara Hayashi Kyoko made* (Tokyo: Nihon tosho sentaa, 1991), 451; and Treat, *Writing Ground Zero*, 67, 442n.16. Treat describes Odagiri's thesis in the essay as follows: "While declaring that 'the issue of the hydrogen bomb and literature marks a new dimension in the history of world literature,' Odagiri goes on to claim that atomic-bomb literature is ultimately important because it is a 'step' to a more 'social' and more 'human' literature: in other words a literature that, while descriptive of the bombings, becomes their historical antithesis. This is an argument that posits an odd atomic-energy utopianism. It plots a historical future in which the same process that developed the bomb ('progress') will also lead to an improved society, thus somehow justifying, or at least compensating, the initial and unfortunate violence produced spuriously. The focus of atomic-bomb literature is shifted from a discussion of the details of, and responsibility for, two real historical events to a potential and therefore comfortably intangible future without actual victims and victimizers" (*Writing Ground Zero*, 102).

88. The translated and shortened English version appears in an anthology of the same title. The essay "Genshiryoku mondai to bungaku" originally appeared *Kaizō*, December 1954, 178–89, and was reprinted in Odagiri Hideo, ed., *Genshiryoku to bungaku* (Tokyo: Kōdansha, 1955), 171–94. The abridged English translation was included in the same volume under the title "The Atomic Problem and Japanese Literature," 1–5. No translator is credited. The Japanese essay also is reprinted in *Nihon no genbaku kiroku* (Tokyo: Nihon tosho sentaa, 1991), 16:41–61. In *Kaizō*, the final page of Odagiri's essay also contains a poem called "Bikini no hai" by Yokota Rihei.

89. The "villainization" of U.S. nuclear policy and admiration for the Soviet stance on atomic power had been a common viewpoint in the leftist media since the late 1940s, especially in the Communist Party organ *Akahata*.

90. Odagiri, "Atomic Problem and Japanese Literature" (1955), 1, and "Genshiryoku mondai to bungaku" (1991), 41–42. Boyer notes that "when Truman indicated in December 1950 that he was considering the use of the weapon in

224 I. THE MEANINGS OF WAR AND PEACE AFTER 1945

Korea, the outcry of horror was so great that Prime Minister Attlee had to come to Washington to argue that its use would be inadvisable. In response to the growing anti-war and neutrality trends among the Atlantic bloc nations, the peace movement continued to grow and to broaden" (*Fallout*, 269).

91. Odagiri, "Atomic Problem and Japanese Literature" (1955), 2–3, and "Genshiryoku mondai to bungaku" (1991), 42.

92. Odagiri, "Atomic Problem and Japanese Literature" (1955), 2–3, and "Genshiryoku mondai to bungaku" (1991), 42–43.

93. *Children of Hiroshima* was based on a novel by Osada Arata, and the score of *Children of Hiroshima* was written by Ifukube Akira, who also composed the score for *Godzilla*. Even though the Japan Teachers' Union was one of the sponsors of Shindō Kaneto's film, not all the members agreed with its formal approaches and messages. See Shindō Kaneto, *Genbaku o toru* (Tokyo: Shin Nihon shuppansha, 2005).

94. Odagiri, "Genshiryoku mondai to bungaku" (1991), 42–43.

95. As a scholar of American literature wrote about the process of conceiving of changes in the arts, film, and literature rather than exclusively as formal or aesthetic grounds, "In the process of renegotiating the relationship between politics and aesthetics, . . . I began to think that what I had been researching as a confrontation between forms of writing, or aesthetic values, was really an expression of political turmoil, in which the nature and obligations of writing were altered in response to the decline of the left, to the fact of Hiroshima, Nagasaki, and the Holocaust, and to the anticommunism which dominated politics and culture for some years afterward" (Thomas Hill Schaub, *American Fiction in the Cold War* [Madison: University of Wisconsin Press, 1991], vii).

2. Sex and Democracy

1. Many of the early reform-minded Occupation personnel were New Dealers, whose work was critiqued during the Red purge. The witness's comment is from Itō Sei's *Saiban* (Tokyo: Chikuma shobō, 1958), 85.

2. The *Chatterley* trial was not the first highly publicized legal case after the war, but it was the first to focus on literature or art. In 1949, the famous "political trial" (*seiji saiban*) known as the Matsukawa incident dominated the headlines. In the Matsukawa case, the prosecution attempted to blame labor union members for a train derailment, about which the novelist Hirotsu Kazuo (1891–1968) wrote the well-known book *Matsukawa saiban* (1954–1958). See also a special tenth-year anniversary issue of *Chūō kōron: Matsukawa jiken tokushū gō* 13 (1959).

3. I call this trend "expansiveness" because of the claiming of other cultural heritages as Japan's own. Inclusivity is another way of understanding the high rate of import of text, image, and sound from outside Japan's borders.

4. Doug Slaymaker, *Confluences: Postwar Japan and France* (Ann Arbor: Center for Japanese Studies, University of Michigan, 2002).

5. Peter D. McDonald, "Modernist Publishing: 'Nomads and Mapmakers,'" in

A Concise Companion to Modernism, ed. David Bradshaw (Malden, Mass.: Blackwell, 2003), 240.

6. McDonald writes, "It is a matter of recognizing the volatility of material *contexts* and the unpredictability of *readings.* Produced and reproduced by new cultural mediators, in new contexts and for new readers, the successive versions of texts represent unique episodes in the constitution of meaning. . . . If the Derridean reader is a permanent nomad who refuses to accept the finality of any border, the documentalist's ideal reader is a stateless cartographer mapping the frontiers as they change. The point, then, is not to celebrate the document at the expense of writing—in Derrida's sense of the term—but to study its attempts to contain the disruptive energies of dissemination" ("Modernist Publishing," 231–32, italics in original). My approach is indebted to the scholarship of Roger Chartier and Pierre Bourdieu. See Pierre Bourdieu, *The Field of Cultural Production: Essays on Art and Literature,* ed. Randal Johnson (New York: Columbia University Press, 1993); and Roger Chartier, "Texts, Printing, Readings," in *The New Cultural History,* ed. Lynn Hunt (Berkeley: University of California Press, 1989), 154–75.

7. The first copies of *Lady Chatterley's Lover* entered Japan in the 1930s. One notable portrait of Itō Sei was written by his son Itō Rei, a Lawrence scholar and translator. See *Funtō no shōgai: Itō Sei shi [A Life of Struggle: Mr. Itō Sei]* (Tokyo: Kōdansha, 1985). The Japanese title of Lawrence's novel is literal: *Chatarei fujin no koibito.*

8. From its start in the late 1930s and even, surprisingly, during the height of the militarist period, Oyama shoten had always focused its list on *junbungaku* (pure literature, as opposed to popular fiction). During the Occupation, Oyama's president, Oyama Hisajirō (b. 1905), quickly expanded his list to include European and American novelists that the militarist regime had banned.

9. Dantō Shigemitsu, "Chatarei saiban no hihan," *Chūō kōron,* June 1957, 47.

10. Jay Rubin, "The Impact of the Occupation on Literature, or Lady Chatterley and Lt. Col. Verness," in *The Occupation of Japan: Arts and Culture: The Proceedings of the Sixth Symposium Sponsored by the MacArthur Memorial,* ed. Thomas W. Burkman (Norfolk, Va.: General Douglas MacArthur Foundation, 1988), 170. Iida Takeo also provides an illuminating overview in "The Reception of D. H. Lawrence in Japan," in *The Reception of D. H. Lawrence Around the World,* ed. Takeo Iida (Fukuoka: Kyushu University Press, 1999), 233–54. Another important analysis of Itō's work and the trial is Keiko Kockum, *Itō Sei: Self-Analysis and the Modern Japanese Novel,* Stockholm East Asian Monographs, no. 7 (Stockholm: Institute of Oriental Languages, Stockholm University, 1984).

11. John W. Dower explored the antileftist focus of Occupation censorship policies: "The thrust of CCD policy . . . was to weaken socialist, communist, and Marxist influence by example, through the harassment and vetting of the most influential and prestigious purveyors of such views" (*Embracing Defeat: Japan in the Wake of World War II* [New York: Norton / New Press, 1999], 435). Although the CCD ceased operation in 1949, the Occupation's censorship continued after that year (432–33). Monica Braw details the Occupation's limits on A-bomb writings in *The Atomic Bomb Suppressed: American Censorship in Occupied Japan* (Armonk, N.Y.: Sharpe, 1991).

12. Christoph Zuschlag, "Censorship in the Visual Arts in Nazi Germany," in *Suspended License: Censorship and the Visual Arts,* ed. Elizabeth C. Childs (Seattle: University of Washington Press, 1997), 217.

13. Rubin, "Impact of the Occupation on Literature," 170. Rubin notes that the police's early use of Article 175 on a popular novel by Ishizaka Yōjirō resulted in public protest and showed in poor light the prosecutor's attempt to censor sexually explicit material written by a Japanese author. Thus the Tokyo police decided to use a translation of a novel by a non-Japanese author in order to assert to citizens its power to control the publication of literary materials.

14. Powerful antivice societies and their supporters in the United States similarly labeled Lawrence as "a diseased mind and a soul so black that he would even obscure the darkness of hell" (Paul Boyer, *Purity in Print: The Vice-Society Movement and Book Censorship in America* [New York: Scribner, 1968], 228).

15. Of the huge scholarly literature on Lawrence, useful writings include Anne Fernihough, ed., *The Cambridge Companion to D. H. Lawrence* (Cambridge: Cambridge University Press, 2001); Paul Poplawski, ed., *Writing the Body in D. H. Lawrence: Essays on Language, Representation, and Sexuality* (Westport, Conn.: Greenwood Press, 2001); and Douglas Mao and Rebecca L. Walkowitz, eds., *Bad Modernisms* (Durham, N.C.: Duke University Press, 2006).

16. D. H. Lawrence, *A Propos of "Lady Chatterley's Lover"* (New York: Haskell House, 1930), 123.

17. I also recognize the importance of reading Lawrence's linking of sex and the nation in relation to shifting social constructions of sexuality, narrative, and taboo. As David Saunders commented in a Foucauldian reading of Victorian obscenity laws and of Lawrence in particular: "Until a circle of highly specialized literary intellectuals embraced what doctors had installed in medically regulated conducts of living—the centrality of sex—and transposed it into the sphere of serious literature, there was no confusing pornography and 'fine literature.' What for the Victorians was problematic social conduct—the use of pornography—underwent mutation to become the object of a discipline whereby sex was aestheticized and aesthetics sexualized. . . . The sexual personae elaborated by Victorian doctors provided the avenue to what literary intellectuals thus came to envisage as a pristine sexual subjectivity long subjugated by repression and censorship" ("Victorian Obscenity Law: Negative Censorship or Positive Administration?" in *Writing and Censorship in Britain,* ed. Paul Hyland and Neil Sammells [New York: Routledge, 1992], 163). See also Damian Grant, "D. H. Lawrence: A Suitable Case for Censorship," in *Writing and Censorship in Britain,* ed. Hyland and Sammells, 200–218.

18. D. H. Lawrence, *Lady Chatterley's Lover* (New York: Random House, 1993), 3.

19. Lawrence, *Lady Chatterley's Lover,* 3, 14–15.

20. Lawrence's hyperbolic claims about the power of sex reflect the extent to which the author had to battle for open representation of sex, among the many ideas he sought to communicate in his writing. It is also an index of the price he had paid by writing purposely provocative texts and publishing them privately,

without copyright protection, which resulted in the rampant piracy of *Lady Chatterley's Lover* and a tremendous loss of income for Lawrence.

21. Many scholars have explored Lawrence's complex and often contradictory views about sex.

22. See also the informative special issue "Itō Sei to Nihon no modanizumu" of *Kokubungaku: Kaishaku to kanshō,* November 1995.

23. Donald Keene discusses Itō's wartime activities in *Dawn to the West: Japanese Literature in the Modern Era,* vol. 1, *Fiction* (New York: Holt, 1984), 676.

24. Keene, *Dawn to the West,* 683. I quote extensively from the court transcript as presented in Itō's *Saiban.* I also compared the quotations with those in court records housed in the Nihon kindai bungakukan in Tokyo in order to confirm their accuracy.

25. What about modernism in general and Lawrence in particular would Itō have found so compelling? In his own fiction, Itō experimented extensively with different formal narrative techniques, such as stream of consciousness. Much of Anglo-European modernist writing is characterized by "continually enacted negotiations between new formal strategies and the unprecedented social matter that [artists in the early twentieth century] sought to absorb" (Michael Levenson, introduction to *The Cambridge Companion to Modernism,* ed. Michael Levenson [Cambridge: Cambridge University Press, 1999], 3). See also William J. Tyler, *Modanizumu in Japanese Fiction: An Anthology of Modernist Prose from Japan, 1914–1938* (Honolulu: University of Hawai'i Press, 2008).

26. Levenson, introduction to *Cambridge Companion to Modernism,* 5.

27. Lawrence, *A Propos of "Lady Chatterley's Lover,"* 85.

28. Lawrence, *A Propos of "Lady Chatterley's Lover,"* 84.

29. McDonald, "Modernist Publishing," 228.

30. "Appendix: United States District Court, Southern District of New York: *Grove Press, Inc., and Readers' Subscription, Inc., v. Robert K. Christenberry,*" in D. H. Lawrence, *Lady Chatterley's Lover* (New York: Signet, 1959), 355–78.

31. The Soviet state and state-controlled media, in contrast, emphasized sexuality in service of the nation and shunned explicit and erotic representations of sex as bourgeois and not in keeping with revolutionary ideals. See Eric Naiman, *Sex in Public: The Incarnation of Early Soviet Ideology* (Princeton, N.J.: Princeton University Press, 1997); Igor Kon, *The Sexual Revolution in Russia: From the Age of the Czars to Today* (New York: Free Press, 1995); and Igor Kon and James Riordan, eds., *Sex and Russian Society* (Bloomington: Indiana University Press, 1993).

32. Bourdieu uses the term "consecrate." He writes, "The art object . . . is an artifact whose foundation can only be found in an artworld, that is, in a social universe that confers upon it the status of a candidate for aesthetic appreciation" (*Field of Cultural Production,* 75, 254).

33. The significant shift effected by the high modernists in the generic categorization and aesthetic reception of words, rhetoric, style, titles, themes, and institutional settings of modes previously classified as pornography is established in Allison Pease, *Modernism, Mass Culture, and the Aesthetics of Obscenity* (Cambridge: Cambridge University Press, 2000); Lawrence Rainey, "The Cultural Economy of

Modernism," in *Cambridge Companion to Modernism*, ed. Levenson, 34–78; and Jay Gertzman, "Contemporary Censors and Publishers of *Lady Chatterley's Lover: Prohibiting the Body with Just Another Dirty Book*," in *Writing the Body in D. H. Lawrence*, ed. Poplawski, 133–48.

34. For a publication history of *Lady Chatterley's Lover*, see Harry T. Moore, "D. H. Lawrence and the 'Censor-Morons,'" in D. H. Lawrence, *Sex, Literature, and Censorship*, ed. Harry T. Moore (New York: Viking, 1959), 9–30. Moore takes note of the "recent *Lady Chatterley* trial in Japan" and observes that "if the trial had its comic aspects, well, sex has always been a subject that has thrown people off center—even the poised ancients" (26–27). Two delegates of the Japan PEN Club reported to an international PEN conference in Scotland about the trials in the 1950s, and the English press in Japan covered the trial as well. Elisabeth Ladenson presents an insightful, comparative view of the *Chatterley* trials in *Dirt for Art's Sake: Books on Trial from Madame Bovary to Lolita* (Ithaca, N.Y.: Cornell University Press, 2007), 131–56. Kirsten Cather offers a groundbreaking study of censorship trials in Japan in "The Great Censorship Trials of Literature and Film in Postwar Japan" (Ph.D. diss., University of California at Berkeley, 2004).

35. On the reception and legal history of *Ulysses*, see Julie Sloan Brannon, *Who Reads Ulysses? The Rhetoric of the Joyce Wars and the Common Reader* (New York: Routledge, 2003), 12–19; and Ladenson, *Dirt for Art's Sake*, 78–106.

36. Quoted in Brannon, *Who Reads Ulysses?* 16.

37. Joyce Wexler, quoted in Brannon, *Who Reads Ulysses?* 32–33. Pease notes that between *Ulysses* and *Lady Chatterley's Lover*, "Lawrence's novel is more widely read outside of the university, distinctly because of its reputations as pornography. Both novels could be said to be equally pornographic in the sense that they position the reader as a voyeur to their representations of explicitly sexualized bodies engaged in sexual acts, and engage in equal amounts of historically accurate pornographic tropes and images. . . . [Lawrence's] alignment of sexuality with health, and with a new social order based on bodies as disinterested bearers of an unconstrained freedom, challenged his readers to agree" (*Modernism, Mass Culture*, 192–93).

38. Pease writes that Lawrence "effected the incorporation of pornographic vocabulary and actions into serious literature, high art, through attempting to reinscribe aesthetic disinterest as a mode of bodily being. He did this as an extension of the sexological project that equated bodily being with health, origins, and truth. Rewritten into the bourgeois ideology of self-knowledge tempered with cultural value . . . sexual representation in the novel, high and low, have become in the twentieth century the norm" (*Modernism, Mass Culture*, 164).

39. Richard Ellis, "Disseminating Desire: Grove Press and 'The End[s] of Obscenity,'" in *Perspectives on Pornography: Sexuality in Film and Literature*, ed. Gary Day and Clive Bloom (New York: St. Martin's Press, 1988), 27.

40. The 1959 *Lady Chatterley* trial in the United States centered on Grove Press's publication of an unexpurgated version of the novel and followed soon after the important and ambiguous 1957 Supreme Court decision in *Roth v. United States*, which defined obscenity as sexually explicit works that have no

"redeeming social importance" and appealed to "community standards." The Supreme Court's decision maintained the 1930s verdict on *Ulysses* that emphasized the need to judge a text in its entirety as a work of art rather than to take passages out of context. In 1960, Penguin's unexpurgated edition of *Lady Chatterley's Lover* became the first case prosecuted in England under the Obscene Publications Act of 1959, which defined pornography in opposition to literature. The courts stipulated that a text containing passages that might "deprave and corrupt persons likely to read it" should not be judged obscene if the text as a whole were aimed at the "public good." In both the British and American cases, the publishers were found not guilty of obscenity. See C. H. Rolph, ed., *The Trial of Lady Chatterley: Regina v. Penguin Books Limited* (1960; repr., New York: Penguin Books, 1991); and Peter Preston, "Lawrence in Britain: An Annotated Chronology, 1930–1998," 1–43, and Keith Cushman, "DHL in the USA," 133–63, both in *Reception of D. H. Lawrence Around the World*, ed. Iida. See also Nicholas Karolides, Margaret Bald, and Dawn B. Sova, *100 Banned Books: Censorship Histories of World Literature* (New York: Checkmark Books / Facts on File, 1999), 299–303; and, on the *Roth* decision, Harry M. Clor, *Obscenity and Public Morality: Censorship in a Liberal Society* (Chicago: University of Chicago Press, 1969), 23–43.

For detailed accounts of the Japanese case, see Jay Rubin, "From Wholesomeness to Decadence: The Censorship of Literature Under the Allied Occupation," *Journal of Japanese Studies* 1, no. 1 (1985): 102–3, and "Impact of the Occupation on Literature," 167–88; Kockum, *Itō Sei;* and Lawrence Ward Beer, *Freedom of Expression in Japan: A Study in Comparative Law, Politics, and Society* (New York: Kodansha International, 1984). On the history of prewar Japanese censorship, see Jay Rubin, *Injurious to Public Morals: Writers and the Meiji State* (Seattle: University of Washington Press, 1984); Sarah E. Thompson and Harry D. Harootunian, *Undercurrents in the Floating World: Censorship and Japanese Prints* (New York: Asia Society, 1991); and Timon Screech, *Sex and the Floating World: Erotic Images in Japan, 1700–1820* (Honolulu: University of Hawai'i Press, 1999).

41. Lynn Hunt, "Obscenity and the Origins of Modernity, 1500–1800," in *Feminism and Pornography*, ed. Drucilla Cornell (New York: Oxford University Press, 2000), 357–58. Hunt writes about the emergence of the concept of pornography in Anglo-European societies, but many of her insights also apply to twentieth-century Japan. See also Anne Allison, *Permitted and Prohibited Desires: Mothers, Comics, and Censorship in Japan* (Boulder, Colo.: Westview Press, 1996). On the nineteenth- and early-twentieth-century American struggle over pornography and Lawrence's place in that debate, see Boyer, *Purity in Print.*

42. Pease, *Modernism, Mass Culture*, 1–36; Lynn Hunt, introduction to *The Invention of Pornography: Obscenity and the Origins of Modernity*, ed. Lynn Hunt (New York: Zone Books, 1993); Michel Foucault, *The History of Sexuality: An Introduction*, vol. 1 (New York: Random House, 1978). Ladenson points out that "the figure of Sade returns to us in edulcorated form as reassurance that ours is a culture that has shed the pointless repressions of the past and fully embraced transgression as an absolute—and therefore empty—value. Our age is all for subversion, as long as the ideas subverted are other than our own" (*Dirt for Art's Sake*, 236).

43. An invaluable source for the newspaper coverage of the *Lady Chatterley* trials is the Nakajima Kenzō Archives in the Nihon kindai bungakukan, scrapbook no. 28471 and newspaper clippings no. 28465. Itō also lists coverage in newspapers and magazines in *Saiban*, 238–39.

44. Itō, *Saiban*, 9, 27–30. Masaki had also taken part in the recent Mitaka trial concerning labor unions.

45. J. M. Coetzee, *Giving Offense: Essays on Censorship* (Chicago: University of Chicago Press, 1996), 42.

46. On the imperial censorship system, see Rubin's definitive *Injurious to Public Morals*.

47. In contrast, the majority of witnesses in the British *Regina v. Penguin Books* trial were literary critics, literary scholars (including Raymond Williams!), ministers, and the obligatory seventeen-year-old Roman Catholic girl.

48. Suga Hidemi suggests that Itō and Fukuda, known as conservatives, might have harbored deep suspicions about the "enlightenment project" of the early postwar period and that they only reluctantly advocated the trial as a challenge to reactionary forces that threatened to revive the thinking of the Meiji constitution ("Yokuatsu no sochi ni tsuite: Chatarei saiban," *Shinchō*, December 1988, 180–81). In my opinion, despite Itō's jingoistic pronouncements during the war, his youthful interest in Lawrence, his views expressed in detail in *Saiban*, and his agreement to translate *Lady Chatterley's Lover* in its entirety (at the risk of police reprisal) indicated that his belief in the progressive emphases of the defense team was not entirely self-serving or hypocritical. For Fukuda as maverick, see Rikki Kersten, *Democracy in Postwar Japan: Maruyama Masao and the Search for Autonomy* (New York: Routledge, 1996), 36.

49. Kockum suggests the trials as a form of penitence, in *Itō Sei*, 275–76.

50. Ellis, "Disseminating Desire," 35 (Bourdieu uses the term "symbolic capital"). Ellis's fascinating article details the involvement of Grove Press and its owner, Barney Rosset, in publishing *Lady Chatterley's Lover* in the United States, for which it was charged with violating obscenity laws in the important 1959 legal case, as well as surveying the changes in the American publishing industry from the 1950s through the 1980s. Ellis contends that "the anti-censorship campaigns of Grove Press . . . and others need . . . to be placed in the context of publishing's capitalisation dilemmas in the mid twentieth century, and need to be seen as cashing-in on the auratic authority of the freshly decensored" (37).

51. Ishizaka later wrote the wildly popular *Aoi sanmyaku*. SCAP refused to support the police's attempted ban of Mailer's first novel, doubtless because it wanted to read about the experiences of U.S. GIs fighting the Japanese in the South Pacific. On *kasutori* magazines, see Dower, *Embracing Defeat*; and Rubin, "From Wholesomeness to Decadence."

52. Because of the bad press surrounding the prosecution's accusation that Oyama had not obtained proper copyright permission from the Occupation authorities and Frieda Lawrence, Oyama shoten went out of business. Oyama Hisajirō started another publishing company soon thereafter.

53. Rainey, "Cultural Economy of Modernism," 35–62.

54. Ellis, "Disseminating Desire," 27.

55. Lawrence, *A Propos of "Lady Chatterley's Lover,"* 83–84.

56. Michael Bourdaghs, *The Dawn That Never Comes: Shimazaki Tōson and Japanese Nationalism* (New York: Columbia University Press, 2003), 70.

57. Itō, *Saiban*, 5–6.

58. Itō, *Saiban*, 5–7. The 1950s also saw the rise of the inexpensive mass paperback market, and thus publishers and authors could imagine a broader consumer base.

59. Itō, *Saiban*, 6.

60. Oyama Hisajirō writes that the Minshushugi kagakusha kyōkai had received a grant of ¥50,000 from the Ministry of Education to conduct the study on sexual attitudes. According to Oyama, he was reluctant, but Kido's youthful enthusiasm, as well as his desire to help a "new scholarly discipline," won him over (*Hitotsu no jidai: Oyama shoten shishi* [Tokyo: Rokko shuppan, 1982], 275–76).

61. Itō, *Saiban*, 133, 220–23. For the responses, see 221. My gratitude to the Otaru bungakukan for showing me a copy of the survey and the original edition of Itō's translation.

62. Itō, *Saiban*, 133.

63. Itō, *Saiban*, 222.

64. Suga notes the importance of the *Lady Chatterley* trial as the first big sex trial in the postwar but stresses that the sexual attitudes expressed in the later Sade and Yojohan trials differed considerably in that they sought less to emphasize sexual explicitness as an integral aspect of transcendent art (as in *Lady Chatterley's Lover*) and focused more on affirming pornography itself [*waisetsu, naze warui!*] ("Yokuatsu no sochi ni tsuite," 180).

65. Itō, *Saiban*, 40–41.

66. Horace Gregory, *Pilgrim of the Apocalypse* (New York: Viking Press, 1933), quoted in Pease, *Modernism, Mass Culture*, 163.

67. Itō, *Saiban*, 34.

68. Douglas Slaymaker, *The Body in Postwar Japanese Fiction* (New York: Routledge / Curzon, 2004).

69. Michael Molasky, *The American Occupation of Japan and Okinawa: Literature and Memory* (New York: Routledge, 1999). For the "female floodwall" (*onna no bōhatai*), see 103–29.

70. As the culture of the Edo period shows, erotica and pornography and a vigorous public sphere can flourish even in an extraordinarily authoritarian regime. Elizabeth Berry points out the possibility of a vigorous public sphere in an authoritarian regime predicated on severing the link between the "public sphere" and the "telos of democracy" ("Public Life in Authoritarian Japan," *Daedalus* 127, no. 3 [1998]: 133–65).

71. On the antipornography versus anticensorship debates, see Cornell, ed., *Feminism and Pornography*; Linda Williams, *Hard-Core: Power, Pleasure, and the "Frenzy of the Visible"* (Berkeley: University of California Press, 1989); Varda Burstyn, ed., *Women Against Censorship* (Toronto: Douglas & McIntyre, 1985); and Brenda Cossman, Shannon Bell, Lise Gotell, and Becki L. Ross, *Bad Attitude/s*

on Trial: Pornography, Feminism, and the Butler Decision (Toronto: University of Toronto Press, 1997).

72. Itō, *Saiban*, 86–87.

73. Itō, *Saiban*, 97–99.

74. In contrast to the CCD's hands-off salacious materials policy, the Occupation's propaganda section, the Civil Information and Education (CIE), made public statements in 1950 encouraging a "purge" of eroticism. Practically speaking, however, such statements served only to encourage the Tokyo Police Department, because the CCD had already ceased operation. See Rubin, "From Wholesomeness to Decadence," 102–3. Andrew Barshay uses the term "authorizer of discourse" in "Imagining Democracy in Postwar Japan: Reflections on Maruyama Masao and Modernism," *Journal of Japanese Studies* 18, no. 2 (1992): 389.

75. H. Eleanor Kerkham, "Pleading for the Body: Tamura Taijirō's 1947 Korean Comfort Woman Story, *Biography of a Prostitute*," in *War, Occupation, and Creativity: Japan and East Asia, 1920–1960,* ed. Marlene J. Mayo and J. Thomas Rimer (Honolulu: University of Hawai'i Press, 2001), 341.

76. Kockum credits the Japanese police for the increased "control regarding the distribution" of *kasutori* magazines, leading to the decline of the genre in 1947 and 1948 (*Itō Sei*, 274). In contrast, Dower emphasizes the introduction of monthly magazines such as *Fūfu seikatsu,* which include serious "frank discussion of conjugal sex," rather than lurid sexual liaisons, and "emphasized that the family was the fundamental unit of society, . . . [although] despite its serious objectives, *Fūfu seikatsu* proved susceptible to the *kasutori*-magazine disease" (*Embracing Defeat*, 164–65). Given the historical specific circumstances of the *kasutori*'s success, Fukushima Jūrō insists that the genre differed from pornography (*Sengo zasshi hakkutsu* [Tokyo: Yōsen sha, 1985], 196). In other words, the thought of the immediate postwar period—chaotic though it might have been—infused these texts and their uses of the body.

77. A publishers' association attempted to intercede on Oyama's behalf, but the police would not back off.

78. Kerkham notes the publicity surrounding police efforts to control the production and circulation of "obscene books" ("Pleading for the Body," 358n.102).

79. Masaki Hiroshi reveals that one of the prosecution's witnesses contributed pieces to the scandalous *Ningen tankyū* magazine and was hauled in by the police, who in turn used him as a witness. Nakagome observed that Masaki wrote a piece for the same magazine, but Masaki told Itō that in that essay he condemned Nakagome. See Itō, *Saiban*, 54, 51, 57, 60.

80. The prosecution pointed out that defense lawyer Masaki Hiroshi had also written an essay for the same *Ningen tankyū*. The attempt to discredit Masaki passed unnoticed, whereas the exposé of the prosecution's dubious morality remained vivid.

81. Itō, *Saiban*, 18, 22, 141, 406, 88. In the British case, pornography "most certainly had corrupted those charged with enforcing with the law against it," as police accepted bribes and became involved in the "thriving pornographic marketplace" (Rolph, ed., *Trial of Lady Chatterley*, xx).

82. Itō, *Saiban*, 113–14.

83. Itō, *Saiban*, 406.

84. Barshay, "Imagining Democracy in Postwar Japan," 367.

85. Itō, *Saiban*, 242.

86. Kerkham points out that "women's groups were upset by the new free-dom in this area of publishing [pornographic materials]" ("Pleading for the Body," 341).

87. Oyama, *Hitotsu no jidai*, 241.

88. Lawrence, *Sex, Literature, and Censorship*, 69.

89. For example, as Iida points out, three other translators produced unexpur-gated versions of *Lady Chatterley's Lover* in the 1960s, 1970s, and 1996 ("Recep-tion of D. H. Lawrence in Japan," 234). The last translation was by Itō Sei's son, Itō Rei. Despite the supreme court's guilty verdict, no legal action was taken against the translators or publishers. See also Cather, "Great Censorship Trials of Litera-ture and Film in Postwar Japan."

90. Rubin, "Impact of the Occupation on Literature," 171.

91. Rubin, "Impact of the Occupation on Literature," 171.

92. Itō, *Saiban*.

93. From Meiji through 1945, even taking into account the brief but vigorous flourishing of Taishō democracy, the imperial government had consistently been an authoritarian force that kept tight reins over cultural production, using as one of its primary tools censorship by administrative means and without the possibil-ity of appeal. Such a high degree of regulation of cultural production by a central authority was, in turn, the legacy of the Edo period. See Thompson and Harootu-nian, *Undercurrents in the Floating World*.

94. Kersten, *Democracy in Postwar Japan*, 269n.2. Maruyama's thought has heavily influenced Japanese studies in the United States, and in their studies of the Occupation period, Rubin, Gluck, and Dower all use Maruyama's readings of the early postwar period. See Carol Gluck, "The Idea of Showa," in *Showa: The Japan of Hirohito*, ed. Carol Gluck and Stephen R. Graubard (New York: Norton, 1992), 27–48.

95. Barshay, "Imagining Democracy in Postwar Japan," 394.

96. Itō, *Saiban*, 5–6.

97. Itō, *Saiban*, 211.

98. Itō, *Saiban*, 13.

99. Itō, *Saiban*, 109–13.

100. Itō, *Saiban*, 396. Not all present viewed the current state of Japanese de-mocracy in such dim terms. Oyama, for example, thought that the "postwar trans-formation" had "given rise to conditions suitable for the reception of *Lady Chat-terley's Lover*" in Japan (*Hitotsu no jidai*, 29).

101. Itō, *Saiban*, 32.

102. Maruyama Masao, "From Carnal Literature to Carnal Politics," in *Thought and Behavior in Modern Japanese Politics*, ed. Ivan Morris (New York: Oxford Uni-versity Press, 1969), 250, and "Nikutai bungaku kara nikutai seiji made," in *Gendai seiji no shisō to kōdō* (Tokyo: Miraisha, 1957), 2:419. Dower also mentions

Maruyama's essay in relation to the early postwar decadent /kasutori/carnal literature boom.

103. Julia Thomas, *Reconfiguring Modernity: Concepts of Nature in Japanese Political Ideology* (Berkeley: University of California Press, 2001).

104. Maruyama, "From Carnal Literature to Carnal Politics," 250.

105. Maruyama, "From Carnal Literature to Carnal Politics," 264, 252.

106. Dower writes that the "Red Purge involved close collaboration among occupation officials, conservative politicians, government bureaucrats, and corporate
managers. A major objective was to break radical unions . . . and to this end some
eleven thousand activist union members were fired between the end of 1949 and
the outbreak of the Korean War on June 25, 1950. After the war began, the purge
was extended to the private sector (including the mass media). . . . Side by side
with the 'Red Purge' came the 'depurge'—a reference to the return to public activity of individuals previously purged 'for all time' for having actively abetted militarism and ultranationalism" (*Embracing Defeat*, 272–73). At the same time, the Left
(and many aspects of Marxist thought) remained viable in political activism, labor,
and education, as well as government.

107. Kersten, *Democracy in Postwar Japan*, 6.

3. Hara Tamiki

1. Both Paul Hogarth (a British painter), in the epigraph, and John Berger are
quoted in James Hyman, *The Battle for Realism* (New Haven, Conn.: Yale University Press, 2001), 169.

2. In a similar manner, Gijs van Hersbergen calls Pablo Picasso's painting
Guernica "horribly prescient" (*Guernica: The Biography of a Twentieth-Century Icon*
[New York: Bloomsbury, 2004], 5). The fascists' 1937 aerial bombing of a Span-
ish village was widely criticized as barbarian terrorism at the time. After World
War II, though, "*Guernica*'s imagery became more recognizable, indeed painfully
familiar" (5).

3. Although *Summer Flowers* occupies a special place because of its early appearance and canonization, many other professional and amateur writers also
produced compelling accounts of the Hiroshima and Nagasaki bombings through
the postwar period. See the groundbreaking study by John Treat, *Writing Ground
Zero: Japanese Literature and the Atomic Bomb* (Chicago: University of Chicago
Press, 1995). Richard H. Minear offers the best English translation of *Summer
Flowers*, as well as a discussion of the work, in *Hiroshima: Three Witnesses* (Princeton, N.J.: Princeton University Press, 1990). See also Reiko Tachibana, *Narrative
as Counter-Memory: A Half Century of Postwar Writing in Germany and Japan* (Albany: State University of New York Press, 1998).

4. *Hibakusha* is a Japanese word meaning "person exposed to bombing" that
was initially used to refer to survivors of the Hiroshima and Nagasaki bombings.
Now *hibakusha* has come to refer to radiation survivors as well—that is, people
who have been exposed to high doses of radiation from weapons testing, nuclear

weapons production, or nuclear power plant accidents (such as that at Chernobyl). The term has also entered English and other languages. For a thorough and insightful analysis of *Summer Flowers* and its relationship to realism and documentary, see Treat, *Writing Ground Zero*, 125–53. See also Iwasaki Fumito, "*Natsu no hana* 'Hara Tamiki' sanbusaku to sono shūhen," *Kokubungaku kō* 176–177 (2003): 79–90, and *Hara Tamiki: Shi to ai to kodoko* (Tokyo: Benseisha, 2003).

5. Hyman uses the term "healthy pluralism" in his study of Cold War culture in Britain. As Hyman notes, the Western Cold War ideology especially emphasized "the rhetoric of individual freedom and aesthetic autonomy," in opposition to the conformity of the Eastern bloc's demands for socialist realism (*Battle for Realism*, 4–5).

6. A similar emphasis on abstract and modern realist art (the latter defined by Hyman as characterized by a "resistance to story telling and an emphasis on the artwork as metaphoric and allusive" [*Battle for Realism*, 4]) is evident in postwar Japanese visual art as well. See Alexandra Munroe, *Japanese Art After 1945: Scream Against the Sky* (New York: Abrams, 1994). Polarized political systems and ideologies characterize the high Cold War. In the realm of culture, the Soviet Union's policy of "cultural conformity," which valorized socialist realism, dramatically contrasted with abstraction and experimental approaches valued in the Western bloc. Despite the purported opposition of formal approaches in the two spheres, however, strains of realism did persist in the free world. As Hyman writes, the "joint presence" and "inter-relationship" of abstract, experimental art with modernist realism "reinforced a liberal message of tolerance" (*Battle for Realism*, 4). Although literature rarely embraced extreme antinarrative abstraction, a tension existed among the varieties of realism in writing. Recall, for example, the brief yet persistent decadence in the late 1940s espoused by the Burai-ha writers such as Sakaguchi Ango. Was this approach to narrative tolerated by the Allied Occupation because of its largely symbolical value of rejecting both the former Imperial Japan's extreme policy of managing bodies and morality and the ongoing Soviet-style socialist realism?

7. Hyman, *Battle for Realism*, 1.

8. *Asahi Graph*, August 6, 1952, 20. In Tokyo, the Hiroshima photography exhibition was shown in a department store gallery.

9. Nishida Masaru et al., *Ajia kara mita Nagasaki: Higai to kagai* (Tokyo: Iwanami shoten, 1990).

10. On the canonization of *Summer Flowers*, see Kawaguchi Takayuki, "'Genbaku bungaku' to iu mondai ryōiki—Saikō," *Genbaku bungaku kenkyū* 1 (2002): 15–21.

11. Quoted in Nogami Gen, "Hara Tamiki igo: Aruiwa, 'media' to shite genshi bakudan o kangaeru koto no (fu)kanōsei," *Gendai shisō*, August 2003, 105.

12. In a lecture at Tufts University in March 2005, William LaFleur argued convincingly for the aptness of the hell metaphor in the cases of Hiroshima/Nagasaki. Michael S. Sherry proposed that the "creation of an apocalyptic mentality" was both "frightening and reassuring" (*The Rise of American Air Power: The Creation of Armageddon* [New Haven, Conn.: Yale University Press, 1987], x).

13. Nogami, "Hara Tamiki igo," 104–18. He quotes Ōe on 105.

14. Hara Kenchū, "Tsuisō ni yosete," in *Teihon: Hara Tamiki zenshū*, vol. 4, *Bekkan* (Tokyo: Seidosha, 1979), 337–41. Volume 4 of *Teihon: Hara Tamiki zenshū* contains reviews of Hara's works, as well as pieces from memorial issues of journals after his death.

15. Maruoka Akira similarly describes the story and Hara's ability to write in the midst of the horror as rare and exceptional, in "Hara Tamiki ron: Genbaku to chishikijin," in *Nihon no genbaku bungaku*, ed. Kaku sensō no kiki o uttaeru bungakusha no seimei (Tokyo: Horupu shuppan, 1983), 1:52.

16. Dominick LaCapra, *Writing History, Writing Trauma* (Baltimore: Johns Hopkins University Press, 2001), 23.

17. Hara's brother-in-law Sasaki Ki'ichi was a founder of the journal *Kindai bungaku*. Other prominent progressive writers and artists featured in *Kindai bungaku* are Honda Shūgo, Miyamoto Yuriko, Kobayashi Hideo, Odagiri Hideo, Nakano Shigeharu, Akamatsu Toshiko, Fukuda Tsuneari, Hirabayashi Taiko, Katō Shūichi, Itō Sei, and Noma Hiroshi. Paper shortages right after the war meant that the magazine was printed on cheap, rough paper with a simple cover that was the same color as the rest of the pages. Sasaki Ki'ichi was the pen name of Nagai Zenjirō.

18. The role of Hara's A-bomb writings in propelling him to national prominence can be seen in the inclusion of several of his works in the mainstream commercial journal *Gunzō* after 1949. It was not so much that it took four years after the bombing for Hara to gain recognition as a writer as that SCAP did not loosen its restrictions on A-bomb topics until 1949. See Iwasaki, *Hara Tamiki*, 124.

19. Hara Tamiki, "Requiem" (Chinkonka, 1949), quoted in Minear, *Hiroshima*, 30.

20. LaCapra, *Writing History*, 22.

21. In *Writing Ground Zero*, Treat describes Hara as evoking a world utterly changed by nuclear weapons.

22. "Hyōka," in *Hara Tamiki sengo zenshōsetsu* (Tokyo: Kōdansha, 1995), 2:36. Maruoka notes the rebirth metaphor in "Hara Tamiki ron," 51.

23. Minear, *Hiroshima*.

24. Naoki Sakai explores particularism and universalism in *Translation and Subjectivity: On "Japan" and Cultural Nationalism* (Minneapolis: University of Minnesota Press, 1997), 157.

25. Lisa Yoneyama, *Hiroshima Traces: Time, Space, and the Dialectics of Memory* (Berkeley: University of California Press, 1999), 24, 130. Yoneyama analyzes oral and other forms of witnessing by the *hibakusha*.

26. Treat discusses at length the varying criteria for evaluating A-bomb literature in *Writing Ground Zero*, as does Kozawa Setsuko in her book on the Marukis, *"Genbaku no zu" egakareta "kioku," katarareta "kaiga"* (Tokyo: Iwanami shoten, 2002).

27. Hyman, *Battle for Realism*, 170. A contrasting example of art valued for its political and moral message is Picasso's painting *Guernica*. See Hersbergen, *Guernica*.

28. The most important book on the Marukis' art and career is Kozawa, *"Gen-baku no zu."* See also Yoshida Yoshie, *Maruki Iri, Toshi no jikū: Kaiga to shite no "Genbaku no zu"* (Tokyo: Aoki shoten, 1996); and Maruki Toshi, *Onna ekaki no tanjō* (Tokyo: Nihon tosho sentaa, 1997). In English, John Dower and John Junkerman produced printed and film presentations of the Maruki murals. Kyo Maclear discusses the Marukis' work in *Beclouded Visions: Hiroshima-Nagasaki and the Art of Witness* (Albany: State University of New York Press, 1999), 159–79.

29. Hara's prewar and wartime poetry and prose have not received similar accolades.

30. Kawanishi Masaaki, "Hana no Maboroshi—'Natsu no hana' sanbusaku to 'Utsukushi shi no kishi ni' no rensaku ni tsuite," in *Hara Tamiki sengo zen shōsetsu,* 2:302–3, 304.

31. In *Writing Ground Zero,* Treat explores the relationship between Hara's hastily scribbled *katakana* notes written in the immediate aftermath of the bombing and his literary memoirist novella *Summer Flowers.*

32. Hanada Kiyoteru, "Hara Tamiki ron," in *Nihon genbaku kiroku,* vol. 16, ed. Ienaga Saburō, Odagiri Hideo, and Kuroko Kazuno (Tokyo: Nihon toshi sentaa, 1991), 29–30.

33. "After the Bombing" (Genbaku igo) is the title of both a short piece that Hara wrote in 1947 and a collection of short works related to the bombing's aftermath. In volume 2 of the two-volume *Hara Tamiki sengo zenshōsetsu,* for example, the short works included under the title *After the Bombing* make up a collection of more than two hundred pages. Hara wrote the parts of *After the Bombing* from 1947 to 1951, and the final section was originally published posthumously in the year of his death.

34. An illuminating description of *tenkō* (in both the prewar practice and the postwar memory) is in Michael Bourdaghs, *The Dawn That Never Comes: Shimazaki Tōson and Japanese Nationalism* (New York: Columbia University Press, 2003), 39–45.

35. I will not give Hara's biography in detail here, as many others have done so already; for example, Kawanishi Masaaki's annotated "Chronology" of Hara's life outlines Hara's prewar political involvement ("Hana no Maboroshi," in *Hitotsu no unmei: Hara Tamiki ron* [Tokyo: Kōdansha, 1980], 158–62). Hara first studied Marxism and Leninism in 1926, and from 1929 to 1931, he actively participated in the Mopporu and related activist groups. But after being interrogated by the police in April 1931, Hara left the movement and turned to wine and women. His second brush with the police in 1934 apparently resulted from his unconventional schedule (sleeping days, working nights). Minear provides a useful biography of Hara in his translator's introduction to *Summer Flowers* in *Hiroshima.*

36. In the tradition of the "I-novel" (*watakushi shōsetsu*) criticism, it is difficult to disentangle the narrators, protagonists, author's persona, and historical author in Hara's writing and reception. Readers of Hara tend to identify his narrators and protagonists (first and third person) with Hara's literary persona, a habit that Hara did not discourage. I do not claim to be able to sort these out.

37. Kawanishi, *Hitotsu no unmei,* 180.

38. Hanada, "Hara Tamiki ron," 37–39.

39. Maruoka, "Hara Tamiki ron," 49. Maruoka headed the publishing company Nōgaku shorin, which published the first book edition of *Summer Flowers*.

40. Maruoka, "Hara Tamiki ron," 48, 52.

41. Sasaki Ki'ichi, "Shi to yume," in *Teihon: Hara Tamiki zenshū*, 4:278.

42. Sasaki Ki'ichi, "Genbaku to sakka no jisatsu," in *Teihon: Hara Tamiki zenshū*, 4:72.

43. Maruoka, "Hara Tamiki ron," 54.

44. Sasaki, "Genbaku to sakka no jisatsu," 73.

45. "On *Essays on Man*," in *Teihon: Hara Tamiki zenshū* (Tokyo: Seidosha, 1978), 2:572–73.

46. Abe Tomoji, *Genshiryoku to bungaku* (Tokyo: Kōdansha, 1955), 86–88.

47. Unofficial sources acknowledged the development of the hydrogen bomb in 1950, and in the same year, Great Britain announced its possession of the bomb. In February 1951, Japanese newspapers quoted General Dwight D. Eisenhower as saying that he would support the use of atomic bombs in Korea if necessary. See Iwasaki, *Hara Tamiki*, 139.

48. Hara, "On *Essays on Man*," 573.

49. Abé Mark Nornes, *Japanese Documentary Film* (Minneapolis: University of Minnesota Press, 2003).

50. Andreas Huyssen, "Of Mice and Mimesis: Reading Spiegelman with Adorno," in *Rethinking the Frankfurt School: Alternative Legacies of Cultural Critique*, ed. Jeffrey T. Nealon and Caren Irr (Albany: State University of New York Press, 2002), 101.

51. LaCapra, *Writing History*, 22.

52. Hara Tamiki, "Hi no kakato," in *Nihon no genbaku bungaku*, ed. Kaku sensō no kiki o uttaeru bungakusha no seimei, 1:111–12.

53. Kajii Motojirō, "Lemon," in *The Oxford Book of Japanese Short Stories*, ed. Theodore W. Goossen (New York: Oxford University Press, 1997), 153.

54. Nogami, "Hara Tamiki igo," 107.

55. Marshall McLuhan, *Understanding Media: The Extensions of Man* (New York: Signet Books, 1964). McLuhan described the influence of media in the Cold War as "electric persuasion by photo and movie and TV works . . . by dunking entire populations in new imagery" (294–95).

56. Quoted in Iwasaki, *Hara Tamiki*, 134–35.

57. Maruoka, "Hara Tamiki ron," 48.

58. Hotta Yoshie, in *Teihon: Hara Tamiki zenshū*, 4:331. According to Minear, biographer Kokai Eiji "stresses the political context of Hara's suicide." Minear also acknowledges the possible influence of Truman's statements on Hara's thinking but concludes that "internal causes had more to do with his suicide than external causes" (*Hiroshima*, 15–16).

59. Nakamura Shin'ichirō, in *Teihon: Hara Tamiki zenshū*, 4:310–11.

60. Sasaki, "Genbaku to sakka no jisatsu," 71.

61. Michael Yavenditti, "John Hersey and the American Conscience," in *Hiroshima's Shadow: Writings on the Denial of History and the Smithsonian Controversy*, ed. Kai Bird and Lawrence Lifschultz (Stony Creek, Conn.: Pamphleteer's Press, 1998), 288–302.

62. Itō Sei, "Hara Tamiki no omoide," in *Teihon: Hara Tamiki zenshū*, 4:346–47.

63. See, for example, Sasaki, "Shi to yume," 276–80.

64. "Utsukushiki shi no kishi ni," in *Hara Tamiki sengo zenshōsetsu*, 2:297.

65. Suzuki Shigeo, "Hara Tamiki e no akogare," in *Teihon: Hara Tamiki zenshū*, 4:340–41.

66. There is a large literature on Akutagawa in English, so I will cite only Masao Miyoshi, *Accomplices of Silence: The Modern Japanese Novel* (Berkeley: University of California Press, 1974); Alan S. Wolfe, *Suicidal Narrative in Modern Japan: The Case of Dazai Osamu* (Princeton, N.J.: Princeton University Press, 1990); and Seiji Lippit, *Topographies of Japanese Modernity* (New York: Columbia University Press, 2002).

67. Several translations of "Hagurama" exist, including Jay Rubin, "Spinning Gears," in Ryūnosuke Akutagawa, *Rashōmon and Seventeen Other Stories*, trans. Jay Rubin (New York: Penguin Books, 2006), 206–36.

68. Quoted in Suzuki, "Hara Tamiki e no akogare," 340–41.

69. Ōta Yōko, "Hara Tamiki no shi ni tsuite," in *Teihon: Hara Tamiki zenshū*, 4:350, quoted in Kokai Eiji, *Shijin no shi* (Tokyo: Kokubunsha, 1984), 166–67.

70. Hara, "Utsukushiki shi no kishi ni," 270.

71. The image of the *"hana no maboroshi"* vision of a flower is echoed in the poem by Satō Haruo that is inscribed on the memorial stele for Hara in the Hiroshima Peace Park. The stele was built in November 1951.

72. This line is from the posthumously published "Shi ni tsuite," in *Hara Tamiki sengo zenshōsetsu*, 2:275–76. Treat discusses the way that Hara regards death as an "object" and states that Hara's "early handing of death as an overwhelmingly powerful and observable entity will coincide with the manner in which conventional documentary would seek to depict nuclear attack" (*Writing Ground Zero*, 132).

73. Hara Tamiki, "Ue," in *Nihon no genbaku bungaku*, ed. Kaku sensō no kiki o uttaeru bungakusha no seimei, 1:103.

74. Hara Tamiki, "Bidōro gakushi," in *Nihon no genbaku bungaku*, ed. Kaku sensō no kiki o uttaeru bungakusha no seimei, 1:93. Light also appears in "Ue": "I am light, light, and float in the void. Transparent?" (*Nihon no genbaku bungaku*, 1:102).

75. Hara, "Bidōro gakushi," 95.

76. Hanada, "Hara Tamiki ron," 29–30. Hanada mentions Godzilla on 35–36. See also Kuroko Kazuo, *Genbaku to kotoba (shō): Hara Tamiki kara Hayashi Kyoko made* (Tokyo: Nihon tosho sentaa, 1991).

77. Hara Tamiki, "Natsu no hana," in *Natsu no hana, Shingan no kuni* (Tokyo: Shinchōsha, 1973), 123.

4. "The World Lives in Fear"

1. On peace movements, see Mari Yamamoto, *Grassroots Pacifism in Post-War Japan* (New York: Routledge, 2004).

2. Readers may be familiar with *A Japanese Tragedy*'s famous scene of the emperor transformed from military man to civilian through overlapping still photographs. In John W. Dower's words, Kamei "came to personify the forbidden terrain of the new censored democracy" (*Embracing Defeat: Japan in the Wake of World War II* [New York: Norton / New Press, 1999], 427–29). See also Kyoko Hirano, *Mr. Smith Goes to Tokyo: Japanese Cinema Under the American Occupation, 1945–1952* (Washington, D.C.: Smithsonian Institution Press, 1992); and Abé Mark Nornes, "The Body at the Center: The Effects of the Atomic Bomb on Hiroshima and Nagasaki," in *Hibakusha Cinema: Hiroshima, Nagasaki and the Nuclear Image in Japanese Film,* ed. Mick Broderick (New York: Kegan Paul, 1996). Dower gives *Nihon no higeki* the English title *The Tragedy of Japan,* while the *Kamei Fumio tokushū* calls the film *A Japanese Tragedy.* See Yamagata International Documentary Film Festival, ed., *Kamei Fumio tokushū / Kamei Fumio Retrospective* (Tokyo: YIDFF Organizing Committee, Tokyo Office, 2001).

3. Nornes acknowledges Resnais's use of the 1946 film but not Kamei's documentary.

4. Public concern about the effects of fallout faded after the treaty, which banned atmospheric testing by signatory nations. The limited test ban treaty did not decrease the number of nuclear weapons tests but simply took them underground and made them less visible. See Samuel J. Walker, *Permissible Dose: A History of Radiation Protection in the Twentieth Century* (Berkeley: University of California Press, 2000), 19.

Kamei's antibase films include *The People of Sunagawa (Sunagawa no hitobito: Kichi hantai tōsō no kiroku,* 1955), *Wheat Will Never Fall (Sunagawa no hitobito: Mugi shinazu,* 1955), and *Record of Blood: Sunagawa (Ryūketsu no kiroku: Sunagawa,* 1956). Kamei made his first antibase film, *Children of the Base (Kichi no kotachi),* in 1953. While the Sunagawa anti–U.S. military base films narrate a struggle centering on a specific place, *Kichi no kotachi* is an exposé of the effects of bases on communities in Yokosuka, Yamagata Prefecture, and Ishikawa Prefecture.

5. Martin J. Medhurst, "Atoms for Peace and Nuclear Hegemony: The Rhetorical Structure of a Cold War Campaign," in *The Cold War,* vol. 2, *National Security Policy Planning from Truman to Reagan and from Stalin to Gorbachev,* ed. Lori Lyn Bogle (New York: Routledge, 2001), 148.

6. In response to the burgeoning capitalist economy, Kamei Fumio threw himself wholeheartedly into PR films, including *The Whole Story of the New Mitsubishi* [*Heavy Industries*] (*Shin Mitsubishi zenbō,* 1956) and *Underwear Makes the Woman* (*Onna wa shitagi de tsukureru,* 1958).

7. Nornes, "Body at the Center"; Yamagata International Documentary Film Festival, ed., *Kamei Fumio tokushū.*

8. John W. Dower, "The Bombed: Hiroshimas and Nagasakis in Japanese Memory," in *Hiroshima in History and Memory,* ed. Michael J. Hogan (Cambridge:

Cambridge University Press, 1996), 137. See also James J. Orr, "Yasui Kaoru: Citizen-Scholar in War and Peace," *Japan Forum* 12 (2000): 1–14.

9. Quoted in Medhurst, "Atoms for Peace and Nuclear Hegemony," 146.

10. Evidence that the Eisenhower administration itself recognized this image of the United States as pursuing nuclear war can be found in Stefan Possony's 1955 White House memo: "In its reliance on nuclear strategy the United States inevitably must pay a considerable penalty in the psychological and political fields. The Atoms for Peace Program has reduced the extent of this penalty and has detracted popular attention away from the position of a United States bent on nuclear holocaust. . . . We are beginning to create an image of America as the guardian of peace and the foremost promoter of progress" (quoted in Medhurst, "Atoms for Peace and Nuclear Hegemony," 154). The mid-1950s was also the height of U.S. stockpiling of its unrivaled cache of nuclear weapons.

11. Although he does not remark on Resnais's borrowing from Kamei's film, Nornes does note that Resnais "cannibalized " parts of the "silent print [of *The Effects of the Atomic Bomb on Hiroshima and Nagasaki*] saved by the Nichiei conspirators" ("Body at the Center," 147).

12. It took the Peace Museum in Hiroshima nearly sixty years to offer an exhibition featuring a detailed and comprehensible explanation of the damage caused by high doses of radiation to replace the displays of melted roof tiles and manikins of people with dripping flesh. This change reflects more than shifts in museum installation and curatorial practices, as it shows the realization of the need to educate the public in the ways that nuclear weapons differ from conventional weapons.

13. On the *Enola Gay* controversy, see Martin Sherwin, "Memory, Myth and History," and other essays in the section "Censoring History at the Smithsonian," in *Hiroshima's Shadow: Writings on the Denial of History and the Smithsonian Controversy*, ed. Kai Bird and Lawrence Lifschultz (Stony Creek, Conn.: Pamphleteer's Press, 1998), 317–409.

14. Even the image of *pika-don* (flash and bang) prominent in most *hibakusha* narratives refers to the intense heat and mechanical energy released by the bomb, not the pulse of radioactive waves.

15. Soon after the Occupation ended, some in the scientific community spoke out publicly about the dangers of radiation. See Kokusai Ishi kaigi Nihon junbi iinkai and Kusano Nobuo, "Shikabane wa kōgi suru," in *Nihon genbaku ron taikei* (Tokyo: Nihon tosho sentaa, 1999), 1:123, and in *Nihon genbaku hyōron taikei* (Tokyo: Nihon tosho sentaa, 1999), 1:120–34. It was first published in *Kaizō* on November 5, 1952. Kusano also participated in making *The World Is Terrified* and wrote about it in *Kinema junpō* in July 1957. See also Kusano Nobuo, *Atomic Bomb Injuries* (Tokyo: Tsukiji shokan, 1953).

16. Ubuki Satoru, *Heiwa kinen shikiten no ayumi* (Hiroshima: Hiroshima heiwa bunka Center, 1992).

17. Does the oft-repeated fear that it would be seventy years before trees and plants would grow again in Hiroshima and Nagasaki arise from the clean sweep around the epicenter caused by the mechanical energy and extreme heat released

by the explosion? Or does the anxiety show an understanding of the effects of the pulse of radioactive rays that swept over the cities in seconds and then lingered there for a while, especially in the corpses and the bodies of the injured who could not flee, and even in those who were seemingly unscathed?

18. Lisa Yoneyama similarly notes that "the survivors' narratives were instrumental in promoting the antinuclear campaign" (*Hiroshima Traces: Time, Space, and the Dialectics of Memory* [Berkeley: University of California Press, 1999], 96).

19. Kamei Fumio, *Tatakau eiga: Dokyūmentarisuto no Shōwa shi* (Tokyo: Iwanami shoten, 1989), 161.

20. Anticommunism in 1950s and 1960s Japan was much less overt and institutionalized than in South Korea during the same period.

21. James J. Orr writes that Fukuda "faulted the activists—in protests against military base expansion, for example—for essentially trying to establish a link even in local issues that were more easily solved in isolation from national issues" (*The Victim as Hero: Ideologies of Peace and National Identity in Postwar Japan* [Honolulu: University of Hawai'i Press, 2001], 206n.101).

22. David S. Painter, *The Cold War: An International History* (New York: Routledge, 1999), 40–41. On U.S. military bases in Japan, see also Michael Molasky, *The American Occupation of Japan and Okinawa: Literature and Memory* (New York: Routledge, 1999).

23. The use of bases to house nuclear weapons would violate Japan's three nonnuclear principles.

24. Tsuzuki Masaaki, *Tori ni natta ningen: Hankotsu no eiga kantoku, Kamei Fumio no shōgai* (Tokyo: Kōdansha, 1992), 234–35; Yasui Kaoru, *Minshū to heiwa: Mirai o tsukuru mono* (Tokyo: Ōtsuki shoten, 1955).

25. Gensuibaku kinshi sekai taikai Nihon junbi kai, ed., *Genbaku yurusu maji: Gensuibaku kinshi sekai taikai no kiroku* (Tokyo: Gensuibaku kinshi sekai taikai Nihon junbi kai and Nihon rōdō kumiai sōhyō gikai, 1955), third page of unpaginated "Declaration."

26. James S. Allen, *Atomic Imperialism: The State, Monopoly, and the Bomb* (New York: International Publishers, 1952); the Japanese translation is *Genbaku teikokushugi*, ed. Sekai kezai kenkyūjo (Tōkyō: Ōtsuki shoten, 1953). Yoneyama discusses the "any and all nations predicament" (*ikanaru kuni*) debate, in *Hiroshima Traces*, 21–23.

27. Abé Mark Nornes writes about Ogawa in *Forest of Pressure: Ogawa Shinsuke and Postwar Japanese Documentary* (Minneapolis: University of Minnesota Press, 2007).

28. Miyamoto Kenji, "Genbaku gisei minzoku no chisei," in *Bikini suibaku hisai shiryō shū*, ed. Miyake Yasuo, Daigo Fukuryūmaru heiwa kyōkai, et al. (Tokyo: Tōkyō daigaku shuppankai, 1976), 615, 606–19. It was first published in *Kaizō* in May 1954.

29. David Alan Rosenberg, "The Origins of Overkill: Nuclear Weapons and American Strategy, 1945–1960," in *Cold War*, ed. Bogle, 2:43–71.

30. My reading of leftism and the antinuclear movement contrasts with that of

Orr, who judges the Left and the communists primarily as divisive forces in the antinuclear movement.

31. In his memoirs, W. E. B. DuBois described the U.S. government's attacks on the Stockholm Appeal, which had been circulated by the Peace Information Center, an American organization with which DuBois was affiliated, as follows: "The first direct public attack on the Peace Information Center came in a broadside from the United States Secretary of State, Dean Acheson, released July 12 (*New York Times,* July 13, 1950): 'I am sure that the American people will not be fooled by the so-called "world peace appeal" or "Stockholm resolution" now being circulated in this country for signatures. It should be recognized for what it is—a propaganda trick in the spurious "peace offensive" of the Soviet Union.'" DuBois rejected Acheson's condemnation: "The main burden of your opposition to this Appeal and to our efforts lies in the charge that we are part of a 'spurious peace offensive' of the Soviet Union. Is it our strategy that when the Soviet Union asks for peace, we insist on war?" He also commented on the abuses of anticommunist forces in 1950s America: "Today in this country it is becoming standard reaction to call anything 'communist' and therefore subversive and unpatriotic, which anybody for any reason dislikes. We feel strongly that this tactic has already gone too far; that it is not sufficient today to trace a proposal to a communist source in order to dismiss it with contempt. . . . We are a group of Americans, who upon reading this Peace Appeal, regard it as a true, fair statement of what we ourselves and many countless other Americans believed. Regardless of our other beliefs and affiliations, we united in this organization for the one and only purpose of informing the American people on the issues of peace" (*The Autobiography of W. E. B. DuBois: A Soliloquy on Viewing My Life from the Last Decade of Its First Century* [New York: International Publishers, 1968], 343–60, available at http://www2.pfeiffer.edu/~lridener/DSS/DuBois/DUBOISW4.html).

32. The thermonuclear test by the United States took place on March 1, 1954, on the Bikini atoll in the South Pacific. The initial "shot," called Bravo, was part of the Castle series of thermonuclear explosions. The magnitude of the blast far exceeded the planners' expectations and resulted in radioactive fallout contaminating places far beyond the security area designated by the U.S. government. As a result, many residents of the Marshall Islands were exposed to high levels of radiation and suffered ill effects as well. News of the fallout spread around the world, and although the test series was "a public relations disaster, it proved to be a scientific and military bonanza" leading to the design innovations and a new "family" of superpowered weapons that rendered the existing stockpile obsolete. In Japanese, the events surrounding Bravo are most often referred to as the Bikini incident (*Bikini jiken*), after the location. In English, the designation "*Lucky Dragon* incident" is commonly used. I choose to use the term "Bikini incident." For the names of the Castle series tests and the names of "targeting categories" of Soviet cities and industry, see Rosenberg, "Origins of Overkill," 16–17, 56–57.

33. Wesley Sasaki-Uemura, *Organizing the Spontaneous: Citizen Protest in Postwar Japan* (Honolulu: University of Hawai'i Press, 2001), 96–97.

34. *Asahi News* newsreel, September 30, 1954, quoted in *Bikini suibaku hisai shiryō* are in *Kamei Fumio . . .*, ed. yamogata, 79 *shū*, ed. Miyake et al., 593.

35. Sasaki-Uemura similarly notes that that many histories of the bomb movement emphasize the so-called homemakers' groups and "ignore the numerous other peace groups that had formed around the country" (*Organizing the Spontaneous*, 95).

36. Stills from the documentaries are in *Kamei Fumio tokushū*, ed. Yamagata International Documentary Film Festival, 79, 82, 86. Also, the Maruki petition painting shows diversity, even though a female figure stands front and center.

37. The medical, social, and psychological needs of the *hibakusha* were also, in a sense, local issues, but ones that took much longer to be addressed.

38. Thomas R. H. Havens, *Fire Across the Sea: The Vietnam War and Japan: 1965–1975* (Princeton, N.J.: Princeton University Press, 1987), 9–11.

39. *Jinmin bungaku*, July 1951.

40. See, for example, *Shin Nihon bungaku*, June, July, and August 1949 and May 1950. Also, on the Stockholm Appeal, see Kangaeru kai, ed., *Hirakareta "pandora no hako" to kaku haizetsu e no tatakai: Genshiryoku kaihatsu to Nihon no hikaku undō* (Tokyo: Nanatsu-mori shokan, 2002), 82–83. The English translation JAMP for Heiwa o mamoru-kai is from Orr. Many comparable European groups used the name Defenders of Peace, which may have inspired the phrase *heiwa o mamoru kai*.

41. For a negative but detailed account of French communists and leftists after the war, see Volker R. Berghahn, *America and the Intellectual Cold Wars in Europe: Shepard Stone Between Philanthropy, Academy, and Diplomacy* (Princeton, N.J.: Princeton University Press, 2001), 118–21.

42. On the purges, see Dower, *Embracing Defeat*, 170–273, 437–38; and Richard B. Finn, *Winners in Peace: MacArthur, Yoshida, and Postwar Japan* (Berkeley: University of California Press, 1992), 228–39. In postwar Japanese academia, Marxism still enjoyed unchallenged prestige.

43. Kido Shigeru, Yanagisawa Jirō, and Murakami Kimitoshi, *Sekai hewa undō-shi* (Tokyo: San'ichi shobō, 1961), 58–59. Many commentators on the Stockholm Appeal claim that controversies within the global movement inevitably resulted in a split between the Eastern and Western blocs in the antinuclear movement, which may have some validity on a very general level. That is, insofar as grassroots political movements can never be entirely independent from global politics and spheres of power, the viability of a peace movement absolutely separate from the Cold War's bipolar power struggle is unimaginable.

44. *Shin Nihon bungaku*, June 1949, 66–67. Occupation authorities did not allow the Japanese delegates to go to Paris, and so they had their own meeting in Japan instead.

45. Maruyama Masao wrote extensively about de-Stalinization in this period.

46. Gensuibaku kinshi sekai taikai Nihon junbi kai, ed., *Genbaku yurusu maji*, 95–96.

47. Orr, *Victim as Hero*, and "Yasui Kaoru: Citizen-Scholar."

48. Yasui Kaoru, foreword to *Genbaku yurusu maji*, second page.

49. Kamei, *Tatakau eiga*, 146–47.

50. Lee Pennington notes a similar image of Japanese disabled veterans during World War II in "War-Torn Japan: Disabled Veterans and Society, 1931–1952" (Ph.D. diss., Columbia University, 2005).

51. Kamei's treatment of the *hibakusha* contrasts considerably with that of Ōe in *Hiroshima Notes*. See John Treat's incisive critique of Ōe's work in *Writing Ground Zero: Japanese Literature and the Atomic Bomb* (Chicago: University of Chicago Press, 1995), esp. 236–58.

52. Yoneyama, *Hiroshima Traces*, 193.

53. Orr credits Yasui Kaoru for the antinuclear movement's "celebration of women's special role in pacifist activism" (*Victim as Hero*, 50). Yoneyama discusses the gendered imagination of the antinuclear movement as well, in *Hiroshima Traces*, 192–96, 187–210. Yoneyama credits women with initiating the "Gensuikin movements that swept the entire nation" (192).

54. Treat, *Writing Ground Zero*, 255.

55. It took years for the government to offer adequate medical benefits to the *hibakusha*. See M. Susan Lindee, *Suffering Made Real: American Science and the Survivors of Hiroshima* (Chicago: University of Chicago Press, 1994).

56. Hanada Kiyoteru et al., "Senkyūhyaku gojū gonen no mondai," *Shin Nihon bungaku*, January 1955, 142.

57. Of the many fishing boats and companies whose catch was contaminated by testing, only the *Lucky Dragon* received compensation.

58. Nornes uses the term "political terror" in "Body at the Center," 190.

59. Immediately after the surrender and before the Occupation forces settled in, some coverage of the Nagasaki and Hiroshima bombings did appear in the mainstream Japanese newspapers.

60. Dower, "Bombed," 116–42.

61. In the 1950s, the U.S. government's Atoms for Peace Program was overshadowed domestically by the fear-inspiring civil defense program. Atoms for Peace was important as a diplomatic tool.

62. On the conceptual fields and discourses of nuclear strategists, see Carol Cohn, "Sex and Death in the Rational World of Defense Intellectuals," *Signs* 12, no. 4 (1987): 687–718. On Eisenhower's weapons expertise, see Rosenberg, "Origins of Overkill," 67–68.

63. Walker, *Permissible Dose*, 20.

64. Walker, *Permissible Dose*, 10.

65. Walker, *Permissible Dose;* Lawrence Badash, *Radioactivity in America: Growth and Decay of a Science* (Baltimore: Johns Hopkins University Press, 1979).

66. *Kinema junpō*, July 1957, 118.

67. The fission and fusion of atoms were not the only jealously guarded technologies. The exceedingly complex mechanisms of military technology, such as the detonation and delivery of nuclear bombs, were fiercely guarded as well.

68. Scientist Takada Jun notes the continuing lack of understanding of the dangers of radiation in *Sekai no hōshasen hibakuchi chōsa* (Tokyo: Kōdansha, 2002).

246 4. "THE WORLD LIVES IN FEAR"

69. Wilfred Burchett, "The First Nuclear War," in *Hiroshima's Shadow*, ed. Bird and Lifschultz, 63–73.

70. Bertrand Russell, "The Bomb and Civilization," 1945, available at http://www.humanities.mcmaster.ca/~russell/brbomb.htm. See also the contemporary critiques written by many prominent people, including Mahatma Gandhi, Albert Camus, Reinhold Niebuhr, Mary McCarthy, and Lewis Mumford, in *Hiroshima's Shadow*, ed. Bird and Lifschultz, 237–316.

71. Quoted in Murao Seiichi, "'Shi no hai' sukuupu made," *Bungei shunjū*, July 1954, 38–40.

72. See also Barton C. Hacker, *Elements of Controversy: The Atomic Energy Commission and Radiation Safety in Nuclear Weapons Testing, 1947–1974* (Berkeley: University of California Press, 1994).

73. Dan O'Neill, "Alaska and the Firecracker Boys: The Story of Project Chariot," in *The Atomic West*, ed. Bruce Hevly and John M. Findlay (Seattle: University of Washington Press, 1998), 179–99.

74. Takada, *Sekai no hōshasen hibakuchi chōsa*; Arjun Makhijani, Howard Hu, and Katherine Yih, eds., *Nuclear Wastelands: A Global Guide to Nuclear Weapons Production and Its Health and Environmental Effects* (Cambridge, Mass.: MIT Press, 2000). Throughout the 1990s in Japan, there were various nuclear power plant–related incidents, the most serious at Tōkaimura in 1999.

75. The original English subtitles of *Godzilla* use the term "atomic bomb testing," but the original dialogue clearly says hydrogen bomb tests, or *suibaku jikken*. The difference between the two types of bombs was highly significant in the 1950s. More recent DVD versions of the movie have more accurate subtitles.

76. *Kinema junpō*, November 1957, 43.

77. Lindee, *Suffering Made Real*, 256.

78. Shimizu Keiko, "'Shi no hai' to hahaoya tachi," *Kinema junpō*, July 1957, 40.

79. Shimizu, "'Shi no hai' to hahaoya tachi," 40.

80. Kamei Fumio, "Anata no ningen teki jikaku ni uttaeru: Osoru beki jijitsu no satsuei o owatte," *Kinema junpō*, November 1957, 44–45.

81. Nornes, "Body at the Center," 207.

82. Nornes, "Body at the Center," 209–10. Kyoko Hirano discusses the 1946 film *The Effect of the Atomic Bomb* in "Depiction of the Atomic Bombings in Japanese Cinema," in *Hibakusha Cinema*, ed. Broderick, 107–10.

83. Nornes, "Body at the Center," 207.

84. For Kamei on Kamei, see Yamagata International Documentary Film Festival, ed., *Kamei Fumio tokushū*, 82. During the late 1940s and early 1950s, Kamei also tried his hand at feature films.

85. Tsuzuki, *Tori ni natta ningen*, 250.

86. The Doomsday Clock dates back to 1947.

87. See the review in *Kinema junpo*,

88. Takakuwa Sumio, review of *The World Is Terrified*, *Kinema junpō*, November 1957, 44. Takakuwa also states that "we are powerless [*muryoku*]" (36), but then later in the film, he asserts optimism: people can change things. Decades

later, Yukawa Hideki, who won the Nobel Prize in physics, mourned "our power-lessness" in the antinuclear movement to abolish nuclear weapons. Nonetheless, Yukawa still lobbied against nuclear weapons, objecting to the common stance that they are a "necessary evil" ("Kaku yokushi ka kaku haizetsu ka," *Nihon gen-baku ron taikei* [Tokyo: Nihon tosho sentaa, 1999], 5:339, 344).

89. Honma Naoya, in *Kamei Fumio tokushū*, ed. Yamagata International Documentary Film Festival, 23.

90. Kyoko, "Depiction of the Atomic Bombings," 103–19; Horiba Kiyoko, *Gen-baku hyōgen to ken'etsu: Nihonjin wa doo taioo shita ka* (Tokyo: Asahi shinbunsha, 1995). Oba Hideo also made the heavily censored *The Bells of Nagasaki* (*Nagasaki no kane*, 1950). Films about fallout and the Bikini incident are surveyed in *Bikini suibaku hisai shiryō shū*, ed. Miyake et al., 592–95.

91. Takakuwa, review of *World Is Terrified*, 37.

92. Kamei Fumio, "Aete 'Hiroshima, Nagasaki no himitsu' o hagu: *Sekai wa kyōfu suru* satsuei urabanashi," *Chūō kōron*, December 1957, 85.

93. During the 1940s, the American scientific community agreed for the most part with scientific findings indicating that "reproductive cells were especially vulnerable to even small amounts of radiation and that mutant genes could be inherited from a parent with no obvious radiation-induced injuries" (Walker, *Per-missible Dose*, 10–11).

94. To explain the sources of "our moral world," in her famous essay on John Hersey's *Hiroshima*, Mary McCarthy wrote that the "hell" of Hiroshima was not Hersey's "sphere." She continued, "Yet it is precisely in this sphere—that is, in the moral world—that the atom bomb exploded" ("The 'Hiroshima' *New Yorker*," in *Hiroshima's Shadow*, ed. Bird and Lifschultz, 303–4). Richard H. Minear ex-pands on her notion: "Our willingness to listen now to these witnesses may mean that we acknowledge the justice of [Mary] McCarthy's assertion that the atomic bomb exploded in *our* moral world" (*Hiroshima: Three Witnesses* [Princeton, N.J.: Princeton University Press, 1990], 8).

95. Tsuzuki, *Tori ni natta ningen*, 237–40. Kamei describes his interactions with *hibakusha* in *Tatakau eiga*, 164–69.

96. Tsuzuki, *Tori ni natta ningen*, 237.

97. Ogura Mami, "Shinbun hihyō no sekinin o tou," *Kinema junpō*, December 1957, 138.

98. In the early 1960s, the so-called Tale of Two Cities issue of *Time* magazine praised Nagasaki for its lack of a "disagreeable" antinuclear movement.

99. On Kamei and the Japan Communist Party, see Tsuchimoto Noriaki, "Obituary: Kamei Fumio—Who Buried Kamei Fumio?" in *Kamei Fumio tokushū*, ed. Yamagata International Documentary Film Festival, 66–68. In 1987, the Japanese Communist Party criticized both Kamei and Maruki. According to both Tsuchimoto and Tsuzuki (Kamei's biographer), Kamei maintained that he kept his membership in the party.

100. Makino Mamoru, "Dokyumentarii sakka Kamei Fumio no ikita jidai," in *Kamei Fumio tokushū*, ed. Yamagata International Documentary Film Festival, 41.

5. The Aesthetics of Speed and the Illogicality of Politics

1. For a detailed discussion of Kurosawa's *Record of a Living Being*, see chapter 1.

2. In a similarly outrageous manner, Ishihara (as mayor/novelist) exclaimed in an interview, "I would like to be Hitler!" ("Taidan: Ishikawa Yoshimi—Ishihara Shintarō," *Ronza*, May 2001, 21).

3. Richard J. Samuels, *Machiavelli's Children: Leaders and Their Legacies in Italy and Japan* (Ithaca, N.Y.: Cornell University Press, 2003), 333–40.

4. For rebellious youth in other cultures, see Leerom Medovoi, *Rebels: Youth and the Cold War Origins of Identity* (Durham, N.C.: Duke University Press, 2005). Studies of James Dean's iconic movie include J. David Slocum, ed., *Rebel Without a Cause: Approaches to a Maverick Masterwork* (Albany: State University of New York Press, 2005); and Claudia Springer, *James Dean Transfigured: The Many Faces of Rebel Iconography* (Austin: University of Texas Press, 2007).

5. Slocum, "Introduction: *Rebel Without a Cause* Fifty Years Later," in *Rebel Without a Cause*, ed. Slocum, 2 (italics in original).

6. For a view of a similar "postwar acceleration," in Europe, see Kristin Ross, *Fast Cars, Clean Bodies: Decolonization and the Reordering of French Culture* (Cambridge, Mass.: MIT Press, 1999). Seiji Lippit and others also have explored the first flush of fast-living culture and aestheticization of speed in the first half of the twentieth century.

7. Togaeri's assertion is problematic because it suggests that a literary text possesses authority only in relation to the elite arbiters of the cultural canon.

8. On reader reception theory, see James L. Machor and Philip Goldstein, eds., *Reception Study: From Literary Theory to Cultural Studies* (New York: Routledge, 2001); Maeda Ai, *Kindai dokusha no seiritsu* (Tokyo: Iwanami shoten, 2001); Hans Robert Jauss, *Toward an Aesthetics of Reception Theory*, trans. Timothy Bahti (Minneapolis: University of Minnesota Press, 1982); Pierre Bourdieu, *The Field of Cultural Production: Essays on Art and Literature*, ed. Randal Johnson (New York: Columbia University Press, 1993); Kohno Kensuke, *Shomotsu no kindai: Media no bungakushi* (Tokyo: Chikuma shobō, 1992).

9. For an illuminating portrait of Ishihara the mayor and politician in English, see John Nathan's excellent "Tokyo Story: Shintaro Ishihara's Flamboyant Nationalism Appeals to Many Japanese Voters Who Are Looking for a Change in Government," *New Yorker*, April 9, 2001, 108–15. Nathan frankly assesses the reasons that Ishihara has frequently been labeled a fascist and also considers Ishihara's relationship with Mishima Yukio.

10. Ishihara himself asserted that he was not just a novelist "sleeping with the age" ("Taidan," 20). By 2008, Ishihara's jingoistic and militaristic political pronouncements, formerly considered on the fringes, had become acceptable to the Liberal Democratic Party's power structure as it sought to revise the constitution and Article 9.

11. Wesley Sasaki-Uemura examines the grassroots protests in *Organizing the Spontaneous: Citizen Protest in Postwar Japan* (Honolulu: University of Hawai'i Press, 2001).

12. In 1968, Ishihara was elected to the Diet's House of Representatives (lower house) and then in 1972 to the House of Councillors (upper house). In 1973, he joined with thirty other right-wing Liberal Democratic Party members of the Diet to form the party's anticommunist Seirankai (Blue Wave Group) faction. He served as director general of the Environment Agency and held a ministerial post in the Ministry of Transport. In 1995, Ishihara stepped down from the Diet and became mayor (governor) of Tokyo in 1999. His political career was undoubtedly enhanced by his friendship with the prominent politician Satō Eisaku (1901–1975), who served as prime minister from 1964 to 1972 and was awarded the Nobel Peace Prize in 1974 for his role in the reversion of Okinawa to Japan. Uesugi Takashi explores Ishihara's relationship with Satō in "Jin'myaku o toku yottsu no kiiwaado," *Ronza*, May 2001, 40–45.

13. Unless otherwise specified, I use the English translation from Ishihara Shintarō, *Season of Violence, The Punishment Room, The Yacht and the Boy,* trans. Jon G. Mills, Toshie Takahama, and Ken Tremayne (Rutland, Vt.: Tuttle, 1966), 13. The original Japanese text is from Ishihara Shintarō, *Kaseki no mori; Taiyō no kisetsu* (Tokyo: Shinchōsha, 1981), 334.

14. Oshima Nagisa, *Cinema, Censorship, and the State: The Writings of Nagisa Oshima, 1956–1978,* ed. Annete Michelson and trans. Dawn Lawson (Cambridge, Mass.: MIT Press, 1992), 26. See also David Desser, *Eros plus Massacre* (Bloomington: Indiana University Press, 1988), 40; Donald Richie, *The Japanese Movie,* rev. ed. (Tokyo: Kodansha, 1982), 128; and Michael Raine, "Ishihara Yūjirō: Youth, Celebrity, and the Male Body in Late-1950s Japan," in *Word and Image in Japanese Cinema,* ed. Dennis Washburn and Carole Cavanaugh (Cambridge: Cambridge University Press, 2001), 220. The film version of *Season of the Sun,* directed by Furukawa Takumi, followed a conventional film form. It was only with *Crazed Fruit,* directed by Nakahira Ko, that an innovative cinematic version of Ishihara's fiction appeared. Nikkatsu produced both films. Odagiri Hideo comments that after Ishihara was elected to the Diet on the Liberal Democratic Party ticket, he became a "conservative politician utterly lacking in imagination and compassion and who advocated re-armament of Japan" ("Nihon bungaku ni okeru 'sengo,'" in *Nihon bungaku no sengo,* ed. Nihon kindai bungakukan [Tokyo: Yomiuri shinbunsha, 1972], 26).

15. Daniel Biltereyst, "Youth, Moral Panics, and the End of Cinema: On the Reception of *Rebel Without a Cause* in Europe," in *Rebel Without a Cause,* ed. Slocum, 186.

16. For the history of the censorship board Eirin, see Desser, *Eros plus Massacre.*

17. Raine explores Ishihara career and the "social and aesthetic conditions of . . . mass culture" in the 1950s in his informative "Ishihara Yūjirō," 202–25. See also Tadao Sato, *Currents in Japanese Cinema,* trans. Gregory Barrett (Tokyo: Kodansha, 1982).

18. If sales are an indicator of a novel's critical or commercial staying power, then the absence of copies of *Season of the Sun* in Tokyo bookstores even during Ishihara's term as governor of Tokyo is significant.

19. In addition to the importance of Ishihara's novels to film, he gained recognition as a promoter of the film world and especially of youth films popular in the 1950s and 1960s. See his best-selling memoir *Otōto* [*My Little Brother*] (Tokyo: Gentōsha, 1996).

20. Donald Keene does not mention Ishihara in his massive survey of modern Japanese literature, *Dawn to the West: Japanese Literature in the Modern Era*, 2 vols. (New York: Holt, 1984).

21. Van Gessel, *The Sting of Life: Four Contemporary Japanese Novelists* (New York: Columbia University Press, 1989), 51–52.

22. Ozaki Hotsuki asserts that the publishing world's battle to win audiences back from television (or perhaps to preserve its audiences against the new medium of television, which the publishers correctly predicted would become the great obsession of audiences and consumers) started in the mid-1950s with the rise of high-stakes consumer culture ("Sengo no taishū bungaku," in *Nihon bungaku no sengo*, ed. Nihon kindai bungakukan, 175). He offers as evidence of this fight to retain audiences the tremendous publicity given to the Akutagawa Prize in 1956; the transformation of Ishihara into an instant and stylish celebrity as he appeared repeatedly in both elite magazines and the glossy *shūkanshi* (which featured copious photos of celebrities, their fashions, and their hairstyles).

23. Raine reports that in addition to the PTA, "regional housewives' groups" and even the Ministry of Education condemned the Taiyōzoku films ("Ishihara Yūjirō," 211). As a result, the producer Nikkatsu and other films that were profiting heavily from such productions sought to reformulate the image of their youth genre films in the mid-1950s. See also Michael Raine, "Contemporary Japan as Punishment Room in Kon Ichikawa's *Shokei no heya*," in *Kon Ichikawa*, ed. James Quandt (Toronto: Cinematheque Ontario, 2001), 175.

24. Wada Natto, "The 'Sun Tribe' and Their Parents," in *Kon Ichikawa*, ed. Quandt, 192.

25. Wada, "'Sun Tribe' and Their Parents," 192. She further naturalized *The Punishment Room* by adding a new character to her screenplay based on the novel: the young protagonist Katsumi's mother.

26. Satō Haruo, "Ryōfu bizoku to geijutsuka: furyō shōnenteki bungaku o haisu," *Yomiuri shinbun*, February 8, 1956. Also see Togaeri Hajime, "Taiyō bungaku ronsō no yukue," in *Togaeri Hajime chosaku shū* (Tokyo: Kōdansha, 1969), 1:282.

27. Bilтereyst examines these controversies in the West in "Youth, Moral Panics, and the End of Cinema," 172–82. Depending on the European country, *Rebel Without a Cause* either was rated for adults only or was censored.

28. Taiyōzoku (Sun Tribe) refers to journalism's name for the young admirers of *Taiyō no kisetsu* (the book, the movie, and other narratives of the youth genre). This style emphasized *après-guerre* youth who were fond of sex and violence, who adored hanging out at the beach, and who at least pretended to have no money cares. Magazines depicted the range of Taiyōzoku fashions (from aloha shirts to white suits) and haircuts (for men, the short-cropped Shintarō-gari, or Shintarō cut). See Raine, "Ishihara Yūjirō," 205–8; and Michael Bourdaghs, "The Japan

That Can Say 'Yes': Bubblegum Music in a Post-Bubble Economy," *literature and psychology* 44, no. 4 (1998): 61. Yoshida Tsukasa claimed that the designation Taiyōzoku also connoted an "American-style" consumer ethic (*Sutaa tanjō: Hibari, Kinnosuke, Yūjirō, Atsumi Kiyoshi, soshite shin-fukkōki no seishin* [Tokyo: Kōdansha, 1999], 182–83). Thus just as the Occupation forces had "colonized" Japan, so the Taiyōzoku youth had "colonized" the Shōnan coastline. The Ishihara brothers may not have worried about money, but many Taiyōzoku in the mid-1950s still were struggling to scrape together money in order to pursue the transient pleasures of fashion, sex, boating, sports, mass media culture, and bar hopping. Yoshida even calls the Japan of the 1960s, with its enormously high production and consumption, the "Taiyōzoku nation" (Taiyōzoku kokka).

29. The second Bungakukai shinjinshō judges included Yoshida Ken'ichi (critic and novelist, 1912–1977), Inoue Yasushi (novelist, 1907–1991), Itō Sei (novelist, critic, and translator, 1905–1969), Takeda Taijun (novelist, 1912–1976), and Hirano Ken (critic, 1907–1978). At age forty-three, Yoshida and Takeda were the youngest members of the committee.

30. Yamamoto Kenkichi recognized as problematic the mania for newness in literature in the mid-1950s, in "Shinjin no 'shin' no morosa," *Asahi shinbun*, March 22, 1956 (evening edition), 6.

31. Odagiri, "Nihon bungaku ni okeru 'sengo,'" 25.

32. Jon Lewis, *The Road to Romance and Ruin: Teen Films and Youth Culture* (New York: Routledge, 1992), 20.

33. Margot A. Henriksen, *Dr. Strangelove's America: Society and Culture in the Atomic Age* (Berkeley: University of California Press, 1997), 162. Stuart Hylton identifies the Taiyōzoku youth as the Japanese equivalent of the teddy boy, the British version of disaffected youth, and the French *zazous*, in *From Rationing to Rock: The 1950s Revisited* (Stroud, Eng.: Sutton, 1998), 49.

34. Lewis, *Road to Romance and Ruin*, 5, 10–11. Also see James Gilbert's excellent *A Cycle of Outrage: America's Reaction to the Juvenile Delinquent in the 1950s* (New York: Oxford University Press, 1986), 175–76, 199–201.

35. Gilbert, *Cycle of Outrage*, 198.

36. The phrase "rebel without a cause" is used in the title of a controversial scholarly book on criminally psychopathic personalities that was written during World War II. The author, a psychologist at a Pennsylvania penitentiary, describes case studies of a mentally ill youth, not a social rebel: "The psychopath is a rebel without a cause, an agitator without a slogan, a revolutionary without a program; in other words, his rebelliousness is aimed to achieve goals satisfactory to himself alone" (Robert M. Lindner, *Rebel Without a Cause: The Hypnoanalysis of a Criminal Psychopath* [New York: Grune & Stratton, 1944], 2).

37. "Bungakukai shinjin shō," *Bungakukai*, April 1955, 134–37.

38. "Bungakukai shinjin shō," 134.

39. "Bungakukai shinjin shō," 137.

40. The lack of controversy over *Taiyō* is evident in the calm delivery of the 1955 Bungakukai selection committee's judgments. See "Bungakukai shinjin shō," 134–37. Itō Sei also commented on the lack of controversy in Itō Sei, Takeda

Taijun, and Mishima Yukio, "Shōsetsu no shinjin ni nozomu," *Chūō kōron*, June 1956, 289. Part of the difference in reactions may be attributed to the fact that the Bungakukai Prize was relatively new.

41. Edward Mack, *Manufacturing Japanese Literature* (Durham, N.C.: Duke University Press, forthcoming).

42. Nakano Shigeharu, "Akutagawa shō ni tsuite omoide," *Chūō kōron*, June 1956, 282–87.

43. The thirty-fourth Akutagawa Prize committee included Ishikawa Tatsuzō (novelist, 1905–1985), Inoue Yasushi (who was also on the Bungakukai shinjin-shō committee), Nakamura Mitsuo (critic, 1911–1988), Niwa Fumio (novelist, b. 1904), Satō Haruo (novelist and critic, 1892–1964), Takii Kōsaku (novelist, 1894–1984), Uno Kōji (novelist, 1891–1961), Kawabata Yasunari (novelist, 1899–1972), and Funahashi Seiichi (novelist and playwright, 1904–1976). Similar to the Bungakukai committee, all the Akutagawa judges were male writers in their forties to sixties.

44. Senuma Shigeki claimed that *masu komi bungaku* (mass media literature) came about partly through the entrance of book publishers into the production of the *shūkanshi* weekly magazines ("Masu komi to bungaku," in *Nihon bungaku no sengo*, ed. Nihon kindai bungakukan, 262). Whereas previously only newspapers published *shūkanshi*, in 1956 the publisher Shinchōsha (and the publisher of the bound version of *Season of the Sun* the same year) started a new trend with its creation of *Shūkan shinchō*, which contained serialized novels. Even in the mid-1950s, individual *shūkanshi* had circulations of more than 1 million. See also Ozaki, "Sengo no taishū bungaku," 175; and Raine, "Ishihara Yūjirō," 205–11.

45. Paradoxically, Nakano also excused one of the other times that the Akutagawa Prize committee erred on the side of caution because of the "political situation" in 1941. Wandering even further from the Akutagawa Prize, Nakano then launched into a criticism of the media for creating a national mania over the Crown Prince's engagement to Michiko, a type of manipulation that Nakano feared as "potentially fascistic and criminal"—even akin to the social engineering of the wartime. Although he did not say so openly, Nakano was also reacting against journalism's willingness to cooperate in the Imperial Household's effort to make celebrities out of the controversial imperial family ("Akutagawa sho ni tsuite omoide," 284, 285–86). The question of the Crown Prince's father's war guilt was still far from resolved even ten years after the end of the war.

46. "Akutagawa shō kettei happyō," *Bungei shunjū*, March 1956, 285.

47. "Akutagawa shō kettei happyō," 284.

48. Ishihara, *Season of Violence*, 41, and *Taiyō no kisetsu*, 355.

49. Togaeri, "Taiyō bungaku ronsō no yukue," 281.

50. In 1958, Takeda wrote that the vitality of Japan's consumer culture, symbolized fittingly by the Sun Tribe culture, would not have been possible without the erasure of memories of mobilizing for war and colonialization, as well as the pornographic body (*nikutai*) imagined by the war and its aftermath. See Marukawa Tetsushi, *Reisen bunka ron: Wasurerareta aimaina sensō no genzaisei* (Tokyo: Sofūsha, 2005), 83; and Yoshikuni Igarashi, *Bodies of Memory: Narratives of War in*

Postwar Japanese Culture, 1945–1970 (Princeton, N.J.: Princeton University Press, 2000), 47–72.

51. Ishihara, *Season of Violence*, 29–30, and *Taiyō no kisetsu*, 347.

52. "Akutagawa shō kettei happyō," 287–88.

53. W. T. Lhamon Jr., *Deliberate Speed: The Origins of a Cultural Style in the American 1950s* (Washington, D.C.: Smithsonian Institution Press, 1990), xi.

54. Ishihara, *Taiyō no kisetsu*, 350.

55. Ishihara, *Taiyō no kisetsu*, 354.

56. Ishihara, *Taiyō no kisetsu*, 349 (my translation). See also Ishihara, *Season of Violence*, 32.

57. Lhamon, *Deliberate Speed*, 7.

58. "Akutagawa shō kettei happyō," 287. Takeda Taijun commented on the debate on the virtues and evils of pleasure (*kairaku*) between Funabashi and Satō Haruo in "'Kairaku-ron' ni tsuite," *Bungakukai*, May 1956, 108–11. In a published roundtable discussion, one of Ishihara's fellow college students (from Tokyo University) uses the English word "speed" (or "speedy" [*supiido ga hayai*]) to describe his romantic relationships. The topic of discussion was "The Views of Pleasure (*kairaku*) of the Super-Modern Youth." See Aoshima Yukio, Ishihara Shintarō, et al., "Chō-gendai ha no kairaku kan," *Chūō kōron*, April 1956, 222.

59. "Akutagawa shō kettei happyō," 284. Raine asserts that the youth in the Taiyōzoku "make a mockery of Japan's postwar egalitarianism," but there is little sign of such class or social conscience in either the novel or Ishihara's discussion of his own writing ("Ishihara Yūjirō," 205).

60. George M. Wilson, "Nicholas Ray's *Rebel Without a Cause*," in *Rebel Without a Cause*, ed. Slocum, 111.

61. Ishihara, *Season of Violence*, 28, and *Taiyō no kisetsu*, 346.

62. American and British sociologists, psychoanalysts, and psychologists pioneered research on alienation, youth gangs, and delinquency in the 1940s, 1950s, and 1960s. Social scientists in Japan and other Western European countries also became heavily involved in such research. Key figures included Eric and Mary Josephson, Kenneth Keniston, Erik Erikson, Robert K. Merton, and David Riesman. See Jon Lewis, "Rebel Without a Cause: Growing Up Male in Jim's Mom's World," in *Rebel Without a Cause*, ed. Slocum, 100–101.

63. Biltereyst offers a fascinating examination of the reception of *Rebel Without a Cause*, in "Youth, Moral Panics, and the End of Cinema," 171–89.

64. Dick Hebdige, *Subculture: The Meaning of Style* (New York: Routledge, 1998), 76.

65. A 1955 television advertisement for *Rebel Without a Cause* features the film's story executive, Walter McKuen of Warner Brothers, who explains that the inspiration for the movie was newspaper stories about lower-class youth such as "Slum Youth Stomp Party" and "Youth Kills Cop." Although *Rebel Without a Cause* is not about "slum kids," the Warner Brothers writers "made a discovery . . . we took a look into some privileged homes, far from the slums, nice homes, very respectable, well clothed, no slum kids here . . . but beneath the surface, trouble, plenty of it." In an interview packaged with the movie, director Nicholas Ray claims

that he had found "part of the story that not even the newspapers had told. . . . What makes kids from nice homes do things like this?"

66. Although the characters in *Season of the Sun* rebel against the adult world, they do not regard their mothers as part of the adult world and leave themselves the option of depending on their mothers when it is convenient to do so. See Awanaka Goro, "Nihirizumu to egoizumu to: Ishihara Shintarō no bungaku ni tsuite," *Purometeusu* 36 (2000): 111.

67. Ishihara, *Season of Violence*, 29, and *Taiyō no kisetsu*, 346. The father says literally, "I'm not that rich."

68. *Season of the Sun* brought excitement as it restored literature to the present forward-looking and potentially prosperous moment. As Bourdaghs has noted, the Hawaiian strains of Yūjirō's song made the United States, and specifically Hawaii, an exotic destination ("Japan That Can Say 'Yes'," 61–86). The South Pacific could now be viewed as a vacation land and not as a place to die in battle. *Season of the Sun* thus distracts readers from both the postwar wallowing in wartime guilt and the Occupation's phobias about Japanese–U.S. relations and away from the mundanity and domesticity of *daisan no shinjin* (for example, the troubled home in *Still Life*).

69. Aoshima, Ishihara, et al., "Chō-gendai ha no kairaku kan," 221.

70. Lhamon, *Deliberate Speed*, 8.

71. Mick Broderick, "'Armageddon Without a Cause': Playing 'Chicken' in the Atomic Age," in *Rebel Without a Cause*, ed. Slocum, 166.

72. "Akutagawa shō kettei happyō," 281.

73. Sharalyn Orbaugh, "The Body in Contemporary Japanese Women's Fiction," in *The Woman's Hand: Gender and Theory in Japanese Women's Writing*, ed. Paul G. Schalow and Janet A. Walker (Stanford, Calif.: Stanford University Press, 1996), 119–64. Also see Michael Molasky, *The American Occupation of Japan and Okinawa: Literature and Memory* (New York: Routledge, 1999).

74. Ishihara, *Season of Violence*, 55–56, and *Taiyō no kisetsu*, 364–65.

75. Ishihara, *Taiyō no kisetsu*, 75.

76. "Kaisetsu," in Ishihara, *Taiyō no kisetsu*, 367–68.

77. "Akutagawa shō kettei happyō," 284.

78. Itō, Takeda, and Mishima, "Shōsetsu no shinjin ni nozomu," 290.

79. *Asahi shinbun*, February 10, 1956, 2.

80. Nakano, "Akutagawa shō ni tsuite omoide," 283.

81. The debates between Satō and Funabashi took place in the *Yomiuri shinbun* from February through March 1956, and the discussion over "gambling" among Kamei Katsuichirō, Nakamura Mitsuo, and Yamamoto Kenkichi ran in the *Tokyo shinbun* from February through March 1956. Furui Yoshimi and Takeda Taijun also published criticism of the Taiyōzoku literary phenomenon in 1956.

82. Ishihara Shintarō, Oda Makoto, et al., "'Shinjin' no teikō: Shōwa umare no sakka tachi," *Bungakukai*, June 1956, 133; Ishihara Shintarō, Etō Jun, et al., "Okoreru wakamono tachi." *Bungakukai*, October 1959, 143; Aoshima, Ishihara, et al., "Chō-gendai ha no kairaku kan," 218. Broderick analyzes the "chickie run" (race to the edge of the cliff in stolen cars) game in the context of mutually assured

destruction and the arms race, as well as the "apocalyptic sensibility" expressed in the astronomy lecture sequence in "Armageddon Without a Cause," 153–61.

83. Gessel, *Sting of Life*, 51.

84. Ishihara, Etō, et al., "Okoreru wakamono tachi," 132.

85. Ishihara, Oda, et al., "'Shinjin' no teikō," 133.

86. Ishihara, Oda, et al., "'Shinjin' no teikō," 133–34.

87. John W. Dower, "Peace and Democracy," in *Postwar Japan as History*, ed. Andrew Gordon (Berkeley: University of California Press, 1993), 15, 20. Kishi was the grandfather of Abe Shinzō, the prime minister of Japan from 2006 to 2007 and successor to Koizumi Jun'ichirō.

88. In 1958, "a national council was formed to opposed revision of the Police Duties Law, which would have expanded police prerogatives to search and intervene in anticipation of a crime. The movement included labor unions, women's groups, cultural organizations, and the Socialist Party. It culminated in a general strike by four million workers and a Socialist boycott of Diet sessions that ultimately defeated a government effort to force the revision through" (J. Victor Koschmann, "Intellectuals and Politics," in *Postwar Japan as History*, ed. Gordon, 406).

89. During the Occupation, the government and SCAP had, of course, also enforced limitations on Japanese legal rights and freedom of speech. See John W. Dower's illuminating *Embracing Defeat: Japan in the Wake of World War II* (New York: Norton / New Press, 1999).

90. Sasaki-Uemura, *Organizing the Spontaneous*, 172–73. Proposals for revising the constitution, and especially Article 9, appeared during the mid-1950s.

91. Ōe states that Wakai Nihon no kai was started by Etō Jun and others with the encouragement of older people like Hirano Ken and Nakajima Kenzō: "Hirano and Nakajima's generation had experienced the dark experiences under the Peace Preservation Law in the prewar days, and thus were compelled to oppose the proposed revisions of the Police Duties law. The older generation understood clearly the implications of the revisions, but young people without such experiences only had a vague notion of what might result" (quoted in Hirano Ken et al., "Bungakusha to seijiteki jōkyō," *Bungakukai*, January 1959, 162).

92. Many established writers participated in antirevision meetings and assemblies. Among them were Sata Ineko, Ishikawa Tatsuzō, and Hotta Yoshie. See "'Nihon bunka no tame ni' Bungei kyōkai no iinkai," *Asahi shinbun*, October 19, 2001 (evening edition), 1; and "Keishoku-hō kaisei hantai: Bunkajin no chomei zoku zoku," *Asahi shinbun*, October 21, 1958 (evening edition), 11.

93. Hirano et al., "Bungakusha to seijiteki jōkyō," 162.

94. Ishihara Shintarō, Ōe Kenzaburō, et al., "Warera minshūshugi no ko ra," *Chūō kōron*, January 1959, 120.

95. Ōe Kenzaburō, "Bungaku chokugen: Jōkyō—1959," *Bungakukai*, February 1959, 5–7.

96. Slocum, "Introduction: *Rebel Without a Cause* Fifty Years Later," 18.

97. Leerom Medovoi, "Democracy, Capitalism, and American Literature: The

Cold War Construction of J. D. Salinger's Paperback Hero," in *The Other Fifties: Interrogating Midcentury American Icons,* ed. Joel Foreman (Chicago: University of Illinois Press, 1997), 257.

Conclusion: Cold War as Culture

1. Marukawa Tetsushi, *Reisen bunka ron: Wasurerareta aimaina sensō no genzai-sei* (Tokyo: Sofūsha, 2005), 12; interview with Marukawa Tetsushi, Tokyo, July 27, 2007.

2. Marukawa, *Reisen bunka ron,* 12.

3. Marukawa discusses Takeuchi's thought in detail in *Reisen bunka ron,* 22–39. See Richard Calichman's incisive analysis of Takeuchi Yoshimi's thought in his introduction to *What Is Modernity? Writings of Takeuchi Yoshimi,* ed. and trans. Richard F. Calichman (New York: Columbia University Press, 2004).

4. Marukawa, *Reisen bunka ron,* 22–23. Chen himself had been jailed for political activities from 1968 to 1975.

5. Harry D. Harootunian, *Overcome by Modernity: History, Culture, and Community in Interwar Japan* (Princeton, N.J.: Princeton University Press, 2000), xxxi, xv, xxi.

6. Takashi Murakami, ed., *Little Boy: The Arts of Japan's Exploding Subculture* (New York: Japan Society; New Haven, Conn.: Yale University Press, 2005).

7. Murakami, "Earth in My Window," in *Little Boy,* ed. Murakami, 100, 141.

8. Murakami, "Superflat Trilogy: Greetings, You Are Alive," in *Little Boy,* ed. Murakami, 152. An interesting but problematic historical overview of Murakami's works and the "Super-Flat Manifesto" is Sawaragi Noi, "On the Battlefield of 'Superflat': Subculture and Art in Postwar Japan," in *Little Boy,* ed. Murakami, 186–207. Sawaragi summarizes Murakami's significance in this way: "It may be argued that Murakami has attempted to create 'defeat record painting' [*haisen kiroku-ga*], ironically commenting on a postwar Japan that is oblivious to its wartime history and has become Superflat, so to speak, with no clear boundary between high art and subculture—which are, in fact, intricately entwined" (201).

Bibliography

Abe Tomoji. *Abe Tomoji zenshū*. 13 vols. Tokyo: Kawade shobō, 1975.

——. Introduction to *Genshiryoku to bungaku,* edited by Odagiri Hideo. Tokyo: Kōdansha, 1955.

——, ed. *Rorensu kenkyū*. Tokyo: Eihōsha, 1955.

Abrams, Nathan, and Julie Hughes. *Containing America: Cultural Production and Consumption in Fifties America*. Birmingham: University of Birmingham Press, 2000.

"Akutagawa shō kettei happyō." *Bungei shunjū,* March 1956, 280–89.

Allen, James S. *Atomic Imperialism: The State, Monopoly, and the Bomb*. New York: International Publishers, 1952.

——. *Genbaku teikokushugi: Kokka dokusen bakudan*. Translated by Sekai keizai kenkyūjo. Tokyo: Ōtsuki shoten, 1953.

Allison, Anne. *Permitted and Prohibited Desires: Mothers, Comics, and Censorship in Japan*. Boulder, Colo.: Westview Press, 1996.

Ambaras, David R. *Bad Youth: Juvenile Delinquency and the Politics of Everyday Life in Modern Japan*. Berkeley: University of California Press, 2006.

Aoshima Yukio, Ishihara Shintarō, et al. "Chō-gendai ha no kairaku kan." *Chūō kōron,* April 1956, 216–23.

Arjun, Makhijani, Howard Hu, and Katherine Yih, eds. *Nuclear Wastelands: A Global Guide to Nuclear Weapons Production and Its Health and Environmental Effects*. Cambridge, Mass.: MIT Press, 2000.

Armstrong, Charles. "The Cultural Cold War in Korea, 1945–1950." *Journal of Asian Studies* 62, no. 1 (2003): 71–99.

Awanaka Goro. "Nihirizumu to egoizumu to: Ishihara Shintarō no bungaku ni tsuite." *Purometeusu* 36 (2000): 109–19.

Badash, Lawrence. *Radioactivity in America: Growth and Decay of a Science.* Baltimore: Johns Hopkins University Press, 1979.

Barshay, Andrew E. "Imagining Democracy in Postwar Japan: Reflections on Maruyama Masao and Modernism." *Journal of Japanese Studies* 18, no. 2 (1992): 365–406.

——. *The Social Sciences and Modern Japan: The Marxian and Modernist Traditions.* Berkeley: University of California Press, 2004.

Baudrillard, Jean. *Simulacra and Simulation.* Ann Arbor: University of Michigan Press, 1994.

Beer, Lawrence Ward. *Freedom of Expression in Japan: A Study in Comparative Law, Politics, and Society.* New York: Kodansha International, 1984.

Berghahn, Volker R. *America and the Intellectual Cold Wars in Europe: Shepard Stone Between Philanthropy, Academy, and Diplomacy.* Princeton, N.J.: Princeton University Press, 2001.

Berry, Elizabeth. "Public Life in Authoritarian Japan." *Daedalus* 127, no. 3 (1998): 133–65.

Biltereyst, Daniel. "Youth, Moral Panics, and the End of Cinema: On the Reception of *Rebel Without a Cause* in Europe." In *Rebel Without a Cause: Approaches to a Maverick Masterwork,* edited by J. David Slocum. Albany: State University of New York Press, 2005.

Bird, Kai, and Lawrence Lifschultz, eds. *Hiroshima's Shadow: Writings on the Denial of History and the Smithsonian Controversy.* Stony Creek, Conn.: Pamphleteer's Press, 1998.

Blackett, P. M. S. "The Decision to Use the Bombs." In *Hiroshima's Shadow: Writings on the Denial of History and the Smithsonian Controversy,* edited by Kai Bird and Lawrence Lifschultz. Stony Creek, Conn.: Pamphleteer's Press, 1998.

Bogle, Lori Lyn, ed. *The Cold War.* 5 vols. New York: Routledge, 2001.

Bourdaghs, Michael. *The Dawn That Never Comes: Shimazaki Tōson and Japanese Nationalism.* New York: Columbia University Press, 2003.

——. "The Japan That Can Say 'Yes': Bubblegum Music in a Post-Bubble Economy." *literature and psychology* 44, no. 4 (1998): 61–86.

Bourdieu, Pierre. *The Field of Cultural Production: Essays on Art and Literature.* Edited by Randal Johnson. New York: Columbia University Press, 1993.

Boyer, Paul. *By the Bomb's Early Light: American Thought and Culture at the Dawn of the Atomic Age.* Chapel Hill: University of North Carolina Press, 1994.

——. *Fallout: A Historian Reflects on America's Half-Century Encounter with Nuclear Weapons.* Columbus: Ohio State University Press, 1998.

——. *Purity in Print: The Vice-Society Movement and Book Censorship in America.* New York: Scribner, 1968.

Bradley, David. *No Place to Hide.* Tokyo: Kodansha, 1949.

Bradshaw, David, ed. *A Concise Companion to Modernism.* Malden, Mass.: Blackwell, 2003.

Brannon, Julie Sloan. *Who Reads Ulysses? The Rhetoric of the Joyce Wars and the Common Reader.* New York: Routledge, 2003.

Braw, Monica. *The Atomic Bomb Suppressed: American Censorship in Occupied Japan.* Armonk, N.Y.: Sharpe, 1991.

Broderick, Mick. "'Armageddon Without a Cause': Playing 'Chicken' in the Atomic Age." In *Rebel Without a Cause: Approaches to a Maverick Masterwork,* edited by J. David Slocum. Albany: State University of New York Press, 2005.

——, ed. *Hibakusha Cinema: Hiroshima, Nagasaki and the Nuclear Image in Japanese Film.* New York: Kegan Paul, 1996.

"Bungakukai shinjin shō." *Bungakukai,* April 1955, 134–37.

Burchett, Wilfred. "The First Nuclear War." In *Hiroshima's Shadow: Writings on the Denial of History and the Smithsonian Controversy,* edited by Kai Bird and Lawrence Lifschultz. Stony Creek, Conn.: Pamphleteer's Press, 1998.

Burstyn, Varda, ed. *Women Against Censorship.* Toronto: Douglas & McIntyre, 1985.

Calichman, Richard F., ed. and trans. *What Is Modernity? Writings of Takeuchi Yoshimi.* New York: Columbia University Press, 2004.

Cather, Kirsten. "The Great Censorship Trials of Literature and Film in Postwar Japan." Ph.D. diss., University of California at Berkeley, 2004.

Chartier, Roger. "Texts, Printing, Readings." In *The New Cultural History,* edited by Lynn Hunt. Berkeley: University of California Press, 1989.

Childs, Elizabeth C., ed. *Suspended License: Censorship and the Visual Arts.* Seattle: University of Washington Press, 1997.

Chūgoku shinbunsha, ed. *Nenpyō Hiroshima 40-nen no kiroku.* Tokyo: Miraisha, 1986.

Clor, Harry M. *Obscenity and Public Morality: Censorship in a Liberal Society.* Chicago: University of Chicago Press, 1969.

Coetzee, J. M. *Giving Offense: Essays on Censorship.* Chicago: University of Chicago Press, 1996.

Cohn, Carol. "Sex and Death in the Rational World of Defense Intellectuals." *Signs* 12, no. 4 (1987): 687–718.

Corber, Robert J. *In the Name of National Security: Hitchcock, Homophobia, and the Political Construction of Gender in Postwar America.* Durham, N.C.: Duke University Press, 1993.

Cornell, Drucilla, ed. *Feminism and Pornography.* New York: Oxford University Press, 2000.

Cossman, Brenda, Shannon Bell, Lise Gotell, and Becki L. Ross. *Bad Attitude/s on Trial: Pornography, Feminism, and the* Butler *Decision.* Toronto: University of Toronto Press, 1997.

Cummings, Bruce. "Japan's Position in the World System." In *Postwar Japan as History,* edited by Andrew Gordon. Berkeley: University of California Press, 1993.

Cushman, Keith. "DHL in the USA." In *The Reception of D. H. Lawrence Around the World,* edited by Takeo Iida. Fukuoka: Kyushu University Press, 1999.

Daigo Fukyuryūmaru heiwa kyōkai (Daigo Fukuryūmaru Foundation), ed. *Shashin de tadoru Daigo Fukuryūmaru*. Tokyo: Heiwa no atorie, 2004.

Dantō Shigemitsu. "Chatarei saiban no hihan." *Chūō kōron*, June 1957, 47–48.

Davis, Tracy C. *Stages of Emergency: Cold War Nuclear Civil Defense*. Durham, N.C.: Duke University Press, 2007.

Day, Gary, and Clive Bloom, eds. *Perspectives on Pornography: Sexuality in Film and Literature*. New York: St. Martin's Press, 1988.

Desser, David. *Eros plus Massacre*. Bloomington: Indiana University Press, 1988.

Doherty, Thomas. *Cold War, Cool Medium: Television, McCarthyism, and American Culture*. New York: Columbia University Press, 2003.

Dower, John W. "The Bombed: Hiroshimas and Nagasakis in Japanese Memory." In *Hiroshima in History and Memory*, edited by Michael J. Hogan. Cambridge: Cambridge University Press, 1996.

——. *Embracing Defeat: Japan in the Wake of World War II*. New York: Norton / New Press, 1999.

——. *Japan in War and Peace: Selected Essays*. New York: New Press, 1993.

——. "Peace and Democracy." In *Postwar Japan as History*, edited by Andrew Gordon. Berkeley: University of California Press, 1993.

Dower, John W., and John Junkerman, eds. *Hiroshima Murals: The Art of Iri Maruki and Toshi Maruki*. Tokyo: Kodansha, 1985.

DuBois, W. E. B. *The Autobiography of W. E. B. DuBois: A Soliloquy on Viewing My Life from the Last Decade of Its First Century*. New York: International Publishers, 1968.

Dudziak, Mary L. *Cold War Civil Rights: Race and the Image of American Democracy*. Princeton, N.J.: Princeton University Press, 2000.

Dunham, Vera. *In Stalin's Time: Middleclass Values in Soviet Fiction*. Cambridge: Cambridge University Press, 1976.

Ellis, Richard. "Disseminating Desire: Grove Press and 'The End[s] of Obscenity.'" In *Perspectives on Pornography: Sexuality in Film and Literature*, edited by Gary Day and Clive Bloom. New York: St. Martin's Press, 1988.

Etō Jun. "Dazai Osamu." In *Hōkai kara no sōzō*. Tokyo: Keisō shobō, 1969.

Fehrenbach, Heide, and Uta G. Poiger. *Transactions, Transgressions, Transformations: American Culture in Western Europe and Japan*. New York: Berghahn Books, 2000.

Fernihough, Anne, ed. *The Cambridge Companion to D. H. Lawrence*. Cambridge: Cambridge University Press, 2001.

Field, Deborah. "Irreconcilable Differences: Divorce and Conceptions of Private Life in the Khrushchev Era." *Russian Review* 57, no. 4 (1998): 599–613.

Finn, Richard B. *Winners in Peace: MacArthur, Yoshida, and Postwar Japan*. Berkeley: University of California Press, 1992.

Foreman, Joel, ed. *The Other Fifties: Interrogating Midcentury American Icons*. Urbana: University of Illinois Press, 1997.

Foucault, Michel. *The History of Sexuality*. Vol. 1, *An Introduction*. Translated by Robert Hurley. New York: Random House, 1978.

Fukushima Jūrō. *Sengo zasshi hakkutsu*. Tokyo: Yōsensha, 1985.

Gaddis, John Lewis. "On Starting Over Again: A Naïve Approach to the Study of the Cold War." In *Reviewing the Cold War: Approaches, Interpretations, Theory*, edited by Odd Arne Westad. Portland, Ore.: Frank Cass, 2000.

——. *We Now Know: Rethinking Cold War History*. New York: Oxford University Press, 1997.

Galbraith, Stuart, IV. *The Emperor and the Wolf: The Lives and Films of Akira Kurosawa and Toshiro Mifune*. New York: Faber & Faber, 2001.

Gardner, William. *Advertising Tower: Japanese Modernism and Modernity in the 1920s*. Cambridge, Mass.: Harvard University Asia Center, 2006.

Geerhart, Bill, and Ken Sitz. *Atomic Platters: Cold War Music from the Golden Age of Homeland Security*. Hamburg: Bear Family Records, 2005. [Book and compact discs]

Gensuibaku kinshi Nihon kokumin kaigi 21-seiki no gensui kin undō o kangaeru kai, eds. *Hirakareta "Pandora no hako" to kaku haizetsu e no tatakai: Genshiryoku kaihatsu to Nihon no hikaku undō*. Tokyo: Nanatsu-mori shokan, 2002.

Gensuibaku kinshi sekai taikai Nihon junbikai, ed. *Genbaku yurusu maji: Gensuibaku kinshi taikai no kiroku*. Tokyo: Gensuibaku kinshi sekai taikai Nihon junbikai and Nihon rōdō kumiai sōhyō gikai, 1955.

Gerteis, Christopher. "Japanese Women, Their Unions and the Security Treaty Struggle, 1945–1960." Ph.D. diss., University of Iowa, 2001.

Gertzman, Jay. "Contemporary Censors and Publishers of *Lady Chatterley's Lover*: Prohibiting the Body with Just Another Dirty Book." In *Writing the Body in D. H. Lawrence: Essays on Language, Representation, and Sexuality*, edited by Paul Poplawski. Westport, Conn.: Greenwood Press, 2001.

Gessel, Van. *The Sting of Life: Four Contemporary Japanese Novelists*. New York: Columbia University Press, 1989.

Gilbert, James. *A Cycle of Outrage: America's Reaction to the Juvenile Delinquent in the 1950s*. New York: Oxford University Press, 1986.

Gluck, Carol, and Stephen R. Graubard, eds. *Showa: The Japan of Hirohito*. New York: Norton, 1992.

Goldman, Merle, and Andrew Gordon, eds. *Historical Perspectives on Contemporary East Asia*. Cambridge, Mass.: Harvard University Press, 2000.

Gordon, Andrew, ed. *Postwar Japan as History*. Berkeley: University of California Press, 1993.

Grant, Damian. "D. H. Lawrence: A Suitable Case for Censorship." In *Writing and Censorship in Britain*, edited by Paul Hyland and Neil Sammells. New York: Routledge, 1992.

Gregory, Horace. *Pilgrim of the Apocalypse*. New York: Viking Press, 1933.

Guilbaut, Serge. *How New York Stole the Idea of Modern Art: Abstract Expressionism, Freedom, and the Cold War*. Translated by Arthur Goldhammer. Chicago: University of Chicago Press, 1983.

Gusterson, Hugh. *Nuclear Rites: An Anthropologist Among Weapons Scientists*. Berkeley: University of California Press, 1996.

——. "Nuclear Weapons Testing: Scientific Experiment as Political Ritual." In *Naked Science: Anthropological Inquiry into Boundaries, Power, and Knowledge*, edited by Laura Nader. New York: Routledge, 1996.

Hacker, Barton C. *Elements of Controversy: The Atomic Energy Commission and Radiation Safety in Nuclear Weapons Testing, 1947–1974*. Berkeley: University of California Press, 1994.

Hanada Kiyoteru. "Hara Tamiki ron." In *Nihon genbaku kiroku*, vol. 16, edited by Ienaga Saburō, Odagiri Hideo, and Kuroko Kazuo. Tokyo: Nihon toshi sentaa, 1991.

Hanada Kiyoteru et al. "Senkyūhyaku gojū gonen no mondai." *Shin Nihon bungaku*, January 1955, 138–53.

Hara Kenchū. "Tsuisō ni yosete." In *Teihon: Hara Tamiki zenshū*. Vol. 4, *Bekkan*. Tokyo: Seidosha, 1978–1979.

Hara Tamiki. *Hara Tamiki sengo zenshōsetsu*. 2 vols. Tokyo: Kōdansha, 1995.

——. *Natsu no hana, Shingan no kuni*. Tokyo: Shinchōsha, 1973.

——. *Teihon: Hara Tamiki zenshū*. 4 vols. Tokyo: Seidosha, 1978–1979.

Harootunian, Harry D. "The Black Cat in the Dark Room." *positions* 13, no. 1 (2005): 137–55.

——. *Overcome by Modernity: History, Culture, and Community in Interwar Japan*. Princeton, N.J.: Princeton University Press, 2000.

Havens, Thomas R. H. *Fire Across the Sea: The Vietnam War and Japan, 1965–1975*. Princeton, N.J.: Princeton University Press, 1987.

Hebdige, Dick. *Subculture: The Meaning of Style*. New York: Routledge, 1998.

Hein, Laura. "Growth Versus Success: Japan's Economic Policy in Historical Perspective." In *Postwar Japan as History*, edited by Andrew Gordon. Berkeley: University of California Press, 1993.

Henriksen, Margot A. *Dr. Strangelove's America: Society and Culture in the Atomic Age*. Berkeley: University of California Press, 1997.

Herman, Ellen. *The Romance of American Psychology: Political Culture in the Age of Experts*. Berkeley: University of California Press, 1995.

Hersbergen, Gijs van. *Guernica: The Biography of a Twentieth-Century Icon*. New York: Bloomsbury, 2004.

Hershberg, James G. "The Crisis Years, 1958–1963." In *Reviewing the Cold War: Approaches, Interpretations, Theory*, edited by Odd Arne Westad. Portland, Ore.: Frank Cass, 2000.

Hersey, John. *Hiroshima*. New York: Knopf, 1946

Hevly, Bruce, and John M. Findlay. *The Atomic West*. Seattle: University of Washington Press, 1998.

Hirano Ken et al. "Bungakusha to seijiteki jōkyō." *Bungakukai*, January 1959, 162–75.

Hirano, Kyoko. "Depiction of the Atomic Bombings in Japanese Cinema." In *Hibakusha Cinema: Hiroshima, Nagasaki and the Nuclear Image in Japanese Film*, edited by Mick Broderick. New York: Kegan Paul, 1996.

Hixson, Walter. *Parting the Curtain: Propaganda, Culture, and the Cold War*. New York: St. Martin's Press, 1997.

Hogan, Michael J., ed. *Hiroshima in History and Memory*. Cambridge: Cambridge University Press, 1996.

Holloway, David. *Stalin and the Bomb: The Soviet Union and Atomic Energy, 1939–1956*. New Haven, Conn.: Yale University Press, 1994.

Horiba Kiyoko. *Genbaku hyōgen to ken'etsu: Nihonjin wa doo taioo shita ka*. Tokyo: Asahi shinbunsha, 1995.

——. *Kinjirareta genbaku taiken*. Tokyo: Iwanami shoten, 1995.

Hunt, Lynn, ed. *The Invention of Pornography: Obscenity and the Origins of Modernity*. New York: Zone Books, 1993.

——, ed. *The New Cultural History*. Berkeley: University of California Press, 1989.

——. "Obscenity and the Origins of Modernity, 1500–1800." In *Feminism and Pornography*, edited by Drucilla Cornell. New York: Oxford University Press, 2000.

Huyssen, Andreas. "Of Mice and Mimesis: Reading Spiegelman with Adorno." In *Rethinking the Frankfurt School: Alternative Legacies of Cultural Critique*, edited by Jeffrey T. Nealon and Caren Irr. Albany: State University of New York Press, 2002.

Hyland, Paul, and Neil Sammells. *Writing and Censorship in Britain*. New York: Routledge, 1992.

Hylton, Stuart. *From Rationing to Rock: The 1950s Revisited*. Stroud, Eng.: Sutton, 1998.

Hyman, James. *The Battle for Realism*. New Haven, Conn.: Yale University Press, 2001.

Ienaga Saburō, Odagiri Hideo, and Kuroko Kazuo, eds. *Nihon no genbaku kiroku*. 20 vols. Tokyo: Nihon tosho sentaa, 1991.

Igarashi, Yoshikuni. *Bodies of Memory: Narratives of War in Postwar Japanese Culture, 1945–1970*. Princeton, N.J.: Princeton University Press, 2000.

Iida, Takeo. "The Reception of D. H. Lawrence in Japan." In *The Reception of D. H. Lawrence Around the World*, edited by Takeo Iida. Fukuoka: Kyushu University Press, 1999.

Ishihara Shintarō. *Kaseki no mori; Taiyō no kisetsu*. Tokyo: Shinchōsha, 1981.

——. *Otōto*. Tokyo: Gentōsha, 1996.

——. *Season of Violence, The Punishment Room, The Yacht and the Boy*. Translated by Jon G. Mills, Toshie Takahama, and Ken Tremayne. Rutland, Vt.: Tuttle, 1966.

Ishihara Shintarō, Etō Jun, et al. "Okoreru wakamono tachi." *Bungakukai*, October 1959, 132–43.

Ishihara Shintarō and Ishikawa Yoshimi. "Taidan: Ishikawa Yoshimi—Ishihara Shintarō." *Ronza*, May 2001, 21–25.

Ishihara Shintarō, Oda Makoto, et al. "'Shinjin' no teikō: Shōwa umare no sakka tachi." *Bungakukai*, June 1956, 130–36.

Ishihara Shintarō, Ōe Kenzaburō, et al. "Warera minshūshugi no ko ra." *Chūō kōron*, January 1959, 114–23.

Itō Rei. *Funtō no shōgai: Itō Sei shi*. Tokyo: Kōdansha, 1985.

Itō Sei. "Hara Tamiki no omoide." In *Teihon: Hara Tamiki zenshū.* Vol. 4, *Bekkan.* Tokyo: Seidosha, 1979.

——. *Saiban.* Tokyo: Chikuma shobō, 1958.

Itō Sei, Takeda Taijun, and Mishima Yukio. "Shōsetsu no shinjin ni nozomu." *Chūō kōron,* June 1956, 288–97.

Ivy, Marilyn. "Formations of Mass Culture." In *Postwar Japan as History,* edited by Andrew Gordon. Berkeley: University of California Press, 1993.

Iwasaki Fumito. *Hara Tamiki: Hito to bungaku.* Tokyo: Bensei shuppan, 2003.

——. "*Natsu no hana* 'Hara Tamiki' sanbusaku to sono shūhen." *Kokubungaku kō* 176–177 (2003): 79–90.

Jauss, Hans Robert. *Toward an Aesthetics of Reception Theory.* Translated by Timothy Bahti. Minneapolis: University of Minnesota Press, 1982.

Junkerman, John, producer, director, and writer. *Hellfire: A Journey from Hiroshima,* 1986. Broadcast on PBS, 1987. [Documentary on Japanese atomic-bomb artists Iri Maruki and Toshi Maruki]

Kaikō Takeshi (Ken). *Kami no naka no sensō.* Tokyo: Iwanami shoten, 1996.

Kajii Motojirō. "Lemon." In *The Oxford Book of Japanese Short Stories,* edited by Theodore W. Goossen. New York: Oxford University Press, 1997.

Kaku sensō no kiki o uttaeru bungakusha no seimei, ed. *Nihon no genbaku bungaku: Hyōron/essei.* Vol. 15. Tokyo: Horubu shuppan, 1983.

Kamei Fumio. "Aete 'Hiroshima, Nagasaki no himitsu' o hagu: *Sekai wa kyōfu suru* satsuei urabanashi." *Chūō kōron,* December 1957, 77–85.

——. "Anata no ningen jikaku ni uttaeru." *Kinema junpō,* November 1957, 44–45.

——. *Tatakau eiga: Dokyūmentarisuto no Shōwa shi.* Tokyo: Iwanami shoten, 1989.

Karolides, Nicholas, Margaret Bald, and Dawn B. Sova. *100 Banned Books: Censorship Histories of World Literature.* New York: Checkmark Books / Facts on File, 1999.

Kawaguchi Takayuki. "'Genbaku bungaku' to iu mondai ryōiki—Saikō." *Genbaku bungaku kenkyū* 1 (2002): 15–21.

Kawanishi Masaaki. "Hana no Maboroshi—'Natsu no hana' sanbusaku to 'Utsukushi shi no kishi ni' no rensaku ni tsuite." In *Hara Tamiki sengo zen shōsetsu.* Vol. 2. Tokyo: Kōdansha, 1995.

Kawanishi Takaaki. *Hitotsu no unmei: Hara Tamiki ron.* Tokyo: Kōdansha, 1980.

Keene, Donald. *Dawn to the West: Japanese Literature in the Modern Era.* 2 vols. New York: Holt, 1984.

Kelly, William W. "Finding a Place in Metropolitan Japan: Ideologies, Institutions, and Everyday Life." In *Postwar Japan as History,* edited by Andrew Gordon. Berkeley: University of California Press, 1993.

Kerkham, H. Eleanor. "Pleading for the Body: Tamura Taijirō's 1947 Korean Comfort Woman Story, *Biography of a Prostitute.*" In *War, Occupation, and Creativity: Japan and East Asia, 1920–1960,* edited by Marlene J. Mayo and J. Thomas Rimer. Honolulu: University of Hawai'i Press, 2001.

Kersten, Rikki. *Democracy in Postwar Japan: Maruyama Masao and the Search for Autonomy.* New York: Routledge, 1996.

Kido Shigeru, Yanagisawa Jirō, and Murakami Kimitoshi. *Sekai heiwa undō-shi*. Tokyo: San'ichi shobō, 1961.

Kleeman, Faye. *Under an Imperial Sun: Japanese Colonial Literature of Taiwan and the South*. Honolulu: University of Hawai'i Press, 2003.

Kockum, Keiko. *Itō Sei: Self-Analysis and the Modern Japanese Novel*. Stockholm East Asian Monographs, no. 7. Stockholm: Institute of Oriental Languages, Stockholm University, 1984.

Kohno Kensuke. "'Gojūnen mondai' to tantei shōsetsu: Sengo bungaku ni okeru janru." In *Tantei shōsetsu to Nihon kindai*, edited by Yoshida Morio. Tokyo: Seikyusha, 2004.

———. *Shomotsu no kindai: Media no bungakushi*. Tokyo: Chikuma shobō, 1992.

Kokai Eiji. *Shijin no shi*. Tokyo: Kokubunsha, 1984.

Kokusai Ishi kaigi Nihon junbi iinkai and Kusano Nobuo. "Shikabane wa kōgi suru." In *Nihon genbaku hyōron taikei*. Vol. 1. Tokyo: Nihon tosho sentaa, 1999.

Kon, Igor. *The Sexual Revolution in Russia: From the Age of the Czars to Today*. New York: Free Press, 1995.

Kon, Igor, and James Riordan, eds. *Sex and Russian Society*. Bloomington: Indiana University Press, 1993.

Koschmann, J. Victor. "Intellectuals and Politics." In *Postwar Japan as History*, edited by Andrew Gordon. Berkeley: University of California Press, 1993.

Kotek, Joel. *Students and the Cold War*. Translated by Ralph Blumenau. New York: St. Martin's Press, 1996.

Kozawa Setsuko. *"Genbaku no zu" egakareta "kioku," katarareta "kaiga."* Tokyo: Iwanami shoten, 2002.

Kurihara, Sadako. *Black Eggs*. Translated by Richard H. Minear. Ann Arbor: Center for Japanese Studies, University of Michigan, 1994.

———. *Kaku jidai ni ikiru*. Tokyo: San'ichi shobō, 1982.

Kuroko Kazuo. *Genbaku to kotoba (shō): Hara Tamiki kara Hayashi Kyōko made*. Tokyo: Nihon tosho sentaa, 1991.

Kusano, Nobuo. *Atomic Bomb Injuries*. Tokyo: Tsukiji shokan, 1953.

LaCapra, Dominick. *Writing History, Writing Trauma*. Baltimore: Johns Hopkins University Press, 2001.

Ladenson, Elisabeth. *Dirt for Art's Sake: Books on Trial from Madame Bovary to Lolita*. Ithaca, N.Y.: Cornell University Press, 2007.

Lauter, Paul. *From Walden Pond to Jurassic Park: Activism, Culture and American Studies*. Durham, N.C.: Duke University Press, 2001.

Lawrence, D. H. *A Propos of "Lady Chatterley's Lover."* New York: Haskell House, 1930.

———. *Chatarei fujin no koibito*. Translated by Itō Sei. 2 vols. Tokyo: Oyama shoten, 1950.

———. *Lady Chatterley's Lover*. New York: Random House, 1993.

———. *Sex, Literature, and Censorship*. Edited by Harry T. Moore. New York: Viking Press, 1959.

Leffler, Melvyn P. "Bringing It Together: The Parts and the Whole." In *Reviewing the Cold War: Approaches, Interpretations, Theory*, edited by Odd Arne Westad. Portland, Ore.: Frank Cass, 2000.

Levenson, Michael, ed. *The Cambridge Companion to Modernism*. Cambridge: Cambridge University Press, 1999.

Lewis, Jon. "Rebel Without a Cause: Growing Up Male in Jim's Mom's World." In *Rebel Without a Cause: Approaches to a Maverick Masterwork*, edited by J. David Slocum. Albany: State University of New York Press, 2005.

———. *The Road to Romance and Ruin: Teen Films and Youth Culture*. New York: Routledge, 1992.

Lhamon, W. T., Jr. *Deliberate Speed: The Origins of a Cultural Style in the American 1950s*. Washington, D.C.: Smithsonian Institution Press, 1990.

Lindee, M. Susan. *Suffering Made Real: American Science and the Survivors of Hiroshima*. Chicago: University of Chicago Press, 1994.

Lindner, Robert M. *Rebel Without a Cause: The Hypnoanalysis of a Criminal Psychopath*. New York: Grune & Stratton, 1944.

Lippit, Seiji. *Topographies of Japanese Modernism*. New York: Columbia University Press, 2002.

Lisle, Rose A. *The Cold War Comes to Main Street: America in 1950*. Lawrence: University Press of Kansas, 1999.

Machor, James L., and Philip Goldstein, eds. *Reception Study: From Literary Theory to Cultural Studies*. New York: Routledge, 2001.

Mack, Edward. *Manufacturing Japanese Literature*. Durham, N.C.: Duke University Press, forthcoming.

Maclear, Kyo. *Beclouded Visions: Hiroshima-Nagasaki and the Art of Witness*. Albany: State University of New York Press, 1999.

Maeda Ai. *Kindai dokusha no seiritsu*. Tokyo: Iwanami shoten, 2001.

———. *Text and the City: Essays on Japanese Modernity*. Edited and with an introduction by James A. Fujii. Durham, N.C.: Duke University Press, 2004.

Makino, Mamoru. "Documentary Filmmaker: The Times in Which Kamei Fumio Lived." In *Kamei Fumio tokushū / Kamei Fumio Retrospective*, edited by Yamagata International Documentary Film Festival. Tokyo: YIDFF Organizing Committee, Tokyo Office, 2001.

Mao, Douglas, and Rebecca L. Walkowitz, eds. *Bad Modernisms*. Durham, N.C.: Duke University Press, 2006.

Marukawa Tetsushi. *Reisen bunka ron: Wasurerareta aimaina sensō no genzaisei*. Tokyo: Sofūsha, 2005.

Maruki Toshi. *Onna egaki no tanjō*. Tokyo: Nihon tosho sentaa, 1997.

Maruoka Akira. "Hara Tamiki ron: Genbaku to chishikijin." In *Nihon no genbaku bungaku*, vol. 1, edited by Kaku sensō no kiki o uttaeru bungakusha no seimei. Tokyo: Horupu shuppan, 1983.

Maruyama, Masao. "From Carnal Literature to Carnal Politics." In *Thought and Behavior in Modern Japanese Politics*, edited by Ivan Morris. New York: Oxford University Press, 1969.

———. "Nikutai bungaku kara nikutai seiji made." In *Gendai seiji no shisō to kōdō*. Vol. 2. Tokyo: Miraisha, 1957.

Masco, Joseph. *The Nuclear Borderlands: The Manhattan Project in Post–Cold War New Mexico*. Princeton, N.J.: Princeton University Press, 2006.

Maxfield, James. "'The Earth Is Burning': Kurosawa's *Record of a Living Being.*" *Literature/Film Quarterly* 26, no. 2 (1998). Available at http://findarticles.com/p/articles/mi-qu3768.

May, Elaine Tyler. *Homeward Bound: American Families in the Cold War.* New York: Basic Books, 1988.

Mayo, Marlene J., and J. Thomas Rimer, eds. *War, Occupation, and Creativity: Japan and East Asia, 1920–1960.* Honolulu: University of Hawai'i Press, 2001.

McCarthy, Mary. "The 'Hiroshima' *New Yorker.*" In *Hiroshima's Shadow: Writings on the Denial of History and the Smithsonian Controversy,* edited by Kai Bird and Lawrence Lifschultz. Stony Creek, Conn.: Pamphleteer's Press, 1998.

McDonald, Peter D. "Modernist Publishing: 'Nomads and Mapmakers.'" In *A Concise Companion to Modernism,* edited by David Bradshaw. Malden, Mass.: Blackwell, 2003.

McLuhan, Marshall. *Understanding Media: The Extensions of Man.* New York: Signet Books, 1964.

Medhurst, Martin J. "Atoms for Peace and Nuclear Hegemony: The Rhetorical Structure of a Cold War Campaign." In *The Cold War,* edited by Lori Lyn Bogle. Vol. 2, *National Security Policy Planning from Truman to Reagan and from Stalin to Gorbachev.* New York: Routledge, 2001.

Medovoi, Leerom. "Democracy, Capitalism, and American Literature: The Cold War Construction of J. D. Salinger's Paperback Hero." In *The Other Fifties: Interrogating Midcentury American Icons,* edited by Joel Foreman. Chicago: University of Illinois Press, 1997.

——. *Rebels: Youth and the Cold War Origins of Identity.* Durham, N.C.: Duke University Press, 2005.

Minear, Richard H., ed. and trans. *Hiroshima: Three Witnesses.* Princeton, N.J.: Princeton University Press, 1990.

Mitter, Rana, and Patrick Major, eds. *Across the Blocs: Cold War Cultural and Social History.* Portland, Ore.: Frank Cass, 2004.

Miyake Yasuo. *Kaere Bikini e: Gensuibaku kinshi undō no genten o kangaeru.* Tokyo: Suiyōsha, 1984.

Miyake Yasuo, Daigo Fukuryūmaru heiwa kyōkai, et al., eds. *Bikini suibaku hisai shiryō shū.* Tokyo: Tōkyō daigaku shuppankai, 1976.

Miyamoto Kenji. "Genbaku gisei minzoku no chisei." In *Bikini suibaku hisai shiryo shū,* edited by Miyake Yasuo, Daigo Fukuryūmaru heiwa kyōkai, et al. Tokyo: Tōkyō daigaku shuppankai, 1976.

Miyoshi, Masao *Accomplices of Silence: The Modern Japanese Novel.* Berkeley: University of California Press, 1974.

Mizukami Isao. "Abe Tomoji to Jaba chōyō taiken." *Bulletin of Tezukayama University* 23 (1986): 34–54.

Molasky, Michael. *The American Occupation of Japan and Okinawa: Literature and Memory.* New York: Routledge, 1999.

Moore, Harry T. "D. H. Lawrence and the 'Censor-Morons.'" In *D. H. Lawrence, Sex, Literature, and Censorship.* Edited by Harry T. Moore. New York: Viking Press, 1959.

Motohashi Seiichi. *Futari no gaka: Maruki Iri, Maruki Toshi no sekai.* Tokyo: Shōbunsha, 1987.

Mukai Junkichi. *Kyōshū Nihon no minka.* Tokyo: Kōdansha, 1996.

Munroe, Alexandra. *Japanese Art After 1945: Scream Against the Sky.* New York: Abrams, 1994.

Murakami, Takashi. *Little Boy: The Arts of Japan's Exploding Subculture.* New York: Japan Society; New Haven, Conn.: Yale University Press, 2005.

Murao Seiichi. "'Shi no hai' sukuupu made." *Bungei shunjū,* July 1954, 38–40.

Nadel, Alan. *Containment Culture: American Narratives, Postmodernism, and the Atomic Age.* Durham, N.C.: Duke University Press, 1995.

Naiman, Eric. *Sex in Public: The Incarnation of Early Soviet Ideology.* Princeton, N.J.: Princeton University Press, 1997.

Naitō Makoto. *Shōwa eigashi nōto: Goraku eiga to sensō no kage.* Tokyo: Heibonsha, 2001.

Nakamura Hiroshi. *Nakamura Hiroshi gashū: Tableau Machine.* Tokyo: Bijutsu shuppansha, 1995.

Nakano Shigeharu. "Akutagawa shō ni tsuite omoide." *Chūō kōron,* June 1956, 282–87.

Naoki Sakai. *Translation and Subjectivity: On "Japan" and Cultural Nationalism.* Minneapolis: University of Minnesota Press, 1997.

Nathan, John. "Tokyo Story: Shintaro Ishihara's Flamboyant Nationalism Appeals to Many Japanese Voters Who Are Looking for a Change in Government." *New Yorker,* April 9, 2001, 108–15.

Nihon genbaku ron taikei. 7 vols. Tokyo: Nihon tosho sentaa, 1999.

Nihon kindai bungakukan, ed. *Hara Tamiki shiryō mokuroku.* Tokyo: Nihon kindai bungakukan, 1983.

Nishida Masaru et al. *Ajia kara mita Nagasaki: Higai to kagai.* Tokyo: Iwanami shoten, 1990.

Nogami Gen. "Hara Tamiki igo: Aruiwa, 'media' to shite genshi bakudan o kangaeru koto no (fu)kanōsei." *Gendai shisō,* August 2003, 104–18.

Nornes, Abé Mark. "The Body at the Center—The Effects of the Atomic Bomb on Hiroshima and Nagasaki." In *Hibakusha Cinema: Hiroshima, Nagasaki and the Nuclear Image in Japanese Film,* edited by Mick Broderick. New York: Kegan Paul, 1996.

——. *Forest of Pressure: Ogawa Shinsuke and Postwar Japanese Documentary.* Minneapolis: University of Minnesota Press, 2007.

——. *Japanese Documentary Film.* Minneapolis: University of Minnesota Press, 2003.

——. "The Typical Genius of Kamei Fumio." In *Kamei Fumio tokushū / Kamei Fumio Retrospective,* edited by Yamagata International Documentary Film Festival. Tokyo: YIDFF Organizing Committee, Tokyo Office, 2001.

Oakes, Guy. *The Imaginary War: Civil Defense and American Cold War Culture.* New York: Oxford University Press, 1994.

Odagiri Hideo, ed. *Genshiryoku to bungaku.* Tokyo: Kōdansha, 1955.

———. "Nihon bungaku ni okeru 'sengo.'" In *Nihon bungaku no sengo,* edited by Nihon kindai bungakukan. Tokyo: Yomiuri shinbunsha, 1972.

———. *Odagiri Hideo chosaku zenshū.* 7 vols. Tokyo: Hōsei daigaku shuppan kyoku, 1972.

———. *Watashi no mita Shōwa no shisō to bungaku no gojūnen.* 2 vols. Tokyo: Shūeisha, 1988.

Ōe Kenzaburō. "Bungaku chokugen: Jōkyō—1959." *Bungakukai,* February 1959, 5–7.

———. *Hiroshima nōto.* Tokyo: Iwanami shoten, 1965.

Ōkubō Tsuneo. "Hara Tamiki to Dazai Osamu." In *Dazai Osamu ronshū—Sakka ron,* vol. 9, edited by Yamanouchi Shoshi. Tokyo: Yumani shobō, 1994.

Omori, Kyoko. "Detecting Japanese Vernacular Modernism: *Shinseinen* Magazine and the Development of the Tantei Shōsetsu Genre, 1920–1931." Ph.D. diss., Ohio State University, 2003.

O'Neill, Dan. "Alaska and the Firecracker Boys: The Story of Project Chariot." In *The Atomic West,* edited by Bruce Hevly and John M. Findlay. Seattle: University of Washington Press, 1998.

Orbaugh, Sharalyn. "The Body in Contemporary Japanese Women's Fiction." In *The Woman's Hand: Gender and Theory in Japanese Women's Writing,* edited by Paul G. Schalow and Janet A. Walker. Stanford, Calif.: Stanford University Press, 1996.

Orr, James J. *The Victim as Hero: Ideologies of Peace and National Identity in Postwar Japan.* Honolulu: University of Hawai'i Press, 2001.

———. "Yasui Kaoru: Citizen-Scholar in War and Peace." *Japan Forum* 12 (2000): 1–14.

Oshima Nagisa. *Cinema, Censorship, and the State: The Writings of Nagisa Oshima, 1956–1978.* Edited by Annette Michelson. Translated by Dawn Lawson. Cambridge, Mass.: MIT Press, 1992.

Ōta Yōko. "Hara Tamiki no shi ni tsuite." In *Teihon: Hara Tamiki zenshū.* Vol. 4, *Bekkan.* Tokyo: Seidosha, 1979.

Oyama Hisajiro⁻. *Hitotsu no jidai: Oyama shoten shishi.* Tokyo: Rokko shuppan, 1982.

Ozaki, Hotsuki. "Sengo no taishū bungaku." In *Nihon bungaku no sengo,* ed. Nihon kindai bungakukan. Tokyo: Yomiuri shinbunsha, 1972.

Painter, David S. *The Cold War: An International History.* New York: Routledge, 1999.

Pease, Allison. *Modernism, Mass Culture, and the Aesthetics of Obscenity.* Cambridge: Cambridge University Press, 2000.

Pennington, Lee. "War-Torn Japan: Disabled Veterans and Society, 1931–1952." Ph.D. diss., Columbia University, 2005.

Poiger, Uta. *Jazz, Rock, and Rebels: Cold War Politics and American Culture in a Divided Germany.* Berkeley: University of California Press, 1999.

Poplawski, Paul, ed. *Writing the Body in D. H. Lawrence: Essays on Language, Representation, and Sexuality.* Westport, Conn.: Greenwood Press, 2001.

Preston, Peter. "Lawrence in Britain: An Annotated Chronology, 1930–1998." In *The Reception of D. H. Lawrence Around the World,* edited by Takeo Iida. Fukuoka: Kyushu University Press, 1999.

Prince, Stephen. *The Warrior's Camera: The Cinema of Akira Kurosawa.* Rev. ed. Princeton, N.J.: Princeton University Press, 1991.

Quandt, James, ed. *Kon Ichikawa.* Toronto: Cinematheque Ontario, 2001.

Raine, Michael. "Contemporary Japan as Punishment Room in Kon Ichikawa's *Shokei no heya.*" In *Kon Ichikawa,* edited by James Quandt. Toronto: Cinematheque Ontario, 2001.

———. "Ishihara Yūjirō: Youth, Celebrity, and the Male Body in Late-1950s Japan." In *Word and Image in Japanese Cinema,* edited by Dennis Washburn and Carole Cavanaugh. Cambridge: Cambridge University Press, 2001.

Rainey, Lawrence. "The Cultural Economy of Modernism." In *The Cambridge Companion to Modernism,* edited by Michael Levenson. Cambridge: Cambridge University Press, 1999.

Rawnsley, Gary D. *Cold-War Propaganda in the 1950s.* New York: St. Martin's Press, 1999.

Rhodes, Richard. *Dark Sun: The Making of the Hydrogen Bomb.* New York: Simon and Schuster, 1995.

Richie, Donald. *The Films of Akira Kurosawa.* 3rd ed. Berkeley: University of California Press, 1984.

———. *The Japanese Movie.* Rev. ed. Tokyo: Kodansha, 1982.

Rolph, C. H., ed. *The Trial of Lady Chatterley: Regina v. Penguin Books Limited.* 1960. Reprint, New York: Penguin Books, 1991.

Rose, Lisle. *The Cold War Comes to Main Street.* Lawrence: University Press of Kansas, 1999.

Rosenberg, David Alan. "The Origins of Overkill: Nuclear Weapons and American Strategy, 1945–1960." In *The Cold War,* edited by Lori Lyn Bogle. Vol. 2, *National Security Policy Planning from Truman to Reagan and from Stalin to Gorbachev.* New York: Routledge, 2001.

Ross, Kristin. *Fast Cars, Clean Bodies: Decolonization and the Reordering of French Culture.* Cambridge, Mass.: MIT Press, 1999.

Rubin, Jay. "From Wholesomeness to Decadence: The Censorship of Literature Under the Allied Occupation." *Journal of Japanese Studies* 1, no. 1 (1985): 102–3.

———. "The Impact of the Occupation on Literature, or Lady Chatterley and Lt. Col. Verness." In *The Occupation of Japan: Arts and Culture: The Proceedings of the Sixth Symposium Sponsored by the MacArthur Memorial,* edited by Thomas W. Burkman. Norfolk, Va.: General Douglas MacArthur Foundation, 1988.

———. *Injurious to Public Morals: Writers and the Meiji State.* Seattle: University of Washington Press, 1984.

Russell, Bertrand. "The Bomb and Civilization." Available at http://www.humanities.mcmaster.ca/~russell/brbomb.htm.

Sagano Ryokichi. *Genshi bakudan no hanashi.* Tokyo: Kōdansha, 1949.

Sakai, Naoki. *Translation and Subjectivity: On "Japan" and Cultural Nationalism.* Minneapolis: University of Minnesota Press, 1997.

Samuels, Richard J. *Machiavelli's Children: Leaders and Their Legacies in Italy and Japan*. Ithaca, N.Y.: Cornell University Press, 2003.

Sandler, Mark H. *The Confusion Era: Art and Culture of Japan During the Allied Occupation, 1945–1952*. Seattle: University of Washington Press, 1997.

Sasaki Ki'ichi. "Genbaku to sakka no jisatsu." In *Teihon: Hara Tamiki zenshū*. Vol. 4, *Bekkan*. Tokyo: Seidosha, 1979.

——. "Shi to yume." In *Teihon: Hara Tamiki zenshū*. Vol. 4, *Bekkan*. Tokyo: Seidosha, 1979.

Sasaki-Uemura, Wesley. *Organizing the Spontaneous: Citizen Protest in Postwar Japan*. Honolulu: University of Hawai'i Press. 2001.

Satō Haruo. "Ryōfu bizoku to geijutsuka: Furyō shōnenteki bungaku o haisu." *Yomiuri shinbun*, February 8, 1956, 8.

Sato, Tadao. *Currents in Japanese Cinema*. Translated by Gregory Barrett. Tokyo: Kodansha, 1982.

Saull, Richard. *The Cold War and After: Capitalism, Revolution and Superpower Politics*. Ann Arbor, Mich.: Pluto Press, 2007.

Saunders, David. "Victorian Obscenity Law: Negative Censorship or Positive Administration?" In *Writing and Censorship in Britain*, edited by Paul Hyland and Neil Sammells. New York: Routledge, 1992.

Saunders, Frances Stonor. *The Cultural Cold War: The CIA and the World of Arts and Letters*. New York: New Press, 1999.

Schalow, Paul G., and Janet A. Walker, eds. *The Woman's Hand: Gender and Theory in Japanese Women's Writing*. Stanford, Calif.: Stanford University Press, 1996.

Schaub, Thomas Hill. *American Fiction in the Cold War*. Madison: University of Wisconsin Press, 1991.

Screech, Timon. *Sex and the Floating World: Erotic Images in Japan, 1700–1820*. Honolulu: University of Hawai'i Press, 1999.

Selden, Mark. "The Logic of Mass Destruction." In *Hiroshima's Shadow: Writings on the Denial of History and the Smithsonian Controversy*, edited by Kai Bird and Lawrence Lifschultz. Stony Creek, Conn.: Pamphleteer's Press, 1998.

Senuma Shigeki. "Masu komi to bungaku." In *Nihon bungaku no sengo*, edited by Nihon kindai bungakukan. Tokyo: Yomiuri shinbunsha, 1972.

Sherry, Michael S. *The Rise of American Air Power: The Creation of Armageddon*. New Haven, Conn.: Yale University Press, 1987.

Sherwin, Martin. "Memory, Myth and History." In *Hiroshima's Shadow: Writings on the Denial of History and the Smithsonian Controversy*, edited by Kai Bird and Lawrence Lifschultz. Stony Creek, Conn.: Pamphleteer's Press, 1998.

Shih, Shu-Mei. *The Lure of the Modern: Writing Modernism in Semi-Colonial China, 1917–1937*. Berkeley: University of California Press, 2001.

Shimizu Keiko. "'Shi no hai' to hahaoya tachi." *Kinema junpō*, July 1957, 40.

Shindō Kaneto. *Genbaku o toru*. Tokyo: Shin Nihon shuppansha, 2005.

Shōno Naomi, ed. *Hiroshima wa mukashibanashi ka: Gensuibaku no shashin to kiroku*. Tokyo: Shinchōsha, 1984.

Silverberg, Miriam. "War Responsibility Revisited: Auschwitz in Japan" (2007). Available at Japan Forum.org.

Slaymaker, Douglas. *The Body in Postwar Japanese Fiction*. New York: Routledge / Curzon, 2004.

———. *Confluences: Postwar Japan and France*. Ann Arbor: Center for Japanese Studies, University of Michigan, 2002.

Slocum, J. David, ed. *Rebel Without a Cause: Approaches to a Maverick Masterwork*. Albany: State University of New York Press, 2005.

Sontag, Susan. *Regarding the Pain of Others*. New York: Farrar, Strauss and Giroux, 2003.

Springer, Claudia. *James Dean Transfigured: The Many Faces of Rebel Iconography*. Austin: University of Texas Press, 2007.

Stites, Richard. "Heaven and Hell: Soviet Propaganda Constructs the World." In *Cold War Propaganda in the 1950s*, edited by Gary D. Rawnsley. New York: St. Martin's Press, 1999.

Suga Hidemi. "Yokuatsu no sochi ni tsuite: Chatarei saiban." *Shinchō*, December 1988, 180–81.

Suzuki Shigeo. "Hara Tamiki e no akogare." In *Teihon: Hara Tamiki zenshū*. Vol. 4, *Bekkan*. Tokyo: Seidosha, 1979.

Tachibana, Reiko. *Narrative as Counter-Memory: A Half Century of Postwar Writing in Germany and Japan*. Albany: State University of New York Press, 1998.

Takada Jun. *Sekai hōshasen hibakuchi chōsa*. Tokyo: Kōdansha, 2002.

Takeda Taijun. "'Kairaku-ron' ni tsuite." *Bungakukai*, May 1956, 108–11.

Takeuchi Yoshimi. *What Is Modernity? Writings of Takeuchi Yoshimi*. Edited and translated by Richard F. Calichman. New York: Columbia University Press, 2004.

Thomas, Julia. *Reconfiguring Modernity: Concepts of Nature in Japanese Political Ideology*. Berkeley: University of California Press, 2001.

Thompson, Sarah E., and Harry D. Harootunian. *Undercurrents in the Floating World: Censorship and Japanese Prints*. New York: Asia Society, 1991.

Togaeri Hajime. "Taiyō bungaku ronsō no yukue." In *Togaeri Hajime chosaku shū*. Vol. 1. Tokyo: Kōdansha, 1969.

Treat, John. *Writing Ground Zero: Japanese Literature and the Atomic Bomb*. Chicago: University of Chicago Press, 1995.

Tsuchimoto, Noriaki. "Obituary: Kamei Fumio—Who Buried Kamei Fumio?" In *Kamei Fumio tokushū / Kamei Fumio Retrospective*, edited by Yamagata International Documentary Film Festival. Tokyo: YIDFF Organizing Committee, Tokyo Office, 2001.

Tsutsui, William, and Michiko Ito, eds. *In Godzilla's Footsteps: Japanese Pop Culture Icons on the Global Stage*. New York: Palgrave Macmillan, 2006.

Tsuzuki Masaaki. *Kurosawa Akira: "Issaku isshō" zensaku jissakuhin*. Tokyo: Kōdansha, 1998.

———. *Tori ni natta ningen: Hankotsu no eiga kantoku, Kamei Fumio no shōgai*. Tokyo: Kōdansha, 1992.

Tyler, William J., ed. *Modanizumu in Japanese Fiction: An Anthology of Modernist Prose from Japan, 1914–1938*. Honolulu: University of Hawai'i Press, 2008.

Ubuki Satoru. *Heiwa kinen shikiten no ayumi*. Hiroshima: Hiroshima Heiwa Bunka Center, 1992.

Uesugi Takashi. "Jin'myaku o toku yottsu no kiiwaado." *Ronza*, May 2001, 40–45.

Wada Natto. "The 'Sun Tribe' and Their Parents." In *Kon Ichikawa*, edited by James Quandt. Toronto: Cinematheque Ontario, 2001.

Wald, Alan M. *The New York Intellectuals: The Rise and Decline of the Anti-Stalinist Left from the 1930s to the 1980s*. Chapel Hill: University of North Carolina Press, 1987.

Walker, J. Samuel. *Permissible Dose: A History of Radiation Protection in the Twentieth Century*. Berkeley: University of California Press, 2000.

Watanabe Kazuo. *"Tachidokoro ni taiyō wa kieru de aroo" Bikini suibaku hisai shiryō shū*. Tokyo: Tokyo daigaku shuppan kai, 1976. [Originally published in *Chūō kōron*, June 1954]

Westad, Odd Arne, ed. *Reviewing the Cold War: Approaches, Interpretations, Theory*. Portland, Ore.: Frank Cass, 2000.

Whitfield, Stephen J. *The Culture of the Cold War*. 2nd ed. Baltimore: Johns Hopkins University Press, 1996.

Williams, Linda. *Hard-Core: Power, Pleasure, and the "Frenzy of the Visible."* Berkeley: University of California Press, 1989.

Winther-Tamaki, Bert. *Art in the Encounter of Nations: Japanese and American Artists in the Early Postwar Years*. Honolulu: University of Hawai'i Press, 2001.

Wittner, Lawrence S. *One World or None: A History of the World Nuclear Disarmament Movement Through 1953*. Stanford, Calif.: Stanford University Press, 1993.

Wolfe, Alan S. *Suicidal Narrative in Modern Japan: The Case of Dazai Osamu*. Princeton, N.J.: Princeton University Press, 1990.

Yamada Kazuo. *Kurosawa Akira: Hito to geijutsu*. Tokyo: Shin Nihon shuppan, 1999.

Yamagata International Documentary Film Festival, ed. *Kamei Fumio tokushū / Kamei Fumio Retrospective*. Tokyo: YIDFF Organizing Committee, Tokyo Office, 2001.

Yamamoto Kenkichi. "Shinjin no 'shin' no morosa." *Asahi shinbun*, March 22, 1956 (evening edition), 6.

Yamamoto Kenkichi, Chō Kōta, and Sasaki Kiichi, eds. *Teihon: Hara Tamiki zenshū*. 4 vols. Tokyo: Seidosha, 1978.

Yamamoto, Mari. *Grassroots Pacifism in Post-War Japan*. New York: Routledge, 2004.

Yasui Kaoru. *Minshū to heiwa: Mirai o tsukuru mono*. Tokyo: Ōtsuki shoten, 1955.

Yavenditti, Michael. "John Hersey and the American Conscience." In *Hiroshima's Shadow: Writings on the Denial of History and the Smithsonian Controversy*, edited by Kai Bird and Lawrence Lifschultz. Stony Creek, Conn.: Pamphleteer's Press, 1998.

Yoneyama, Lisa. *Hiroshima Traces: Time, Space, and the Dialectics of Memory*. Berkeley: University of California Press, 1999.

Yoshida Fumihiko. *Shōgen: Kaku yokushi no seiki: kagaku to seiji wa koo ugoita*. Tokyo: Asahi shinbunsha, 2000.

Yoshida Tsukasa. *Sutaa tanjō: Hibari, Kinnosuke, Yūjirō, Atsumi Kiyoshi, soshite shin-fukkōki no seishin.* Tokyo: Kōdansha, 1999.

Yoshida Yoshie. *Maruki Iri, Toshi no jikū kaiga toshite no "Genbaku no zu."* Tokyo: Aoki shoten, 1996.

Yoshimoto, Mitsuhiro. *Kurosawa: Film Studies and Japanese Cinema.* Durham, N.C.: Duke University Press, 2000.

Yuasa Ichirō. *"Heiwa toshi Hiroshima" o tou: Hiroshima to kaku, kichi, sensō.* Tokyo: Gijutsu to ningen, 1995.

Zuschlag, Christoph. "Censorship in the Visual Arts in Nazi Germany." In *Suspended License: Censorship and the Visual Arts,* edited by Elizabeth C. Childs. Seattle: University of Washington Press, 1997.

Index

DATE DUE

MAY 0 1 2014			
2014 -05- 12			
			PRINTED IN U.S.A.